PRIVACY

Paul Weiss

SOUTHERN ILLINOIS UNIVERSITY PRESS
Carbondale & Edwardsville

Library of Congress Cataloging in Publication Data

Weiss, Paul, 1901-

    Includes index.
    1. Philosophical anthropology. I. Title
BD450.W463   128   81-21513
ISBN 0-8093-1066-X   AACR2

83 84 85 86 6 5 4 3 2 1

FOR NEIL WELLIVER
great painter, teacher, and friend

BOOKS *by Paul Weiss*

BEYOND ALL APPEARANCES *(1974)*

CINEMATICS *(1975)*

THE COMMONHEALTH *(forthcoming)*

FIRST CONSIDERATIONS *(1977)*

THE GOD WE SEEK *(1964)*

HISTORY: WRITTEN AND LIVED *(1962)*

THE MAKING OF MEN *(1967)*

MAN'S FREEDOM *(1950)*

MODES OF BEING *(1958)*

NATURE AND MAN *(1947)*

NINE BASIC ARTS *(1961)*

OUR PUBLIC LIFE *(1959)*

PHILOSOPHY IN PROCESS, Vol. 1: 1955–1960 *(1966)*

PHILOSOPHY IN PROCESS, Vol. 2: 1960–1964 *(1966)*

PHILOSOPHY IN PROCESS, Vol. 3: 1964 *(1968)*

PHILOSOPHY IN PROCESS, Vol. 4: 1964–1965 *(1969)*

PHILOSOPHY IN PROCESS, Vol. 5: 1965–1968 *(1971)*

PHILOSOPHY IN PROCESS, Vol. 6: 1968–1971 *(1975)*

PHILOSOPHY IN PROCESS, Vol. 7: 1975–1976 *(1978)*

REALITY *(1938)*

RELIGION AND ART *(1963)*

RIGHT AND WRONG: A *Philosophical Dialogue Between Father and Son, with Jonathan Weiss (1967)*

SPORT: A *Philosophic Inquiry (1969)*

THE WORLD OF ART *(1961)*

YOU, I, AND THE OTHERS *(1980)*

PRIVACY *(1983)*

PRINCIPAL CONTRIBUTIONS *by Paul Weiss*

AMERICAN PHILOSOPHERS AT WORK, *edited by Sidney Hook (1956)*

AMERICAN PHILOSOPHY TODAY AND TOMORROW, *edited by H. M. Kallen and Sidney Hook (1935)*

THE CONCEPT OF ORDER, *edited by Paul Kuntz (1968)*

CONTEMPORARY AMERICAN PHILOSOPHY, *edited by John E. Smith (1970)*

DESIGN AND AESTHETICS OF WOOD, *edited by Eric A. Anderson and George F. Earl (1972)*

DETERMINISM AND FREEDOM, *edited by Sidney Hook (1958)*

THE DIMENSIONS OF JOB, *edited by Nahum N. Glatzer (1969)*

DIMENSIONS OF MIND: A SYMPOSIUM, *edited by Sidney Hook (1960)*

EVOLUTION IN PERSPECTIVE, *edited by G. Schuster and G. Thorson (1971)*

THE FUTURE OF METAPHYSICS, *edited by Robert Wood (1970)*

HUMAN VALUES AND ECONOMIC POLICY: PROCEEDINGS, *edited by Sidney Hook (1967)*

LAW AND PHILOSOPHY, *edited by Sidney Hook (1964)*

MID/TWENTIETH CENTURY AMERICAN PHILOSOPHY, *edited by Peter A. Bertocci (1974)*

MOMENTS OF PERSONAL DISCOVERY, *edited by R. M. MacIver (1952)*

MORAL PRINCIPLES IN ACTION, *edited by R. Anshen (1952)*

PERSPECTIVES ON PEIRCE, *edited by R. Bernstein (1965)*

PHILOSOPHERS ON THEIR WORK, *edited by André Mercier (1979)*

PHILOSOPHICAL ESSAYS FOR A. N. WHITEHEAD, *edited by O. Lee (1936)*

PHILOSOPHICAL INTERROGATIONS, *edited by S. and B. Rome (1964)*

PHILOSOPHY AND HISTORY, *edited by Sidney Hook (1963)*

THE PHILOSOPHY OF BARUCH SPINOZA *edited by R. Kennington (1980)*

THE RELEVANCE OF WHITEHEAD, *edited by I. Leclerc (1961)*

SCIENCE, PHILOSOPHY, AND RELIGION: PROCEEDINGS *(1941–)*

STUDIES IN THE PHILOSOPHY OF CHARLES SANDERS PEIRCE, *edited by C. P. Weiner and F. H. Young (1952)*

EDITED WORKS *by Paul Weiss*

COLLECTED PAPERS OF CHARLES SANDERS PEIRCE (six volumes), *editor, with Charles Hartshorne (1931–35)*

Contents

Preface

In *Beyond All Appearances* I began what, for me at least, was a comparatively new range of philosophic inquiries. I there sought to isolate unmistakable evidences of what was ultimately real, and to trace these back to their original sources. In the attempt to make the view clear to colleagues and students, I have, since its publication some seven years ago, subjected it to a number of highly critical readings. It has been pleasant to find that a great deal of what it maintained requires no significant alterations. Still, there are crudities and errors in it. The last part, particularly, is not in clear focus. Most of the difficulties pivot about my understanding of the final realities which condition everything else; others reflect an inadequate grasp of the nature of man. The main defects in the account of the finalities were, I think, eventually noted, thereby making possible a better entrenched, more defensible formulation. This was presented in *First Considerations*. I have since tried to provide a correspondingly precise and systematic treatment of man, as able to be apart from and to oppose and interplay with those final realities. The issue was opened up in *You, I, and the Others*. The present work continues the venture. It seeks to isolate evidences of human privacy in the body and the world, to understand what then becomes knowable, and to explore the result.

'Privacy' will be used throughout this work to refer to the initial source of a man's activities. What he initiates may not be given a bodily expression. It may make a difference to the body's functioning. Or it may bear on what is outside the body. If either of the last two occurs, even if not observed or even if it is without interest to the state or to anyone else, it will be referred to as 'public'. The term 'privacy', when used by lawyers and political scientists, refers instead to the right to live without interference by the state. Or it marks off an area where the state does not justifiably intrude and where its laws do not apply. But that area, more often than not, is quite exposed. In one's home, with one's family, defenses are down; each person is there involved with others to a degree he is not when engaged in activities which are legally and politically 'public'.

Men who are private, legally or politically, are always private and always public in the senses that will be here employed, since they always manifest some of their privacy—but only some of it—in their bodies and the world beyond. Evidence of the presence, functioning, and nature of that privacy becomes available whenever it is possible to distinguish what a human body does from what it does not contribute to some observable activity. When the portion which the body does not contribute is traced back to a particular expression of privacy, it becomes possible to explain what is occurring without having to affirm anything more than what the evidence warrants.

The clarification, elaboration, and grounding of what is initially discerned in an activity, makes conspicuous the fact that we all know much more about the nature of man than most specialists, whether they be linguists, psychologists, anthropologists, biologists, or philosophers, explain or are even interested in explaining. Cherishing clarity, control, tests, and confirmations supported by practice, these theorists restrict themselves to studies of words, behaviors, customs, cells, genes, subatomic particles, and their combinations. Much that is important is discovered and clarified. It is true also that not much of importance is learned about that unitary, complex being we all know as man. Something is also learned and clarity is gained—but content lost—when man is interpreted in terms derived from studies of the less mature, the subhuman, or the inanimate. It is better to keep mature man in mind, even when an attempt is made to understand what he is at earlier stages.

An understanding of what man is and does, from the vantage point of what is known of him at his most complex and developed, need not preclude an examination of the earlier stages by themselves, nor need it preclude a sound grasp of beings below the level of humans. Indeed, it should instead encourage an understanding of these, allowing us to detect what is involved in quite different tasks.

If there be someone who does not know that he has come to be at a particular time and place, that he is a person, and that he knows other persons; if there is someone who is not sensitive, who does not and cannot assume roles in a social setting, who has no native rights, and who is not responsible; if there is someone who does not know himself as a me and others as you's; who does not know that each mature man has a self and an

I, that each makes decisions, is self-same over time, and is conscious a good part of the day, he is of course not one who could now be addressed. But it is quite another thing to explain, clarify, interrelate, and justify what is so well-known. That is what is here attempted.

Washington, D.C.
July, 1982

Introduction

Considerable emphasis in the intellectual world today is placed on attempts to understand what is familiar, experienced, or complex in terms of simpler, more precisely characterized units. When these are treated as alone real, as the necessary predecessors or sources of the complexes, or are supposed to provide exhaustive explanations for whatever else occurs, an attitude, which can ground brilliantly successful investigations of great daring, becomes rigidified. The result is a reductionism in which the originally acknowledged items no longer have any role. Five forms are current.

a. *Physical.* Physical reductionism is perhaps the oldest and the most widely accepted of all. It is to be found in pre-Socratic Greece and at the center of modern science, from its Galilean beginnings until today. More resolutely and precisely than other reductionisms do, it reduces its rivals as well as the objects of daily life. Accepting as correct the reduction of man and other living beings to biological units, and the reduction of these to chemical units, it goes on to hold that these are nothing more than combinations of physical entities—particles, waves, or combinations of these. It would be both foolish and idle for one who was not a theoretical physicist—or more accurately, a knowledgeable theorist of physics—to object. It would be foolish because he would be trying to impose external restraints on a discipline which has its own rationale, objectives, and requirements, and it would be idle because no one of its practioners would find the objection relevant to his tasks or discoveries.

Within the compass of its own interests, every discipline will do what it must in order to understand, in terms of its own tradition, ideals, and agencies, the data with which it is occupied. But this is not enough to warrant the supposition that what it takes to be irreducible, basic, or final is so in fact. If it is so for the discipline, it cannot be so in fact unless that discipline is actually dealing with what will enable one to account for all else.

Like every other reductionism, a physical reductionism has to take for granted the presence of the items which it seeks to reduce. They are its initial data, its check, and its warrant. In addition, as Peirce long ago observed, physical reductionism cannot account for the distribution of the entities with which it rests. This it takes for granted. It makes no difference whether or not one traces the current distribution back to an original, sudden production, 'a big bang', or supposes that it is just a continuation of the adventures of ultimate units over the course of endless time. Why the units are where they are is, for it, just an inexplicable 'given'.

The distribution of which Peirce spoke was a distribution of all supposed ultimate units. There is another distribution, more relevant to our study. The adventures of ultimate units, whatever they be, are affected by the adventures of the particular complexes in which they are—especially if those complexes are individuals. The units in me are to be found where I am. When I move, I move not the short distances that are possible to those units, but distances that are appropriate to my concerns. When I go to the door I walk at a rate and in a direction which requires a reference to me as a single being. The units within me will be located at the door in a second or so, not because they independently moved there—if one could speak properly of a 'there' for them—but because I went there. No physical reductionism can explain why the units within me are where they are, precisely because the where is dictated not by them but by the being whose body embraces them. That body, of course, is limited in its acts, and some of the limitations are due to the nature and functioning of the units within it. But those limitations are not absolute; they merely qualify the ways in which the complex unit can itself act, on its own terms, in its own way, in its own time scheme, and in its characteristic space.

b. *Technological.* The most popular of reductionisms today is the technological, the attempt to understand all gross and some subtler occurrences in terms of the activities of machines. Today, the machine to which reference is usually made is the computer, an agency by which open and shut circuits follow one another in rapid order, and whose outcomes can be expressed in conventional numbers and eventually in conventional language. At a speed previously unknown, a computer can carry out a very complicated and sophisticated program and do it accurately.

If one supposes that a mind is a brain and that a brain is a computer, one is ready to speak as though whatever was known or knowable was the work of a computer. But no computer can ever bring anything to a close. All it can do is come to an end. It can put a dot at the end of a series of combinations of marks which one might be willing to call letters and words. It cannot produce a period. A period does not merely come at the end of a series; it is related to the beginning of a sentence and, with the capital letter there, helps make a sentence a single whole. Only one who knows what a sentence is knows how to program a computer, how to utilize its productions, and how to take its results to be correct or incorrect, good or bad, right or wrong, and not simply permitted or rejected.

A man, not a computer, is able to infer, reflect, judge, and claim; only a man, therefore, and not a computer, has a mind, can think, assert, and know. A man can be trained and habituated; he can agree or disagree without reflection. All the while, he will be able, and sometimes will make evident, that he can affirm and deny regardless of the state his body is in, or what he had previously been prepared to do. Only a man can accept or deny this contention. A computer will just accommodate it or not, depending on how it had been prepared for it.

There is no difference in principle between the most complicated, advanced computer and the most primitive adding machine. The one is quicker and more efficient; it can yield results with an accuracy and rapidity nothing else can. But like its primitive predecessor, the computer has nothing to do with numbers. Both it and the adding machine deal solely with numerals. Neither could ever tell one how much money he has received, how much he has spent, or what his balance is, since all that either could provide are numerals which he has to translate into numbers and relate to purchases and sales.

c. *Biological*. Biological reductionists resist the trend to speak of men and other living beings as though they were sums of ultimate units, or were kinds of machines. They are neo-Darwinians, convinced that mankind had an animal origin, and that man differs from all other living beings only in degree. That difference in degree, it is allowed, may be enough to make possible the production of tools and eventually of complicated machines, and the creation of language, society, the arts, and sciences. It might be conceded that some of these have natures, careers, and consequences which cannot be given a biological meaning—but only if one also abandons the idea that the living body is the only source and offers a complete explanation of what is and of what is done.

Men, in this reductionistic view, are held to be nothing other than living bodies whose differences in degree do not stand in the way of understanding them fully as subject to laws governing bodies, and as having constituents like those possessed by other living beings. Two great obstacles stand in the way. The view ignores the fact that bodies are not only living but lived; not only active or reactive but used; and that any pains and pleasures, and therefore also more complex experiences—hopes, fears, beliefs, ideas, memories, and expectations—are not bodily occurrences. All these can be undergone apart from and sometimes in the absence of or in defiance of any change in the body or circumstance.

Biological reductionism also ignores the fact that the achievement of new forms of experiencing make a difference to the quality, meaning, and import of the old. An animal's pain is never equatable with a man's, if for no other reason than that a man's pain, and not the animal's, is undergone by him as a person, having rights and powers which the animal does not and cannot have.

A biological reductionist begins by begging his question, if he supposes that because a man has an animal origin he can differ only in degree from an animal. Even if it were granted that there is only a difference in degree in their living bodies, they still can and do differ in kind, and quite radically, because of the ways in which their bodies are lived and used.

Man is a proper topic for biology, and what it knows of him can be brought under principles applicable to other living bodies—but only so far as one ignores what else is true of him and, therefore, the fact that he makes his body function in ways that biology cannot understand. He has prospects in view, some of which are dealt with privately without achieving any public expression. And he may publicly express other prospects in such a way that they prevent his body or the species from continuing or prospering.

d. *Psychological.* The history of psychology has been characterized as one in which it first lost its soul, then its mind, and subsequently its consciousness. Later it became irritable. Now it is reactionary. The last is the status enjoyed by a dominant school, behaviorism. Eschewing all attempts to speak of what goes on in a 'black box' or a supposed mind, it attends solely to reinforcements of activities by rewarding those that the experimenter endorses, and by punishing or refraining from rewarding those that he wants not to recur. The view seeks to state in as precise and predictable a manner as possible just how reinforcements are to be administered in order to achieve desired results most efficiently. It has proved to be an effective device for training stupid animals and birds; these have been made to engage in odd behaviors, quite different from anything they might otherwise do, solely by having their accidental moves reinforced again and again.

Behaviorists are positivistic in mentality; they seek to stay with facts and to eschew all interpretations. References to ideas, prospects, purposes, wills, even desires or appetites are, for them, signs of looseness in thinking or, at least, in talking. It is therefore astonishing to find them endorsing purpose, teleology, the control of the present by the future, to a degree no one else seems ever to have done. Rewards, they maintain, are given by them at the end of an activity in order to promote the repetition of the activity, which is to say, in order to increase the probability that the activity will be begun again. But to suppose that what is done at the end of an activity helps bring about that end is to give the end the status of a guiding control. It is to take the activity to be purposive in nature, even when it seems to be mechanical and to occur without control. And, of course, the behaviorist himself, like his subject, acts purposively, controlling his experiments in the light of the results he seeks to obtain.

A behavioristic reductionism removes all the intelligible ways in which one might be able to connect consequent with antecedent activity, to leave the behaviorist accepting an inexplicable governance of the beginnings of acts by their prospective endings. The results are then offered to others in the form of hypotheses, truths, and theories, which those others are to think about in privacy, and not just react to as irritants or stimuli. Like other reductionists, the behaviorist evidently operates within a non-reductionist frame. His embraces experimenter, subject, the community of investigators, what can be observed, and what can, at the very least, be presented as plausible and perhaps true. This would not be possible were there only bodies 'emitting' behaviors which were reinforced by 'rewards'.

e. *Linguistic*. There is a large segment of the Anglo-Saxon philosophical community which has taken its stand with linguistic reductionism, the attempt to understand everything in terms of language. For some, the language is that of logic, mathematics, or science; for others, it is the language of a society; for still others, it is an idealized language constructed to accord with the needs of a theory of knowledge, observation, or commonsense. Starting with the idea that all that is left of a distinction between men and animals is the possession of a mind by the former (Descartes' thesis), they accept the reduction of that mind to the status of a feeling of pain or pleasure, and then the reduction of this to a viable report that a pain or pleasure is being undergone. As a consequence, these thinkers find themselves left with nothing but words or sentences which they interchange. Or, starting with the idea that what is well-expressed in mathematical or logical terms or which is in accord with the most recent theories of science alone is intelligible or reliable, they find themselves unable to justify the claim that there is something to which the expressions refer. All are therefore left facing 'the problem of reference', the problem of how they could make contact with something to which some expressions in language supposedly lead us.

The boldest of these thinkers are the clearest and most rigorous. Unable to find any device by which they could escape the bounds of language, they have summarily decided that the world was well lost. All that one could properly do, they hold, is to remain within the confines of a language, and refine it as much as possible. More clearly than the rest, they see that such a simple claim as 'predicates are predicated of subjects' is mistaken, since a subject (of a sentence) is just as much a part of language as a predicate, and that in any case a predicate does not characterize the subject of the sentence in which the predicate occurs, but either something else or nothing at all.

A language is often used by someone to talk to someone else, often about something different from either of them. Neither speaker nor listener is part of the language. And if either is speaking of anything other than words and sentences, he is evidently involved with something other than these. The language reductionist could never present his case to anyone if there were nothing but language.

Reductionisms are parasitical on the data, observations, and confirmations of what they had presumably replaced. They presuppose that there are men who use their bodies as agencies for the realization of prospects which may have no bodily value. Each is offered as a truth for others to accept as a truth. All exist only so far as they at least tacitly cling to what was supposedly reduced, if only to provide the reductionists with a world in which they too can live and where their reduction can have a heuristic role.

References to reductionism will crop up again and again throughout this work. It will be faced with the fact that we already know more than any reductionism allows. Without this more no reductionism would be possible. One of the things we know is that men live their bodies to realize prospects not within the purview, and outside the reach of physics, technology, biology, psychology, or language.

II

A well-entrenched, non-reductionist method for learning about men begins with the supposition that each man has a sure knowledge of himself, acquired through observation or introspection, or by supplementing and correcting the one by the other. When the result is taken by one man to apply to all the rest with only the changes that are needed to accommodate differences in opportunity, genesis, experience, and habit, a touch of arrogance and condescension will usually taint the conclusions. Left unexamined will be what is unimportant for that individual, though perhaps of considerable importance to others.

To avoid just supposing that others are like what one takes oneself to be, it is desirable to attend to what other men—and therefore oneself as well—publicly show themselves to be. If it is possible to then extricate evidence of the existence of powers present in any man, it will be possible to learn about the nature of human privacy. Different kinds of evidence will enable one to remark on the main divisions of that privacy, and to expose the differences they make to the body and the world. Evidences are continuous with their sources. To be acquainted with the one is already to be in contact with the other, and in a position to make an intensive, convergent, insistent further move into the sources as not yet expressed.

Our enterprise will go astray if it fails to take account of the fact that there are a number of living and non-living actualities, quite different in nature and activity from man, existing alongside, affecting, and being used by him. Though distinctive in nature, power, promise, and achievement, man is still but one kind of being among many.

There is a single public world occupied by men and other actualities because their expressions are countered by and united with universal conditions, themselves expressions of ubiquitous realities—'finalities,' I call them. The expressions of the actualities, and the conditions expressing the finalities, together constitute a single world of objective appearances. It is these which we daily face, but never as entirely separated from the actualities and the finalities. The constituents of appearances are actualities and finalities in attenuated forms, limiting and interplaying with one another.

One cannot, I think, avoid the acknowledgement of these two types of reality, one actual, limited, individual, and governed, the other final and persistent. The actualities resist one another and express themselves in opposition to conditions, themselves expressing and empowered by the finalities. I was not always aware of the fact. In my first book, *Reality*, I made a strenuous effort to present a naturalistic metaphysics which acknowledged only actualities. But the more I reflected on the view, the more evident it became that it could not be maintained. It did not and could not provide a warrant for its admission that actualities are together in a common space and time, able to act on one another. It was unable to explain how complex entities could arise, have distinctive natures, and function as single units. Nor did it or could it account for the future and the role this played in the present, and therefore for the difference that prospects, objectives, goals, and ends make to what is directed toward and occupied with realizing these. A view which affirms that there are actualities must sooner or later also affirm that there are finalities, different in range and kind, effectively conditioning those actualities and their expressions.

Were final realities all-powerful, or were they alone ultimately and irreducibly real, actualities would at best be offshoots, faint copies, or subdivisions of them. Were actualities all-powerful, or were they alone ultimate, there would be no power able to condition them. Laws, space, and time would then have to be treated as abstractions from the actualities, or as illusory. But were they abstractions, they would not make it possible for anything to be with anything else. And if they were illusions, actualities would not be governed by a common rationale, and would not be spatially distant from one another. Nor would any really come to be earlier or later than others.

Both finalities and actualities must be acknowledged. Nothing less than a knowledge of how they interplay through their expressions will account for the world we daily know and in which we daily live—the 'mixed' Plato called it—unless that world is necessarily without explanation, does not exist at all, or alone is real. The presence of evidence defeats the first of these suggestions; the claim itself defeats the second; while our decisions, the resistance our efforts encounter when we act, and common conditions, such as laws, space, and time, which encompass all actualities, defeat the third. The daily world is the product of the interplay of diverse realities distinct from it.

The presence and roles of one or the other, and sometimes of both types of reality, have been acknowledged in the past, though often misconstrued even by great thinkers. Kant took that which was conditioned to be an undifferentiated stuff, with the result that the conditions he insisted on had nothing which could resist them. This left him with a world in which his categories were displayed without hindrance. He should then have said that they were never modified, limited, or could make a difference, the opposite of what he in fact did claim. Berkeley and Leibniz both supposed that there were many different units, but could make them form a single set only by calling on God for help. God, being omnipotent, was able to make good the intrinsic defects of their systems. Taking the human mind to be a final reality, Hume could not acknowledge a world un-thought, or one able to exist before there were men. Nor could he show that there was anything to be experienced or known, or available for use by his mind. To get his empiricism working, he inevitably rested his case on what he could not empirically determine. Aquinas and Spinoza both acknowledged finite entities; in addition, the one maintained that there was one final reality, a free, loving God, while the other took God to be both loving and unfree. For both, the supposed finality was all-powerful. But then no finite entity could conceivably oppose or interplay with it, or have a genuine career of its own. Were their God real, neither of these men could have existed.

Even a cursory examination of the works of these great thinkers shows that my summary statements require multiple modifications. But they hold in the main. In any case, it is hard to find in any of these men unmistakable references to two kinds of realities, each with a number of members, interplaying through their expressions in such a way as to constitute the mixed world in which we daily live.

We know the mixed, of course, only because we bring our interpreta-tions to bear on it. The epistemological pair of interpretation and inter-preted that is here to the fore, however, is quite different from the ontolog-ical pair of finalities and actualities. The mixed to which an interpretation is directed is the joint product of the ontological pair. Although we cannot avoid confronting the mixed, a world of appearances, since this is where we must begin and from which we can never entirely escape, that does not prevent us from reflecting on and thereby coming to know it to be con-stituted, apart from our interpretations, by the interplay of real finalities and actualities. Any account we give of it will, of course, be affected by ideas of our own making. But it is possible to rid oneself of what is arbitrary and false, or even only tentative, by allowing the real to dictate what should and should not be affirmed. And this it can do the more what is claimed is presented to the real as that which it is to accept or reject in its own way and on its own terms. We know that we think correctly of the real when we find that the real accepts without alteration what we claim is true of it. When the irrelevant, the willful, and the false are assimilated by the real they are altered.

To remain with the mixed is to remain with what is confused, some-what unintelligible, and overrun with contingency. The situation can be dealt with in at least four ways. With some phenomenologists, we may be content to describe it. With the 'soft sciences,' sociology particularly, we can try to reorganize it with the help of statistics. With the 'hard sciences,' particularly theoretical physics, we can look for highly general structures which all items instance. Or, with metaphysicians, we can try to get to the ultimate sources of the constituents of the mixed. The last is what I ventured in other places. The outcome provides a background for the present attempt to focus on the actuality, man, with a special emphasis on what he is privately. Though one need not attend to that background in order to understand man, it is surely presupposed in this as well as in any other effort that might be made to provide a justifiable, systematic characterization of him or any other actuality.

The ontological route is to be taken if one wishes to get to the irreducible sources of the factors which are joined in the mixed. This may be done in order to escape from the confusions, irrelevancies, and imprecisions which mar what is originally confronted, or because one wants to get to bedrock. The first of these motivations is also exhibited by the soft and hard sciences. But the soft sciences have no reason for the supposition that what happens here or today will happen or be pertinent to what happens there or tomorrow, while the hard sciences not only strive to understand complex actualities as combinations of less complex units, with the reality of the initial actualities left undetermined or denied, but suppose that the less complex units are just instances of variables in universal laws. Left undecided, because unexamined, is the question of the nature of the application of the laws to the units and to the more complex actualities. Does the application make a difference either to the actualities or to the laws? Is it possible warrantedly to deny that the expressions of both are altered when they mesh? These questions can be answered only if we know something about the expressions of both actualities and finalities, and how those expressions combine.

A philosophic inquiry shares with the hard sciences a refusal to remain with the mixed. But it should not dismiss it as illusory or 'mental'. Instead, the mixed is to be acknowledged, even embraced and insisted on, at the same time that it is dissected, and the results traced back to their more basic sources. Philosophy should also resist the attempt to reduce complex actualities to the status of combinations of their parts just as strongly as it resists the attempt to convert effective, objective conditions into supposed ideas or other products of the mind.

There is little gained if one replaces what can be encountered and what is demonstrable by what is dubious. The integrity of the mixed and the complex, as well as of their components, should always be respected. Steadfast and honest inquiry demands that nothing be explained away, that the facts be respected, and that the struggle toward the light never be brought to an arbitrary end.

Because a resolute philosophic study seeks to know what is presupposed by every occurrence in the daily world and in the cosmos; what accounts for appearances, both those that mislead and those that do not; what the final conditioning realities are like and how they act; what actualities are, what they can do, and how the main kinds differ from one another; what human beings are, severally and together; because it takes seriously the existence of ultimate units, complexities of all sorts, inanimate and animate; and because it seeks to understand man both in his individual privacy and as a being together with others in a common world, it can do no less than acknowledge that the two distinct kinds of irreducible reality, actualities and finalities, are exhibited in a number of independent ways.

Where the expressions of the actualities and finalities meet is where they are at their most attenuated. It is from that meeting point one can, ought, and must begin an intensive move into them. But the more closely we come to one of them, the more surely will we come to the point where it is necessary to turn back toward the other.

A satisfactory account cannot rest with only hypothetical formulations. These have alternatives, no less basic. What is needed is reliable evidence and the careful and precise use of it. The evidences enable one to move to and into the actualities and finalities beyond any pre-assignable point. If one rejects the idea that actualities are just places where hypotheses are instanced and variables have values, one is in a position to attend to the ways in which the expressions of actualities, together with the conditions that the finalities insistently empower and impose, constitute appearances.

Instead of supposing that conditions are just present, or are introduced by a mind, one should attend to the objective ways the conditions are made to affect, and are met by expressions of equally irreducible, but finite, transient actualities.

The mixed is explicable, not brute, not beyond questioning or analysis. Man is located there at the same time that, like every other actuality, he stands outside it. At both places, he functions in ways no other actualities do or can.

Like the hard sciences, philosophy is not content to describe, to classify, or to reorganize. What it seeks are the sources of those factors that constitute and explain what is daily encountered. With the soft sciences, it refuses to treat compounds, thoughts, responsibilities, and societies as non-existents, or as being beyond all knowing or understanding. It sees that these, though not ultimately real in the sense in which actualities and finalities are, have their own integrities and careers and that a view, which has no place for them and their properties and functions, has no place for what men are and do, and for the ways they in fact live together.

Hypotheses, formulae, and limited, local conditions apply to a number of actualities. None tells whether or not, apart from it, actualities are together, or how. Nor can we learn from a study of the way in which actualities are together how they originate or what kinds of groups they form.

We can learn about the nature of the finalities which empower conditions that relate all actualities, about the nature of actualities, and about the outcome of the meshing of the expressions of actualities with the expressions of finalities. We can also learn about the nature of privacy and its epitomizations, both those which do and those which do not achieve a bodily guise and, of course, that portion of them which, though not manifested, is continuous with what is being manifested. The knowledge we seek becomes available once we separate out the contributions that men and other actualities make to what appears, and use the result as the beginning of a move into their sources.

We seem unable to use evidences to get far into inanimate beings. Occasionally, it is possible to make sympathetic contact with some of the higher animals and to then understand the nature of their privacies by discovering what could have made the evidences available. We can do better with men. Not only is it possible for us to sympathize with humans more deeply than we can with animals, but it is possible to begin with evidences available in what men publicly are and do, and to proceed intellectually with considerable surety toward what sympathy had impinged upon. The intellectual adventure follows the same route that sympathy traverses, but moves more cautiously, arriving only at what might be a source in animals, and what is close to a source in men.

The privacy of animals, though never without a bodily form, is too indeterminate to enable one to make it intelligible without introducing illegitimate additions, but the privacy of a man is available to a thinking which proceeds convergently and intensively toward the source of what he exhibits. At both times, it is necessary to distinguish a publicly presented content from what sustains this; to extricate the distinguished item; to recognize the relation that the evidence has to its origin; to have one's thoughts follow the course of the relation; and, finally, to attend to what is not manifested bodily.

Supplementing an earlier study of the finalities as lying beyond and grounding what conditions actualities, the present work places its stress on the private origins of what men bodily express. Occupied initially with the distinguishing of the required evidences, it then makes use of them to promote the understanding of the nature and activity of human privacy and of its epitomizations. Man, it makes apparent, has a distinctive privacy specialized in a person and a self, able to function apart from the body, and epitomized in multiple ways. That privacy and its epitomizations lie behind and make possible sensitivity, desire, and other ways in which men express themselves in and through their bodies.

The private control man exercises stands athwart attempts to understand him solely in terms of genes, brains, behavior, or language—or other efforts to treat him as though he were wholly public. Such endeavors are self-annihilating, presupposing as they do the presence and activity of complex unified men who privately formulate the theories, cling to them, and urge their acceptance by others who are also exercising their privacies in acts of thinking and deciding.

Privately produced claims sustain the affirmations that public occurrences are or are not present. The theory that the occurrences are the counterparts, accompaniments, duplicates, causes, or criteria of what is private, refers to such occurrences from a private position. Replacements of what is private by what is public, denials that there is anything private, and claims that what is private is unintelligible or unavailable, are all privately produced and sustained.

What is observed could not warrantedly serve as a substitute for what was supposedly being privately undergone if it was not in fact relevant to the pains, fears, hopes, and thoughts which were to be replaced. If these were absent, we could not find out whether or not the chosen public occurrence was a proper substitute. No one knows whether or not this or that bodily occurrence in another is the right replacement or counterpart of what is privately undergone by him, except by engaging in a private act and looking to that other for confirmation that one has made the correct identification. What we can know of others is rooted in what is publicly available, but this is not yet to say that it was not made available by a privacy, or that it could be separated from this.

Conceivably, every one of a man's thoughts, beliefs, memories, fears, hopes, and fantasies might have a public form, enabling one to read off what had been privately entertained. Although there does not seem to be a good warrant for holding that this supposition answers to the facts, let it be granted. One could then suppose that a man expresses his privacy in an otherwise neutral body. His *lived* body—the body he privately possesses, governs, and acts on and through—could then be said to be produced by his imposing that privacy on what is understandable in terms applicable to all bodies. On the hypothesis, the result could not tell us what had been uniquely and privately begun and, therefore, what was transformed in the course of expressing it and giving it a publicly observable form. To understand men, we must be able to refer to what is not duplicated, and that requires us to move intensively and convergently toward the singular private origins of whatever was bodily manifested by them.

A man's body makes a difference to what he uniquely intrudes on it from his privacy. Sometimes his body overwhelms or obscures what intrudes on it, but it never converts the intruded into just a public occurrence. That is why it is possible to extricate evidence of an act that was privately begun and carried out. The setting in which a private expression is imbedded can be understood in universal objective terms, appropriate to any public occurrence, but that setting is quickened and enriched by an unduplicable insistence which originates in and remains continuous with what is unduplicable and unitary, not yet in any setting.

There are publicly available evidences that a man has a privacy and that this is specialized in a number of distinguishable ways. But the discovery of the evidences, the separating of them out of the mixed and from their public, bodily settings, the use of them, and the grasp of what they terminate in, is so difficult that one is readily tempted to slip over the fact that the evidences can be found and used, and to be content to acknowledge only what can be publicly observed. This would not justify the claim that all one can or need know—or only the reputable, intelligible, or verifiable—is what is common and expressible in either formal or public terms. It is not wise to privately think and decide that all that is or can be known is entirely public.

The attempt to discover and communicate the nature of man presupposes that one engages in an activity over a period of time; tries to live up to the demands of a radical honesty; dedicates himself to the effort to reach what is irreducible; and takes himself to be accountable for what he says. It should keep to the fore the fact that other men are sensitive and conscious of what they bodily undergo; that they have private rights to whatever truth is available; and that they too have needs, desires, aims, and beliefs. The rejection or distortion of these spoils the aim of philosophic inquiry, the clarification and explanation of what all dimly but surely know.

Though the privacy of no man can be replaced by another, what is said of one may nevertheless be pertinent to all. It will of course still be grounded in and by each in a distinctive way. Every assertion about a man has a general form; it becomes pertinent to him as an individual only if it is singularized. The singularization can be known because what is publicly available is continuous with its intensive, unitary source. That source can be reached so far as one, through sympathy or thought, moves from what is publicly available to what makes it so. The limits of these moves are approached when we say what it is that we know, as well as when we address another. In the one way, a privacy is met as an adumbrated unit which we articulate by separating and relating what we experientially distinguish in it; in the other, it is that in which our address comes to rest.

Beings are and do what they are then able to be and do. They have careers because they can still be and do what they then are not able to be and do. And, so far as there is a possibly more developed stage which they can attain, they are inseparable from the promise of this, making them quite different in kind from any other being which lacks such a promise. Even if there were nothing that an infant could do that was not duplicable by an animal, it still would not be possible to equate the two, for the infant, but not the animal, has a promise to be a child. An infant, consequently, is always more than just an infant. Able to be a child, it has a promise to be one, and is so far more than what it actually is. It is not then able to be a mature man. Only a youth has that promise, and then only because he realized a promise possessed by himself as a child and, in that act, acquired the promise to become a mature man. The promises are all partial determinations of a single constant privacy.

Because there is only one privacy from the beginning to the end of life, a mature man is necessarily the same being who was once an embryo. Over the course of his life, though his privacy remains self-same, the area of its indeterminacy is narrowed. As he develops, part of his indeterminate privacy is specialized in the form of person and self and their epitomizations, each with it own distinctive promise. His maturity is measured by a realization of a succession of instituted and realized promises, each originating with and sustained by a realized, preceding promise.

An infant's epitomizations use only a very limited portion of its privacy. It makes a part of the rest of its privacy partially determinate in the form of a promise whose realization brings it to the stage of childhood. The realization of its promise is not sudden; there is no jumping from one stage to the next. But once a promise is realized, there is an epitomization of privacy that had not been and could not have been present before. The new epitomization makes a difference to the epitomizations that had been realized earlier and are now exercised together with what is newly produced, affecting it and thereby making it be and act as it could not before.

Because a realized promise makes a difference to what had been realized earlier, the presence of those earlier epitomizations in a more developed being are not equatable with what they were at an earlier stage. A child's sensitivity is different from the sensitivity of an infant, for the child has made determinate what was only promissory in the infant, thereby making a difference to the functioning of the sensitivity that had been present in the infant. The infant's pain, consequently, is not only different from the pain undergone by anything non-human, but is not equatable with the pain of a child. Related observations apply to a youth and adult, and finally to a mature man, able to become a full member of a civilized world.

A man's constant, indeterminate privacy is unitary, intensive, and controlling. Insistent and effective, it cannot be properly attributed to or identified with a passive matter, or even with a body, dynamic and living. His body provides occasions which enable him to realize what he privately promises in the form of a new power, until he arrives at the stage where all he can do is to refine, redirect, and exercise greater control, to make himself function excellently in a world with other men. Much of what he privately initiates is considerably transformed when it is expressed in and through his body. And what he bodily does has repercussions on what he privately is and how he privately functions. He can also sometimes avoid expressing some of his private epitomizations in his body, and may at times have them act on one another. His wishes, hopes, and memory may never be made publicly manifest; he can act publicly, reacting and carrying out bodily processes without apparent affect on what he is or does privately. He can think about the way he decides, and decide to think. Unitary, alive, expressive, and active, he is never just a bundle of smaller units or acts. Though there are many regions in him where items function in considerable independence of one another, and from others elsewhere, no one of these regions is neatly marked off from the rest. Distinctions are produced in act, his epitomizations being separated off from one another through the help of what is external to them.

III

Our study begins with an examination of evidences of the human person, and particularly of its most primitive, persistent epitomization, sensitivity. It goes on to examine more and more advanced epitomizations, arriving at and passing beyond the stage where a self comes to be, with its epitomizing assumed accountability, responsibility, and I. In a mature man, all epitomizations of his privacy may be present and active at the same time. To determine whether or not they are correctly ordered in relation to one another, it will help to attend to their genesis. That in turn will require us to understand how individual human beings can come to be.

Each man is at once individual and complex. As individual he has a singular, unduplicable privacy. As complex he encompasses a plurality of units—organs, cells, genes. These, too, are individual and complex. Without supposing that there ever was a time when there were actualities which were not complex, we must nevertheless also affirm that there were and now also are irreducible, unit items within the compass of the complex. To be sure, no one has identified them; every particle that has been isolated not only has an extension and could conceivably be divided, but might itself be a complex within whose confines we may later distinguish smaller units. Still, bodies fall at the rate that unit items within them fall. If those units were themselves complex, their fall would in turn depend on the movements of whatever units were within them.

We cannot avoid holding that there are unit irreducibles, unless we are prepared to allow that there are only complexes of complexes without end. That is an alternative which, as Kant remarked, should guide our inquiries, leading us to search forever for smaller and still smaller units within smaller and smaller complexes. But it is not necessary to identify unit irreducibles in order to understand how they could make it possible not only for complexes to be but for those complexes to have privacies of their own, providing that we also grant that the conjoint activity of the units makes possible the fragmentation of an aboriginal, active continuum. Although the examination of that continuum is somewhat outside the central concern of the present study, it does help ground this. Before proceeding with the main task, it is therefore desirable to at least remark on the nature of the continuum, the relation of the irreducible ultimate units to it, the ways in which the units can function together, and the kind of subdivisions of the continuum that their conjoint activity makes possible. Man will then be seen to be, despite his privacy and his uniqueness, despite his difference in kind from all other living and of course non-living beings, one whose privacy originates from the same base out of which the privacies of animals, wholes, colonies, and ultimate units also emerge.

Amoebas produce new amoebas. But animals and humans can do no more through their activity than bring about sperm and eggs, quite different from the animals and humans in power, nature, and role. When a child asks, "Where did I come from?", therefore, we do not answer its question if we reply that it came from a sperm (as Aristotle thought), from an egg (as Pincus implied), or from their union (as men today are inclined to say). A sperm is not a human being. An egg is not a human being. The piercing of an egg by a sperm does not produce a human being. Nor is the cluster of cells that quickly follows on the piercing, human. And if these are not human, they are of course also not individual persons.

Just what takes place and what this entails must be brought out. But we are already in a position to say that the child's "Where did I come from?" is a question that is not answered if one allows explanations dealing only with cells. At the very least, we must give an account of the origin of a single, complex, living embryo with a privacy and a body, both of which can become more specialized with time. We must also explain how the embryo can grow into a fetus, this into a publicly functioning human, and this into a still more developed human being, until we finally come to a matured man able to represent others and to engage in purely private activities.

Some hold that a man is one who is able to be conscious of another consciousness, can feel shame, use a language, or love. But, like others who hold that what is distinctively human is produced by a divine act, or that men necessarily think or remember, these theorists have difficulty in accounting for abysmal idiots and monstrosities. Though human, such unfortunates may not be conscious of other consciousnesses, may feel no shame, may never speak, may love no one, and may neither think nor remember.

Biology confines itself to observable occasions and to the ways in which cells and combinations of them function. Individual privacies that express themselves in and through lived bodies, and the complex, maturing individuals whose lived bodies change in power, role, appearance, capacity, and act from stage to stage, are outside its provenance. It passes by the question of the origin of individuals; or it treats that origin as somehow covered in an account of bodily growth, contenting itself with the discovery of the occasions which prompt one stage to give way to another. That knowledge is precious. But it needs supplementation if the nature and origin of individuals are to be understood.

The first men to appear on earth were individuals. Like us, they had to pass from embryo to fetus before they were born. But no knowledge of the circumstances that made their existence possible could tell us how each, as an unduplicable being, originated. Nor can we get help from psychology, sociology, or anthropology, for when these tell us how men are affected by environment, milieu, training, and the like, they not only speak in terms applicable to a number, but all the while presuppose that there are individuals to which the terms are somehow pertinent, and who somehow give these a unique import.

A study of genes, cells, and the like, will let us know why a man has blue eyes, flat feet, large ears, and so forth. If it be allowed that any one of these features could be duplicated, allowance has been made for the possible duplication of all. Were it supposed that an individual were nothing more than a collection of such features it would, therefore, also have to be supposed that he could have any number of duplicates throughout the world. But an individual has no duplicates; he is never equatable with a collection of features. Even if the experiences of a number were the same in content, each would still privately and uniquely feel, need, and desire and, through these and other means, live his body.

One can learn from a study of bodies and their public adventures, whether in native settings or in the laboratory, the kind of duplicable occasions that make it possible for non-human bodies to turn into human embryonic bodies, these into fetal bodies, and these into the bodies of infants, and so on. One will not yet know anything about the individual privacy of any one of them. No one can discover how an unduplicable human being arises by knowing how cells, or smaller or larger bodies divide and combine.

A concordant set of entities is contained within a *whole*, such as a stone, if the entities jointly sustain a single, bounded, encompassing nature; they are contained within a *colony*, such as a purple sail, if the entities are alive and function cooperatively. Neither whole nor colony can act. What is done is a function of what they encompass or range over. The moves of the entities within them set limits to where they can be and what they can do, dictating when and how they will change in place or state. When a *living being* is viewed as a whole, abstraction is necessarily made from the effective bodily presence of its insistent, singular privacy.

The privacy of a living being is expressed in and through its body, constraining and dictating to the entities confined there. When it moves, what it encompasses also moves, and that quite suddenly, to places rather distant for them. While it rests, most of the entities it had encompassed remain confined at the place where it is. To be sure, the entities in it also have some independence and have an effect on it. They, too, are realities. They also exist independently of it and one another. What they are and how they act affects the being within whose body they are confined. Their mass, magnitude, and moves set limits to where the complex unitary body can be and how it can change. But all the while that they are constrained by that body, they continue to determine the functioning of a whole whose nature partly coincides with the nature of the living being. When the body is no longer lived, what is left is that whole, with an appearance something like that of the living being, but no longer controlled by a single privacy, unable to constrain the entities within its bodily confines.

A whole might encompass living as well as non-living beings. So may a complex living individual. But unlike a whole, a living being has an effective privacy. If it is the most primitive of living beings, it was produced

through the action of what was not alive; if more advanced, it was produced through the action of what was alive, but different in nature and
kind from itself.

Wholes and complex living beings encompass other entities. The living are produced through the action of what is no longer found within
them. Only they are not constituted by what they happen to confine.

A complex living being arises through the joint action of living beings
which are no longer. Unlike a whole, it cannot be accounted for solely by
understanding what it happens to encompass, not only because it affects
these, but because it presupposes the action of other entities. The problem of the origin of an individual man, in particular, comes down to
understanding how he could have originated from a joining of a living
sperm and egg, neither of which is a human being. That problem will not
be adequately dealt with unless a number of difficult questions are answered:

1. What happens to the individual sperm and egg on their successful
   meeting?
2. How does a fetus come to replace an embryo?
3. What happens to an embryo's privacy when the embryo gives way
   to a fetus?
4. Is the embryo a human? Is the fetus?

1. Neither the egg nor the sperm of a human can be found in the
embryo which eventually exists. They cannot continue to be there just as
privacies, for privacies require appropriate bodies. They have privacies of
their own, but once they give way to a single living being that being has its
own privacy, quite different in nature and power from theirs. The new
being depends for its presence on the conjoint activity of entities in the
sperm and egg. But its privacy is unique, and must have a source distinct
from those entities. One way of accounting for that privacy—and for any
other—is by showing each to be a condensation of a primal, insistent
continuum, primitive, unbounded, and indeterminate. Plato referred to
this as 'the receptacle'; Aristotle called it a 'prime matter'; Whitehead
spoke of it as 'Creativity'. Schopenhauer, Bergson, and Jung referred to it
in other ways. The most elementary condensations of it are the privacies
of irreducible unit actualities, each fragmenting it in a distinctive way,
and leaving untouched most of it. The conjoint activity of those units
promotes another fractionization of the continuum. If the units enable
the fractionated portion to be expressed, the outcome is a unitary being,
privately lived; if they do not, the outcome is a colony or whole, with a
privacy unable to control the body from which it is inseparable.

The Greek for 'power' is *dunamis*. *Dunamis* is also Greek for 'potentiality' and for 'dynamic'. The primal continuum is all three at once; 'dunamis' therefore is an ideal technical name for it. The dunamis has the vitality of Plato's receptacle, but it needs no demiurgos to divide it. One can identify it with Aristotle's prime matter, but only if, contrary to him, this is recognized to be insistent. Unlike Whitehead's Creativity it does not make everything its creature. It is not more real but only more subterranean than individuals. The irreducible units which condense it are in turn to be understood in both Democritean and Leibnizian terms, the one emphasizing the bodily side of them, the other the private.

Ultimate units are *atomic monads*, each with its own privacy and body. When a number of those atomic monads act in consonance, their monadic sides elicit a new fragmentation of the dunamis in the form of a new privacy. That privacy is inseparable from a single body within which the atomic sides of the initial units are at once confined and bunched. The new body has a nature, specializing common conditions, and a mass obtained from the atoms. If the body merely expressed the fact that the monadic atoms were in consonance, it would constitute the body of a whole. Only when a privacy in fact governs the body from which it is inseparable is there a single complex body lived by a single privacy.

To envisage monadic atoms acting in consonance it is necessary to make a double abstraction from them as they coexist in the cosmos under common cosmic conditions. One must abstract not only from the ways they are distributed under the governance of the conditions, but also from the ways they are distributed through the actions of the more complex bodies in which they function as units. We engage in the first of these abstractions when we accept whatever distributions we find. We engage in the second when we take notice of the motions of complex bodies, since these help determine where their contained items will be located in public space.

Monadic atoms may so function together that they fragment the dunamis into the ineffective privacy of a whole, into the copresence of a number of effective privacies in a colony, or into the effective privacy of a single living being. Those living beings which exist within the confines of another are parasites, aliens, independent beings with their own privacies, functioning there under limitations but still independently of the larger living being. Or they are organic, not separated from the unitary being. Though they may play an important role in the life of what contains them, they are there without the ability to make possible the isolation and mediation of the privacy of the including being.

The product of sperm and egg is not a unitary living being. Like a

Portuguese man-of-war, it is a colony, without its own effective privacy. Nowhere in that colony can the sperm and egg be found. In their place are the genes and cells that had existed within the confines of the sperm and egg. Did the sperm and egg directly produce a new individual with a distinctive privacy, this would have a body which it lived and thereby unified. But this is not what results or could result when sperm and egg are successfully joined. Together they produce a conjunction of smaller units in a colony, the privacies of the sperm and egg sinking back into the primal continuum where they can no longer be distinguished, their natures merging into the conditions that they had separately specialized, and their bodies dividing into an aggregate of bodies of smaller units. On uniting, sperm and egg vanish, leaving behind the independently functioning items that had been in them.

Nothing survives the union of sperm and egg unless it has a privacy of its own, inseparable from a body. It can then become no more than a member of a colony. For that colony to give way to an embryo, the members of the colony will have to become nuances in the embryonic complex living being, with its own distinctive privacy and lived organic body, or they will have to become independent units existing within the boundaries of that being.

A gene or cell is a genuine, independent, living being only if it can exercise a distinctive privacy in and through its own body. If it has a body which it lives, it can exist within the confines of one that is larger, affecting and being affected by this in the way in which entities in a whole or colony are affected by and affect these. In wholes and colonies units are bunched with others by what contains them, while they make a difference to the way this acts.

Process philosophers are among the few who recognize that atomic monads are not eternal. But they tend to minimize the atomic side of these, and for the most part suppose that the units last for only a moment, to be replaced by others with similar, short temporal spans. At the very least, it should have been said that the units have atomic bodies, and that these, together with and inseparable from monadic privacies, exist for indefinite periods, with some passing away while others continue or come to be. So many in fact continue, that most of the atomic monads that are present at one moment are present at the next, whether or not there are newly produced wholes, colonies, or unitary living beings within which those atomic monads exist.

The coming together of sperm and egg involves a loss in one sense and a gain in another. It requires the cessation of two living beings with their privacies, and the coming to be of a colony. This has an ineffective privacy, one unable to live a single unified body.

Might not sperm and eggs themselves be just colonies? Might there not be just a plurality of independent, actual, atomic monads which make possible, not sperm and egg, each lived by its own effective privacy, but a single colony with a single ineffective privacy? No. Were sperm and egg just colonies, they would not be individuals. Though the most primitive of complex living beings arise solely because some atomic monads act concordantly and thereby permit the isolation and expression of a fragment of the common dunamis, it is the joint activity of the individual sperm and egg that makes possible the conjoint activity of the atomic monads in them both. The result is a new privacy living its own distinctive body, a body which encompasses the atomic monads that were in the sperm and egg.

2. Well before they fully function in a public world, living beings pass through a number of stages. Ignoring refinements, and attending mainly to man, a colony gives way to a unitary embryo, this to a non-viable fetus, this to a viable fetus, and this finally to an infant.

An embryo takes nourishment and excretes. A fetus has a distinctive structure and organs. The one grows into the other, but there is no precise point where one can say a fetus replaced an embryo. Throughout there is a single privacy. From the first, this is expressed in some way, and at every stage provides a background and an opportunity for a later stage to be present, until we arrive at a man at his most mature.

Although a man's privacy remains self-same over the course of his life, at different times it expresses itself differently, manifesting itself in different specialized epitomizations. As a consequence, it is able to provide different and appropriate controls over the course of the body's development.

An earlier stage contains the promise of what is next able to be realized. An embryo has the promise to become a fetus, this to become viable, and this to become an infant. An infant has the promise to sustain social roles. It becomes a child when it is able to assume the roles; it then has the promise to become a youth, one in a position to function in accord with private dictates that it act in various social contexts. The youth has the promise to become a mature human, one who is able to perfect himself at the same time that he carries out a representative role in a society. At each stage the next is foreshadowed and gradually realized as a capacity to act in a distinctive way. The acquisition of the capacity is one with the attainment of a power to act at the next stage. One lives at that stage by exercising that power.

Although superior in one way, because of the promise it grounds, the sensitivity of a human embryo is also inferior to the sensitivity of an animal, particularly one well-matured and intelligent. The latter alone has realized a promise to have a consciousness—a promise that the embryo does not have. Also, the human embryo must pass through a number of stages before its sensitivity can be radically modified; an animal's sensitivity is already modified by other powers.

A fetus realizes what was only promissory in the embryo. The exercise of powers by the embryo makes possible the fetal realization of what the embryo promises. That realization provides the fetal promise with determinations enabling a distinctive fetal capacity to be exercised. The exercise of the fetal power makes possible the realization of another promise whose realization characterizes a viable human. Since an embryo does not have the promise that a fetus has—a promise which is relative to what the fetus has already realized—the embryo and fetus are necessarily identical in one sense and not in another. There is the same privacy in both, but this is specialized in the form of a promise in the one and a power exercised in the other.

The privacy of a mature man is the very privacy possessed by an embryo, but with determinations and a promise this does not have. At both times there is sensitivity; at both times the body is lived sensitively. But the mature man's sensitivity is different from the embryo's, for the promise which is grounded in the embryo's sensitivity has first to be actualized in the fetus, itself connected with a distinctive promise for some other private power. That power can be so realized that it affects the sensitivity, changes its course, alters its emphasis and effectiveness. Since the other powers that are achieved as the individual matures also make a difference to the functioning of its sensitivity, the sensitivity of the embryo and the mature man must differ. They are quite different in tone and effectiveness.

3. The privacy of a human being remains self-same from embryo to death. To suppose that the privacy begins earlier is to suppose that it was already present in a colony. This would allow it to be replaced by two or more new privacies, since at that stage it is possible to generate multiple fetuses, each able to develop into a live birth. To suppose instead that the privacy begins with the fetus, or with the infant, or later, is to take a stage of fulfilled promise to be essential to the presence of a privacy. Were this warranted, if we could legitimately deny that the privacy was already present in the embryo, we would have a good warrant for denying that it was present in the infant, child, and youth, for these too have only in a promissory form what is later actualized in the privacy of a mature man.

Unless the same individual human privacy could somehow be in each identical twin, a pre-embryonic being must be a colony, lacking the singular privacy of an individual. Destroying a colony of human cells denies life to what necessarily precedes a singular human, but the destruction of such a predecessor is not the destruction of a human. The exact point where a human comes to be is where multiple identical births are no longer possible. The fact that we cannot mark the exact moment when the impossibility comes about does not mean that we cannot clearly specify times when a human can and when a human cannot have come to be. Once a human has come to be, he persists with a single privacy, acquiring new epitomizing determinations and expressions as he matures. Throughout, he will have rights and abilities not available to a colony.

4. An embryo and a fetus, like a full-grown man, are human, though they lack his powers, some of his rights, and do not have his ability to know, decide, and control. Alternatively, only he is fully human, for though they have bodies through which the self-same privacy is expressed, that privacy lacks the determinations that a mature man's epitomizing powers provide.

There is just a single human privacy, the same at every stage, from its origin in an embryo until it dies. But when viewed in terms of the particular epitomizations that can be exercised, the roles that can be assumed and carried out, the rights that are possessed, the rights that are expressed, and what can be done with the body, one must say that only when fully matured is there a true man. But the very same privacy is present all the while, even though there are times when this is relatively unspecialized, and when the body could not be controlled or used as well as it could later.

At each stage, a living being necessarily, but not consciously or deliberately, insists on being what it is, and on growing to the degree that it can. The insistencies are so many essential claims, expressing rights that can be justifiably overridden only if they stand in the way of superior claims. The right of a fetus is greater than the right of an embryo, for this has only the promise to act as a fetus can. Similarly, the right of an infant is greater than the right of a fetus that can become an infant, for the infant, and not the fetus, can become a member of a human society with its distinctive alliances and opportunities; its different dignities and ranks; its language, rules, and customs; its tasks, demands, and play; its morality, ritual, values, and pervading myths. An infant does not, of course, function as a member of a society. It has only the right to be a member of one. The membership accrues to it after it is born. Before that time, it can at most be what is able to arrive at the position where it can freely sustain, carry out, and eventually assume social roles.

We have no more warrant for crediting an embryo or fetus with the rights of an infant than we have for giving the rewards of a victor to all who enter a contest. The matter assumes considerable importance when the fetus becomes viable. Before then it was not, but now it is a person with a right to become a social unit. It is not, however, a functioning person. To be this, it will have to be born. Only then will there be one who is able to be a social being who can subsequently assume social roles. Only then will it be possible for there to be one who can fill, sustain, adopt, and enrich social roles. As the individual matures, he will be able to assume still other roles, and fill them out in ways he could not before. Gradually, he will move toward the stage where he can produce new epitomizations of his privacy, and sometimes impose them on another without expressing them bodily.

Without taking thought, a cat becomes acquainted with other cats. Rarely does it confuse another cat with a dog, a pig, or a man. It neither guesses nor infers. It knows nothing about traditions. It does not know how to argue by analogy. A male elephant has little trouble in identifying female elephants, and in distinguishing them from other animals, even ones as large as a rhinoceros. Men are no less successful in their recognition of others as men—and therefore as at least persons, loci of human rights. Yet dominant theories speak as though the knowledge of other persons was at best hazardous and at most impossible.

The brain is not sensitive; it has no desires; nothing interests it. No study of the way the brain functions can tell us about the existence, nature, or activities of a person. If it has rights, they are surely not as many or as great as those which a person possesses, or to which he gives lodgement on behalf of other aspects of his privacy. A person is neither encapsulated in some bodily part nor engaged in just physical or biological operations.

Men and other living beings can be fooled for a while by wax figures, mirror images, statues. No one of us is altogether sure how to speak precisely of mass murderers or of embryos just formed. There was a time when men were unsure whether or not the Indians in South America had souls and therefore were true humans. There are some today who say that dolphins and chimpanzees differ only in appearance, degree of promise, and size of vocabularies from those whom most of us call men. Still, some of us know others who are persons, and know that these are quite different from animals. The knowledge has a double prong. When another is known to be a person, he is known as one who can both be with other persons and interact with them, at the same time that he is known to have a private status. He may have features and abilities like those possessed by others, but he also stands apart from them, not altogether penetrable. Existing in a public world with others he is, at the same time, radically alone. Confronted as a you held on to from a dense, insistent, resistant side away from us, we face him as a public person inseparable from a private, one who is together with us in a social context at the same time that he stands away, possessing rights that may not have been publicly expressed or acknowledged.

Physical and chemical laws and other conditions apply to both living and non-living beings. But they are too general in character and too broad in range to be able to account for the growth and decay, procreation, nourishment, and excretion of living beings. These, with their distinctive natures and careers, are governed by conditions having a greater specificity and a more restricted scope than those that embrace chemical or physical units.

The realm of biology falls inside the compass of chemistry and physics, where it is occupied with distinctive types of entities, and the conditions appropriate to these. Inside the realm of biology, the fact of growth requires a new way of understanding how items can function together. But biology must itself be left behind if one is to understand what a full human being is. The privacy of man is to the side of its scope and interest; it can therefore know man only in part. It does not and it cannot tell us about his ability to engage in activities independent of, and at times in opposition to, his body. Nor does it concern itself with him in the role of a representative of all the others, offering them truths, bringing tradition to bear, and the like.

Just as physical and chemical laws are specialized and limited by living beings, biological laws are contracted in the form of limited natures, and as relations connecting these. With an increase in the complexity of a pre-embryonic colony, the biological laws that apply to it give way to those that are singularly pertinent to what will give way to a human embryo. Although this must become a viable fetus before there can be a publicly functioning human, with roles relative to those assumed by other humans, it can be anticipatorily dealt with as having a social import. But though it can be named and cherished, only after it is born is there a human able to carry out social roles—initially unconsciously and just by being part of a family—in relation to the roles assumed by other humans.

As just a member of the species 'man', a human being has a promise inseparable from the prospect of being a social unit. As having that promise, he has the status of a person. Were he only viable, no more could be claimed for him than that he was a unit in a social setting, for only later, after birth, can he take on a social, and eventually a representative role.

If we attend to an infant, or even to a viable fetus, in a social setting, we deal with it as a person able to have a self. Do we not have to go on and hold that some animals, since they live in groups and even in quite tightly bound communities, are also able to have selves? We would, if they could, then or later, become privately accountable or responsible for what they do. Only a person can take upon himself the carrying out of a role, and only a newborn human has the promise of maturing toward the state where he could take upon himself the carrying out of such a role. Only a person can privately initiate an act which is to take him through a common context to other men, faced as having correlative roles. Were all other humans to perish, he would still continue to be a person, and even to have a self. The absence of other persons would deny him only a context in which he could act as a person, but all the while he would be able to act as a person toward other persons, identified imaginatively or retrospectively.

A lived body is a living body governed privately. As living, it is an object for biology; as lived, it is not. Did he not make a living body into his lived body, a man's body would be somewhat more complicated than others, but would not sustain and help carry out decisions or other activities of no necessary biological import. A human body is lived, with different degrees of intensity throughout the day, relaxed at one moment and tensed at another, sometimes through the imagined confrontation of what is pleasant or threatening, but always through expressions of a distinctive privacy.

We are now in a position to give a firm answer to the child's question. We can say to it: "When you were tiny, parts of your body were joined together by something special that was separated off from the larger world, and made you. Since then, you have been helping your body grow, and it has been helping you grow." If the child goes on to ask where its body came from, it invites a foreshortened biological report. In the course of this, it would have to be remarked that its body is always accompanied by a single, unduplicable privacy, and that this is expressed in and through the body. The recital may also have to be backed by the observation that the child is able to ask its question because it has reached the stage where the privacy, without losing connection with the body, is able to engage in some activities apart from that body. It may then be enough to add to the initial remarks, "You were you when you couldn't ask the question. You are you when you ask it. You are you all the time in between. You will be you when you answer it. As your body grows, you will continue to be, and will be able to ask other questions, and even to answer many of them yourself."

No adult will or should be satisfied with the first part of this answer, and all should be past the stage where they need the rest of it. An adult will want 'the something special', which was intended to convey to the child the presence of a privacy, to be explained. And that would lead the adult far from where he would perhaps like to be. If he were willing to accept a short answer, one may conceivably have to say no more to him than, "The body is affected by a distinctive privacy which may eventually act in considerable independence of the body."

Not until much later, and often enough never, does a child or adult ask just how one knows that he or any other human is a person. It is a question which should be asked and answered. Otherwise one will fail to take adequate account of the extraordinary status that men have, and will leave unexplained or unexamined an item of knowledge that is within the reach of a child. For the moment, it is enough to repeat that though only humans are persons, there are humans who are not fully functioning persons. A fetus and an infant have a human privacy in too promissory, too indeterminate a guise to enable them to be functioning persons in a common world.

PART ONE

ONE

The Person and Its Epitomizations

a. Some Important Distinctions

Traditional psychology took as one of its main tasks the understanding of what had been previously been referred to as 'soul', and is now called 'mind'. The one term carries overtones reflecting religious suppositions; the other is occupied with what is consciously entertained or has some reference to this. The one, but not the other, makes provision for character and decisions; the second, but not the first, makes provision for what apparently is partly duplicated in subhumans. Both overemphasize specialized activities originating in human privacies.

Like the supposed soul, a man's privacy persists from the beginning to the end of his life. Unlike that soul, its origin does not require a reference to an act of divine creating, nor allow one to suppose that a man could have some kind of existence without a body. Like the mind, his privacy can engage in activities independently of his body but, unlike the mind, it is able to be and function without thinking.

In recent times, the entire issue has been reduced by some to the question of how to understand pain, as though pain exhausted the content of privacies or even of the traditional 'mind'. Those who cling to some remnant of the traditional view take all pain to be ineluctably private, requiring the acknowledgment of more than bodies, public activity, or a common language. Their opponents either try to deny the presence of those private pains, to exhaust their meaning in physiological terms, to treat them as interpretations of otherwise unspecifiable feelings, or to make them the objects of the same kind of knowing that is pertinent to more public and palpable items. The issue of the difference between the private and public occurrences is not fully faced in any of these views, mainly because a number of distinctions are overlooked:

Privileged and secret access. I alone feel my pains and think my thoughts. My decisions are made only by me in privacy. I may of course yield to the demands of others, follow their suggestions, copy their ways. Whether I do or not, I have an access to my pains and thoughts that no one else has, even when what I confront is accompanied by bodily occurrences that others might note and duplicate. My access is privileged. But that does not mean it is secret, never yielding data that others could possibly note and use. If what I privately produce is not revealed or communicated to others, they of course will not know of it. It is sometimes contended, though, that some manifestation or communication is inevitable, on the grounds that nothing ever occurs in privacy without a distinctive, eventual, observable occurrence taking place in the body. But this is just a dictum, backed by no evidence or persuasive reason.

Whatever I confront, and this whether it occurs in my privacy, in my body, or in the world beyond, *I* confront. I have a privileged access to whatever I attend, no matter where it be. The point has been exploited by solipsism, though it is difficult to know whether or not its advocates think of themselves as alone having a privileged access, or whether they allow that such an access characterizes each man's approach to the items with which he deals. If the first, the solipsists should provide reasons for taking themselves alone to have that capacity; if the second, they abandon their solipsistic thesis in favor of a supposed truth about other real men existing independently of them.

A privileged access on the part of different men need not terminate in different items. All can attend to the same objects. Each will then act from a private base, all his own, but each will still be able to attend to himself as in the public world, as a me. Each, too, will be able to know himself via that me. Since every man is faced as a you which partly coincides with his me, others can come to know at least part of the person at which each can arrive in a privileged act. Of course, the others will not know what was not publicly expressed, but they may still have good grounds for inferring it. Certainly, no one knows the hidden thoughts of others. Nor can he be sure of them, even when he notes the inadvertencies that accompany their deliberate acts. But anyone can know that thoughts can be hidden, for all can know that what men express are attenuated continuations of private powers which can be directed at other private powers, as well as elsewhere.

Though I privately constitute my pains—and my dreams, responsibility, and thoughts—I do not have a secret access to them. That would require my experiencing and knowing to hold on to their own termini.

But both I and another can attend to my body, and although I alone feel my pain, he can sympathetically move toward it as that which was occasioned by something in or affecting my body. When I and he attend to what I make publicly available, the privileged access that each of us has to what he then notes, will allow each of us to make contact with what I constitute. Because our advances toward my I are resisted by my outward thrusting privacy, he and I can have a publicly grounded, direct acquaintance with an increasingly intensive version of what we both impinge upon.

Usually, I can penetrate further into myself from a public position than others can. Whether I do or not, I alone sustain what I made publicly available to myself and others. I do this through the act of the very power by means of which I publicly arrive at me. My private privileged access is therefore one from which I can benefit in ways others cannot, even when they have a ready access to me.

Adumbrative and direct references. It is a commonplace in grammar and logic that some terms—'this' and 'here' and 'that' and 'there'—are denotative, referential, directing us to something external to themselves. But no terms could possibly denote, refer, take one to something outside them. All are on a footing, just words, as much a part of language as 'if', 'but', 'horse', and 'brown'. When it is claimed instead that some terms are predicates and that these are predicated of subjects, one has to embrace the absurdity of maintaining that 'cat' in "This is a cat" is predicated of the word 'this' or that the word 'cat' attaches to what is sleeping in the corner. Nothing in principle is altered when one here exchanges words or terms for concepts or ideas. All are used in articulations where they are related to one another as coordinate units. Were this the end of the matter, there would be little more that men could do but try to speak to one another by exchanging sentences or other articulations. But then no account could be given of the individuals who were making the exchange. Nor would there be anything external to what was exchanged that could be acknowledged to make the articulations be true or false. Men would talk, but nothing would be spoken about. Nor would anything be communicated to another.

Denotative terms are components in articulations. Those articulations have the status of assertions when they are offered as truths or falsehoods. Both as articulations and as assertions, they are inseparable from what is external to them, the articulations offering an analysis of it and the assertions thrusting toward it. Neither hurls itself out of language or moves way from speaker and listener toward some neutral object; neither is attached by the user to what lies outside both of them. Both are inseparable from an adumbrative component terminating at what enables the terms in them to converge at it.

What is spoken about provides a single, undivided locus for the units in articulated assertions. Those units are distinct but related factors. In the assertion, "This is a cat", the 'this' and the 'cat' are distinct but joined; they are units in an assertion about a this-cat, adumbratively reached.

It makes little difference to the issue whether one takes account only of what is observable or of what is imagined, or of what could be confronted by others or only by oneself. We can speak about anything, and in the act of doing this we will necessarily adumbratively make contact with what is real. If what we express is a fantasy, a fiction, a work of art, it will be connected with what Rilke called 'the all', with existence, or with mankind. Metaphysical assertions, instead, will be adumbratively joined to privacies, finalities, or the primal dunamis which is behind all. Whatever it is about, an assertion will join its terms syntactically in an articulation, while it relates them adumbratively to what is being articulated by means of the terms. Because the adumbration is continuous with the assertion, it is possible to pass beyond the assertion toward what makes it true or shows it to be false. The fact is implicitly denied when one takes "I am in pain" to be equatable with a moaning or a groaning. Were it one of these, others would not be told about something privately undergone, an actual pain.

Assertions about what we encounter are sometimes sharply distinguished from what is encountered. Sometimes the one hides the other, in whole or part. When I have a severe pain, I usually keep the pain to the fore, and do not allow the assertion, "I am in pain" to hide what I am undergoing. Sometimes, though, a pain is so slight or inconsequential that I readily ignore it to attend to the assertion that it is present, using this as a reminder perhaps, or as an occasion for drawing consequences.

When I attend to what is to be attended to by others, I sometimes allow my assertion and its adumbration to overlay the direct relation that I have to what I confront. But sometimes what I encounter in the public world is so startling or important that I do not allow any assertion to stand in the way. Usually, though, I keep the two apart, refusing to allow assertions to hide from me what I adumbratively reach, and not letting my experiences stand in the way of my formulating intelligible claims about what I confront.

An unexamined rationalistic supposition, accepted by many empiricists, treats assertions as though they were adequate substitutes for what is undergone. An equally unexamined, empirical supposition, accepted by most rationalists, treats directly encountered content as though it were identical with what was asserted of it. Distinguishing the two allows one to say that we can know what we confront without denying that we privately forge, accept, and use assertions.

Intentionality and Constitutionalizing. Whatever we confront is constituted both by us privately and by what is other than ourselves. The constituting is not always consciously carried out. Since it depends for its operation on given content, it is necessarily distinct from a supposed 'intentionality', a private complete constituting by a mind or self.

Every act is in part a constituting, and partly forced to work with and against oppositional factors. If either component is dominant, the other will have at least the role of its bearer; if they are more or less of equal strength, something new will be produced in which neither component may be discerned. If an intentionality is to produce something, it too must be met by a counteracting agent. Were intentionality to meet no opposition, it would simply peter out or come to an end; there would be nothing at which it ended, nothing which was 'intentionally' produced.

Pains, no less than any other occurrence, in or outside privacy, are constituted occurrences. One of their components is privately begun; the other is bodily occasioned. The privately produced component may be so overwhelmingly dominant that the contribution occasioned by the body may be obscured. Consequently, it will not be known by anyone who attends to that body.

What is constituted from within terminates at content externally sustained. A feeling of pain ends at the point where it is bodily supported. Here the experience of it comes to a focal point which the body, from its side, sustains. An intention is a special case of such constituting, requiring as it does not only a terminating, insistent constituting, but one which is conscious, perhaps deliberate, and peculiar to men.

The body, both when we feel pain and when we intend, acts not as an antecedent cause of a bodily outcome, but as one contributor to the production of what is different from itself and from what privacy contributes. A pain is constituted primarily by a privacy which ends with the pain as that which is being limited by a body. Despite the great role that the body plays, the pain is possessed and felt from within. When, instead, a color or an apple is in focus, there is a reverse stress. What the color or apple contribute to the result is not overwhelmingly subject to what is privately insisted on. As a consequence, the experiences of the color or apple terminate in what is available to others. These, in their experiencing, contribute their own distinctive, privately initiated components, to constitute their own privately experienced, but objective, color and apple. The color and apple cling to what is outside the experiencing. Pains, instead, cling to constituting privacies. An occasional poet, though, seems to find the emphases reversed.

To make evident what one is privately contributing, it is necessary to intrude this on what is distinct from it, accessible to others. Were this never done, men would not make their privacies evident. They would lead completely secret existences, at the same time that they had public careers. In effect, they would be two beings which might have nothing to do with one another. Their bodies could then have their own tasks, and might interact with other bodies, regardless of what the men privately were, did, and sought. Conceivably, the men could take note of what their bodies needed or of the encounters these had with other bodies but since, on the hypothesis, no one would ever make his privacy evident, it would not be possible for anyone else to know whether or not this was done. Such supposed, forever hidden privacies are quite different from the privacies that men in fact have. But it is also true that their privacies are not always nor completely manifest in or through their bodies. Must we not therefore conclude that just so far as a man's privacy is not publicly manifested it is unknown? Not if he can tell us the nature of his experiencing. Suppose he does not? His silence will also express his privacy, contrasting with other expressions of it. We will not then know, of course, what he is being silent about, unless, say, his silence is a reply to a specific question. But we will know that he can express his privacy by means of his silence, once we know that silences can connect terms in assertions.

Men own their bodies, express themselves by means of their bodies, and use them. Their privacies are never fully probed or exhaustively known, for their expressions are overlaid and modified by occurrences which originate with their bodies and elsewhere. One can penetrate into their privacies, but not fully. The further one penetrates the greater is the resistance encountered, until one is finally blocked. That there is more to another's privacy than what one makes contact with, the resistance makes evident. Since something is learned about the privacy by discovering what was already manifested and what this presupposes, it is just as dogmatic to claim that we can know nothing of the privacy, even that it is present and makes a difference to what is bodily occurring, as it is to claim that we can grasp that privacy completely.

We may be deceived, misled, lied to. If we are, we will of course not know exactly what had been privately entertained, believed, known. We may never find out what occurred. But if we know that deceptions and lies had been produced, or if we mistake them for truths, we necessarily know that there had been private activities, and that private use had been made of the body and public language. We may even come to know some of the more specialized forms through which privacy was evidenced. And what we may not be able to discern in some particular man at some one time may sometimes be surmised from what we learned about others. Occasionally, the correctness of a surmise is confirmed.

Animals do not lie. They do not deceive. They do not have the kind of privacy which permits the forging of ideas, intentions, purposes, and beliefs. They therefore cannot offer any of these in a good or in a misleading form. Subhumans, to be sure, provide miscues, make errors, feint. These, and protective colorations, allurements, and misdirections, are unreflecting expressions of their privacies in and through their bodies. They are not equatable with falsehoods. Only men can produce these.

Deny that a man can determine some of the ways in which his privacy is to be publicized, and you deny that he could ever lie. By glance and grimace he might even betray what he preferred to keep hidden, thereby making it possible to know that he was lying. Such self-betrayal is beyond the power of an animal. Since it never is able to set its privacy in opposition to its body, it could not decide to keep something hidden, and then have this inadvertently evidenced. An animal can wait, and even refuse to satisfy or protect itself in order to benefit others. Hungry, it may remain quiet, waiting patiently for the moment when it can pounce most effectively. It might give food to its young though it needs the food itself. Such acts require no deliberation, no ideas, no intentions, no self-determinations, no private expressions which are denied a public role.

It is possible to train an animal by taking account of the fact that some of its bodily acts can be triggered by other acts. The discovery does not require the supposition that there is anything the animal can do which lacks a bodily occasion or expression. A hungry man seems to act somewhat similarly. Much of what he does can be explained in ways similar to those that have proved illuminating in connection with an animal. We can note how his bodily acts affect one another and, backing this with a knowledge of the ways he had been disciplined, educated, and socialized, can get a good idea of what he will subsequently do. But not always. He can oppose his bodily tendencies and can act on behalf of beliefs and ideals. An examination of his body will not tell us that he does so act, and surely will not tell us what he is accepting as a guiding control.

Cats seem to have secrets of their own; chimpanzees play with their keepers; horses take scolding badly. Why deny that these have privacies like man's, only not as well developed? Why deny that some animals have private lives and that they express part of it apart from their bodies? Or, taking the opposite tack, why not deny that any man has more than a capacity to act bodily, though in more complicated ways than are possible to an animal? A single answer suffices for both questions: We should affirm whatever, but nothing more than the available evidences warrant.

There seems to be nothing we cannot explain in the behavior of animals that cannot in principle be expressed by referring to the observable functioning of their bodies. But there is much that a man does which remains inexplicable if one overlooks the fact that he can be privately occupied with objectives that are not pertinent to the body, and may be entertained and be effective within his privacy.

We are precipitate if we credit the privacies of animals with powers and roles for which we can provide no evidence. We unnecessarily confine ourselves if we refuse to follow the lead of the evidences that men publicly provide, back to their sources, and if we fail to recognize the capacity of some of those sources to produce what does not have a bodily expression. Although we come to know those sources only from what is publicly manifested, what we then can also come to know is that they can act in non-bodily ways.

Men do not express their privacies all at once. At no time do they make their privacies altogether evident. Nor do animals. But men not only bolster one expression by another; they occasionally restrain their expressions and occasionally express themselves deliberately. Most often, though, what they privately begin achieves a bodily expression without reflection. And when they are clear as to just what they would like to express in and through their bodies, they do not usually know exactly how to do so, or how to do it most effectively. There is considerable slippage between what a man privately initiates and what he publicly does.

It is also true that a privately initiated act may be expressed in such a way that it is obscured in what is bodily manifested. If a man decides to stand and does stand, it may not be possible, from an examination of what he does, to know why or that he had so decided. Not knowing or being able to discover the causes or reasons for his standing at just that moment, we really do not know whether or not his standing was due to some hidden bodily cause which has not yet been found, or to some external provocation which no one has detected. Even if a man said that he had decided to stand, and even if we add that when we so decide we correctly report what we did, it still may be true that he never did decide or that, if he did, his decision did not have anything to do with his getting up. The statement, "If a man decides to stand, he does stand", has a consequent that may have nothing to do with the antecedent.

Our confidence that there is an independently functioning, distinctive, human privacy does not depend on the reports of other men or on the supposed knowledge we have of what we ourselves do, though both of these may lend it support. It is possible that the reports are in error, or that hope has been allowed to pass for knowledge. After all, many of us are quite confident that we are immortal, that there is a God who loves us, and that virtue will triumph. None of these is obviously true. May we not have outstripped the reach of all evidence in a similar way when we take men to have distinctive privacies, and when we claim that men alone can use their privacies to realize ends of no bodily value? A short answer to questions like these has already been indicated. The claim that we may be mistaken in supposing that there is a distinctive human privacy is itself privately grounded. Without that grounding, there could be only a series of sounds or words uttered. Nothing would be offered as a truth.

To claim that anything is true is to set the thesis that there is a distinctive, human privacy in an invulnerable position, making it quite different from the claim that one is immortal, that there is a God who loves men, or that virtue will triumph. But one does not then know much about the nature of that privacy, how it functions, and what its main divisions are. Evidently, a much longer answer must be provided and justified. And that requires us to attend to evidences that cannot, even in principle, be accounted for in purely bodily terms, and which can, unlike the evidences that an animal provides, take us to what is not inescapably expressed on behalf of the body or a group.

It is not possible to account for everything that a man does by attending only to what can be known about his biology, physiology, chemistry, mechanics, psychology, or social life, separately or together. The contention seems over-bold, too uncompromising. It surely will make the intelligent reader skeptical, on the alert for flaws. That result, however, instead of being regrettable, is eminently desirable and intended.

Nothing in a philosophic account should be accepted—even the most cautious and most widely endorsed claims—unless it can be justified. Let it now, though, be supposed that there will be a time when everything that a man does can be explained by making reference only to the body by itself or to its interactions with other bodies. It will still have to be admitted that this cannot now be done. Explanations today of what men do require a reference to a distinctive human privacy. We can hold on to the explanations—indeed, we must do so—while we continue to look for other explanations which take account only of bodies and the situations in which they interact. We will of course know what we are looking for, only because we already have knowledge of the nature and functioning of human privacy.

Could we find a satisfactory set of bodily grounded explanations for all that a man does, we would be tempted to take him to be a living body exhibiting distinctive powers. But we would not then know where those powers originated and if or how they were able to act on what was apart from them. If we replace a reference to his privacy by the evidence it enables us to use, we will lose what justified the quest and warrants the replacement, for justifications, when cut off from what they are supposed to justify, cease to be justifications. A replacement of what one seeks to understand by what enables us to understand it, must remain attached to what it replaces; if it does not, the replacement loses its warranted status.

What we learn can be used in place of what was to be explained only if it is sustained by what it replaces. There is a need to hold on to what is replaced if only to guarantee that the replacement is appropriate and complete. We could not get rid of a reference to a man's privacy even if what we learned from a study of his body showed that all references to such a privacy were arbitrary, misleading, willful, harmful, unnecessary, confused, and the like. The reference is needed if we are to legitimately claim that a proper replacement had been found. And, of course, were one to reject all references to the privacies of any other man, the claim that an adequate replacement for his supposed privacy had been produced would still require one to make use of his own privacy.

It is desirable to replace the obscure and arbitrary by the coherent, clearer, and verifiable, but we still have to presuppose something. The claim that a disease was caused by witches or a curse can be justifiably rejected since we have found better, more satisfactorily verified causes. The replacement of the private by the publicly known, even if this were better substantiated, clearer, and more coherent, requires the continued presence and tacit acknowledgment of what was to be replaced. Indeed, not only does the replacement require the presence of what was supposed to have been eliminated; it is privately performed and depends on the private acknowledgment of the privacy that is to be replaced.

Both today and tomorrow a satisfactory account of a man requires a reference to a distinctive privacy, the source and explanation of what he publicly exhibits in and through his body. He owns that body because he imposes his privacy on it and thereby lives it. But surely, not every one of a man's bodily acts has its explanation and source in what he privately is and does? When he falls from a height he falls at the rate that stones do. When he eats, his digestive fluids begin to operate in somewhat the way digestive fluids do in other types of being, and even in test tubes. When he burns his finger it blisters; so does the burned finger of an ape. His blood courses through his body when he sleeps and when he wakes, whether he knows or does not know that it does. Were he in a complete stupor, tossed about by a storm, or paralyzed, he would provide little reason for anyone to believe that he had a privacy or that it was operative. But it is also true that an adequate understanding of his fall, digestion, burns, and the movement of his blood requires a reference to other occurrences in his body.

Were a man unconscious and tossed about by a storm, his privacy would have little efficacy. It might then not be possible to discern it. Nevertheless, it would still be present and operative. If it were not, he would cease to be human at that time. His recovery of his normal state would then be indistinguishable from the achievement of the status of a human by one who was not human, though perhaps possessed of a highly developed body. Conceivably, such a man might pass back and forth any number of times during a lifetime, from the stage of living a body by means of a privacy to the stage of being just a unified body. If so, he would change back and forth from one type of being to another.

The many occurrences that take place outside the body, where they are kept in consonance with one another through the effective operation of an accepted and controlling objective outside the purview of the body, remain inexplicable facts as long as we refuse to take account of what is not to be found in bodies. This is not yet, of course, to say that when bodily occurrences take place, a man has or uses a distinctive privacy. The unity of all the bodily occurrences, even their guidance and control, might be due to a force having a source other than an individual's privacy—a governing organism, a God, a devil, a cosmic force, society. Eventually, though, one will have to grant the existence of individual privacies if only to make sense of the fact that it is individuals who feel pains, think, and decide, and refer to an organism, God, a devil, a cosmic force, society, or a world of bodies.

From the moment he becomes an embryo, a man expresses his sensitivity, if only to a minimal degree, thereby making his body a lived body. This he is able to live by means of further expressions of his sensitivity, or by other epitomizations of his privacy. That privacy possesses, guides, controls, and thereby lives his body. The unity that his body has as living, or in abstraction from this, as a mere extended mass, is not equatable with that privacy, for it lacks depth, interiority, intensity, and a capacity to feel or know.

Either there is no distinctive, persistent, governing human privacy, or as long as a man is alive it is present, making a difference to what he bodily is and does. Even if he were only minimally alive, his privacy would be expressed, and thereby affect what was happening in and to his body. His bodily acts and misadventures consequently have a quite different meaning from that characteristic of similar acts and misadventures undergone in similar circumstances by a stick, a corpse, or a cat.

A man's body often makes a great difference to what he is, can do, and does. Sometimes there is a reverse emphasis, with his body serving primarily as a vehicle for what is being privately insisted on. Each makes some difference to the other's functioning. His lived body is their joint product. Unlike the privacy of an animal, his is a privacy that is not always directed at the body to make this able to obtain satisfactions for itself or a group. Unlike the privacy of an atomic monad, his is a privacy which is not always expressed in his body.

When a man passes from hearing to listening, from looking to seeing, he does not replace a purely bodily occurrence by another. His hearing and seeing differ from his listening and looking as the more from the less privately initiated, directed, and controlled. When his privacy is only minimally effective, we are not able to know anything more than that it is present and living his body. If we did not know this much we would not know that he was human, able to feel, with some of the rights we have. We would not know that he could express other privately initiated powers, some of which have no counterpart in any other type of being.

Privacy lays down no fixed conditions. The specific ways it acts on the body and what is outside this, enable a man to take advantage of what happens to be present. But even though his privacy lives the body in its own way and is not a product or a function of the body, that privacy may alter its emphasis and course in the light of what is encountered through the body's help. Despite all that one might say along these lines on behalf of the presence and efficacy of a human privacy, however, it is an inescapable fact that the only warrant that one has or could have that others have privacies is to be found in what they express by means of their bodies. It is also true that much of what anyone knows of himself is known in a similar way. Sometimes we learn what we are thinking by noting what we said; sometimes we learn what we willed by attending to what we do.

We do not know whether or not others despise their bodies or try to ignore them, and whether or not they pursue unrealizable prospects, unless they provide evidence that they do. We will therefore keep close to the nub of truth only if we try to understand what they privately are by paying careful attention to their bodies, what these make available, and the ways they interact with what is external to them.

If we are to learn about the privacies of men, we can do nothing less than find evidences for those privacies in what is publicly available. And we ought to do no more than affirm what is then inescapably implied by what we warrantedly reach. Not all the evidences will be found by attending just to bodies. The species, the environment, and society also affect and are affected by man's privacy. All must be considered if we are to

obtain the fullest and most reliable knowledge of man's privacy and therefore of his ability to be guided by goals, objectives, and ends. Some of
these we can come to know because they are presupposed by what is
already known or because they enable one to explain what otherwise
would be inexplicable. To know just what human privacies are like and
what they can do, we must initially attend to quite specific occurrences,
not only in but outside their bodies.

Some organized acts and efforts promote the welfare of the body.
Others may not promote it or the individual's welfare. When 'the wisdom
of the body' is exaggerated, one tends to treat private expressions as either
normal or aberrational, the one benefitting, the other not benefitting and
perhaps getting in the way of benefits to the body. When, instead, the role
of the body is unduly minimized, it will be viewed as though it were a
creature of the environment, an agent for the species, or an instrument for
the privacy, without requirements of its own which it acts to satisfy. To
preserve the difference between a refusal to eat because one is bodily
surfeited and a refusal to eat because one is obeying a privately instituted
injunction, it is necessary to recognize both that the body has its own
insistent requirements and that it is used by privacy to bring about results
that may be to its detriment. What is publicly done, is not only the
product of a private use of bodily channels; it is sustained and often
overwhelmed by the body's structure and functioning. Whether the privacy plays a major or a minor role in what is thereby produced, it could
result in injury to the body, jeopardy to the species, or opposition to the
society. Whatever occurs, it will have its route, rhythm, direction, and
outcome determined by both the privacy and the body.

Were one to credit to the body alone all the powers expressed through
the body, it would still be necessary to distinguish those powers which
help the body to continue and prosper from those that do not. The latter
would have to be classified as causes or effects of the body's failure to
function properly, even if others benefitted. Were it supposed, with
socio-biologists, that bodily acts were the work of special genes, one
would so far take the body to be a function of its parts. If the body
prevented the successful action of the supposed genes, it would then once
again have to be said to act improperly, no matter who benefitted. Yet the
act may be just what is demanded by the privacy, occupied with a prospect
whose realization may hurt oneself or others.

That there is a persistent privacy in man, and that this has a number of
specialized forms has now, I think, become patent. But before going on to
a detailed examination of the evidences leading to the acknowledgment of
the privacy and an understanding of its nature and main divisions, it will

be well to remark on a number of specialized ways in which the term and its cognates will be used. In its most widely applicable form 'privacy' will refer to an independently maintained insistence, a mere privacy, partly undifferentiated. Such a privacy is present in every actuality. In man, the privacy, while still indeterminate, has a different nature and power from that possessed by the privacy of other types of being. But no matter what the type, privacy differs in being and action from individual to individual. And in each, the privacy has a number of more determinate forms. It is epitomized initially as the privacy of an unduplicable person, itself epitomized as the privacy of a sensitivity, sensibility, need, desire, orientation, sociality, understanding, and resolution. Part of the remaining indeterminacy of the privacy of a man is later epitomized as the privacy of a self, itself epitomized in a private autonomy, responsibility, and an I. Most of the rest of the privacy is epitomized as the privacy of an idios, occupied with accepting and using pervasive conditions so as to be able to dictate how the other specializations of the privacy are to function in relation to one another. Person and self, and their epitomizations, will all be referred to as 'privacies' since they differ mainly in their degree of determinateness, power, and act. The context should make it comparatively easy to keep the different uses of 'privacy' distinct.

In every instance, if we try to make direct contact with a privacy, we find that the more deeply we penetrate it, the greater is the resistance that we encounter. Our move, into ourselves or another, eventually meets a growing resistance to further progress. We would be left with an unknowable residue were there a point at which we came to a full stop. But no matter with what content we rest, we always thrust beyond it into what is more and more resistant. Consequently, though what we become acquainted with is what we stop at, we still continue beyond that point, meeting greater and greater resistance. Sometimes we can move into the area into which we had thrust to make a stop with content at a further point, beyond which we thrust still further. There is no set limit where we are completely cut off from a further advance. Our thrust is into an indeterminate stretch, more and more subject to privacy on its own terms. Reflections on the nature of privacy and what it can do must take account of that fact.

Many attempts have been made in the past to give a detailed account of the major distinctions that must be acknowledged if man's privacy is to be adequately understood. Apparently, the most widely accepted is the trichotomy of thinking, willing, and judging. Its advocates leave unexplained how these are known. There is a tendency also to separate the three, even at times to attribute them to distinct faculties. Though thought, will, and judgment can be exercised independently, they are not cut off from one another. While carrying out their characteristic functions, they are also interlinked. And they affect one another. Men can will what they think and think of what they will, and in other ways have one epitomization bear on another. There are also a number of other private powers, such as autonomy and responsibility, which are at least as basic as the chosen three. Initially, too, no matter what their dignity, all epitomizations are no more than nuances in one privacy, separated out from it only in act.

The long-established triplet deals with some expressions of the person and self, ignoring all others. Having failed to consider the I, it is unable to show how the private and public activities of a man can be his, or how he could attend to himself as a me, and present a you to others. The fact that one can know that someone else not only engages in private activities, but controls what he publicly does, and can come to know what conditions him, is also passed over. So is the difference between decisions made by the will and those due to preference and choice.

More subtle accounts have been advanced by Plato, Aristotle, Hegel, and Freud. They provide better ways of understanding how it is possible for there to be knowledge, ethics, and social life. It is difficult, though, to find grounds in justified principles for all they maintain. And when such principles are advanced, they often fail to show that or how a man's bodily existence is at once distinguished from, affects, and is affected by his privacy and its expressions. A knowledge of the strengths and weaknesses of these views point up the need for systematically grasping what all of us already know, but most of us poorly though surely understand.

Person and self make a constant privacy be more and more determinate. The epitomizations of these add further determinations. The indeterminacy that still remains in the privacy after the achievement of person and self, and the indeterminations that still remain in these after epitomizations of them are achieved, all acquire a new import, because the acquired determinations sustain promises there for still other determinations.

Epitomizations are a consequence of an effort to act with greater definiteness and efficacy—an effort which is itself a specialization of a man's primal attempt to complete himself. In the absence of all epitomizations, he would have only an indeterminate privacy acting on his body. But from the very beginning, his privacy is specialized in the form of a private person, itself specialized in a privately expressed sensitivity. That sensitivity is inseparable from his person, and this in turn is qualified by the effort to have the sensitivity function in some consonance with other epitomizations. The self, in turn, makes possible the existence of an idios, with its ability to deal with all the others together.

Each epitomization not only has rights of its own, but has them joined to other rights within the compass of the person. If one makes a man feel pain, he makes not just a privacy but a private person feel pain. If one makes an animal feel pain, he makes a being with just a privacy feel it. The rights violated are different, the one violating the rights of what can engage in purely private activities; the other, the rights possessed by what is alive, but without even the promise to be a person.

Promises are not reflexive. They also are not transitive. Sensitivity does not sustain a promise that there will be an I, or even a desire. An embryo has the promise to be a fetus but does not have the promise to be a child, for its privacy is expressed only as a sensitivity; it has other epitomizations, as the fetus and the child do. We have as much warrant for taking the embryo to be a child, or even to have a promise to be a child, as we have to take a new born child to be a doctor or have the promise to be one. Just as a child must first attain the stage where it can take on and carry out the requisite medical training, before it can become a doctor, so an embryo must first give way to a non-viable fetus before there can be a viable one.

Promises are inseparable from actual epitomizations. No promise can be realized except by the being passing to a higher stage. The realization of the promises depends on many contingent circumstances; no stage in the growth of a man is inevitable, irresistibly coming to pass. Death may intervene. Distortions occur. There are delays, stoppages, and disorders. But if maturation is to occur, a human must pass through various stages, each of which satisfies a promise grounded in a predecessor. The activities at one stage help realize a higher stage, one that is usually more powerful and more deeply rooted in the privacy. Sensitivity, the first epitomization, can realize only a promise to feel; the idios, the last epitomization, can realize only a promise to govern. Neither, nor any other epitomization is initially well-marked off from the others. Each is differentiated in use. But once the sensitivity is distinguished, it usually continues to remain so. It is almost always in act. So is the I. Once achieved, this too continues to insist on itself for an indefinite period. Other epitomizations remain distinct for shorter stretches. "I don't remember" reports one such occurrence with startling accuracy.

A person is a locus of rights. When the self comes to be, the person carries its rights as well, and thereby is able to act as its representative, not simply by functioning on behalf of the I, but by carrying within itself the claims that the self makes. A self enables one to hold on, in the form of a relevant past, to what has been and, in the form of a relevant future, to what is about to be; it can acquire character, and it has duties. More insistent than the person, it tends to override it, but it can never do this completely.

Although there are humans and therefore persons who have not yet acquired selves, there are no selves where there are no persons. Both are privacy, contracted and limited. Neither exists or acts apart from it. Privacy is single and singular, specialized in a number of independently functioning private epitomizations, themselves privately epitomized in more specialized ways.

b. Sensitivity

When we feel, we privately make contact with what our bodies make available. At those times, our activities both terminate and are limited, sustained by what is beyond the termini. Were there only termini each of us would be wholly confined within his own privacy. But limits are two-sided. We arrive at them from one side and are inescapably opposed by them from the other.

Because we come to limits, we are able to make contact with what is externally determined. At the same time, because we then thrust beyond the limits, we are faced with further limits, where we are involved with what is distinct from the initial termini and limits. The further limits may have others beyond them. The last limit is that into which our thrust imperceptibly fades, the being of others as blocking our advance.

Private activities are limited. That is why no one is confined within his privacy, entirely cut off from what is external. The tree we see is experienced by us as a terminus. As known and knowable, it is at successive limits beyond what is initially experienced. When we experience the tree we also face it as known; when we attend to the tree as known we also face it as knowable. It is not uncommon to remain indefinitely with or to use one of these results, and neglect the others.

From the first, as embryos, we are sensitive, able to discriminate among qualitative differences in what is bodily undergone. As embryos, our sensitivities are different in nature and promise from the sensitivities of other kinds of beings, as well as from those expressed by us when we have matured beyond the embryonic stage. Not only are the ranges of discrimination of the different sensitivities markedly different; their import is changed in a distinctive way by the promises they ground.

Initially crude in its operation, sensitivity privately records, in the form of pain and pleasure, the presence of different kinds of disturbances in the body. Nothing bodily is added to it by the body—that would require it to be a body in a world of bodies. Sensitivity is and always remains a private act but one that is in contact with what is not private.

Pain is felt because sensitivity makes discriminations in what is occasioned by the body which limits it. Consequently, privacy does not have to be joined to what is entirely cut off from it, as a Cartesian mind is supposed to be joined to a Cartesian body. A limit for a privacy is a privately met restraint, produced by what is other than that privacy. Otherwise, the limit would be identical with the terminus of the privacy. Because it is limited, a privacy is necessarily involved with what is setting a limit for it.

Sensitivity, like every other epitomization, insistently thrusts into what sets a limit for it. If it could not do this it would terminate, but not be stopped. Because it is stopped, it is at a limit, making contact with what is producing the limit. As a consequence, it has painful or pleasurable content, while passing indefinitely beyond this. When feeling pain and pleasure one is acquainted with disturbing bodily occasions for them. Those occasions are not grasped as distinct objects, as causes, or as bodily events. They are encountered as blocking the insistent sensitivity and, with this, constituting part of a sensitively lived body.

When we ask for evidence warranting the affirmation that someone else is sensitive, an apparently serious difficulty looms before us: either that other's sensitivity could not be known, or we are directly acquainted with what he is as a private individual. The first of these alternatives is embraced when it is said that all that can be known is public, palpable, common; the second, when it is held that we can know the privacy of another. The two, though, are compatible. If accepted together, they qualify one another.

Evidence of sensitivity is first encountered as imbedded in a body. With this, it constitutes a single unit. When freed from the body the evidence is identical with a privacy in its most attenuated form. We are acquainted with another's sensitivity, but not at its origin nor as being insisted on and living his body.

The public behavior of another is in part constituted by what evidences privately undergone pain or pleasure. Isolating that evidence is one with the confrontation of that pain or pleasure at the extreme of a stretch privately undergone. But because we cannot approach either pain or pleasure from the position of another's sensitivity, what we discern of either will be differently toned, and available to us in a different way. If he observes his body, he will be able to do what we can, in addition to being able to sensitively insist on himself and thereby live through a pain or pleasure. We feel another's pain or pleasure intropathically, sharing in its rhythms, abrasiveness, and tonality without possessing it as he does, as at the most extreme portion of his sensitivity. Attending to what he made most explicit by his involving it with the body which occasioned it, we become acquainted with what he had privately enabled us to find.

Usually our extractive and penetrative acts are not well controlled. We are not persistent, steady enough, or very clear. We are too ready to accept the resistance we meet as though it were throughout of the same degree, and beyond our mastering. And when we reflect, we are both dismayed by theoretical difficulties and inclined to affirm what we hope we will find. Again and again we express what we discover in terms that we had picked up elsewhere. To reduce the confusion and error, and to be able to explain, as well as to sympathize, we must become more cautious, more reflective, and more resolute than we usually are. We must extricate more decisively the contribution that another's privacy makes to the constitution of public occurrences, and must use with finesse the evidence then obtained, making sure that its source is in this rather than that particular epitomization of the person or self.

The scientifically-minded are right: what we confront are resistant forces. So are the existentialists: we privately terminate in what we constitute. Because both are right, it is correct to say that we privately terminate in what we constitute, and that this is limited by what acts independently of and counter to us. Except when we are interested in just experiencing, and therefore in just coming to a terminus, we are attentive to what is being constituted both by us and by what is independent of us.

It is not enough to extricate evidence; what we separate out and use must also be purified. This requires the help of the very privacy we are trying to reach. If our privately grasped evidence is to take us toward its source in another's privacy, he must supplement our efforts. If he does not, what we use at the beginning of our act of knowing that he is privately discriminating will not carry us far. We need him to help us move effectively and intensively into his sensitivity. A price is paid for that help. The more we succeed in moving into his sensitivity, the more surely will the evidence be caught up in, be affected by, and be taken over by the rest of the sensitivity. We pass into dimmer and dimmer, increasingly denser regions, eventually losing focus, finding our content slipping from our grasp. The other resists our advance. Eventually he denies us further access.

Sensitivity is contoured by the body which it lives. Hard, but not impossible to extricate, its bodily manifestation is to be used at the beginning of an intensive move into it. If we could never do this, we would not be able to know that another was pleased or in pain, actually feeling the one or the other. But because of his resistance, we end somewhere near a midway position, between the evidence as affected by what limits and publicly carries it, and that evidence as an indistinguishable part of the very sensitivity that is undergoing the pain or pleasure.

Sensitivity lives the body. But it is at once more and less than that living—more, because not all of it is expressed in the body, and less, because the body is lived in other ways as well. And though a human always lives his body sensitively, it is possible to have a living being which is not sensitive. A growing cabbage is an instance. It surely is alive, but not sensitive. Were there any being which was sensitive, and nothing more, it would be quite different from a human, for in every human there is a promise to be more than sensitive.

We speak metaphorically when we refer to the 'sensitivity' of a photographic plate. The term is unnecessarily stretched if we use 'sensitivity' to refer to what is only a discernible reaction to a bodily disturbance. When a frog's head is cut off, the frog is no longer sensitive, not because the head made it sensitive, but because the frog is no longer alive. To be sure, if acid is put on its leg, that leg will twitch in somewhat the way in which a living frog's does. Despite the similarity between the two twitches, the one is nevertheless to be credited to a living and the other to a non-living being, for the one is a twitch sensitively produced, while the other is a twitch due to a sudden contraction of a muscle. Although the latter cannot be understood without some reference to what is private, there is no need to hold that it is the privacy of a the frog that is making the leg react. Only when the frog is alive is the muscle, and secondarily some of the muscle's parts, governed, directed, related and constrained by the frog's privacy. In a decapitated frog, the muscle has either the status of a whole or a colony, since the privacy it has is not expressed in a single, controlling activity. What the muscle then does is a function of its parts, themselves perhaps understandable as a function of still other units. Consequently, the muscle will not behave exactly in the way that it did when the frog was alive.

It is possible to imagine and perhaps produce cases where one would be hard put to say whether or not sensitivity was present. But one thing is sure. For a pain to be present, it must be felt, and for it to be felt, one must be sensitive. That pain is not identifiable with a bodily injury or with a bodily effect of this. There are pains even in the absence of discernible bodily injuries or effects, and there can be bodily injuries and the effects of these without any pain being felt. Pains are privately undergone; injuries are bodily occurrences. But if the injury is inflicted on a living body, it will usually entrench upon a private undergoing, usually of pain.

Although both injury and pain may have clear public and private guises, we may not learn of either. Often enough we are unaware that someone is undergoing pain. His bodily activity, too, may so obscure the sensitivity being expressed that he may not feel anything. Or we may not be able to discover that he feels pains because they are hardly noticed by him. He may be in a state of shock, or we may be absorbed in noting how his body acts. It is one thing to painfully press one's finger and another to be pained when one attends to the pressed finger. The first yields a pain which is incidentally located; the second has the pain as an incidental accompaniment. Pain does not always have an unmistakable public occasion and an unmistakable public expression.

The awareness by another of the presence and functioning of our sensitivity awaits an act by us. But we already know that we are sensitively discriminating. While others can know that we are sensitive no earlier than at the time at which we are making that sensitivity publicly evident, we can know of it before then. If we live through a pain without producing any public indication of the fact, no one else, of course, will then know of it. Others would, so far, be justified in hesitating to credit us with a sensitivity. They could continue to be hesitant even when we acted in strict consonance with disturbances in our bodies. Whatever we did, they could contend, might conceivably be bodily produced—until they found us discriminating in ways which had no bearing on the body's welfare, or otherwise learned that we were living persons. They would then have to suppose that our bodies were malfunctioning, or would have to allow that our bodies were being privately used.

Initially, and most of the time afterwards, one learns about the nature and functioning of his sensitivity in the way others do, by taking account of what he can discern in his publicly observable body. The infant cries and thereby learns that it is in pain. If it did not, it would just undergo an unlocated private disturbance at the back of a noise issuing from a body it had not yet learned was its own. Introspection follows on and follows the lead of what is learned from what is publicly evident to oneself and others. That, of course, does not deny its legitimacy, accuracy, or warrant.

Physically manifested discriminations provide evidence of a sensitivity at work. If the discriminations are viewed as purely behavioral units, the discriminated items would not, so far, be related. There would then be no real discriminations acknowledged, but only isolated acts of focusing.

Reactions to injury in the form of cries, grimaces, rubbings, withdrawals, and attacks are occupied with what is publicly occurring. They are not expressions of pain, but alarms, preparations, replies, triggered by pain. Instead of making evident the pain that one is undergoing, they exhibit privately initiated efforts to deal with its occasions, or to elicit help or consideration from others. They are not criteria, that is, measures or rules for determining that a pain occurred. Were they expressions or criteria of pain, they would vary with it. Instead, they keep more or less in accord with conventions, where they are not aimed at removing a cause, or where they do not exhibit an uncontrolled or impulsive act. Even when spontaneously and seriously produced, they do not express a pain, give it a public role. Instead, cries and other similar expressions assess the pain, often in social terms.

Evidences of sensitive undergoings are to be found in discriminative activities. To know that others are experiencing pains and pleasures, we must attend to what is publicly exhibited by them. Though there are many grades, and though they divide into many kinds, the pains and pleasures bundle together private experiences that could have been discriminated had the sensitivity been used with more subtlety. Pains and pleasures record quite crude discriminations within which one can sometimes deliberately remark on otherwise ignored nuances, rhythms, stresses, and changes.

Acts are privately initiated, unit occurrences, stretching out temporally and spatially. Within their confines, there may or may not be a number of others with shorter spans. All relate a temporal beginning and ending, and group a number of otherwise separate units. Although some are performed without consciousness or sensitivity, they too carry out what was privately begun.

We can learn that another man is sensitive when he shows that he is discriminating among items occurring within the confines of such acts. We make contact with his sensitivity by following the route of the expressions of his sensitivity backward to their more intensive, singular source, and can come to know that this functions independently of his body when we discover that some of his discriminations do not benefit his body, but, instead, enable him to work better with others, help the species continue, or support his pursuit of some prospect. When we have no knowledge that anything else is being promoted, and when no indications are provided which allow us to know that another is pleased or pained, or that pleasure or pain accompany his focusing on some item and a neglect of others, we would not be able to know that he was sensitive, did we not also know that he was a living human.

An actor leads us to share in his apparent pain or pleasure. He then incidentally enables us to know that he is sensitive, for acting requires expressions of sensitivity. When we misread what he is sensitive to, we still correctly take him to be a living human and therefore to be expressing his sensitivity, as well as other powers which exist only because he is sensitive.

He is, of course, pained or pleased as an actor, which is to say, as involved in his portrayal. Concerned with producing an effect, he denies his sensitivity a separate expression and, instead, makes it subservient to a more basic effort to express understanding and decisions. He then is closer to one who holds his feelings in check than to one who makes his pains and pleasures evident without reserve, for like the former he denies his feelings adequate expression, giving preference to the imaginative portrayal. We can be deceived, consequently, about his feelings at the time, but only so far as we, perhaps unknowingly, are attending to more deeply grounded expressions of his privacy. These expressions use his sensitivity, and compel this to be exercised in special ways. Having denied a privately felt pain or pleasure a direct expression, the actor favors what is not sensitively discriminated. As a consequence, he provides evidences leading to the knowledge of some deeper expression of his privacy and, incidentally, of his sensitivity as well. What we will not then know is the pain or pleasure that he undergoes while he is acting out his role.

Only if we are unable to distinguish rough from fine discriminations is there no knowing whether or not a man is primarily or only incidentally pleased or pained. Only if we are unable to know that a man is making fine discriminations or doing something else, is there no knowing whether or not he is more than sensitive. The fact that he undergoes his own pains and pleasures, that he may privately discriminate what his pains and pleasures might otherwise obscure, and that he may not provide any indication of what he is privately doing, prevents us from knowing all we might like to know about him at that time. But once he provides us with evidence, we will be able to make sympathetic contact with him and, reflecting on what we then discern, understand his privacy to be the intensive unity of what he had expressed, and which his body countered, sustained, and helped transform into what we confronted.

For those who are willing to identify mind with a feeling of pleasure or pain, there need be no 'mind-body' problem, and no problem of 'knowing other minds', though it is mainly those who make this identification who seem to think these are difficult and perhaps insoluble issues. If the identification is made, the mind will be in the body in an attenuated, diversified form, and could be directly and reflectively known by proceeding in a reverse direction, intensively or through inference, along the route by which the mind was manifested.

What is sensitively begun is more than any of its evidenced expressions. The sensitivity can be expressed again, not necessarily in the way it had been. And since what is expressed is the epitomization of a more basic power—a person—that power could be epitomized in other ways as well.

To know if epitomizations other than sensitivity occur one must of course find evidences of private expressions not produced by sensitivity.

A man can be subject to various stimuli at the same time that he is prepared for what is a source of pains and pleasures. When reference is made to a 'reflex arc' in which a stimulus is viewed as being inseparable from a reply, the sensitivized body, of which account has already been taken, is substituted for externally produced causes. A man's body, as capable of being assaulted from without, is not to be identified with his body as already connected with occasions for pains and pleasures.

Were a man just occupied solely with maintaining himself, he could do nothing more than overwhelm whatever happened to intrude. Were he to do no more than to move insistently toward whatever there was, he would be radically open to whatever was encountered. Because he both maintains himself and insists on himself, there is an inclination for him to control what intrudes, and an opposing inclination to accept whatever is encountered. But there is no conversion of the latter into the former, no encountering of something in the external world and a translation of it into oneself, any more than there is a conversion of the former into the latter, a private determination of what intrudes followed by an attempt to see if it matches what is encountered. At the very same time that provision is made for what might be made available, there is an outward thrust toward what makes its own demands. What intrudes on an epitiomization is accepted as filling out the place that a directed insistence opened up; what is encountered in the external world is faced as contrasting with a private self-insistence. Privacy and what is beyond it act independently, but what takes place in one can be in consonance with what takes place in the other. One can consequently act in accord with a sensitively constituted world, a world faced as a source of pains and pleasures.

Reference is not a jump from privacy into an alien world. It is an act by which one acknowledges an occurrence for whose presence provision had already been made. A specific reference, of course, will need a specific referent, and depend on one's ability to locate this. But that referent must have already been accounted for in principle; otherwise it would not be known that there was anything to which a reference was made.

Sources of pains and pleasures are quite unlike those pains and pleasures. Were one unprepared to deal with pains and pleasures, the world might provide occasions for the occurrence of either, but it would not be dealt with as containing their occasions. We learn from experience that we will be pained if we touch fire. But we could not learn this if we had not already been in contact with what was external to us, and made some provision for its effect on us.

The world to which we are able to refer is one in which we already are. Were we not in contact with it, we would be left with words like 'it' and 'this' and 'here'. Instead of helping us mark out something, they would be just words alongside others. To be used as references they must apply to delimited regions within an area of which we had already taken account. The fact is underscored when we address other men. Because we are already prepared to deal with them, we are in a position to address them as individuals and make proper use of their proper names. We do not first attend to men in general, or begin with a knowledge of personhood, and then proceed to know individuals. As will become evident, we make use of epitomizations other than sensitivity to reach what is beyond us and are thereupon in a position to deal with delimited regions by means of specialized terms, names, and other personal references.

A privacy which is prepared for encounters with external sources of pains and pleasures stands apart, not only from the external world into which it insistently moves, but from the sensitized body and the sensitivity as well. It contrasts with these, just so far as its own effort at maintaining itself has been affected by its own insistence. Continuing to thrust into the body and the world beyond, it is able to stand in contrast with these only so far as its act of self-maintenance is qualified by the way in which it insists on itself. Prepared for encounters with external sources of pleasures and pains, it stands apart from these and from the sensitized body and sensitivity as well.

Fire burns the hand and a searing pain takes over. In a man, the pain can be consciously attended to, and can be possessed by him as one who is readied to deal with its occasion. A failure to locate or identify that occasion does not compromise the fact that the pain is then and there possessed as an intensive form of the outcome of a previous move away from the position where a man just maintains himself.

c. Sensibility

Schopenhauer remarked that, if accompanied by a cry for help, a pain will sometimes be responded to without hesitation, before it is known what might have occasioned the pain or the cry. Before there is a reflection on or a looking about to see what may have brought about the pain or occasioned the cry, others may unreflectingly begin an intensive move into a man, usually backing this with attempts to come to his aid. What is then initially known is that he is in pain, but little is known of its tonality. From his side, there is just a sudden and sharp discrimination privately made, and an outburst and perhaps a surge of fear which preclude any focussing on the tonality, or any attempt to notice its rhythms. Sometimes, though, men make finer discriminations than these, discriminations beyond the power of sensitivity.

Some discriminations have neither a positive nor a negative bearing on what the body requires, seeks, or utilizes. They are aesthetic. Expressed in acts which are bodily sustained, they are not bodily oriented. Making use of eyes, ears, nose, tongue, or hands, they express a sensibility, acting in independence of and sometimes in opposition to the ways the senses and other parts of the body act on behalf of or in opposition to the body.

Sometimes it is necessary to allow the sensibility a greater role than sensitivity has. Sometimes there is a need to reverse the emphasis and even to suppress the expression of sensibility. Despite a sudden withdrawal and feeling of unpleasantness, we might like the tonality of what we are drinking; or we may be pleased by what we taste and disdain what we there might aesthetically discern.

The discriminations which others make can be known only so far as these provide evidence that they do make the discriminations. Some of the evidence, though sustained by the body, may make no difference to the body's functioning or prosperity. A resolute naturalism will nevertheless try to understand the discriminations as somehow serving bodily needs. The aesthetically satisfying will then be supposed to offer resting points, relaxation, or stimuli serving to make subsequent, more vital bodily activities possible or better. The position is faced with the fact that the aesthetically satisfying does not always contribute positively to the body's subsequent functioning, and that it sometimes keeps the body from carrying out more pressing and more important tasks, then and later.

Birds are attracted by bright colors. Certain sounds soothe some animals. Insects take note of fine differences in light, weight, and size. Are they engaged in making purely aesthetic discriminations? We do not know. All of their discriminations might conceivably be derivatives, translations, anticipations, or residua of what is bodily efficacious. Conceivably, the discriminations might benefit groups in which different bodies functioned as so many parts. There seems to be no warrant for dogmatism on the point. All the discriminations of subhumans may or may not be directly or indirectly at the service of their bodies. But with man the same indecisiveness need no longer continue, for there are times when his aesthetic discriminations are set sharply against all other expressions and are then subjected to a greater and greater refinements. One sound may not only be distinguished from another, but may itself be made subject to discriminating activity marking out different facets of it. These, and the initial sound itself, may then be related to quite different sounds and sometimes to occurrences in other sensible modalities. All this may be done in the face of pain, bodily stress, and possible irreparable damage. Often enough, the discriminations are culturally qualified. The fact that some of them are so determined or are functions of tradition, training, or expreience, however, does not stand in the way of the truth that one man may explicitly discriminate what others do not, and may then relate the result so as to make an aesthetically satisfying whole.

Some men have more acute sensibilities than others. Occasionally an attempt is made to view them as though they had poorly functioning bodies. If, as that view suggests, they were bodily defective when their discriminations were made independently of what their bodies need to distinguish if these are to continue or to prosper, connoisseurs, scholars, and spectators, musicians, painters, and poets would all have to be taken to have malfunctioning bodies. Instead, these men often provide evidences that they have well-trained, efficient bodies, and that they use these to promote and sustain privately produced discriminations. But, though they use and depend on the excellent functioning of various organs and parts of their bodies, these dictate neither the nicety nor the range of what is discriminated. A body provides preconditions for what in fact is privately done; what is sensitively discriminated is occasioned, not determined by the body.

The discriminations made by sensibility are more or less agreeable, not just more or less pleasurable or painful. They are approved or disapproved, not merely accepted or suffered. What is encountered continues to play a dominant role. The sensibility makes its presence felt by giving the discriminated new functions, and occasionally marking the degree to which a bodily occurrence accords with what was privately discriminated.

A man who is hard of hearing will miss what one with acute hearing does not. There will be much that he cannot, but the other can discriminate. Still, distinctions possible to one who has acute hearing may be unnoted, while the less able remark on rather small differences. Where one with acute hearing may have expressions of his sensitivity radically transformed by his body and may, therefore, do no more than discriminate pleasurably or painfully in accord with the demands of that body, the other may give a new import to what he confronts, as that which more or less accords with his sensibility's functioning. A dissonant sound for him or for one with a more active sensibility need not be heard with displeasure, but as disagreeable by itself and yet perhaps agreeable as fitting in with other sounds.

A bodily oriented sensitivity discriminates in accord with the body's requirements, unless there is something amiss with the body's functioning. But a bodily sustained sensibility imposes, on what might be painful, an acceptance of what is approved or a rejection of what is not. Consequently, for sensibility to be clearly evidenced even while its expressions are being bodily transformed, there must be something publicly available, having no necessary bodily role or function, that is idle, not needed by the body.

A man is alerted to another's sensibility when some bodily agency of the other—such as his voice—duplicates, refines, or plays variations on what he himself might express. If his own discriminations have no relation to what the other is expressing, he has to be content with attending to what is just presented—to a singing, a humming, or a reporting—in order to be able to begin a move into the other's sensibility.

The distinctive nature and functioning of sensibility provides some warrant for the view that aesthetic discriminations are the work of a distinctive sense, whose functioning need have no bodily import. That view, though, will claim more than the facts justify if it adds, to a proper emphasis on aesthetic discriminations made independently of what the body needs and does, a denial that the discriminations use the very bodily senses that the sensitivity uses when it acts on behalf of the body. But if a supposed aesthetic sense uses the very bodily senses that sensitivity does, there is no real need to suppose that there is a distinctive aesthetic sense.

Nothing is gained by postulating the existence of an aesthetic sense making no use of the others. Nor is there a need to suppose there is one in order to account for aesthetic discriminations, severally or together, or for the fact that some of these end in the agreeable or disagreeable, in considerable independence of the pain or pleasure that might accompany them. If it were the intent of those who speak of a special aesthetic sense to do no more than refer to a private power able to discriminate between the agreeable and disagreeable, what was being maintained would be identical with what is here affirmed—provided that it was also held that the supposed aesthetic sense had a private origin; that there were other privately initiated activities; that the various private activities, including the aesthetic, affected one another; and that all the senses made use of the body, though in quite different ways.

Men express discriminations because they had already made distinctions in what they had confronted, or because they are then and there producing these. At both times, they make it possible for another to know that a privacy is being expressed. At both times, they make it possible to know that a sensibility is at work.

The shift from a bodily oriented sensitivity to a bodily sustained sensibility is at once a progression and a retrogression. Sensibility is occupied with what has a larger range and often a higher value than what is available to sensitivity; at the same time, it fails to focus on what is most beneficial to and may be desperately needed by the body. A man reaches a higher stage of maturity when he is able to avoid such losses. That requires him to start further back within his privacy and bring other, more independently functioning and wider ranging epitomizations to bear. He will not then annihilate his sensitivity or sensibility. These may not only continue to be active but may be incidentally enriched by more comprehensive, more lasting, independent powers.

Evidence of sensibility is to be found in those occurrences in which distinguishable qualities are agreeably or disagreeably related, no matter what the bodily demands. That evidence is just as difficult to extricate as is evidence of sensitivity. We never get to the point where we can just face the evidence and thereupon simply have its private source in an attenuated form. We do find the evidence, and do find it quickly, making use of it to start a penetrative act or an inferential move to its private origin. But this evidence is not neatly cut off from all else, just awaiting our attending to it. Sensitivity often has its expressions so submerged in the body that it is difficult to extricate it.

Sensibility is less subject to the body than sensitivity is. Unlike sensitivity, it reaches to, focuses on, and keeps together or separates discriminated items which may have no bodily value, the bodily senses serving only as carriers which enable the sensibility to be involved with the external causes and sustainers of what is discriminated. Sensibility is a private power epitomizing a person, living a body already sensitized. But while it may not take account of what is primarily constituted by or needed by the sensitively qualified body, the aesthetic content with which it is occupied is never wholly detached from what is sensitively encountered.

Sensibility can be cultivated. One can be taught to distinguish more than one otherwise would. But there is a point beyond which most cannot go. Try as they may, they cannot note all the subtleties that others do. The former and the latter differ amongst themselves, making it proper to say that the sensibilities of men differ in degree, if not in one particular modality, then in some other. Even if two musicians were to be equally able to distinguish sounds in exactly the same way they would undoubtedly diverge when they came to colors or smells, although there is nothing in principle which precludes the sensibility of one acting exactly as the other does, were it possible to keep it completely unaffected by any other epitomization and by what is remembered and expected.

It is consistent with the position of Marxists and Freudians to understand the directions and activities of sensibility to be a function of social and familial situations as well as of the experiences that individuals undergo. But it is not clear from their accounts why a sensibility should be at work. Sensibility leaves a man open to futile annoyances, irritations, and feelings of disgust and revulsion as surely as it enables him to have a heightened and exquisite satisfaction beyond the reach of one who is just sensitive. Not needed by the body, it does not usually promote the body's welfare or its place in the world.

It is hard, on any pragmatic, evolutionary, or calculative grounds, to see why sensibility should be present, or why it is exercised. Its presence and activity will always remain a mystery to anyone who refuses to acknowledge that men have privacies epitomized independently of what their bodies might require or need to avoid, particularly since its exercise may get in the way of a proper concern with what the body, the species, or one's group may urgently demand or require.

Creative men have heightened sensibilities, but these are not necessarily better nuanced than the sensibilities of connoiseurs, critics, curators, or historians of art. And when creative men have the most developed of sensibilities, they may be prevented by disabilities and circumstances from expressing those sensibilities adequately, thereby precluding anyone else from knowing how well developed the sensibilities are. To be sure, an occasional Beethoven, denied the opportunity to express his sensibility as a listener, may make its presence evident in his compositions. Some men are able to hear imaginatively what they are unable to compose. Many are able to give excellent expression to their sensibilities when they compose, and are able to appreciate what is heard when the compositions are splendidly played.

Creative work can be produced in a frenzy, when one is drugged or drunk, though it is doubtful that the process can then be carried out for long with much distinction. But the fact that it can at times and for a while outstrip actual discriminations points up the impossibility of identifying or strictly correlating creativity and sensibility. Sometimes a painter's or sculptor's, and perhaps even a composer's or a poet's hands take over for a while, to produce a work which only later is properly appreciated. It is possible, of course—indeed, it is usual—for an artist to be in full control, using training, technique, and insight in consonance with what is sensitively discerned.

Sensibility does not require an I to enable it to be or to act. If it did, subhumans would have I's, or would be unable to privately distinguish anything more than pains and pleasures. But since there are no discriminations unless there is something to discriminate, it would seem as if sensibility differed from sensitivity only in its ability to make distinctions additional to those needed in order to contrast pains and pleasures, and perhaps certain types of pain and certain types of pleasure as well. Sensibility, like sensitivity, does reach into and beyond the body. But, unlike sensitivity, sensibility does not just await content within which it makes distinctions. Instead, it imposes itself on the content, intent on making discriminations. Sensitivity stops with only rough discriminations in what it happens to confront; sensibility endeavors to make finer discriminations, even searching for content where finer discriminations can be made.

Sensibility makes it possible to produce discriminations which have no necessary bearing on what is pleasurable or painful. But since it overlaps sensitivity, it can make contact with the pleasurable and painful. As independently operative, it goes further, encountering the agreeable or disagreeable, that which elates or disappoints. It is a power most certainly present in primitive men, and sometimes is most acutely exhibited by child prodigies. One who is inattentive allows it only a minimal role; a discriminating man gives it maximum play. To be in between these extremes is to be just appreciative, not altogether inattentive or discriminative.

No one is so inattentive but that he makes some provision for some of the discriminations which sensibility provides. None is so discriminating that every possible distinction is already prepared for. Could a man be completely inattentive, he would be caught by surprise, thrown back, shocked by every distinction. Were he perfectly discriminative, nothing would be unprepared for; the discriminations provided by sensibility would simply alight on what was already demarcated.

As not yet caught up in the affairs of the body, sensibility is rather like a refined consciousness. Like that consciousness, it is devoid of content. Unless something is given to it, it is unable to operate. Separating out and focusing on differences in what it encounters, it exists and functions no matter what the body does, making distinctions which have no necessary pertinence to what the body undergoes or requires. And where sensitivity accepts a bodily occurrence as painful or pleasurable, sensibility attends only to what is agreeable or disagreeable. It is, therefore, more superficial, less serious than sensitivity. This does not mean that its products may not have greater value than sensitivity's.

Why should, how could useless qualities, differences, aspects, sometimes of the very items that make a difference to the body, its continuance and prosperity, loom so large in the lives of some men? Dewey's answer is that the aesthetic is the culmination of, the fulfillment of what had gone before and which, without it, would have been incomplete, too slack or too tight, uninteresting, vapid, not a genuine single experience. The answer neglects the fact that aesthetic discriminations are directly made, and usually made with reference to what is perceived when and as it appears. Use of sensibility means that one is not inattentive. But it does not require that a multiplicity of threads be pulled together. It is possible to be sensible of what is immediately before one.

Nuances, refinements, differences, contrasts, can be directly noted without preliminaries. A musician distinguishes among sounds as readily as another hears noise. What the musician notes are usually not isolated units. His discriminations do not require him to remain fixated at separate sounds just following one after the other. What he discriminates is often faced within the very same setting that others yield to as a single whole but, because he makes his discriminations in that whole, what otherwise would be lived through as something pleasant or unpleasant is discriminatingly appreciated.

Sensibility is a distinct epitomization of the person, having its own distinctive nature, mode of operation, and products. It adds to what sensitivity produces, not by acting on and enriching this, but by functioning independently of it and, often enough, on what the sensitivity does not reach. Its presence and operation do not need and cannot always obtain pragmatic warrant. Discrimination beyond the point that sensitivity permits is not always desirable; an exquisite sensibility may unsuit a man for the rough tumble of practical existence, and it may distract him from matters which are important for his peace and continuance. But sensibility does enable a person to be more determinate and diversified than sensitivity permits; it provides him with a larger and richer variety of experience, and entrains satisfactions more subtle than those that mere pleasure provides.

Could there be a person who had a sensibility but no sensitivity, he would of course fall short of one who had both. But such a person is not possible, for sensibility arises by realizing a promise that sensitivity grounds. The interderminate but promissory privacy into which a human sensitivity continues is specialized by the sensibility. In most subhuman beings, if sensitivity grounds a promise to have a sensibility, that promise is not (and apparently in some of the lower living beings will never be) realized as a sensibility. Life is too precarious for them. Insufficient protection and storage compels them to spend most of their energies living as just sensitive beings.

When a subhuman acquires a sensibility, this will be different from that which a man has, for his is mediated by his person and can be directed at other epitomizations of this, and even at epitomizations of his self. The sensiblity of a non-human is tied down to perceptions and, when it is not at the services of the body or limited to what this provides, is occupied with what helps its kind. Sensibility for it is mainly an agent for working on behalf of sexual selection; a man's is expressed for other reasons as well.

Sensibility yields outcomes which are unpredictable in their particularity; often no adequate provision is made for those outcomes even as being of such and such a type. Other unanticipatable results are produced by sensitivity. But in contrast with sensitivity, sensibility may search for that to which it will be subject. But, for the most part, it discriminates mainly within the content that the senses make available.

Men differ not only in the refinements and use of their sensibilities but in the types of things of which they are most acutely sensible. One man is especially sensible of differences in colors; another of differences in sounds, and a third of differences in tastes. Their sensibilities are not passive; rarely do any of them attend to punctuate items. Instead, each relates what it discriminates, often modifying one item by what it has discerned in another.

Although sensibility acts with the help of the body and can therefore be found to be involved with the senses, it is not identifiable with the bodily available evidence of it. Still, when sensibility is identified within a complex bodily occurrence, contact, through an intensive convergent move, can be made with it as the private source of what is publicly manifested. The evidence for it is that part of the sensibility which is being expressed, located at the forefront and continuous with the sensibility as a private epitomization of the person.

If a man makes minimal allowance for sensibility, he is crude, too insistent on himself to make adequate provision for what the sensibility might encounter. He is flexible if he makes maximum provision for the reception of whatever the sensibility might provide. But he is never just crude or perfectly flexible. Instead, he is always somewhere in between, able to express a more or less refined selectivity with reference to what sensibility makes available. His position is self-determined, the outcome of his adjustment to an insistence on himself and the limitations to which the sensibility's content imposes on that insistence. Consequently, although sensibility's achievements are its own, and although in their particularity they are unanticipatable, a man is not entirely unprepared for them. So far, his use of sensibility parallels his use of sensitivity.

Sensibility is ready to make distinctions which have no bearing on what enables the body to be satisfied or to prosper. Still it makes use of the body. Most of what it discriminates is made available by means of the different senses. The body is used by it, but not without the body dictating where and how sensibility will be expressed. If sensibility makes inadequate provision for what the body does, it will be prevented from making the discriminations it otherwise could. To avoid being crude, it must anticipate, in the form of an accommodation, the limitations to which the body might subject its activity. The closer it comes to being flexible, the better prepared it is for the limitations which the body introduces. It must maintain itself between these extremes, be selective, at once insisting on itself and making allowance for what the body sets in its path. In all three ways, sensibility can be prepared for what the body does. When it in fact insistently acts on the body, and is effectively countered by this, it and the body come into active interplay.

The body provides an occasion, a vehicle, a means by which sensibility can deal with content qualified by the body's nature, structure, and functioning. For other epitomizations to take account of the presence of the sensibility as sustained and qualified by the body, their insistence must be modulated, and thereby brought into closer harmony with a selectivity which is to the fore.

Selectivity is not a floating power within the privacy; it expresses a readiness for sensibility to encounter what the senses make available. The claim rests on the fact that sensibility can make a difference to every epitomization, and conversely.

A number of familiar but not well-explored corners of human experience now come into focus. Every one of us, again and again, shifts from an idle noting of differences amongst colors, for example, to a conscious awareness of those differences. Each of us brings his sensibility to bear more and more on what is distinct from it, a sensibility which had already been prepared to act on what is made available. Nothing is learned when it is said that one first makes use of an unconscious in order to mark differences, and that this then pushes its way into consciousness. Not making use of consciousness is not the same thing as making use of an unconscious. We do much privately and publicly by means of powers functioning independently of consciousness and of any unconscious that one might suppose is then operative. Also, what is not consciously faced does not suddenly emerge into consciousness; content already discriminated is maintained in the face of an encroaching consciousness.

Sometimes a man realizes that he had already made discriminations, and then takes possession, accepting the discriminations as his, enjoying them, holding on to them, and privately savoring them even after their bodily occasions have passed away. It would be an error to appeal here to a faculty of memory. First, there is no remembering except of what one had previously faced. No one can remember what he had not himself dealt with. Second, the discriminations are just accepted, not located as having occurred at a previous time. One is compelled to deal with discriminations with which one had not had anything to do.

The various encounters that men's preparations partly anticipate often make a considerable difference to one another. As a consequence, one's experiences become the unpredictable product of a number of interplaying, largely unknown inclinations joined to the unpredictable product of a number of interactive effects, each making a distinctive contribution to the constitution of the resulting experience. The surprises are usually not very great; rough approximations of what will ensue are often quite reliable. And they are, of course, more reliable the more observant one is.

Although creative men in particular areas are more observant of what occurs than others are, and though they make distinctions that others fail to note, they are not necessarily as discriminative as others who devote themselves to a life of aesthetic appreciation. The former put their aesthetic experiences at the service of their creative acts. They transform material so that it allows what is privately produced to be copresent with what lies beyond the particulars of the world. Aesthetic appreciation begins with that result. It may enable one to discern much that the creative man does not note, since often enough he urgently passes from one position to another without allowing himself sufficient time to savor what is at each. But the appreciative will not do more than enjoy the subtlety of a completed work if they do not also come to it with an awareness of what lies beyond all particulars. One who appreciatively deals with an artist's work, not as something merely aesthetic, as just an organized set of discriminated items, but as that which had been creatively produced, will subordinate what he brings to bear to what he discerns. His embodied sensibility will then be enriched by being joined to what he has already glimpsed of what is beyond all particularity.

Whether engaged in producing a work of art, in appreciating a work already produced, or in attending to the achievements of an embodied sensibility, a man must be selective, moderating a tendency to be crude by an effort to be flexible. Only if he were absolutely crude, completely unaccommodative, would he be entirely unprepared for what his sensibility provides. Only if he were absolutely flexible, completely accommodative, placing no emphasis on himself, would he accept its products without qualification. His selectivity protects him doubly; it allows him to stand apart from all else, and to qualify what is then obtained.

A man is well prepared to use his sensibility only if he is selective in every sense modality. He must be tensed as much toward touch as toward sight, as much toward hearing as toward touch or taste. This is not likely. Also, a man's different senses have different degrees of acuity. Training and learning will sometimes make it possible for him to discriminate what could not be discriminated before. But the mitigations are only partial and, in any case, await opportunities, interests, and the functioning of a body which makes demands of its own. One is fortunate if he is ready to make more discriminations in a few areas than most men do. This will require his sensibility to use the body as a source of content, and not to be blocked, distorted, or overwhelmed by it.

Sensibility provides clear evidence that men have privacies, for no matter how tied in sensibility is with the workings of the body and particular senses, it is manifestly occupied with what has little, no, or even an adverse bodily value. When Darwin, in his attempt to show the continuity between animals and man, claimed that subhumans make aesthetic distinctions, he supported one of his theses while undermining another. If, as he thought, both humans and subhumans have similar sensibilities, both would have to be occupied with more than the survival of themselves or of their kind.

Discriminations in what is seen and heard are made in present content. So are the discriminations that are made in what is tasted, touched, and smelled. Yet what is seen and heard appear to be at a distance, objects of a sensibility which is involved in the world beyond the body, rather than at or in the body. To this, it would not be improper to reply that what is heard is heard here as well as there, and that it is heard there only because it is heard here. This still leaves sight as an agency for dealing with what is beyond the body. But it too operates here as well as there. As Whitehead observed, we see with our eyes at the same time that we see what is at a distance. What is seen is therefore somewhat like what is heard, with one role at the body and another at a distance. The movement of the eyes, even if this be unnoticed, or be denied to yield anything but sensitized rather than sensibilized content, can be made the object of a discriminatory sensibility, though not one which is attending to colors.

Both what is being tasted and what is being seen may but need not be qualified by the body. So far as they are so qualified, the sensibility, while still freely acting, is affected by the body. What is beyond the body may, of course, be seen by a man who approaches the world from the standpoint of his sensibility. Something similar is true of what is tasted or otherwise sensed. One may not only be sensible of what the body makes available but of what is distinct from it.

Apple growers know there is a difference between sweet and sour apples. It would be difficult for them to make sense of the claim that apples are neither sweet nor sour, and that they are just assumed to be so when they are tasted. The growers would not even say that apples are potentially sweet or sour, unless what was meant was that the apples themselves become so, that they eventually could really become sweet or sour apples. The apples are sweet or sour before they are tasted. This they are as surely as they are young or old apart from any calendar. And what is true of the taste of apples is true also of their colors, shapes, smells, and anything else with which the sensibility can deal.

Men relativize the objective world, make its content subject to their private determinations. They do not thereby make it something subjective, somehow in their minds or feelings. The external world is not internalized but qualified by a sensibility that passes beyond the confines of the body. The insistence of that sensibility is inevitably limited by what is in the world, just as surely as the insistence on one's person is limited by the sensibility. The apples dictate what will be available to the sensibility, and the sensibility, as so dictated to, determines what one will be able to make his own.

By means of sensibility men relativize the world, make it theirs. They do something similar when they make use of their sensitivities and other private powers. So do subhumans. But their sensitivities are inescapably oriented toward their bodies and the world. Also, because they lack the promise that men have, the outcomes of their relativizations of what is external to them are necessarily different from those that men provide. And each, like the humans, inevitably adds further notes reflecting its own stresses and experiences.

The external world, which it is the object of a cosmology and a cosmological science to understand, is multiply relativized in ways that cannot be understood without taking account of how living beings qualify that world. Even were no one to disagree with this claim, disagreements would quickly surface in replies to the question whether or not the outcome of a qualification of the world by sensibility ends with what is real, external, objective, or with what is unreal, 'psychological', personal. Cosmologically-minded thinkers will answer directly and bluntly with a sharp negative: what is real is what occurs apart from man or any other living being; relativizations, for them, report merely what appears, what terminates a private, inaccessible distortion of what occurs in fact. Putting aside the difficulty that this answer depends on the acceptance of realities which no one in fact encounters, it requires in the end the affirmation that all our instruments and data—indeed even the world as cosmologically understood—are relativized, even humanized, made into the qualified termini of men's involvement with them. Since the supposed, unaffected cosmos itself could not then be known, they would also be left with the paradoxical consequence that they could not justifiably claim that it existed, available for a relativization.

The presence of sensibility does not make apples sweet; it makes the sweetness oriented toward a privacy. If sweetness and other relativizable characteristics were held not to be present in the apple, the apple would be reduced to a mere 'it' and therefore become indistinguishable from other similarly denuded entities, or it would be reduced to a plurality of irreducible particles or waves. Such particles or waves will be located where the apples are, and under the limitations that the apples impose.

As long as an apple is a single complex unity, it will be more than a set of smaller units; as long as it is more than such a set it will be ripe or unripe; as long as it is ripe or unripe, it will be sweet or not sweet; as long as it is sweet or not sweet, it will, once there is sensibility, be relativized as sweet or sour for taste; as long as it is sweet or sour for taste, different men, and each one of them at different times, will be able to attend to a differently experienced sweet or sour on eating the apple.

To be able to confront a sweet apple, a man must be more or less prepared for the effect that his sensibility, as involved with the apple, will have on him. The more participative he is, the more provision will he make, in some other epitomization, for what his affected sensibility introduces. The more disinterested he is, the less provision he will make. The closer he comes to being in between participation and disinterest, the more appraisive he will be, making as much allowance as he can for what sensibility presents, so far as this is consistent with his continuing undisturbed.

Sensibility does not initially or primarily focus on some particular object. When directed beyond the body, it becomes involved with whatever is present. And it continues to be so involved even while there is a concentration on some limited portion of the world. At the limit of the thrust of sensibility beyond the body is a panorama of interlocked items merging into one another. The items there are distinguished only so far as sensibility is used.

Disinterested, we are environed by a continuum of shapes, sounds, smells, tastes, pressures, all sustained by a faintly discerned background of resistances also sensibly reached. The Rockies and the Grand Canyon are objects of such a disinterested sensibility, a sensibility not prepared for them, no matter how well-read, no matter how well-traveled or imaginative the observer is. The panorama that one first confronts is quickly broken up into vistas themselves able to be broken up. Both at the beginning and at the end of the confrontations, both when faced as single diversified wholes and sensibly discriminated as a multiplicity of inter-locked, subordinated wholes, the eyes will be used. But the outcome cannot be adequately conveyed, if reference is made only to the sensibility as mediated by the eyes. The sensibility is also involved with what the eyes do not reach, with what is not seen. The fact has sometimes been re-marked by referring to the awesome and the sublime as objects of a distinctive power, not grasped solely by using a bodily organ. There is, though, no need to go beyond the acknowledgment that the sensibility at these times, while making use of the eyes, is involved with what grounds the seen. Sensibility then functions in a way that is somewhat similar to its functioning when it discriminates among tastes, though when directed at the awesome, sensibility is involved with and limited by what is external to the body, while when occupied with tastes it is involved with and limited by what the body is then and there making available. Since sensibility is pulled toward the one and accepts the other, where the one seems almost to escape possession, the other does not.

Awe depends on a yielding to what keeps the sensibility in thrall; what is found to be bodily agreeable and disagreeable, instead, is largely what one has been able to hold on to as one's own. The difference is not simply due to the fact that the awesome is distant and the bodily agreeable or disagree-able is close by. We can be negligent of what is at a distance, coldly discriminating what is present there; and we can be caught up in what is bodily available, losing ourselves in what is bodily undergone. The awe-some is distant for a sensibility which has been caught up in the affairs of an external world; the bodily agreeable or disagreeable is reached by a sensibility involved with the body. At both times, sensibility effectively discriminates.

The contention, that sensibility, whether disinterested, participative, or appraisive, can be involved with what is occurring at a distance from the body, goes counter to obtrusive and commonly accepted views of perception, observation, experiment, and science. The established ac-counts agree in holding that what we know comes to us from the outside and, after being somehow converted into mental content from vibrations and other types of physical occurrences impinging on our bodies, is imagined to be, is projected toward, or is sent out into the world. Such an account self-confessedly has no way of being acquainted with the sup-posed intrusive physical occurrences, since it admits no knowing of any-thing but what these have been supposedly transformed into. Nor is it entirely free of the idea that individuals somehow reach what is external to themselves—unless it is also being supposed that they are locked within themselves with idle claims that there is something outside—from which the content was obtained.

If the external world in any sense is supposed to be reached, the alternative offered to the present view will differ from it mainly in supposing that the external world is arrived at only after it has impinged on a man rather than, as is here contended, that sensibility and other private powers are participatively insistent on themselves. Content external to the body is entertained in privacy, but only because the sensibility is able to adopt what is there encountered without subjecting it to possibly distorting factors. Because the sensibility is already involved with content at a distance from the body, there is no need for what is privately received to be projected outwards, and most surely, no need to suppose that the known external world exists only so far as men have somehow managed to externalize what is located within their privacies, somehow confined in their bodies.

As long as sensibility is treated as a physical force moving across distances in public space, one will find justifiable fault with the present view, not only when it deals with sensibility, but with every other epitomization, from sensitivity to responsible action. There is no evidence that such traversals occur. There is no room in what we know of the expenditure of physical energy for an intelligible report of such traversals. Sensibility is not a physical force; it remains private no matter what it is prepared for and what it might discriminate. The distance between one's body and the Rockies is privately bridged in a single expression of sensibility.

There is no passage through a public space from or to a privately used sensiblity. Men are involved in the world beyond them, not by having it first somehow come to them on the first half of a journey which is to return to the point of origin in a more or less altered form. They make direct contact with what is other than themselves by means of sensibility and other insistent epitomizations of privacy. None of these move in public space over a period of objective time. The privacies remain privacies even when they are limited, constrained, and qualified by their bodies and the bodies of others, nearby or at a distance.

To be a man is to be at once self-maintained, persistent, and effective, expressing his privacy in multiple epitomizations. Other actualities also insist on themselves. Were there nothing but actualities, no matter what the kind, they would not be together. Each would be a universe to itself, not bounded by, not reaching any other. It is because they are all subject to common conditions that they are able to be together. Space is one of those conditions. Actualities are in space because they occupy it, and they can occupy it because they exist apart from but are able to reply to its conditioning. Motion, whether it be by men, particles, waves, or rays, is carried out by what is itself not spatial. To move is to be successively spatialized through the private occupation of different public regions of a common conditioning public space.

A man's sensibility, more often than not, terminates at what is itself without sensibility. If what is terminated at is not a complex, unified, single actuality with its own privacy, it is not a living being, but an ultimate physical unit, a plurality of these, or a colony or whole in which a plurality is encompassed. Colonies and wholes have only latent privacies, privacies unable to be insistently expressed, and therefore unable to govern and limit the activities of their contained pluralities. The Rockies and the Grand Canyon are wholes. Sensibility impinges on the privacies characteristic of them, privacies which the vast multiplicity of their encompassed actualities have not succeeded in mediating. We are awed when facing those wholes. Unfortunately, our sensibilities are not acute enough to enable us to reach into the privacies. We, therefore, have to be content with noting the brute resistance which the encompassed items together produce.

Human beings are with one another in ways no other beings are with their fellows, because the humans reach one another via sensibilities of a distinctive type, at once more diversifiable than those possessed by other beings, and inseparable from distinctive promises. Although the sensibility of each reaches to every other, to make them men involved with one another, genocide, slavery, hatred, and prejudice, unfortunately, are not thereby precluded. Men insist on other epitomizations, sometimes in such a way as to hide from themselves the fact that, by means of their sensibilities, and in other ways as well, they are inescapably part of a single humankind.

d. Need

A man moves to a higher stage of maturity when he is able to make use of more deeply grounded, independently acting, wider ranging private powers than he could before. A number of such stages may be moved through at the same time. One or more of them may enrich the others and that with which these are involved. Higher, but not later, stages in a man's development reflect his capacity to deal with what is more and more comprehensive, valuable, and lasting, exhibiting him to be one who uses his body while involved with what is beyond that body. Just what happens publicly all can know, and what happens privately they can learn just so far as what is being privately brought to bear is distinguished from what is objectively contributed, and traced back to its source.

Need expresses a higher though not later stage in the maturation of a human than sensibility does. It has a greater urgency which sometimes awakens a body's organized effort to dampen it. Bodily oriented, it directs the body toward a searching, a focusing on, and finally a possessing and using. Tensional, reaching toward what is able to make good a deficiency, it overcomes a bodily lack. Since it seems to require only bodily acts in order for it to be carried out and satisfied, it is tempting to understand it in purely bodily terms. But no examination of the body ever uncovers a need; the initial experience of a lack, the activity of searching, and the final relief, relaxation, and satisfaction are privately undergone. The move from sensibility to need can be at once a progression and a retrogression, for while need can avoid the loss of bodily pertinent content that the sensibility allows, it can also end with what may be bodily repugnant, unwanted, and perhaps injurious.

Eating and drinking are at once primitive and highly complicated activities. They are overwhelmingly bodily, and are performed readily and successfully. Hemmed in by tradition and custom, affected by training and situation, cushioned, qualified, enriched, and distorted, carried on without supervision, they often occur without an awareness that one is privately involved in them. Yet they too exhibit a privately grounded, bodily oriented need, a need restricted to what the body requires in order to continue and prosper.

A body in the presence of food or drink—even one deprived of food or drink—is not yet a body in need of these. The body must be related to them by a relation which begins in the privacy and ends with what is sought. Need must relate the body to what is to be used to make good some lack in that body. Although the need is not produced by the body, it is also not produced without regard for it. In response to the functioning of the body, it directs the body toward what the body is to have. There is no deliberation here, no conscious private acknowledgment of something sought, no getting the body to obtain it. There is just a private insistence through the body on what is to serve it.

Sometimes what would satisfy a need is not available, and sometimes in the presence of what would satisfy a need nothing is done. We may be aware that we are thirsty or hungry, and give no indication of that fact; others will not then know that we are in need of water or food. Even if an examination of our bodies shows the kinds of deficiencies and disturbances, the kinds of movements and probings that accompanied a previously expressed thirst or hunger, and even if the provision of water or food ended in the overcoming of the lacks, others would still not be able to know whether or not we were in need. Bodies act and react, move and rest as a consequence of the realization of bodily potentialities. Those potentialities are not justifiably identified with need, for this dictates to and makes use of the body, sometimes in considerable independence of what is being sensitively and sensibly undergone.

An infant's cry could conceivably express only a bodily response to a bodily lack. If the scheduled time for its nourishment arrives, its cry will not yet offer evidence of something privately felt. If it then unhesitatingly eats or drinks, its cry would still not provide clear evidence of a need. That it is expressing a need will not be known as long as one does not know that the infant privately relates a bodily lack to what will enable the infant to overcome this.

We cannot credit an infant's need solely to its body without supposing that the infant does not privately experience a lack, that it does not privately relate itself to what would overcome this, and that it does not overcome this by making use of its body. It may, of course, not be conscious of what it is doing. If we are to know that it has a need, we must find evidence in what it bodily does, leading us into and permitting us to infer that it privately began an activity directed at using the body so as to provide the body with what it must have if it is to continue and to prosper.

We must distinguish an effort to reduce the tension between changes in the way a being is related to what would satisfy it, and a possible satisfaction which controls, orders, and directs the functioning of its body. We learn that someone is hungry or thirsty by noting how he focuses and keeps focused on food or drink. We have evidence that he is in need when we can see both that his body is being related to what would satisfy it, and that his acts alter the relation until satisfaction is attained.

Were a man to gulp, devour, uncontrollably eat or drink, he would make evident that he was overcoming a bodily lack in ways which he does not and perhaps cannot control. He will act under the influence of what is satisfying, but will not condition himself, or utilize his body to obtain what the body requires. Conceivably, his body might just be acting after a period of denial, so that there was just a bodily easement, perhaps sensitively felt.

A need is a bodily oriented private insistence directed toward what is not yet possessed. Evidence that a man has a need and that it is being satisfied is provided by his bodily expressed efforts to make good a lack through the use of what is distinct from his body. Although no conscious purpose or deliberateness is being supposed, the fact that what is to be attained is taken into account does show the act to be purposive. Purposiveness is present whenever there is an insistence on a prospect, with a consequent use of agencies for realizing it.

Drinking and eating may occur at a pace and at intervals which have nothing to do with the body's satisfactions, its structure, or its ways of functioning, though these may occasion and support them. It may therefore be difficult to know whether the body is being governed by a need or is just not acting properly. A malfunctioning body has its own rationale. Often enough, it exhibits a pace and a well-ordered set of acts which enable one to discern a distinctive kind of deviation from a normal course. Medicine takes account of that fact. A malfunctioning body, it knows, is quite different from one which is under the governance of a need. Only the latter involves a governance of the body so as to bring about what satisfies this, thereby enabling the body to function well.

Conceivably, one could view an illness as a kind of need requiring the body to obtain what must be had if the body is to continue and to prosper. But then one would also have to say that hunger and thirst express a kind of illness, or that there are no malfunctioning bodies but only normal ones with greater or lesser pressing needs. Malfunctioning is not a kind of satisfactory functioning of low degree; it exhibits the body acting in ways which are not appropriate to need.

In the absence of what would overcome a bodily lack, there may be a period of searching, foraging, struggle. For these to evidence need, they must be so joined to external content that they constitute ordered acts, promoting the attainment and use of what satisfies. The private nature of need makes it possible for need to guide the body over a period of time, so that the body goes toward what might benefit it, and ignores or pushes aside what may not. Another's changes in pace and rhythm, his keeping abreast of circumstance, all serving to benefit the body, let one know of the presence of a need in him.

A need is satisfied when a man makes good a bodily lack by using what he seeks to affect what he does. He could stop short, before a full satisfaction was obtained. Religious taboos, training, custom, superstitions can make him use what would satisfy his thirst or hunger in such a way as to suppress, hide, or distort these. What he does will then not be understood unless account is taken of his assessment of what he seeks and finds, and of the effects these have on what he does.

We come to know of the presence of a man's privately initiated need most surely when we note that what he seeks is used differentially by him, with varying emphases at different times, and with a resultant alteration in his bodily acts. Although what he does will still have its observable side, this will be misconstrued if reference is not made to the effective controls he privately provides.

A need is private in origin, privately directed, and privately satisfied. But it is also publicly manifested and sustained, relating a bodily lack to anything that might overcome it. The inability of the body to do more than be what it is and do what it does when and where it is, requires one to recognize that it is governed by what is able to relate it to something which the body must obtain if it is to continue and prosper. But the satisfaction of the need can be deferred. It could also occur in a manner and at a time determined without adequate regard for what the body must have. Satisfying a need is not identical with satisfying a body, even though it is directed toward what is to benefit this.

As private, a need is singular. It is the body that enables the need to assume the form of a number of quite different and sometimes oppositional stresses. The need is not then divided. It continues to remain single, not only in origin but even as stopping with what is externally sustained. Stopping at water rather than food, need makes the water pertinent to a bodily lack; stopping at food, need makes the food pertinent to a different bodily state.

If need is ignored, the body must be credited with a multiplicity of appetites, each operating without necessary bearing on any others. A reference to a man in need would then be but a blurred and imprecise way of talking about his having many distinct bodily urges. There would be no guiding, controlling, or satisfying of his body, but just a number of distinct occupations with what could bring various tensions to an end. It is necessary to refer to a need to account for the fact that all lacks characterize a single being which is able to govern them in relation to one another, and to relate them to what could overcome them. The fact that a limit for need is provided by a body does not stand in the way of the limit being privately faced and dealt with.

The body does not dictate that there should be a need, or how this is to be expressed. Just as sensitivity is manifested in and through the body antecedent to anything which occasioned feelings of pain and pleasure, so need is expressed in and through the body antecedent to anything that occasions a private focusing on what would satisfy the body. There is a sense, therefore, in which living beings are always in need. Finite, they are necessarily incomplete, thrusting toward what else there is, under limitations which their bodies introduce. Without those limitations, their privacies would be occupied solely with reaching whatever was other than themselves in order to have within them whatever there is, since whatever else there be defines them as just 'others'; to be independent, each must have within itself whatever makes it an 'other.' Actual needs are specialized forms by which privacy attains the state of being self-contained.

What makes necessary a reference to need is not only the fact that the body is directed at what is to satisfy it, but that what could satisfy it is used as a guiding condition, affecting what the body does. A man may not make effective use of the guide. He may deliberately hold it up, modify it, or attend to the satisfaction of his body because of the weight he has given either to what could satisfy it or to the prospective satisfaction itself. These, though, are late achievements. Well before then, he governs his body by what is prospectively satisfying, and does it without training, thought, or the support of dominant mores. His need, while relating his privacy to what satisfies his body, takes on a multiplicity of forms in that body. Despite the fact that need then has a greater range while maintaining a greater independence of the body than sensitivity does, and that it can be more readily distinguished than sensitivity from factors which the body provides, need is so involved with what is important for the body that it is as difficult to recognize its purely private status and functioning as it is to recognize those characteristic of sensitivity.

Because needs lives the body at the same time that this qualifies and channels need, need becomes imbedded in the biosphere—the totality of all that has bearing on the welfare of the body—in the way sensitivity is imbedded in the body itself. It is there that it must be first identified. We will miss it if we suppose that the body has needs, and that it is satisfied when it is replenished, or pained when it is not. If we wish to say that the body searches for what satisfies it, we will also have to say that a body is not just a physical or biological unit.

To speak of a body as though it searched for what would satisfy it is to suppose that the body can direct itself at that which may not exist, and in any case is outside its boundaries and may be beyond its reach. If there is something not present in a body it is not present in it, and that is the end of the matter. If it receives something, it has it, and that too is the end of the matter. A searching would require it to have a unitary purpose, to be guided by a possibility. Let it, though, be granted that a body is able to search for what, if obtained, makes it better able to continue and prosper. Why are there times when the search is held up, when drink or food is not taken in by a body which has been deprived of these for a time? The body could be said to be malfunctioning, to be disordered, sick, not to be acting the way a well-organized body does, though it seems to be functioning as well as it did before. Despite thirst and hunger, men sometimes refuse food and drink, often when their bodies are acting extremely well. What would make a body neglect or reject food and drink, sometimes violently, with great concentration, and without hesitation? Whether or not it makes sense to say that a man's body is satisfied, it surely is true that the man seeks something else which is to him privately pleasing because it enables him to overcome a lack.

Human need is insistent. The more its insistence makes no provision for anything else, the more demanding it is. It yields so far as it makes provision for what it might impinge upon. When adjusted, it remains itself while making maximum provision for what it encounters. A similar set of distinctions is pertinent to any other epitomization as able to be affected by need.

Compared to need, sensitivity and sensibility, apart from the action of other epitomizations and apart from changes produced in the course of experience, are fairly constant. It is the I rather than the sensitivity which is inattentive, the I rather than the sensibility that is judicious. But need, no less than the I, can be demanding, yielding, or adjusted.

Human need initially is a private power, quite apart from any involvement in the world or the world about. As such a private power, it can be directed at other epitomizations. As independent, natively unlimited in range, need insistently expresses the finitude of an unduplicable individual so far as this is consistent with its being limited in its activity by others. It never is as demanding or as yielding as it conceivably could be. But, also, it is never perfectly adjusted, in equilibrium, self-maintained at a stage where it cannot be disturbed.

All men take account of human need. All not only make provision for what it encounters, but for it as an insistence revelatory of an individual finitude. No matter what it subdues, it leaves one still deprived, denied, confronted by what it would but cannot have. Eastern sages, acutely aware of the fact, urge men to pull themselves back from need, to make themselves receptive of and eventually merged into what is still, forever, and featureless. Most, perhaps all, would admit that the goal will not be attained, and perhaps is beyond the capacity of any man to reach. But, they would add that any advance toward that goal is desirable. They differ from most Westerners in trying to get us to turn the need away from the world, toward what is free of the faults of finitude. What they direct us to therefore should not be viewed as requiring the annihilation of need. Indeed, they point up what, in addition to the finite, one ontologically needs to have and which can be obtained not by action or conquest, but by submission only.

A man is finite, not only because there are other finite beings, but also because there are realities which are not finite at all. Even if the finite be

taken to be illusory, it is distinct from what is final. Even if the finite is
taken to be illusory, it is a finite man who is to become enlightened in fact,
and this by really yielding to his need to have in a better way what he now
has in a poorer.

There is wisdom, but also some misunderstanding behind the advice
that one should not allow bodily lacks to dictate what one is to do, where
one's attention is to be directed, or how one is to understand the nature of
human need. In effect, one is being asked to make some other epitomization yield maximally to need as already maximally yielding to what is
eternal, it being tacitly supposed that the need and therefore whatever
takes account of it will then no longer be affected by anything else. But the
rest of privacy, like the rest of the world, pays no attention to a man's
search for enlightenment. Whatever there is continues to limit his need.
If the need is to be overcome, need must make provision for what does
this.

A truly enlightened man has a need which is well adjusted to the
presence of other occurrences. Only he is in a position to yield maximally
to need as that which maximally yields to what is forever. Well before
there is a prospect of need becoming involved with what is eternal, it must
make provision for what else it might encounter.

Initially, human need is identified when involved with the body.
When traced back to its source, it is found to be just one of a number of
private powers. Like every other private power, it is prepared for by others,
and must itself prepare for them and what else might limit and eventually
affect it. An inability by those others to yield to need sufficiently opens
them up to the likelihood that they will be radically transformed by it.

Enlightenment literature speaks usually not of need but of desire as
requiring control or annihilation. Both are in fact dealt with under a
single name, and then sometimes as unitary and sometimes as diversified
in the form of specific insistencies. A unitary need alone is what should be
in focus, not only because specific needs and desires are many, not only
because we do not know what they are until they are in operation, not
only because they must be controlled at their origins in an undiversified
form, but because what is sought is a redirecting of the being as a single
unit whose usual insistency toward what is in the world is to give way to
another that is pointed elsewhere. Consideration should also have been
given to the fact that need has to do with what is lacking to the individual
while desire has to do with what is important for the species. Both, of
course, may be viewed as misdirected powers to be suppressed, and an
occupation with eternity set in their place. Could this be done, men
would somehow have been transformed from actualities, inescapably

distinct and finite, into indistinguishable parts of a single undifferentiated whole. But the most enlightened of men remains individual, finite, with limited insistencies interlocking with others under the control of common conditions. At best, enlightenment is a state which finite individuals achieve while being minimally affected by their bodies and the world about.

If a need for what is eternal is met, an individual must make the result his own or cease to be one who sought and attains enlightenment. There are, to be sure, some who speak as though this is exactly what is not intended. But it is perverse to hold that men are to seek to be so perfected that they are no longer individual human beings who all the while continue to live and breathe, eat and drink, and are related to all other men, particularly those who are not enlightened.

The need of subhumans, like the need of men, is freely biased toward what might intrude, but only so far as the need is mediated by the body. Their freedom is the freedom to be bodily prepared. They have no power to determine what role need will play in their economy, but men can subordinate need, qualify it, hem it in, or expand its scope.

The most conspicuous and familiar form of need is where the initial evidence for it is isolated—when it is involved with, qualified by, and affected by the body. That the need is not native to the body has already been remarked upon. Only a private being has a need that makes demands on, yields to, or is adjusted to the body. The way it, and any other private power, is involved with the body depends on the degree to which it is freely readied for what the body does, and the extent to which the body is more or less receptive to it.

If omnivorous, one makes little provision for need; if lax, one makes maximum allowance for it. So far as need is involved with the body, its adventures there will take one by surprise unless a temperate state is achieved, midway between omnivorousness and laxness. A man is to be judged adversely as defective in character or control when he is lax or omnivorous, just as surely as he is commendable when he is temperate, acting somewhere between these extremes.

Every epitomization is more or less receptive to the presence and activities of need. It is therefore correct to say of any one of them that it freely, though not deliberately, deviates more or less from the stage of being temperate. Men can consequently be judged adversely for failing to be temperate in any number of ways. The fact is ignored by moralists who speak as though temperance was to be commended because it characterized the will or that on which the will was imposed. Aristotle confined it even more narrowly, treating temperance as though it concerned the way men avoided excess or defect in matters of touch and taste, and therefore only so far as they were adjusted to their bodies or were subject to a controlled sensitivity. Temperance is a virtue and virtue is a habit, as Aristotle remarked; but a habit can be acquired by private power either by repeating a type of preparation again and again, or (as Aristotle apparently did not allow) by being maintained steadily in the face of various challenges. Men have a habit of thinking along this or that line both because they have done so frequently in the past, and because they do not allow themselves to be swayed by exterior influences. Because of the independence of the various ways in which privacy can be specialized, and those specializations specialized in turn, it is possible for a man to be temperate in one respect and not in another, to be temperate for example, in desire but intemperate in choice.

The contact that need makes with the external world is not achieved through a traversal over space and time. As has already been observed, such a traversal presupposes a public space and time as well as a private being able to occupy different positions in them. The world beyond the body, of course, is a world which is spatially distant from it. One makes contact with that world, though, just by laying claim to it; at that time, the world limits what is privately reaching it.

Need and other epitomizations are limited in distinctive ways both by the body and by what is beyond the body. It is surely right to speak of each expression as beginning in an individual who was born at a particular time, and who now exists at a particular place. One then identifies him in a public position. But one must not continue to hold on to that mode of identification if one wishes to refer to his privacy.

This account of the limitations to which need and other private powers are subject by the world is not unrelated to Peirce's discussion of Secondness. He held that, in addition to an immediate Firstness and a rational Thirdness, there were obstinancies, oppositions, actions and reactions in experience, and perhaps also in reality. But he never did make clear how one knew that these were not supplied in the very act of expressing oneself, making them facets of either Firstness or Thirdness. He could not know whether or not this occurred, because he did not ask whether or not one was able to face the same content in both a free and a limited way. He tended, too, to give priority to Thirdness, speaking at times as though Secondness were wholly subordinated to this, and conceivably even a degenerate version of it. These misconceptions were perhaps inevitable, because he thought of Secondness as a category, instead of taking it to be what was constituted by a category but still different from this. Were one to take Thirdness to be the basic category, and then understood Secondness to be Thirdness as subject to externally produced limitations, and so far able to stand in contrast with Thirdness itself, there would still be a difference between what is here being maintained and what a Peircean account allows, but the difference would not be as great as before.

Other epitomizations make some accommodation for need as limited by what is beyond the body. The exact nature of the limitations to which need will be subject will not then be anticipated, for the double reason that a preparation comes before an actual contact with particular entities occurs and that the need also suffers limitations due to what provides a condition to which every body is subject.

When need, as involved with the body, is set in contrast with need as involved with the world beyond the body, the body is also set in opposition to the world. Such a body is a lived body, inseparable from the private living of it. Despite the fact that the world with which need is then involved is indefinitely large and encompasses every other body, such a world will differ considerably from one that encompasses all bodies. A world with which one's own body is involved is a world of other bodies; only a world of all bodies contrasts with one's privacy. In the former, need has two independent roles, living the body and insisting on itself everywhere else; in the latter, need is insistently expressed everywhere. The former allows for a privacy which lives a body; the latter adopts the position of privacy by itself.

e. Desire

Men privately initiate bodily sustained acts that are hard to gainsay, despite the fact that their bodies may then function in ways which are injurious to, and which may even destroy those bodies. But while the result may be to their bodies' detriment, men sometimes make their bodies act so as to achieve other than bodily goods. They express private desires, striving to benefit the species, primarily through procreation, and secondarily through the protection and assistance they give to the young and others.

Like need, desire is directed toward what satisfies; unlike need, it is directed toward what may not satisfy the being which initiates it. Like need, it cannot be credited to the body; unlike need, it regularly uses the body to promote what may be indifferent to that body. Like need, desire is given impetus and a new import by being used by the body, at the same time that it makes the body function in ways which cannot be bodily provided; unlike need, it does not always divide into a multiplicity of channeled insistencies governing particular bodily acts.

So-called 'desires' for dominance, fame, money, and the like, are rather late developments, arriving only after a man has passed beyond the stage where he is able to express and consummate a more basic, primitive desire. Quite different in origin and function from it, they are so many different strivings. Sometimes they act in accord with, and sometimes in opposition to, and most of the time without regard for, what desire insistently demands. Were these or other strivings identified with desire, they would still have to be distinguished from an earlier, singular form, since all of them, unlike desire, presuppose some maturation, thought, and resolution, and entail responsibility. Like them, desire operates without necessary pertinence to the body's lacks; unlike them, it is most insistently exhibited in an urgency to copulate. In men, the insistence is affected by tradition and custom, age and opportunity. Bypassing masturbation and homosexuality, frustrated by impotence and menopause, it is often qualified by and can qualify aesthetic discriminations.

Animals act in ways which promote their species. Since they are not affected by tradition and are not subject to deliberation, desire in them cannot be equated with man's desire. Even when a desiring man is overcome by passion, when he pushes on regardless of consequences, his acts are different from what is possible to any other kind of being, if for no other reason than that he cannot act on behalf of his species without passing through the cultural setting in which he daily lives. Although that setting has its analogues in the groupings of animals, and though it is easily overridden at times, it limits and is operative well before and all the while that his desire comes into play. But even apart from such a setting, his desire would be different from any desire an animal could have, for his alone is inseparable from a distinctive promise to occupy a distinctive place in a limited portion of an environment.

Even when radically qualified, even when its time, place, manner, and value are subject to controls, human desire continues to express its own origin and nature, is directed at a distinctive prospect, uses special agencies in distinctive ways, and carries out unduplicable roles. The control that society, tradition, other interests, and reflection introduce may slow or deflect the work that desire does on behalf of the human species, but they neither extinguish it nor make more than a minor difference to it. One should not be surprised, therefore, to find some men maintaining that desire is dangerous or that its dominance reveals a man fallen back to some lower, primitive, unfortunate level, where he then duplicates what is characteristic of brutes. But a man, no matter how bestial, never ceases to be a man. His acts may bring him morally below the level of an animal, but they never change him into one.

Desire may also be well expressed in the most rigidly structured societies. Although these do not annihilate it or even deflect it, they do regulate it, and thereby determine when and how it is to be publicly expressed without penalty. The nature and urgency of the desire will still remain. Consequently, what desire accomplishes in one society will usually not be radically different from what it accomplishes in others, exercising different, stronger, or weaker controls. The fact that desire must at times break through social barriers in order to be adequately expressed is not always regrettable.

The expression of desire is carried out with the help of the body. It ends with a relaxing of tensions, though it is not directed at attaining that result. The supposition that it is so directed has as much warrant as one which takes the perpetuation of the species to be the incidental outcome of a bodily attempt to recover a state of quiescence. Both suppositions tacitly treat desire as though it were just a need, at the service of the body.

The satisfaction of the body is as much a prospect for privacy as is the prosperity of the species. Neither prospect is consciously entertained. Neither is attained without the body's help. Both are exhibited in bodily acts, thereby providing evidence of the prospects' presence and natures. We know that desire is operative because we find a living body acting to bring about results that are advantageous to the species, though not helpful and perhaps disadvantageous to that body.

The Trobriand Islanders are said to make no connection between their sexual acts and procreation. If, as is here claimed, it is possible to have evidence of desire, and if desire is directed at continuing the species, it becomes difficult to see immediately why the Trobriand Islanders should not have made the connection between the expression of desire and the more conspicuous ways in which the species is continued. Nor is it easy to see why it is not known by some among us that the human species may be promoted by the satisfaction of desire. The difficulties dissolve with the realization that it is hard to make a connection between causes and effects which are separated by three quarters of a year, and that if it is supposed that God or some other transcendent power alone makes humans, no matter what men and women do, their sexual interplay will not be tied to activities which promote the continuation of the species. The evidence that desire is operative is present, but naïveté and special doctrines stand in the way of its recognition and use. Once the connection between sexual activity and gestation in subhuman beings is noted, and when man is seen to be as fully in nature as other living beings are, it becomes less difficult to isolate and use evidence of the presence of desire.

The similarity between men and subhumans here must not be allowed to obscure their differences. Only the distinctive privacy of man can operate in independence of the body and the species, and be specialized in the form of a desire that is expressed through and sustained by the body which it lives.

Desire also makes use of the body in order to sustain attachments of men to one another. Without the attachment, there would be no common action, and the species, as a consequence, would at best be the outcome of the adventitious coming together of individuals. Men would not belong together in a species; they would just happen to have it as an incidental product, or as an idle condition. As a result, the species would have neither past nor future, but merely antecedents and replacements, themselves equally adventitious.

The nature of the species and the attachment of men to one another together constitute an actual functioning species, able to interplay with others. It acts as a controlling condition; changes in its nature make a difference to the course of human desire. Were its presence and functioning ignored or misconstrued, there would be no explaining why various activities which do not benefit normal men, as individuals or in groups, are nevertheless insistently carried out by them.

The understandable disinclination of biologists to refer to the presence and action of a privately grounded human desire has left them with no alternative but to suppose that the human species makes individuals serve its ends, or that the activities of genes, severally or together, dictate what men do. The first of these views credits the species with a power for which there is no evidence. It also fails to show how the species affects individuals. The second reverses the emphasis to give power to the genes, with a corresponding lack of warrant and a failure to show how these units could determine what a unitary organism does, or how any act could be privately initiated. Both suppositions ignore actual men, with privacies that are able to make use of their bodies for the benefit of the species.

Desire is directly, though only partly, expressed in individual displays, lures, enticements, struggles. These prompt others to express themselves in relevant ways. The expression by one of them is here matched by reciprocal expressions by others, thereby making it possible for them together to bring about what the species requires.

Each man expresses desire from a unique, private base. Each is limited by and thereby related to the expressions of desire by others. Something analogous occurs in subhumans, particularly those which came into existence late in the history of the world of living beings. Here, even more sharply and successfully than is the case with men, something like desire is answered by desire, with a consequent benefit to the species. Were men to act just as these do, they would match the expressions of desire by others with expressions of their own. Instead, they sometimes just observe others who desire, keeping their own desire in a subordinate role, or they face the others as within the context of a milieu or society, with distinctive traditions, conventions, and other constraining conditions.

If one ignores the role of desire, and the species from which it is inseparable, one will not be able to identify those bodily actions which, though not aberrational, do not help the body, insistently override it, govern and incorporate other bodily acts, and benefit the species. The identification is readily made when one sees that someone is sexually excited or—taking account of the conventional frames in which desire is expressed and may be matched by some selected other—that he is in love.

Bodily expressions of desire can be and have been identified with regrettable impulses of the body. Instead of being seen as evidence that desire is being expressed, is sustained by, and is using the body, the expressions are taken to mark the absence of a genuinely human, privately initiated act. A man is then understood to be a pure spirit yoked to and occasionally but unfortunately at the mercy of an independent body. Held for thousands of years and in more than one culture, subscribed to by great religious leaders and distinguished thinkers, such a view has yet to make clear how the body, supposedly inferior and apparently passive, is able to act independently of and block the excellent and active spirit on which its very life depends. Nevertheless, the fact that the view is so widely held, and by men who are perceptive and presumably observant, should make one hesitate to accept the present claim that there is evidence, available in men's bodily actions, leading one to a privately initiated desire which is living and using the body to obtain trans-bodily outcomes. The two views, that of tradition, and that here presented, are not opposed in principle. Still, they differ, for the present account alone takes desire to have a private origin and its own objective which the body sustains in a modified form, and that it is good to have the desire satisfied. It alone refuses to denigrate desire just because some of its consequences are deplorable, are disdained in canonical works, are rejected by some religious or philosophical thinkers, or because other expressions of privacy help us realize nobler prospects.

Desire is privately initiated. It is not a purely bodily occurrence. Evidence for it is found in acts which may not have value for the body but which are matched by the bodily expressed acts of others. That evidence is available to anyone who is able to identify in what is bodily done, contributing to an attachment of men to one another, whether or not the outcome is regrettable from other positions.

Making use of the body to bring about results not of benefit to that body, the bodily sustained expressions of one man are interlocked with those of another. Comparatively free of his own body, each is aroused, stimulated, and limited by the other. The fact that their desires realize a common prospect which is relevant to and beyond their bodies, remains concealed as long as what one man expresses is not seen to be coordinate with the expressions of the other.

It sounds paradoxical to say that subhumans are readily recognized to function on behalf of their species and not on behalf of their individual bodies, whereas humans, despite the fact that their privacies are exercised in considerable independence of their bodies and are sometimes occupied with non-bodily prospects, are not readily recognized to concern themselves with serving their species. The paradox vanishes with the recognition that the bodies of subhumans are conditioned by their species to a degree that human bodies are not. Subhumans act as units in a species because their bodies are already under the dominance of that species. Humans, instead, use their species to guide and control the use they make of their bodies. Where the one is wholly subject to the species, the other helps make itself subject to it. An evolutionary theory which would account for the coming of man must, therefore, attend not only to the similarities and differences between subhuman and human bodies, but to the similarities and differences in the ways in which diverse species act on the bodies of their members.

There are, and perhaps there will always be two irreconcilable factions in biology. On the one side are the naturalists and vitalists who attend to the activities of gross, unitary living beings as they interact with one another and their environments. Darwin was a naturalist. On the other side are the experimenters who attend to cells, genes, and the like that are found within unitary organic bodies. The experimenters are occupied with showing how those units are interrelated, and sometimes how they are prompted to act by, and to produce results on what is in the larger world. The experimenters say that the position maintained by the others cannot be expressed in biological terms, that discourse about unitary organic bodies is vague, ill-defined, and contains echoes of a religious, non-scientific supposition that there is a non-empirical soul. Though not able to understand all that a complex organism does, these men find it neither necessary nor desirable to look beyond cells, genes, and other experimentally ascertainable units in order to understand how a living being originates, matures, lives, and interacts with others. The others seem unable to answer their opponents convincingly. But whether or not what they say makes sense to other biologists, we cannot deny that they are right in contending that a living being functions in ways, and makes the parts within its body function in ways, no study of the parts explains. To this it will be replied, that though we do not know how to explain everything about living bodies today by referring to what is within their confines, it is to be expected that the explanation will be forthcoming eventually. That hope is unwarranted. There is no particular entity and no interconnection of the entities that could provide the explanation, even in principle, since a living body bunches and separates its encompassed units and makes them function in ways they could not on their own. When a rabbit scurries across the field, it traverses space for distances and at a speed not possible to any one or any collection of the items encompassed within its body. Its genes interact with others nearby, and move short distances all the while that the scurrying rabbit is taking them into a distant region of space. There is no question but that the functioning of the genes and other units in the body have an effect on that body, and where and how it is able to be moved, but that is only to say that the control of the units by the body is not absolute, that there are occasions when it has little, and perhaps even no control over what it encompasses.

These considerations come into play in another form when one tries to understand sexual selection solely in terms of the activities of units encompassed within complex bodies. If there were no privately vitalized, unified, complex bodies, there would be no sexual selections. Mating would be just a product of the ways in which units within different bodies functioned. Sexual, and natural selection as well, would report only the interplay of various units somehow bunched in separate groups. If all that acts are the units, we will have to be content to learn which ones happen to form bonds and somehow have made possible other bunches we call 'offspring.' Whatever bunch happens to survive better than others will just so far have been 'selected' or produced by what 'selects'. 'Selection' in such a view, is shorthand for the acknowledgment that some combination of occurrences happens to fare better in a given region or epoch than others do. Yet sexual selection, the mating with some rather than with others also available, and perhaps even more accessible, does occur. Men, at least, ignore possible mates nearby and compete with one another as single complex beings for others who may not in fact be fertile. It will not do to say that they happened to have the kinds of genes or cells which make them so act, for not only do they compete and act as single beings, but the selection of a mate by one may be triggered solely because it had been selected by another.

Mating is between unitary living beings, with complex bodies, encompassing and governing smaller ones. To ignore that fact is to ignore the only data one has for claiming that genes or cells prompted the act or, paradoxically, that only they really exist, and that selections, matings and of course the biologist who holds this, have no reality.

Once we allow for the reality and actions of complex beings, we are in a position to recognize the presence of desire, a primary private insistence directed at other beings under the controlling condition of their common species. Desires for food, drink, and shelter specialize this, thereby making the occupation with these into particularized ways in which the species is sustained.

How could any being desire? It is attentive only to what is in its vicinity, but most of the other members of its species are distant and unknown. How could its acts make a difference to a species ranging over a vast space and enduring for an indefinite time? Could any being promote anything more than the welfare of other individuals? Could it make a difference to others in that part of the group which it is not focusing on? And if it could affect the group itself, could it do this for any part which is not embracing those particular individuals with which one is directly interplaying?

A being whose actions promote its species functions in ways which are pertinent to many members of which it is oblivious. Once this is allowed, it becomes evident that desire has a great reach. And once it is recognized that a species is a specialized form of a more comprehensive condition ranging over all actualities, it also becomes evident that desire, as operating on behalf of the species, is a specialized form of a desire operating on behalf of a more comprehensive condition. Just as sensibility specializes an effort to realize value, and need specializes an effort to realize a relation of othering, desire specializes the realization of a condition which enables other beings to be coordinate with what seeks to possess and use them. The fact is somewhat obscured by the obtrusive emphasis that desire places on the beings that conspicuously quiet it. As having that emphasis, desire is only one facet of the effort to be coordinated with all else, reaching from one to all other beings. Made specific, it endeavors to utilize some for its own benefit. As both general and specific, it requires that the others it reaches have a reciprocal relation to it. Otherwise they would simply block the desire, to make it function as though it were something like sensitivity. There are, of course, those who seek and those who wait, those who impose themselves and those who receive. Some are relatively active; others are relatively passive. But desire, as mating helps us see, is no less present and effective in those who are sought than in those who seek. The species is promoted by their reciprocal exhibition of the self-same desire.

Each man has a dim, unfocused awareness that he is on a footing with others who have a similar private desire, though those others are so far unknown and the desire not evidenced. While entirely alone, keeping within his own privacy, each is aware that others are connected with him as desiring and, so far, are his equals.

It is a fact, as lamentable as it is inescapable, that for thousands of years, slavery was not condemned by the greatest of intellects, the most perceptive of religious leaders, or the most daring of philosophers. If all men have a sense that every other is an equal, how could slavery be tolerated and sometimes even endorsed by leading thinkers and spiritual guides? Aristotle and Aquinas were quite clear in their affirmations that slaves were human beings and, therefore, so far as their essential nature was concerned, were on a footing with other humans. They took them to be inferior to others in physique, intelligence, belief, and heredity. They did not see that this did not make the men really unequal, because they did not fully grasp, as their own doctrines should have enabled them, the measure that the privacy of men necessarily imposes on the way men function together.

Men live together in public in ways not privately governed. Still, when states are assessed as being unjust, they are judged in part in terms of their failure to promote a public equality matching one privately grounded. The public ways in which men are together does not remove them from an evaluation in terms of what is privately required. It is one thing to recognize that political states have independent groundings, careers, and standards; it is quite another to suppose that their activities and achievements are not to be assessed in terms of the way they do justice to what has a justifying, independent, and privately operative ground. What the inexcusability of slavery makes evident is that public life and the warrant it has do not preclude the existence of an inextinguishable right grounded in the privacy of each man. The reconciliation of the private and public is essential to civilized living. For the moment, it suffices to observe that from the position of the privacy of men, the institution and practice of slavery is completely unjustifiable. No pragmatic or political justification could ever extinguish that fact. This was not seen by men as acute as Aristotle and Aquinas because they failed to evaluate all the public roles of men in the light of what men essentially were as individuals, joined together by virtue of a common condition under which their desires privately functioned. The converse of that error results when men's public status is taken not to have any value. All men are equal as members of the same species, where 'species', as Aristotle saw, does not have to do solely with bodies, but initially and primarily refers to what encompasses private beings. Each man expresses desire in and through his body, often in considerable disregard of his body's prosperity or continuance.

The activities of some living beings serve the continuance of the species even at the price of a loss of their individual lives and heritage. The fact has led some sociobiologists to the desperate measure of speaking of 'altruistic genes' which lead the individual to engage in self-destructive acts that seem to promote the welfare of others. Not only is there no evidence that there are such genes, but the supposed altruism characterizes the beings as single complex units, with privacies. To credit what complex beings do to the genes within their bodies is to carry out the old practice of taking the acts of complex beings to be due mainly to instincts, differing from that practice primarily in sacrificing all reference to what begins, sustains, and directs the acts. The actions of complex beings offer the only basis we have for the claim that there is self-sacrifice, altruism, and the like; these are discovered on the macro-, not the microscopic level. Nothing is gained by reading the action back into some parts, tacitly assumed to effectively determine what a complex being is in fact found to do.

A study of the functioning of encompassed units is perhaps all that a biological experimentalism permits. If there are also activities carried out by a complex being we gain nothing by reading into a number of unspecified units what had been exhibited by what encompasses them. To try to account for the activities of a complex being, whose work makes it possible for the species to maintain itself, by attending to what is or is supposed to be within that being, is but to replace an organism with an effective privacy by a whole with an ineffective privacy.

Desire is insistent, a unitary way in which privacy lives a complex body. As involved with the body, it is inseparable from a more comprehensive, private involvement in that body and the world beyond, an involvement which had already been specialized as an insistent sensitivity, sensibility, and need. As he matures, a man is able to make his body the object of other specializations of his privacy. Those specializations, to be able to remain themselves and still be affected by desire, must be ready for the outcomes of their bodily involvement. They must be more or less supportive of desire, maintaining themselves somewhere between the extremes of inhibition and indulgence.

A body quickened by desire may be tumescent, tensed, oblivious of injuries and dangers, while it acts in ways which serve the interests of the species. Conceivably the states may have been preceded by the use of drugs, but so far as these provide occasions for the body to have possible various chemical reactions, what the body does on behalf of the species will be adventitious. The body must be used by desire if there is to be more than a change in state, or a just readiness to interact with others in species-enhancing ways.

A biological species has no existence apart from living bodies. It therefore differs from an ontological species, for this is involved solely with interlocked private desires. The difference has usually been ignored or slighted. Aristotle focused on the species as that which was rationally defined and, so far, not in time or space. Modern biologists have changed the meaning of the term, taking 'species' to embrace a multiplicity of individual beings capable of interbreeding and sharing a common pool of genes. It is possible to reconcile the two by supposing Aristotle to be attending to privately expressed desires, and the moderns to be attending to them as making use of bodies. Both Aristotle and the moderns encourage the attempt at reconciliation: Aristotle recognized that men form an actual species, one which exists only so far as men do; the modern biologists take a species encompassing actual men to fit neatly within a formal pattern of classification. The two positions, though, are not really comparable. The species that is pertinent to interlocked private desires is basic; it is given a limited special form when desire makes use of the body.

The biological species is made up, not only of interlocked contemporaries but of possible progeny and thus of what cannot in fact be members of the species as it is at any given moment. As merely future, the species is ontological, constituted privately. As related to a biological species with contemporary members, the ontological species is specialized, turned into a prospect whose realization enables it to become an actual biological species in some subsequent present.

A biological species is a present concentration within the ontological, constituted on one side by purely private desire, and on the other by a future germane to the present existence of the biological species. That future is necessarily relevant to the biological species as it is in the present. Consequently, when other epitomizations interact with desire, they are inevitably affected by the biological species as continuing into the possible future, at the same time that they yield to that biological species, as both present and future. A man's biological species is *his* species, one for which he has a responsibility, for which he makes himself accountable, with reference to which he expresses preferences and choices, on which he exercises his will, and within whose scope he functions as a member of a society.

A man's defiance of biological demands, his pursuit of mathematics, art, religion, and speculative knowledge, his private thoughts, his insistence on his individual self, and the like, cannot all be traced back to his experiences, education, tradition, or society. Before these operate, and independently of them when they are effective, a man accepts his participation in a biological species on his own terms. It is an error, therefore, to try to understand what he privately is and does by taking these to be a function of what he, as a member of his biological species —or worse as a member of that species as it was supposed to have been constituted and acted in the remote past—initiates or suffers. Men are not first members of a biological species who somehow read the adventures of that species back into their privacies. Indeed, such reading would require them to be private beings already, able in multiple ways to accommodate what has a biological origin. Unlike units in an Aristotelian, formally defined, eternal species which they cannot affect and which has no bearing on them as living men who more or less prepare themselves for what results from their biological adventures, and unlike the members of a biological species with its specific population and gene pool, constantly changing in numbers and slowly changing in nature, men have desires which together determine how a common ontological species will be actualized.

An actual biological species is made up of unit beings joined together under the governance of a common condition. That common condition as apart from all the members, is their ontological species as purely formal, an object of classification and definition. As joined to individuals, making them members, the ontological species itself becomes the limited, changing nature of an actual biological species. In the absence of the condition, the interlocking of the particular desires of different individuals would at best be an uncontrolled, unbounded adventitious juncture of units—granted that those units could make contact with one another, and that the desires could interlock apart from all conditioning.

The body that is used by desire is not the body of a member of a species unless it is related to other bodies also quickened by desire. Desire interlocks with desire in the world to make an integrated totality of beings belonging to the same biological species. Each individual, from its position, expresses itself through its body, and forms a bond with others when his desire terminates at them as having desires terminating at it. Once again, there is no deliberation, thought, or consciousness involved. A desire is a private power which, through the agency of the body, enables one to form a bond with others having separately grounded desires. The result is the actual biological species with a particular population, made up of whatever actual beings there are, with their own privacies and bodies. It is the biological species as it in fact exists at a particular time, fringed by the desires of its particular members as passing beyond the species toward whatever else there be and, of course, toward the future with which the present biological species is connected.

Were men just bodies, they could conceivably still be just members of an actual biological species, which together interplayed with the nature of that species as a common condition. Each would be a unit term, distinguishable from others, but not necessarily unique, not irreducible, not able to engage in a multiplicity of private acts, not able even to feel pain or pleasure, to have agreeable or disagreeable experiences, to make fine discriminations having no bodily value, not unitary, not privately prepared for what might ensue. They would never be able to think or decide. Nor would they be able to act in ways which had nothing to do with the biological species, or which endangered or precluded its continuance.

When bodies do not act in consonance with the requirements of the biological species, those bodies could be said to be diseased, distorted, perverse. But such characterizations serve only to restate the fact over again, unless one can show that there were malfunctioning parts in those bodies.

Men with excellent bodies sometimes turn away from the world to attend to what has no practical importance. They devote their lives and make their bodies act to sustain long stretches of self-denial. Some pursue unrealizable ideals. Some try to destroy their fellowmen. Others court illness and death. Unable to find anything amiss with their bodies, one might of course contend that what was done by them was due to malfunctioning parts we are not now able to discover, or that there are deep-lying unconscious drives which pervert what men normally and properly do. The first of these alternatives expresses the hope that lies behind all scientific inquiry. But there is no reason for supposing that it will, or must be, or even can be satisfied. The second takes us back to the privacy, evaluating what this demands as being the outcome of what perversely fails to promote the species. One then of course, simply assumes that the only proper private acts are those that sustain or promote the species.

If otherwise healthy men can ignore their bodies or engage in acts which injure these, they are obviously more than bodies, and are occupied with more than quickening their bodies. They will surely make some use of their bodies in the course of their efforts to express their privacies. Since they can ignore their species and can engage in acts which are to its disadvantage, they are obviously more than bodily members of a species. But we will not be able to say that what they do is wrong or perverse until we know what it is that they ought to do and be. And that we cannot know without knowing what they are as privacies, insisting on themselves, both apart from and through their bodies.

There is a difference between a being as merely located, as occupying a place, and as able to occupy it. As merely located, it is just a delimited filled out region. As occupying a place, it fills out a region, taking it to be the limit of itself. As able to occupy the place, it is distended, privately voluminous, indivisible, without parts distinct from one another. An actual population of a biological species depends on the existence of individual privately distended beings, able to occupy, and in fact occupying limited places. Those places reduce to mere locations just so far as they are separated from the beings able to occupy them by privately using their bodies.

Since inanimate beings, no less than subhumans and humans, all occupy places, and since such occupation presupposes that the beings are already distended, the distendedness cannot await differentiations of the privacy. The privacy must itself be distended. When desire or any other epitomization is expressed in or through the body, it fills out that privacy on its way to being bodily expressed. When any other epitomization accommodates desire as involved with what is beyond the body, it is ready for what will be affected by what is encountered in that limited portion of public space within which the members of the species exist.

f. Orientation

Orientation is a bodily expressed private activity enabling a man to have an effective place and role in a humanized portion of an environment, a milieu. Like desire, the orientation is made determinate in act and is elicited by or elicits complementary expressions by other men. But it has both a wider and a narrower range of objects with which it interplays than desire does—wider, since it takes account of what is not relevant to the species, and narrower, since it primarily promotes a better functioning individual and not the continuation of the species. Its emphasis on the individual constitutes a retrogression from desire's service to the species, at the same time that it acts in terms of a more complex and sometimes a more inclusive prospect, the functioning well in a limited part of the world together with others, and with what is available for human use.

A man in his milieu differs from a subhuman in its environment primarily in the way in which his involvement modifies and is modified by the actions of his other private powers, from sensitivity to those which are more private and may never be publicly expressed, and by his being involved with what else has human import. Were his body not quickened by his privately initiated orientation, it might interplay with others and use what it could in the situations in which it happens to be. But it would not occupy a vital place in a humanized portion of the environment, where it affected and was affected by many different kinds of being. Others add determinations to his bodily expressed orientation, supplementing it with expressions of their own. They thereby lend different degrees and kinds of support to the expressions of his need and desire, provide occasions for their exercise and satisfaction, and may lead him to act to benefit others, sometimes at the price of his own continuation.

Both environment and milieu are combinations of limited conditions in shifting relationships, with different ones dominant at different times. As a consequence, orientation, though privately initiated, is elicited in different ways on different occasions, and comes to expression in a variety of different acts. The orientational expressions of men are met and thereby supported, muted, and opposed by other types of expression by other beings, most of which are not human. Although, from the position of each man, other men are at the limits of his unitary act of orientation, making them relevant to him, the total milieu is more than their joint product, for other types of being provide content which orientation humanizes. A man becomes a constituent of and a contributor to a milieu when his occupation with what other men provide has a reciprocal in their occupation with what he provides. Together they constitute a single humanized setting. Other beings are included in this as material, necessities, dangers, oppositions, supports, and occasions.

A man's career as a member of a species is subject to the demands of his milieu as surely as these are subject to the demands of his species. His actions connect the conditions, to which the species and the milieu subject him, to his attachments and associations with others. When the associations are caught within the limits of the attachments, there is an emergence of tribes and families. Shelters, niches, and territory, in contrast, have attachments dominated by associations.

The great role that society plays in the lives and activities of men, and the fact that it seems to be cut off from nature, helps obscure the truth that men are environmental beings as surely as animals are. Even the characteristic human milieu, in which human values and controls are imposed on a limited number of items, thereby turning them into extensions of man, is located in an environment. The conventions of a human society are consequently not altogether unrelated to ecology. The sun and moon, the seasons, the clouds, the rivers, and terrain all make a difference to the ways men act severally and together, and in relation to what is not human. But when men attend to the environment, they attend to it from the position of their individual privacies and particular milieu. As a consequence, what is faced by them is given a new import. The sun shines as it always did, but as a sun that marks the days and the seasons.

It is hard to determine whether or not men ever lived outside some milieu, and thus whether or not they ever were purely environmentally conditioned beings, perhaps with some regard for one another. Even when they are occupied with dealing with the environment in the light of the needs and values of a milieu, the obstinacy and independence of environmental occurrences compels a recognition that the environment has an independent status and role. The objects in the milieu of course— indeed anything that a man might use—have their own independent beings and careers. But only the environment is large and independent enough to provide new objects which allow for continued humanization, and thereby for the indefinite extension of the milieu.

What is in an environment, the different ways in which the items there impinge on one another and man, the radical contingency which characterizes its course, and the effects all of these have on one another, make one inclined to reject the idea that what occurs there has private grounds. One might then try to understand the environment to be just an adventitious outcome whose apparent constancy reflects the fact that terrain and available necessities change slowly. But once again, it would then be necessary to suppose that bodies themselves can act outside their own boundaries, that the prevailing conditions suffice to determine what is done, that associations dictate what men severally do—or some combination of these. Orientation has the power to combine associations and to express the result from a unique position. Not only does it serve and use the body, but it promotes a prospect other than the preservation of the species.

No species can continue unless there is food and shelter for its members. That is provided, not by the members, but by the environment. As in an environment, men make use of more recessive powers than they do as members of their species. Although their successful existence in the environment is a precondition for the continuation of their species at that time and place, they take direct account of what is in the environment without necessarily connecting it with what is required by the species. Not everything that is done by men serves their bodies or their kind.

Through his union of the conditions imposed by his species and environment with his associations and attachments, a man makes connection with a limited number of beings not in his species. His body is then not simply used, made to act as an agency, but is subject to external determinations. When it is made into an instrument having direct pertinence to available opportunities, that body provides a vehicle or agent for the privacy, thereby enabling this to express itself more adequately.

As just in an environment, a man adjusts himself, yielding to the demands of others to some extent while insisting on his own. By intensifying and contracting his environment, he turns part of it into a milieu where all else is assessed in human terms. Due to this, to the way in which the epitomizations of his privacy interplay, and to the promise that enriches them, a man's orientation achieves a distinctive nature and role.

Evidence of a man's orientation is found in those actions which, while not satisfying or supporting his need or desire and, therefore, not required by his body or species, give him an effective place among a multiplicity of other types of being. His use of only some of the available and usable items for food, shelter, shields, supports, competitors, and antagonists, while others of equal suitability are pushed aside or are forced into the background, evidences a power of selectivity in him not traceable to his body or the environment. Although other beings are selective, rejecting what they could have accepted, they do so because of chemistry, experience, habit, and a felt unpleasantness, not because it has been negatively assessed.

The reasons for a man's negative evaluations may well lie in his habits, experience, or the unpleasantness of an encounter, but all are overlaid with privately produced condemnations. A subhuman can reject, but a man can denigrate. Although he behaves differently in different groups, although in one he may eat and drink what others find revolting, and although he can in anger, crises, and perhaps through persuasion or belief, spend his energies in killing, mutilating, or destroying what no other beings do, he usually takes himself to be doing what is right. Consequently, his environment and milieu are not merely lived in by him as fields or settings, but as domains of objects with different degrees of value.

Were the environment not known or its functioning not understood, one would have to be content to note that actions by a body when it is well-functioning, stable, and prospering are not like those it exhibits at other times. Its misadventures would then appear to be mysterious oddities. But in fact they often offer evidence of an involved private orientation. That evidence is to be used by anyone who seeks an intelligible explanation for the occurrence of some unprofitable but not aberrational bodily actions.

The presence of a human orientation is most clearly evidenced when his body is held away from what is most congenial in his environment, and is made to accept something it initially rejected or which it should reject if his body or his species is to prosper. Untaught and untrained, a man may insist on accepting what his body reacts to as repugnant, and which may have no bearing on the continuation of his species. This kind of acceptance is peculiar to men. Able at times to reject what might benefit their bodies or their kind, subhumans apparently cannot make their bodies accept something which is not congenial to those bodies or is not needed to enable the species to continue.

To know a man to orient himself with the help of his body is to know him as a private being who has made himself be together with a number of others at a particular place and time. By being in an environment, he escapes dominance by his body and kind. His expressions are then specialized, diversified, and subject to environmental objects and circumstance. Consequently, it is about as difficult to extricate the contribution which his orientation makes to the environment as it is to extricate the contributions of his sensitivity, sensibility, desire, and need from their particular embodiments. The task is eased if attention is paid to other privately initiated activities which are not so completely affected by the environment. If one were to note the constancy of an act of orientation while the environment changes and, most important, were to understand how diverse parts of the environment are dealt with in diverse ways so as to enable the individual to stand in the same relation to all, one would be in a position to see that a man's activities in a milieu have private origins.

Orientation is purposive just so far as it converts that in which it terminates into a relevant object. When it meshes with the orientation of others, it enables a man to be a member of a group. Reflecting on these results, it might be supposed that orientation aims at them. One will then deal with orientation, not as a separately functioning epitomization of a person, but as just being made use of by some other epitomization of that person or of a self.

Purpose and purposiveness differ as the conscious and deliberate differ from an unreflecting thrusting toward what brings it to an end. The former is a late arrival, and depends on the latter. The former can, the latter cannot be questioned, for purposiveness cannot be avoided once we acknowledge orientation.

The crediting of purposiveness to a judgment is an interpretation of what objectively occurs. Were what objectively occurs merely mechanically produced, such a judgment and its application would not be likely. Nor would there be a prescribed way of relating the components of the judgment, or an appropriateness of the judgment to what was occurring.

An objective purposiveness is presupposed in the formation and use of a judgment of purposiveness.

Purposiveness has a number of specific forms, of which the clearest and most important exhibit the effect of the private intrusion of orientation on later epitomizations. As soon as we have knowledge of the nature and activity of those other epitomizations, the recognition that orientation is involved with them makes it possible to speak of a man making a new purposive use of what purposively functions. Something similar occurs when the body governs the use of organs, themselves governing the activities of their parts. Whether or not one treats what occurs on the lower levels as purposively determined or as mechanical systems, there will always be a governing purposiveness as long as orientation is exercised. If many grades of purposiveness occur, a single complex purposiveness will be expressed, reflecting the presence and interplay of all the grades.

The attempt to deal with a man as though he were one who was essentially in a group is up against the fact that he is privately and publicly often either indifferent to or opposed to being in a group. Although he always is with others, he also quite early thinks privately about matters having nothing to do with them, and engages in other private activities having no public import. He does function as a group member by virtue of his epitomizing orientation, but this is only one of many private powers, and can be blocked, restrained, and utilized by others for other ends.

Because men's group life is the outcome of the expression of their mutual purposive orientations, one would have to credit the so-called social insects and animals with a similar purposiveness, and therefore suppose that they were persons—or one would have to distinguish their form of existence from man's. The latter supposition alone is tenable. Subhumans do not have traditions. None knows that it has grandparents or that its own progeny will have progeny of their own. None dedicates, celebrates, praises, or blames. Obligations, anxieties, depressions are beyond them. None ever expresses or judges the conditions under which all live. They do not educate their young to fit into a group, while also allowing room for deviance, modification, and even for innovation and challenge. When together, they are more than members of a species, but still less than members of a group within which individuals act independently but in consonance.

When orientation is properly utilized by another epitomization there is tolerance, an allowing of both to function maximally together. When, instead, orientation acts in ways which answer to nothing in other epitomizations, the result is alienation. This, a key notion for Marx, has a

long history, and a use in Hegel and Feuerbach on which his own
depended. Marx thought of alienation as essentially marking a discrepancy between the individual as a single unit, and his products. A man, he
thought, was denied these in many different ways. Sooner or later, they
became powers to which he had to submit. So far as a man did this, he was
supposedly turned into less than a man. What was not seen is that the
alienation is to be replaced, not by nothing, but by something positive.
There is little prospect of avoiding some alienation. All that one can hope
to do is to be ready to exercise orientation effectively. The tolerance that
marks such use is not to be identified with the familiar attitude of permitting and respecting other beliefs and practices. It is more like the tolerance
of metals, or the tolerance of the living body, a capacity to continue to
remain as one has been despite what was being encountered.

Were a man to function in accord with an orientation over its entire
length, his activities would have to be altered so that they were in accord
with the difference that the limit for the orientation makes to other
epitomizations—whether or not the other epitomizations act in the light
of that limit or in consonance with the difference the limit makes to the
orientation. Just what happens is a contingent matter, depending on the
actions of the different powers.

A failure to allow for separately originating and functioning epitomizations ends by taking a man's initiated acts to be just privatized, derivative
forms of what he has shown himself to be in his group. That he is affected
by the others is beyond question. This fact, though, is not what is being
maintained by those who take privacy to be the inverse of what one is in
public. Such a view has a place only for what is produced by the group, or
for what is invented by one who takes this alone to be real or basic and
everything else to be an imagined derivative.

The privately instituted not only terminates in what is distinct from it,
but accepts this on its own terms. The result can be characterized as
private or public, depending on whether one is considering it from the
position of an origin or of a sustainer. From the position of an origin, what
sustains its limit is external to it, but what a sustainer does is internal to
that sustainer. We here have a counterpart of the recurrence of double-
sided limits referred to earlier. Every activity remains inseparable from its
source throughout its length, and at its end. Originating privately, it is
private throughout. Were that all, it would not enable one to be in contact
with the external world, and there never would be evidence of its presence. One would then have to deny that there was anything but one's own
private acts or, by starting with what was public, would have to hold that
there was no communicable meaning that could be given to the presence

and activity of any private act—and that would bring down the denial at the same time.

Orientation, like every other epitomization of privacy, is never less than private throughout its length. It becomes publicized only so far as it is attached to independently functioning items. It enables men to turn various objects in their environment into parts of a common milieu. The men are then not yet social beings who carry out traditionalized roles, attend to common tasks, have a morality.

The fact that there are no known men who live wholly in groups does not mean that they do not live in them at all. Indeed, since men can never entirely escape being interlinked with some others in a limited portion of the environment, they inescapably function as members of groups at various times, and always exhibit an aspect of such functioning, even when most completely absorbed in other activities.

g. Sociality

Subhumans can do no better than to find niches in good environments, their privacies being so closely tied to their bodies that they must stop with what their environments provide. Their packs, herds, schools, and the like are not societies, for they have no traditions, conventions, myths, rules, or morality. Their privacies are adequately served when their bodies enable those beings to function as units in a species or in an environment. A man's privacy enables him to go further. But though it cannot be kept from all involvement with his body, it is not limited to what the body must have in order to continue or prosper. Nor need it serve the species or a group. A man's privacy can also face prospects that are of no concern to his body or species and that cannot be realized by him as just a member of a group.

There was a time when the social setting in which men operate was much different from what it is today, but there does not seem to be a time when some social setting was not operative. No matter how far back we go in an evolutionary account, anyone we take to be a man in the past is located in a social setting. Indeed, it is a tautology to say so; if we were to find the skeleton of a being quite like the skeleton of a man today, we would not call it the remains of a human if we could not understand its possessor to have been socially involved with others. It is his existence in a social setting that we take to definitely distinguish him from other kinds of beings. Only there is he one who is accountable for what he does and does not do with and for others.

Everywhere men are together in societies. These are of many kinds and grades. In all, the expressions of sensitivity, sensibility, need, desire, and orientation are modified. In all, men are required to fill various roles, and to carry them out at special times and places, and in prescribed ways. Rewards and penalties make them persist in or change their courses. They there have histories; maintain traditions; act in terms of myths; have prescribed periods for celebration, commemoration, and organized play.

Men alone can avoid carrying out roles that had been carried out over the generations and were determined by the constitution of their bodies or by indurated practice. They alone adopt and transmit novelties introduced at some particular time and for no good purpose. Only they know that they have ancestors. Only they condemn themselves and one another for failures to conform to prescriptions, some of which they themselves may provide. Only they act in terms of what is held to be right or wrong to say, be, or do. Subhumans endorse nothing. At best they duplicate, repeat, change, neglect, or follow, without ever imposing measures or standards determining what is to be done.

A human society has a complex structure, rarely focused on and rarely openly and flagrantly defied without risk. If the society is minimal, it makes relatively few demands whose clear violation entrains severe punishment. The society may be confined within another that encompasses more men and imposes additional requirements. If a society is minimal, it does not necessarily antedate or follow another. Some early societies have relatively complex forms; others have relatively simple ones. The languages, rituals, etiquette, and other governances of what is publicly done may be simple or complex in either.

Each member of a society carries out roles more or less matched by roles carried out by others. The result may not benefit any of them. Nor need the members be occupied with preserving or enhancing the society. Like the lemmings on their death march to the sea, men can jointly act to their individual and common detriment. If they do, they can, unlike the lemmings, still reject some alternatives as unworthy or wrong.

Morality is an inseparable part of a human society. It applies not only to acts which may hurt or help others, or which enable them all to function better though perhaps with regrettable outcomes, but to whatever is done. There are despised ways of speaking, cooking, eating, hunting, dressing, as well as splendid, highly valued ways to engage in these. Yet nothing in either need bear on actual benefits or losses.

In a society, men are required to carry out an interlocked set of prescribed roles. Though each assumes his role from a private position, each carries it out in a common setting. A society leaves most or all of its demands unstated, even by those who have the task of affirming or insisting on conformity to them; in a state, rules are explicitly stated, with some men having the roles of formulators, enforcers, or embodiments of the rules. Because there must be an understanding and statement of rules, and a deliberate acceptance of some roles before there can be a state, it is necessarily a late arrival. But were it, as Plato and Aristotle thought, just the outcome of an increasing complexity in the common lives of men, there would be no very large societies and no very small states, no highly complex societies and no quite simple states.

Society and state share important features. They both have members who act representatively for the rest, exemplifying or expressing standards that all are to meet in different ways and from distinctive positions. And either society or state can, in principle, provide men with all that is required, if the men are to be excellently together as public beings. Neither would necessitate a reference to privacy could the assumption of roles, the insistency of demands, and the assessments of the ways the roles are carried out be otherwise explained. But roles are privately assumed; demands are submitted to privately; assessments are privately made. Without privacy, there would be no referring to the roles that others assume or to men's submission to common prescriptions.

Men help constitute their societies. Were their contributions to the nature and activities of the societies ignored, one would inevitably be caught in the dilemma of trying to provide a purely objective, external account of what in the very nature of the case can be grasped only from within the societies. To see a society of men from without is to see the men as a 'they'—or at the very best, as an 'us', approached from without the society by representative members who begin from within it.

When expressions of a man's sociality are elicited by the expressions of sociality by others, he uses his body to sustain what may not be pertinent to the welfare of his species, that body by itself, or that body in an environment or milieu. Since the elicitation has to be produced by the expression of sociality by another man who presumably also awaits an elicitation, conceivably, a man's sociality might never be elicited. Fortunately, his expression of his sociality need not await such elicitation. But it could stop at his body, thereby precluding others from knowing that it is sociality that is being expressed. To know this, one must know that what is occurring is not something private which is just present in the body, and the body must be known not to be just a place where a role is carried out, awaiting further determinations through an impingement on it by others.

Unless there are accompanying explanatory reports, an unelicited sociality will seem to be adventitious, or to express a privacy whose nature is not yet understood. Evidence of the presence of a private sociality is available only for those who can see that some bodily occurrence, having no value to the individual, species, environment, or milieu, sustains a role that has correlatives in roles carried by others. Evidence of sociality, consequently, is evidence of a private expression of a person which must be traced beyond sensitivity, sensibility, need, desire, and orientation.

To know of the existence and functioning of sociality, one must see that what occurs in the body of another occurs in a society. No question is then begged. Society is not identical with the sociality that men express. It is not identical even with the totality of such expressions. Instead, it is the outcome of the interplay of their interlocked expressions with common conditions.

An examination of a society will not reveal the sociality that the men separately but reciprocally express. To discover that, one must attend to private expressions which cannot be understood except as requiring reciprocals, and whose juncture with these govern the individuals. Society is constituted by men who yield more or less to a common conditioning. When one tries to explain how their different acts interlock to help produce that which is to be governed, one moves to the conditions helping constitute the common society.

We begin to see that men are different from other kinds of beings when we note the distinctive ways in which their bodies are used. But not until we focus on those bodily sustained expressions of privacy that do not serve the body, separately or as joined with others, are we in a position to recognize the radical distinctiveness of human privacy. Only then do we come to know man as having a privacy which can be occupied with what has no public role.

Language, work, and convention reach to a society's limits. Although each is at once inescapable and illuminating, an attempt to understand men in terms of any, or even all of them, invites misconstructions. Each of them is but one of a larger number of equally basic dimensions of the society, forcing a comparative neglect of others. Not even a concentration on all of them is enough, since it leads to the supposition that society is just a complex of languages, work, conventions, and/or other wide-spread factors. If it were this, society would lack a power of its own, and have neither a career nor a history. No genuine advance in principle will then be made over an approach that deals with men as merely biological, ecological, or grouped units, despite the recognition of features and activities which belong to what is more than a unit of a species, an object of an environment, or a part of a milieu.

A society is not an actual entity, like a man or a horse. If it were, it would have a privacy which it only partly expresses at one time, and would be able to constitute appearances through an interplay with common conditions. Nor is any man a society, as Whitehead maintained. If a man were a society, he would have no power to think or to imagine; would not appear or move; would have no single sensitivity, sensibility, need, desire, or any other epitomization expressed persistently over an indefinite stretch of time. He would have no obligations, would not speak or act, and would depend for his nature entirely on the relations of entities whose combination somehow was equated with a living person.

A society is a single complex, produced through the interplay of common conditions and interlinked men. It primarily associates those men, and subordinately relates them in other ways. It is what it does; its coming to to be is one with its functioning. There is nothing hidden or latent in it, though there is much that is hidden and latent in actualities. Nevertheless, it is correct to say that it changes in size, is more or less flexible, is to be found in one place rather than another, and has a history and prospects which may be effective for long periods of time. These and the growth and decline of a society are due in part to the changes that interlinked men independently introduce when they interplay with common traditions and myths.

One society can encompass others. One can, therefore, with some justice, speak of a single society of which Eastern and Western societies are part, and of these as embracing smaller societies of their own. If so, it must be allowed that there is a world history, and that behind the different traditions and myths which characterize the different societies in the East and West there is a common tradition and myth that particular ones specialize and partly distort. The smaller societies would be real parts of a larger, real society of men only if and so far as the larger constrained the smaller. It is not clear that such a state of affairs ever does or does not occur. What we do know is that the constraints societies impose are expressed in the form of constant relations opposing the ways in which men are directly interlinked.

When a man so acts on another that he helps constitute a new interlinkage with him, quite different in its suitability for the constant relations characteristic of a society as a single condition, the new interlinkage must be transformed. The deviations from approved social behavior that he introduces into his society, through its established relations, are inevitably altered. Punishments, rewards, encouragement, and neglect affect the interlinkages, and therefore the import of the contributions which he and others make to society. They may occur without thought or deliberation. When we say that a man is shunned by his society, we have a right to

mean only that there are conforming men within the society who change
their relations to him. If he so acted that the persistent relations of that
society were resisted, the new relations which others have to him would
produce new interlinkages in place of the old.

The interlinkage of a transgressor with those who shun him may fit as
readily within the society as those in which men act with the endorsement
or support of others. The shunning is no more the act of the society than
the deviant behavior is. Both are expressions of directly related men. But it
is the society's persistent relations which allow the shunned deviant and
the shunning conformist to be part of a socially acceptable interlinkage.

When a man steals just to keep alive, he steals as surely as he eats. The
debilitating hunger he suffers may be traced back to the malfunctioning of
the society as a complex embracing common conditions and interlinked
men, but the hunger is his and not the society's. What he does to alleviate
the hunger is also his doing. The reactions of other men to him, too, are
to be traced to them, and not to the society, though often enough what
these others do compensates for the deviant behavior in such a way as to
promote the stability of the society as a complex of common structures
and actual interlinked men.

This view is faced with two difficulties: (1) it seems to suppose some
magical activity on the part of individuals which compensatorily balances
the activity of a deviant; and (2) it apparently violates the stated condition
for a society, that men be together there, since men who are shunned are
denied the liberty they had before, and may in fact be exiled, enslaved, or
imprisoned, denied a part in the society.

1. There is no need to suppose that there is a hidden hand or an
all-seeing eye which sets a plus alongside every minus, a minus alongside
every plus in a society. Deviant behavior is not necessarily countered by
responses such that the outcome is a unit equivalent with the old. Not all
punishment or reward is deserved or appropriate. Men act blindly and
passionately, exaggerating and minimizing, misconstruing and misunderstanding, and the punishments they inflict can reduce the value of an
interlinkage below the level it has when no one is punished. But what is at
issue is not the value of something in a society; it is its functioning there.

The more a man is made to fit in with others, the more readily can he
be assimilated by the society. Sometimes the fit is made by the other
members of the society conforming to a deviant's ways. At all times, the
outcome is unpredictable, a prey to contingencies.

2. Master and slave, jailor and prisoner, citizen and exile have different
degrees and kinds of liberty. So far, they are asymmetrically related. Yet
together they are symmetrically interlinked. There is, of course, a sym-

metrical relation between the minimal liberty enjoyed by the slave, prisoner, or exile and the liberty enjoyed by the master, jailor, or citizen,
but if one were to take the symmetrical relation to unite with a common
condition and thereby constitute a society, one would have so far
abstracted from what in fact makes the relationship between the men one
of master to slave, jailor to prisoner, exile to citizen. Although a slave is
not part of a society of masters, he is part of a society of masters and slaves.
An exile, precisely because he is exiled, is related to those who have set
him apart. Excommunication does not free one from a heretic; it relates
one to him in a new way. No pre-established harmony enables men to be
together with others in a society, and they remain together there even
when some are shunned, degraded, or read out of it.

A monistic concentration on a society as a unit structure takes this to
function in a constant way, no matter how its members change in relation
to one another. An atomistic concentration, instead, takes the society to
have no explanatory status. Inevitably, the one moves to the point where
there is nothing except a single, complete Absolute, while the other ends
with ultimate particles. Both eventually rest with what cannot in principle
be known. A barrier is put in front of the two of them when it is recognized
that a society has a structure and interlinked members in interplay.

Societies have primarily associative structures, requiring that interlinked members be compatible, incompatible, hostile, cooperative, and
the like. The members may be severally related in different ways to their
property, work, and ideals, but all will be subject to the same common
conditions, though usually in distinct ways.

A society does not necessarily expand to include all interlinkages. Nor·
are all men necessarily interlinked so as to be subject to a common
societal governance. Were both outcomes achieved, peace and immobil-
ity would still not be an inescapable outcome, for a society requires men
to so act that they enrich or at least sustain its prescriptions, and the men
require society to provide each with the opportunity to be better than he
otherwise would be in the absence of that society. The Hegelian dialectic
ends with his Absolute forever becalmed, no longer needing or able to
function as it had before, when it supposedly had to oppose itself in order
to articulate itself, and thereby become itself most truly. Only if there are
individuals independent of that Absolute could oppositional moments
acquire the status of entities actually functioning. And what holds of the
supposed Absolute holds of societal and other conditions, since they
constitute ongoing complexes only when supplemented by independently functioning men.

A man is at his best when he is readied to do what he ought; what is pertinent to many men is at its best when it gives to each what each must have. The idea will crop up again and again in new forms, most conspicuously when one comes to consider the state. At all times there is a difference between the import that an interlinkage of men has for the individuals in it and for the societal conditions. Men start from their privacies and interplay with one another apart from society; a society independently sets limits and provides prescriptions for interlinked men.

The common view that it is individuals who are subject to society's conditioning is ambiguous, even self-discrepant. Precisely because men are individuals, they must first be interlinked in order to be subject to the common conditions characteristic of a particular society. Were they not so interlinked, they would be Aristotelian beasts or Gods, incomparable and without common rights. They are in a society, not because they individually enter it as beasts or Gods, or as already full-grown, mature, and considerate of the needs of others, but because they are interlinked apart from it, and interplay with it. In the absence of individual men there would be no interlinkage of them; but, also, without an interlinkage, the men would not be available for social conditioning.

A state, not a society, compels men to conform to its demands. It alone can take account of what individual men are and do. To be sure, we can and do criticize a society for not making adequate provision for the necessities of a full life for individuals; we can and do criticize individuals for going counter to the persistent demands of an established society. But the individuals are then viewed as providing terms in interlinkages, not as just independent realities.

We also can and do criticize a society for not measuring up to the standards of some ideal. But it makes no sense to criticize it for conditioning a particular interlinked set of men. There would be as much sense in criticizing it for doing this as there would be for criticizing a triplet for embracing three units.

A society has a structure intelligibly relating formally definable terms. Like a state prescribing and enforcing political tasks or duties, it dictates how men are to function. But unlike a state it deals with the men only as already interlinked. Despite the fact that it is society which is concerned with character, wisdom, and motives, and that a state attends only to what men are as public beings, it is the latter and not the former which deals with men mainly as distinct beings and not as filling out roles and having positions relative to one another. The difference is not absolute. Society punishes individuals; civil law takes account of positions occupied. But the individuals for a society are related to others; the positions for a state are occupied by separate units.

A social structure is a tissue of such formal relations as kinship lines and rules of protocol. These are effective even when not explicitly formulated or understood. Were men not subject to such formal relations, they might be connected by affection, proximity, or antagonism, but there would be no determining of common paths and limits for their activities. Exogamy would be adventitious, not prescribed. There might be hunters and farmers, but no market or language, or other structuralized conditionings of them.

Sociology and anthropology understandably attend primarily to formal social structures, for these are intelligible, communicable, and abstractable, eminently suitable for treatment by a science. They tend to neglect the actual interlinkage of men, or the way this interplays with the structure. The problem is not peculiar to sociology or anthropology. Every society has a degree of opacity for those who approach it from the outside, at the same time that the outsiders are able to note formal relations and implications that the members of a society thoughtlessly live through and might even deny are present.

A social solipsism hovers on the edge of all investigations of societies. But there is no need to succumb to it, any more than there is a need to succumb to the more familiar individual solipsism which denies that there could be an access to any other men. Both are like the solipsism which supposes that a man is unable to get beyond the limits of his own speaking, thinking, feeling, or ideas. But no matter where, when, and how he stops, a man always adumbratively reaches toward and into what lies beyond. Each knows others to be distinct, and even strange, because they are encountered as existing beyond the limits where he ostensibly stops. Each knows that he is ignorant, knows that he is with strangers, knows that there is something he has not yet understood, because each is already in touch with what is beyond what he observes.

The knowledge that is had of another merges into a density maintained apart from that knowledge. Into this a man can move more and more, subjecting himself to it without ever becoming entirely subject to it. Sympathy, insight, imagination, and participation in crucial events, such as birth, marriage, and death, enable him to move further into depths otherwise not reached.

If anthropologists and sociologists can escape an individual solipsism, as they believe they do, they can also escape a social solipsism, and in analogous ways. And if they can know men in their own societies, they have the power to know what is taking place in other societies as well. Could it be maintained that no one ever knows himself or other men, there would be warrant enough for claiming that no one ever knows the nature of his or any other society. We might then conceivably live in a society, but we would not then know that we did. We could not then rightly claim that we were cut off from other societies, for such a claim would require us to know that the societies exist beyond the point where our knowledge reaches.

No purely formal treatment of society is adequate, for the double reason that social roles are carried out by interlinked men without regard for any structured rules, and that such rules can be violated. But in the absence of a formal account we will not know what is prescribed.

A formal structure may have different embodiments at different times. Without any embodiment at all, it would lack efficacy and be unable to benefit from the presence and functioning of an interlinkage. The embodiment may be obtrusively grounded in a territory or food, or obscurely in a governing tradition, myth, or history, conveyed through story and festival. The fact that the ground may not yet or even eventually be expressible in purely formal terms does not yet or eventually prevent it from providing formal relations. The contention goes counter to a widely held view which takes the formal to set a limit beyond which one cannot or need not go. But if one were to deny that the formal needs to be grounded, or to deny that it can be grounded in anything which was not formal, one would have to credit it with a power, or take it to be subject to something able to impose itself on what is formal. It cannot, though, have a power of its own, since that would mean that it would be realized always, or be somewhere forever, too strong to vanish even when too weak to be embodied. The formal must be realized through the aid of some power, and this obviously cannot itself be formal. It is traditional to say that the power is a mind or God. I have traced it back to a finality. Whatever the source, and no matter how it strengthens the formal, it requires the contributions of interlinked men. Without them there would be no actual society able to interact with other societies, and the world beyond.

Although a society is only what it does, and although it has no interior, no hidden side, what in fact is occurring in it includes and qualifies its formal relations. These are altered when they interplay with interlinked men. Anyone can come to know those relations or abstract formal facets from an ongoing society, since both are available to an approach to the society from outside it.

A society is inseparable from its functioning. Its intelligible structure is one with its formal relating of terms. If one approaches it from the outside, one will be able to know these, but will necessarily fall short of the society as a complex in which structure is united with interlinked men. The coming to be or action of the society will not then be understood. To understand the coming to be or action of a society, one must attend to a single, indivisible complex, constituted by both structure and interlinked men.

It is not the fact that it involves an ongoing that places a society beyond the reach of a complete formalization, but the fact that its formally expressible structure is grounded and empowered on one side, and opposed on another. If a society is at rest and unchanging for a while it will not therefore be turned into a bare structure. It will still be constituted through the agency of powers not caught within any formality. A loosely governed society is no more fully graspable from the outside than is a dynamic, energetic, productive one.

A society with a formal structure defining the roles of men faces those men as already insistently interlinked. If one begins with the structure, one will therefore have to add non-formal specifications and prospects to formally specified roles in order to reflect the ways these can be carried out by the men together. Insistent rationalists, though, will claim that any interlinkage is itself just a set of formal relations. The claim leaves over the fact that the supposed relations are distinct from the several individuals as well as from the structure. Were basketball players reducible to their physiologies, and were their every move explicable in terms of a mechanics of pushes, pulls, imbalances, balances, and the like, it would still be true that while their roles are given in the rule book, they will qualify those roles, filling them out in ways the rule book does not and cannot specify; that they will unite their physiologies and moves in ways neither alone determines; and that their union will effectively dictate how the roles are carried out. If one is interested in understanding the team, and not its presuppositions, the value and promise of a radical rationalistic program will be of little interest.

A society has neither spatial size nor shape. It has no identity maintained over time. Having no power, it has no causal efficacy. Yet it does cover an extended region and is bounded off from others at a distance; it is in the present and has a future and a past; it does make a difference to the functioning of its units and it does affect the functioning of other societies. It both is and is not spatial, temporal, and causal. These opposed characterizations do not altogether vanish with the recognition that society encompasses men who are distanced from one another spatially, temporally, and causally, for the society need not then be spread out in these ways. Not every connection, even between men or their interlinkages, is extended. Men are similar, different, even larger and smaller without thereby being spatially, temporally, or causally related. The two types of relation may be independently grounded, or the extensional relations may be subordinated to the other. A population illustrates the one, a performed program the other. Within a constant territory, a population may grow larger or smaller; a program can be carried out for a period of time.

A society can govern interlinked men independently of their changing distances from one another, though there may well be a distance beyond which its units could not be linked as they had been before. A father does not cease to be part of his family when he goes off to work, though when he is absent for a long time, the power of the family may not be great enough to make him continue to be linked with other members as he had been before.

Although a family or a larger society may grow smaller or larger over the course of its career, it endures through but does not occupy time. It may vary in effectiveness, but it is no causal agent, and is only part of a causal situation. Nor does it stretch or contract with the movements of its members in space. It exists, not as men or their interlinkages do, but as a distinct kind of entity within which temporal, causal, and spatial extensions have subordinate functions. Each of these three types of extension raises distinctive issues, and deserves to be dealt with independently of the others.

Despite the fact that the subjugation of space to interlinkages is a commonplace to architects, sculptors, painters, poets, actors, and dancers, to coaches, players, and spectators of games, it has hardly caught the notice of philosophers. Aware of the cosmic reach of space, most treat every variation in cosmic geometry as a product of localized activities. The spatialized contour of an actual society is then taken to be a modification of space itself, and the society is viewed as a limited region in the whole of space. At the same time, the interlinkage of men is abstracted from and, as a consequence, is denied its own boundaries, and its own governance of its members. Strictly speaking, there is then no society left, but only various groupings within a single cosmic space.

To divide off a portion of space from the whole of it, recourse must be had to actualities. But these help constitute not societies but interlinkages. The men who are interlinked are spatially related, not by space itself but by a portion of it, and are kept within the limits of and subject to the constraints of the interlinkage. Apart from its functioning in a society, an interlinkage is just together with others in a single common space which it bounds off and utilizes in its own way.

Societies are products of limited conditions and a limited number of interlinked men. The space occupied by its members is subject to the conditions expressed in the society's structure. Conversely, the various conditions which a society prescribes are affected by the way in which interlinked men together contour a common space.

When an interlinkage is subjected to spatialization, the men in it are distanced from one another. They are not thereby impoverished. Instead, they are enriched, acquiring the status of units which, without necessarily affecting their interlinkage, will have spatial properties. The solidifying tendency of an interlinkage is there braked by units occupying distinct positions. Although the complex lacks spatial size and shape, it can rightly be said to be where a common space is bounded off, just as the pain within my body can be said to be where by body is maintained apart from the rest of the world. A society is also rightly said to be where the individual members of its interlinkages are. This family is home today; next week it will be spread over the globe, with the parents in Mexico, one of the children in Europe, another in Egypt, and a third in India. But the family does not stretch from one place to the other; it does not expand and contract with the comings and goings of its members. When the parents and children are at a considerable distance from one another, the interlinkage which characterizes the family may not be affected, although its dominance over a region of space may seem to approach the vanishing point. They will still be in their own familial space, separated off from a public space, and lived through by them alone. This does not prevent them from being locatable in the public space, any more than their being at home would prevent them from also being locatable at different parts of a house or room. In the house or room, they are also on the couch, near the window, and far from the clouds, at the same time that they are in the confined, separated, lived-through space of the family. They can be in all because they are able to terminate many different relations.

The socialized space of an interlinkage and the public space of all its members may stop at the same boundaries. But the socialized space will be undivided, with the boundaries serving merely to mark off limits spatially related to other places, no matter where. A society, by possessing those boundaries, makes possible the constitution of a single, unitary, confined space. That space is not carved out of a neutral space. It originates when the interlinked men are kept within a limited socialized region.

If one views a society from the position of the cosmos the space which the society determines will be treated as an irrelevant, inexplicable intensification and distortion of a larger cosmic space. But the two are independent, the society uniting interlinkages with a limited spatial region bounded off from all else, and the cosmic space relating all items, regardless of whether or not there are societies. Together, the two spaces enable a society to have an internally limited space located in a larger. From the position of the larger space, a society has the status of an occupant; from the position of the society, the larger space has the status of an attenuated continuation. When it is remarked that a society has its own spatial contours, with its own distinctive, internally conditioning planes and bends, one approaches it as an occupant. The locating of the occupant from some outside position never enables one to reach that occupant.

It is not possible to know the contour of a society's space if all one does is to locate the society in a larger space. To know the contour one must attend to the space of interlinked men. If one does not grasp the interlinkage which makes players members of a team, the actual space of the game will not be known. Were nothing known about a game, one would see just changes in position. Although no anthropologist ever becomes a full member of the society he studies, all know that they must live as well as they can within it, for only then are they in a position to see that the space inside is subject to the interlinkages that there prevail.

When a family's members are in different parts of the globe, we do not think or say that the family has a global spatiality. Nor do we take the family to be located in the cosmos, or all over the earth. We locate the individual members. If we are not to say that the space of the family has stretched over continents, we now seem forced to hold either that there is no space within the family or that this is a space which has no place for measurable distances. The first of these alternatives is not tenable. Were there no space within the complex family, there would not be distinctive spatial relations amongst its units; they would have only non-extensional relations to one another. Whatever warrant we had for that view would justify a denial that a team or a mob had its own internal space. Yet the members of these are sometimes near and sometimes far from one another. And they are nearer to one another than are some things, not considered, which in fact are physically closer to them than they are to one another. The germs on the soles of his shoes are physically closer to the father than his children, sleeping in the next room. He is spatially related to the children within the confines of the family in a way he is not related to them in a larger space. He is close to them, particularly when he is straining to hear if they are awake, a closeness which is spatial but subordinated to other linkages.

To take care of all these considerations, it is necessary to distinguish the internal space of a family or of a larger social group from the larger neutral space in which their members might be located. Unlike neutral space, the internal space is beyond the reach of any physical measure. It is not divisible, nor can it be occupied, since all it does is to relate terminal points, distanced from one another by a controlling linkage.

Time, even more evidently and familiarly than space, has one nature and import inside, and another outside the confines of a society. The time of a play, symphony, dance, film, or game is also distinct from a common neutral time, a time measured by clocks calibrated to keep in accord with changes or motions of cosmic units. The play and the other events occupy a single temporal moment whose limits are given by a joined beginning and ending, and not by a first and a last member of a set of events that happen to coincide with those limits. Otherwise, on coming late to a performance or leaving early one would share fully in a part of the performance, rather than in the insufficiently articulated whole of it. A performance is no set of disjunct occurrences; it is an undivided unit which approaches perfection the more surely each distinguishable segment reverberates with what has been and with what promises still to be.

The time of a society is its own, produced then and there. Each moment is a limited region in that time. In remarking that a society lasts for a longer or a shorter time than some occurrence elsewhere, one refers not to the time of the society but to the times of other entities, and makes note of the fact that the temporal limits of the society fall inside or outside those of the others.

The time of a society is internal to it in the double sense of being then and there constituted and in being part of an interlinkage. At each moment, one unit there has the status of a precondition for another and, so far, is before that other. This 'before' is not earlier, that whose passing away is a precondition for the presence of the other, but a limit asymmetrically related to that other. The time that is stretched between the limits of a society is a single fixed moment, whose beginning is before, not earlier than, its ending. There is no passage in that time; the whole of it is present in every distinguishable segment, though with different degrees of prominence.

Outside a society, many moments may pass away while the society's moment remains. That moment will be followed by another only when its interlinked men are differently related. The two moments will share a boundary which serves as the end of one of the moments and the beginning of the other. Three such moments will have the first and third separated by the second. The first moment passes with the relating of its end to the end of the second, the measure of the time that passes being given by the distance which separates the first from the third. As a result, there will be a genuine measurable time within a society distinct from the time outside. No stretch of time could conceivably occur in either place if the moments were of zero length.

Outside a society, moments are also extended and indivisible. There, the smallest possible moment is expressible as that fraction of a larger which the smallest particle or wave, moving at the fastest possible speed, takes to occupy an adjacent position. That movement and its moment are indivisible subdivisions of the whole of time. The society itself, when its limits are externally determined, is also in that whole of time, but it lives through its own time without regard for that whole.

A physical particle is more at home in the cosmos than a societal man can be, since it occupies a portion of cosmic time, while his society is only located within this, without every occupying any portion of it, and therefore being in it. Different societies have moments of different lengths, measured by some outside set of occurrences. Nevertheless, they may be contemporaries, existing at the same time and passing into the next moment together. References to the societies will then have to be made, not to them as internally constituted, but to them as located within a neutral time.

A dance and a symphony both begin at 8:00, but the dance ends at 10:00 and the symphony at 10:30. Each stretch is indivisible, one extending from 8:00 to 10:00, the other from 8:00 to 10:30. At 9:00, the dance and symphony are contemporary. Everything that is at 9:00, with just the features it then has, passes away. If anything that was at 9:00 also is at 9:01, it arrives abreast of what also had been at 9:00 and is now at 9:01. The 8:00, 9:00, 9:01, 10:00, and 10:30, though, are all divisions of a common neutral time. Neither the dance nor the symphony is involved with that time; both are turned away from it, stretched over single moments. A moment in a society, like the moment in theirs, is forged apart from the moments in neutral time. Still a society is not a work of art. Its moment is within it, subordinated. A temporal art's moment is filled, vibrant, its entire reality.

The moment of a society stretches over its encompassed interlinkage. Since a moment can begin at any one item in it and end at any other, there evidently are many paths leading from one end of the society to the other. Because there are later moments which define the terminus of one of the moments to be the beginning of a successor, some of the paths become asymmetrically ordered in a time through which the society exists. A father who exists earlier than a child is intermediated by his wife and other children. Apart from determinations by other moments, that child is intermediated by its mother and its siblings. The moment in which the father and child terminate is subdivided into stretches between father and mother, father and other children, mother and children, child and siblings, and so on. These are not subordinate moments of the family but abstractions from this, limited relationships isolated from others in the actual family. Should the father and child form a complex of their own, of course, they will be able to function as termini of the moments of that complex.

Without supposing that everything is an event, it makes sense to remark that every actuality is undergoing change. All the members of a family are growing older. It does not follow from this that all their interlinkages are changing; a husband and wife may form a constant pair. And if all interlinkages change, they need not change concurrently. When every member of the family changes, they change at different rates.

The moment of a society encompasses all its units in an asymmetric order. Since those units are in the space of the society as well, the moment must cover that space. The moment can then be helpfully imaged as a line, or better, as a wedge. Moments are spread sidewise as well as from back to front; otherwise there would be nothing like a single moment in which a number of occurrences were contemporaries, all facing a single common undifferentiated future. If one envisaged neutral space in somewhat the way Aristotle did, as a place enclosed within a sphere, one could take a moment there too to have the shape of a wedge. In such a world, as he saw, there would be no time were there no change of any kind, though this is far from warranting the conclusion that time is but a series of numbers. In any case, the conception of time as a mere line requires one to take units in an order of before and after, and to deny that any are contemporary. The foundation of the view undoubtedly is in our conception of ourselves as in the present with everything else a possible object of future import for us, at which we arrive with effort and perhaps by traversing space. But that conception obscures the fact that space itself already has each of us in symmetrical relations to others, thereby requiring any moment which starts with any of us to spread out spatially as surely as it points toward what is yet to be. Time is expressible as a line when items are arranged simply in an order of before and after. It is not so expressible when a number of copresent units are all before or earlier than some other unit.

A causation that is not constitutive takes time. The fact has been bypassed in a number of ways. Spinoza identified causality with logical necessitation, thereby making it be part of a world where there was no time. Reversing this stress, Hume concentrated on the fact of time. Because he could find no necessity there, he also denied that there was any causality. Kant, in effect, combined the Spinozistic and Humean views, and took causality to be a time subject to necessitation. But like the other two, he made no provision for the transformative power of causality. An effect is a prospect which does not merely achieve a position in a present moment but is in fact made present.

Causality is an exercised power transforming a possible into an actual effect. Since it takes time, all the considerations raised in connection with time, both inside and outside a society, are pertinent to it. But since it contains another factor—the transformative power which changes the status of a possible effect—no account of time will ever do justice to it. Causality adds to time, not a Spinozistic logical necessity or a Kantian irreversibility, but a necessitated transformation of a possible effect.

A cause is a distinctive kind of precondition. Where the beginning of a moment is just distanced from the end, a cause requires an implicative relation between itself and a possible effect. It begins a set of changes which traverse that relation and progressively enable the effect to be realized.

The internal causality of a society is not reducible to physical activities. Because it is a function of the self-maintenance of a relation between units in the face of changes in one or more of them, it is able to serve as an agency by which a society can remain self-same two moments in succession, even when those moments occur only because some unit simply changed relative to the rest. As just temporal a society differs from moment to moment; as causal, it is self-same in structure, but moment after moment it has new terms, some changing and others made to change.

A society persists through the exercise of an internal constitutive condition in defiance of the alterations that its units may undergo. It functions, therefore, somewhat as a living organism does, differing in not being alive, in not having a dense depth, in not necessarily being occupied with what is outside its borders, in not necessarily being involved in an interchange with what is external to it, and in not existing in an environment. It has no causal power of its own, enabling it to alter other societies. If it functions as a unit within some larger unit, it has a causal role there, but only because the larger insistently maintains itself in the face of the changes which the smaller is undergoing.

A society's self-maintenance is partial, a function of the degree of alteration undergone by its units. A great change in them will usually result in considerable change in the nature of the society.

Within the limits of a soceity, all members are graded as more or less well-unified, and thus as having different degrees of excellence relative to one another. Had they been so graded apart from their interlinkage there, they would form a mosaic of individuals differing in the excellence of their lives; were there no ordering of them within the society, they would not have relative values there.

The men who form a particular society are already in a larger setting with others, where they are governed by wider-ranging conditions. They may then share in a common tradition, face a common future, and live in terms of a common myth. But as members of a limited society they are also subject to limited forms of that tradition, ideal, and myth. They have one ranking as members of a particular society; outside this, they may have quite different values. They have values at both times, not because these have been assigned to them, but because they are subject to two orderings. They are value units in societies, not value units as such, though apart from any society, they have a rank in relation to all others, measured by a single standard of excellence. They may judge wrongly, and the principles they use may not be those which are in fact operative apart from that use. Relativity theories of value make much of this fact. Allowing that the members of a particular society may share the same values, the theories remark on the diverse conditions that different societies use in determining the relative values of their members. What is overlooked are the ordered hierarchy of all individuals no matter where they are or to what societies they belong, and the common manner in which each society produces a singular value order amongst its members.

Men caught within their own societies are absolutistic in their judgments. If they are right, they express the values that are there. Those who stand apart from their societies also form absolutistic judgments when they assess their societies. If they are right, they express the values that ought to prevail. Sound judgments can also be made by those who use the values that prevail in their own societies to evaluate other societies or the men in them.

A plan of organization can be framed, ranking positions in a society as more or less important. The men who fill the positions will then be credited with the values which those positions are defined to confer. If the men fill those positions properly, they will deserve to be credited with the values. This does not mean that they in fact have those values. The distinction between values credited and values actually possessed is sometimes missed by men in high office, and, as a result, they have little trouble in believing themselves to have the value conferred by the positions they occupy. They are also encouraged by the press, with its focusing on individual heads of government when referring to primary political moves. It was laudable of Richard Nixon to speak of 'the presidency'. But, as he made evident, such speaking might just barely hide the conceit that the value accorded the position of president was in fact possessed by the man occupying it.

Although one can never fully know what is occurring in some society without being a part of it, the limitation does not preclude a knowledge of its values. What it does preclude is a sharing in those values and a knowledge which is dependent on such sharing.

Since a man is either a unit in an interlinkage or a representative of others who, with him, are members of a society, he is not there assessed as a separate, unduplicable being. When, then, it is said that the value which a man has changes with what he contributes to a society, an abbreviated account is being offered of what in fact occurs. Men do change in value because of what they do. Their society does enable them to have values they did not have before and do not have apart from it. If what they do is done outside the society, affecting what is outside the society's scope, the values that they have will be due to their presence and functioning in some other society, or in a common neutral world. Inside the society, they are faced with an evaluative condition. So far as they sustain the condition, so far are they enhanced or lowered in their value there. Since the condition operates in independence of conditions operating elsewhere, it is possible for men to have one value inside a society and another outside it. No man is all he ought to be unless he is excellent in both places.

h. Mind

For a long time after Descartes, it was common to use 'mind' to refer to private activities, and in particular to refer to feeling, believing, willing, intending as forms of thinking, both when they acted separately and when they acted together. More recently, 'mind' has been identified with the activities of the brain, or whatever part of it one assumes is used when concepts are formed, inferences carried out, or rationally necessitated results produced.

In the attempt to keep in as close an accord as possible with the later usage, it is desirable to use 'mind' to refer to the locus of one's thinking. If one does not reduce thinking to bodily activities one will also be able to take advantage of the older ways of speaking as well. Consequently it will then be possible to say that by the use of the mind one can arrive at valid conclusions, and also achieve an understanding of what exists apart from the mind.

It is now becoming more and more the vogue to speak of computers as having minds. Fed certain data, with great speed and accuracy they present other data which can be shown to be logically necessitated by that with which one began. A computer, of course, does not attend to the rationale justifying the outcome. It just operates along the paths laid out for it. That the results achieved are necessitated is due to the way the computer is designed and programmed. Since its results can be said to be warranted only so far as they match what men obtain when they infer in consonance with what logical rules justify, there is no ground for the claim that a computer thinks, unless it is also correct to say that a stone falling from a height calculates the different positions it will be at in successive moments, and that it reaches the ground at a time and with a velocity it could justify. We can speak of a stone falling and a computer operating along lines warranted by laws acting on them, or which match what occurs at the beginning and the end of an operation, but this is not yet to say that the stone or the computer understands. A falling stone and a computer have minds only in the sense that they have structures, conformity to which yields an outcome that is in accord with what is produced when a man uses his mind.

The structure of a machine is expressible in formulae. It can be outlined in blueprints. Joining various bodies together so as to enable energy to be transmitted through them in a prescribed order, it yields results that men endorse when they think. Were one to take a well-functioning brain to be a kind of machine for producing warranted conclusions, one would treat it as an embodied, logically functioning mind. A privately acting mind would still have to be used to certify the fact. And without the use of a mind, the state of the brain at a subsequent moment would not be produced because some accepted premiss required it; in the absence of a mind, there would be no such accepted premiss. And if the premiss existed, though there might be use of it, there would be no action carried out so as to use it. There could be no knowledge that a conclusion followed from it.

To find an occurrence in the brain, one has to make private use of an idea referring to that occurrence. To refer to an occurrence in the brain as matching that idea, use would have to be made of another idea. By necessity there must always be an idea in a private mind which refers to the brain that is supposed to match some idea. One observes, not the brain which is supposedly used in the observation, but the brain that was used in some other act. Observations of a brain are carried out by a different reality.

Even if a brain and a mind were in accord at every point, there would still have to be a mind different from either to understand that this was so.

The mind that does justice to what is happening in a brain is the mind of an observer of that brain, not the mind of one whose body houses the observed brain. Could one observe the workings of his own brain while he was thinking of it, he would entertain a reference to what was occurring in his brain, but that reference to his brain would not be provided by his brain. Were one willing to tolerate the supposition that observations of the brain are the work of the brain as not then observed, he would still have to face the fact that a brain can change but not infer, react but not know, incorporate a structure but not use it.

The theory that brains are duplicates of or replacements for what is in the mind is evidently not an occurrence in the brain. No such occurrence refers. No such occurrence expresses a claim. It just is.

A computer is designed to present what a man will mentally endorse. When the computer presents the endorsed outcome, it shows that it is functioning properly—or, more accurately, it is defined to be functioning properly. A brain cannot do that much. Because it is not designed, we have to select this or that process or part of the brain and identify it as the right counterpart of what is thought. That act requires the use of a mind. By itself, all the brain does is change. But even that cannot be known unless one makes private use of a mind.

Thinking is and always remains private. In referring to that power by the traditional term 'mind', no supposition need be made of the existence of a substance, an area, a receptacle, or a distinct unit. 'Mind' is just the substantive correlate of the verb 'to think'; 'understanding' is the outcome of successful thinking. None occurs except so far as there is a body. That body is more than a brain. A concentration on what the brain does is a concentration on what at best is inseparable from other organic functionings. A neglect of the rest of the body, consequently, will reduce the brain's events to the status of occurrences dislocated from their causes and effects and, so far, make them inexplicable.

If we are to treat a brain's many interlocked occurrences as the counterparts of what is happening in a mind, we have to separate them out and match the result with mental units. Did we instead try to treat a mental occurrence as if it were interlocked with others, we would have to suppose that the detachment of an idea of a conclusion would necessarily distort it. Were we willing to say this, we would also have to say that our acknowledgement of the distortion would itself be distorted, and so on. Brains are part of an organic unity; a mind allows for distinct units.

We communicate the nature and outcome of thinking through speech and other public devices. These require the use of a body along lines its structure makes possible. The communication is not itself the message.

Privately attained conclusions may or may not be warranted. If not, we think poorly, no matter how the body functions, or what we say.

A child may recite the multiplication table correctly. It does not then think. Thinking does not occur until the child infers in accord with legitimatizing rules. A duplication of its recitation by a machine will not therefore show that the machine thinks. The difference can be exhibited by putting new problems to the child to which a proper answer cannot be obtained unless it does more than recite what it had learned. Since a right answer might still be arrived at by happenstance, the child must be offered many problems to solve if we are to overcome our doubts about its ability to think. But we will not be finally satisfied that it thinks until it can tell us how the solutions it reaches could be justified. To do this, it need not show exactly how it came to the result. That may be beyond its capacity, and even beyond the capacity of anyone else. What it must do is to reveal how its activity is controlled throughout by some such prospect as the possible achievement of truth or proof—and that requires it to be subject to a ruling condition throughout the course of the activity.

Every occurrence in a child's brain, like every occurrence in a computer, could conceivably follow necessarily on what preceded it, even when the child spoke at random, committed blunders, or was thoroughly confused. There need be no violation of laws, no matter what it bodily does. Yet its thinking may be awry and may conclude with what is not warranted. If one act of its body were to follow on another by rigid necessity, its thinking could still end with what is not logically required. Even if a body's actions were taken to exhibit not only laws of nature but the laws of logic, it still could not be held that the body engaged in a thinking, for a body can draw no conclusions.

Conclusions are the outcome of a use of rules, directed toward the objective of getting a justified result. The requirement seems at first to be overly severe, requiring the denial that a child, and perhaps the majority of men, can think. This would be the consequence if rules had to be known in order to be used.

We ask whether rules are known and used when we are in doubt as to whether or not thinking has taken place. But thinking can occur even when the rules are not known and not consciously imposed. Now, it would seem, a child reciting the multiplication table correctly, or even incorrectly, must be said to think. It would, were a rule, terminating in some such prospect as pleasing an adult, to control what the child did. But it would not then think about multiplication. Instead, it would think about a performance which might be satisfactory even if the multiplication table were incorrectly recited. And if the child just recites, without using a rule to help it realize some prospect, it will not think at all. For it to think, it must control the way in which various private activities are joined and distributed, whether or not these are known, and whether or not they have counterparts in the brain. The controlled use of a rule and prospect may not be deliberately carried out. It may not be expressed in a bodily form. But until it is, it will not be known to occur. To know that there has been a thinking, one must begin a move from a public occurrence to a controlled private use of both a prospect and a rule.

A living body is necessary if thinking or any other private activity is to take place. It is necessary, too, if there is to be evidence of the activity. But the body does not decide whether or not what is being privately done or claimed is warranted, is right or wrong, or is true or false.

Understanding, though a wholly private activity, occurs only so far as one has a body. If what it does is expressed, it will be in and by means of the body. That will not make it a bodily occurrence. Although it will use the body, exhibit itself there, what it exhibits will have been and will continue to be a private occurrence. Evidence of understanding has the form of bodily occurrences which remain unintelligible until shown to be required by a sequence of private steps that progress toward the realization of a sought conclusion.

Recursive functions seem to offer a good reason for not accepting this view. Students of that branch of mathematics have obtained brilliant, completely unexpected results by proceeding in a purely mechanical manner, paying no attention to prospective conclusions to be reached in the form of rule-certified outcomes. Machines can be made to work recursively. Still, the discovery of the recursive method and the understanding of how it is to be used are not the work of machines, but of exceptionally gifted thinkers using their understanding. The direction in which the recursive work proceeds, moreover, as well as the nature of that at which it stops, depends on the acceptance of a rationally necessitated prospect, as that at which one seeks to arrive.

A man is credited with an understanding because what he publicly presents is assessed in terms of its consonance with a result which a privately used rule justifies. If it be denied that another can do this, it will be because one has used his privacy to conclude that the other's privacy is not specialized in the form of a controlled understanding. Held to be a man who could not possibly be reasoned with, the other would be taken to be comparatively undeveloped, even if his body were well-formed, and he could tell what rules were used and what prospects were sanctioned by those rules. For no discernible reason he would be placed on a lower level than his judge.

There are some who say that they don't know if anyone else thinks or has an understanding. They are solipsists, holding that everyone is trapped within his own privacy. Could a warrant for this view be produced, it would be in the form of something thought about, and wholly confined within one privacy. It would not therefore be a truth offered to others to understand. The solipsist cannot defend or urge his position. If offered to others, solipsism requires itself to exist only in the form of a stimulus prompting most to reject it as untenable. One who understands it, knows it to be in error precisely because it is offered to him as a supposed truth. A solipsist has no one to whom he could present his view as true. Solipsism is the outcome of a thinking that went astray because it was controlled by an untenable prospective conclusion or because it was poorly controlled by a justified one. In either case, it cannot be offered to another as something true. I am, of course, affirming this because I am using and expressing my mind. If I were not, I would not be able to conclude that solipsism is mistaken. I would be merely prompted to say that I understand the solipsism when I hear someone state the position.

A kind of understanding can be credited to those subhumans which avoid obstacles in a move that brings them closer to what they need, their species requires, or what enables them to become better adjusted to what is in their environment or group. That kind of understanding differs from man's, being necessarily elicited by what their bodies undergo, and terminating in what is important only to individuals, to members of a species, or to units in an environment or group. We have no reason to believe that such subhumans can forge concepts, that they can decide whether or not to think, or that they need to and could live their bodies intelligently.

A computer can be so constructed that it provides an answer to chess problems; a missile can be made to zero in on a target. Both, rapidly bypassing a multiplicity of alternative routes, follow out that path which their construction and program require. It is misleading to call what they do a thinking or a solving of problems, for their courses are built into their designs and are utilized by imposed programs. They do not entertain some prospect and try to realize it. They do not subject themselves to a guiding rule so as to arrive at an outcome which the rule will certify as being right. But a man can provide evidence that this is what he does.

It is conceivable that all thought is for the sake of practice and is, therefore, always pertinent to the body's requirements and functionings. The view was strongly and persistently urged by Dewey over his long, distinguished career. Since theologians and metaphysicians often end with what is not observable, Dewey was inclined to dismiss them and their claims. That attitude made it impossible for him to deal properly with the work of mathematicians. Not only may these begin with premises answering to no matter of fact, but they often end with what has no experienceable counterpart. Since theoretical physicists, too, sometimes end with what is not empirically observable, they too cause a difficulty for one who can find no place for a mind whose conclusions sometimes have no empirical referent. Men can think for no practical purpose, seeking only to arrive at what a logical rule requires them to accept if they have accepted a particular premiss.

Dewey was never able to escape the dilemma: reject formal logic, mathematics, and physics as unwarranted, unintelligible, unnecessary, or futile, or allow a place even for the thinking of theologians and metaphysicians. A solution seems at hand if one follows Kant and Peirce and holds that formal thinkers, and perhaps also physicists, make use of constructions, diagrams, or schemata. This, though, will not show that their thought is already practical, for what is achieved is required not by the body or the world, but by the mind. Also, justified conclusions can be reached without diagrams, etc., and can then be used to alter the way in which the body is to function. Sometimes they help determine how the body is to act to its own disadvantage.

Having privately reached justified conclusions, one may privately use the body to communicate them. One may not then pay attention to the body's needs and roles, or to the world in which it is, but just use the body in order to record and report. If the records and reports are about what is rationally concluded they will tell us what a private mind reaches independently of the body. That the body, through speech and writing, may make the records or reports available, shows that the body is functioning, not on behalf of itself or anything else in the public world, but on behalf of the mind. That mind can itself be made the object of other epitomizations, and may in turn affect the ways in which these are used.

When I conclude that the claims of another express his mind, I incorporate other epitomizations of my privacy on the way to continuing into him. To know my own mind I must go in the opposite direction from what I do when I know his. My mind then, via my publicly reached me, attends to itself. Other epitomizations of my person may also be used in the course of that act.

Men and animals can act mechanically, though their organic natures and complexity makes it difficult for them to continue long in a purely mechanical way. If they focus on prospects, the animals can make these be realized through bodily activities. Men, in addition, can give the prospects the status of what is to be arrived at in a self-prescribed way.

What they then achieve, though, will be difficult occasionally to distinguish from what occurs when no rules are followed. The differences between what men and subhumans do are sharpened the more that prospects are joined to rules and then used by men to govern what is done.

A mind, like every other epitomization, is inseparable from prospects to be realized. And, like every other epitomization, it can realize prospects. This it may do by living a body through acts governed by certifying rules, terminating in the prospects. There is no more difficulty in mind living the body in this way than there is in sensitivity doing so.

When a grammatical rule is applied, words are made to fit in a prescribed order. When it is illustrated, use is made of variables and schemata in order to expose the nature of the rule, freed as much as possible from any application. A mechanical application of a grammatical rule, though it orders words, is usually made on behalf of what is being expressed by those words, while an illustration of the rule is made on behalf of thought. If one's ideas are about rules, the words used may themselves be ordered by a different set of rules and, therefore, while expressing the ideas, will illustrate rules that could be used by other thoughts and be expressed by using other words. Confronted with words ordered grammatically, we do not know whether or not they are being used to illustrate a grammatical rule or, instead, express some idea, even one about grammatical rules, unless we are able to learn how the functioning of the words is being privately determined.

Rules apply to units which are distinct from them. Their application is not contained in themselves or in the units; it could not itself require a reference to a rule without leading one through an infinite regress of rules using rules, using rules . . . . Nor could the application of a rule be identified with that to which the rule applies, without sending one off on still another infinite regress. The difficulty causes little embarrassment as long as rules are framed in terms of variables and their application is treated as just an instantiating, a making of the variables in a rule take on specific values. This occurs when the rules and units are defined in strict accord with one another, making the application of the one to the other just the reverse of a process by which the two can be obtained from their joint product. Computers are designed to conform to this idea. If we have well-defined units and well-defined ways of combining them, energy can be used to provide occasions for the one to instance the other. Since a computer does nothing other than allow energy to be channelled along pre-established paths, it does not and cannot apply a rule. At most, it allows for an instantiation of a program for a rule.

A marriage ceremony can be likened to a rule, with the man and woman to be married having the status of units to which such a rule applies. The couple enables the ceremony to be a distinctive, solemn relation, while it enables the man and woman to be mutually committed in a world where the ceremony has a distinctive import. By virtue of that ceremony, the couple is able to be related in distinctive ways to such other complexes as the home, the tax office, and in-laws.

The mating of some animals seems to be accompanied by ceremonies, but these do not provide the commitments or the social sanctions of a marriage. More important is the fact that animals cannot illustrate a ceremony. When they teach and train their young, though they then seem to illustrate what is to be done, they in fact provide performances that the young are to imitate. An illustration has units which have no other role but to articulate and thereby show what a performance is like; a performance unites the units to constitute a single activity.

The fact that a computer does not apply rules was overlooked by Hubert Dreyfus in his persuasive demonstration that computers can never do everything human minds can. He thought that they could calculate successfully if they were given precise rules, and then followed purely mechanical proof procedures. They failed, he thought, only when they were set the task of duplicating situations which were dependent on non-explicit meanings or situations; tried to play ill-defined games; were faced with problems which required insight; or had to take account of concepts or paradigms. But it is questionable whether any machine can even calculate. To start with one set of numerals and stop with others, after passing through a selected set of steps, is not yet to calculate. It is but to mark out one position after another. A calculation starts and ends with numbers. These are in a mathematical domain into which not even a high-grade animal can enter, since it requires a joining of numerals and rules so as to constitute entirely new units, the numbers. These both fill positions in that domain and are related to other positions there, to be filled out by similarly constituted units.

Machines and animals deal with values of variables. The animals, but not the machines, occasionally are guided by bodily pertinent prospects to be instanced in a final outcome. Neither can produce a premiss or a conclusion. A premiss is a new product, fitting in a domain where there have been or can be other premisses, or what is relevant to them, such as a conclusion. Machines have no domain in which, on their own, they can be constitutive parts. Animals live in natural domains, or in artificial settings provided for them in homes, zoos, or designated habitats, but these are quite unlike the domains occupied by premisses and conclusions.

Men create domains. Their premises and conclusions fill out positions which had been made available by previous human acts. In addition to being able to illustrate what they mean by an arithmetical operation, the men are able to think mathematically because they are able to create formal complexes which can be known only to those who have similar traditions, and who understand proofs, no matter what the situation or environment. The domain of mathematics in which they operate is governed by a prospective certifiable conclusion to which thinking subjects itself.

Mathematics can have a role in the contingent world because the understanding of it is expressed there through the agency of a lived body. The living of that body by thinking preserves the necessities of the mathematical proofs; the particularities of the body's functioning give the necessities specialized, contingent forms. Both the terms and the equality in $E = mc^2$ have unanticipatable particularized forms when the formula is exhibited in fact at a particular time and place.

Galileo's approach to the cosmos does not seem to conform to this view. It seems to be more in harmony with the ways in which computers work, since he took universal laws to apply to units which had the role of values for variables in those laws. Yet, when he applied his idea of law to his idea of particles, which he took to be its proper units, he forged new complexes. These could not be understood simply by understanding the conceived laws or their supposed instantiating items. Their union altered both. When he supposed that the laws, the units to which they applied, and their application duplicated what he envisaged and did, he inevitably took the world to contain more than units instantiating laws. That is one reason why, every once in a while, he looked to the world to see if his thinking was in accord with it. He did not antecedently know whether or not what he mentally produced answered to what occurred in fact.

Having creatively joined conceived law and conceived units to constitute new complexes which belong to an abstract domain of similarly constituted complexes, Galileo minimized his own achievements by supposing that both the laws he discovered and the units he envisaged were mirrors of what occurred in nature. Had he produced mirrors, they would have been in the form of complexes in which his conceived laws and units were modified. Giving operative laws a purely mathematical form does not prevent the laws from having limited ranges over contingent occurrences.

The use of the mind is often taken to be inseparable from consciousness, language, and experience. A well-established tradition underscores the difference between pure and impure forms, calling the one an 'active' or pure reason, and the other a 'passive' or mere understanding. It usually supposes that these are and remain distinct either as quite different powers or as greater and lesser forms of what is taken to be so independent of all else that it seems to take up residence in man only inadvertently and precariously. Radical rationalists treat the latter somewhat in the manner in which romantics treat creativity, as an external power which seizes the individual—with one signal difference. Unlike the creativity, the power is taken by the rationalists to make a man live for a while within a rigid frame, he contributing only errors and mistakes, whereas the intrusive creativity of the romantics is supposed to subject him for a while to an uncontrollable irrational force, bringing about great results beyond anyone's prevision, and to which he can add only narrowness and conceit. Both positions are in accord with the classical theological view that while God produces nothing but what is good, men produce only ugliness and evil. If, instead, one recognizes that mind is an epitomization of privacy, and that its entanglements and errors are due to the way it is affected by other epitomizations and by the body, it is possible to take men to be not only creative, rational, and good, but unimaginative, irrational, and bad as well. He is surely every one of these in different degrees at different times.

Not all intrusions on the mind are regrettable. Were that the case, it would always be better for men to think in the absence of all desire; to ignore their responsibilities; and to have no interest in anyone else. Thinking is occupied with drawing conclusions, regardless of the truth or falsehood of these or their antecedents, but it should and it can take account of the demands made by other powers.

Pure thought is logical thought. To think is to infer, to pass from a premiss to a valid conclusion. Although thinking does not produce implications, one must refer to them in order to show that he does validly arrive where he should. And though the content of thinking may be provided by other agencies, the thinking operates on it in its own way and on its own terms. What it does can be followed by acts by other epitomizations; it can also direct these toward prospects to be realized through reasoning.

Machines—and of course subhuman living beings as well—could be said to have minds whenever their structures are utilized in such a way that the outcomes of valid thinking are achieved. But such minds would be different from the minds of men, since men's minds are privately used, sometimes to achieve results having no bodily import. Only men think about what never was, never will be, and even never could be.

The minds of animals, though different from men's, are in turn different from the minds that could be credited to machines. Like human minds, some animal minds can be infused with consciousness. The used structure of a machine, an animal's conscious use of a bodily structure, and a man's possessive use of a private epitomization of his person are all identifiable as minds, therefore, only if 'mind' is used in three different senses.

Were one to credit a brain with a mind one would have to grant it the ability to infer or reflect, thereby tacitly supposing that there was a private mind imbedded in the brain, or that the parts of the brain were so ordered that they carried out the prescriptions of some mind. In the one way, one would distinguish mind and brain but give a physical location to the former; in the other, one would treat the brain as a kind of machine. Neither makes much sense. A mind takes up no room. A brain is not deliberately designed or programmed by men.

By conflating the claims that the brain is a mind and that computers think, one might conclude that the brain thinks. But no machine, no brain, no body can think. Thinking is a private act, inseparable from private claims of validity, from acts of inferring, from occupations with truth and falsity.

Machines have structures requiring different parts to be employed in distinctive orders if a desired result is to be obtained. Their structures can be utilized to reach and present outcomes that thinking can accept. When their use involves no more than the provision of energy, so that nothing is added except an occasion for parts to function in a determined order, it would not be amiss to say that they have minds impressed on them, that their designs incorporate the minds of their designers or, better still, that they carry out in another domain a process which produces outcomes that a thinking can certify.

Machines are designed by men using their minds. Only a slipshod materialism will slide from a plausible acknowledgment of a derivative mind in a machine to the implausible supposition that the brain is a complicated machine and therefore has a machine-like mind. The 'mind' that a machine has is the outcome of the private use of a human mind. But a man's brain has no mind at all, since he did not put his mind on or into it. Conceivably, there might come a time when a brain could be given a structure designed to bring about various specified outcomes. That brain will then have been given a mind which was somewhat like that creditable to a machine. But before that time, the brain will not have a mind any more than a stomach or a tongue has one.

The mind of a man does not arise until his body has developed considerably. Nor does it operate except under special bodily conditions, one of which is provided by a living brain. If we wish to credit the brain with a mind of its own, we will have to identify that mind with some ordered functioning of the brain. Since the view that the brain by itself has or is a mind is held by one who makes use of his own mind, that identification will require the private use of a mind. If one wishes to speak of the brain as a mind, existing and acting apart from any private control or use, one must then be willing to say that every man has two minds, one in his privacy, the other in his body. We cannot stop there. Since a brain is no more indispensable than a stomach, heart, lungs or other vital parts of a living human body, these too ought to be credited with minds if the brain is, thereby providing a plurality of minds confined within the supposedly larger mind of the organic body. None of these supposed minds makes articulated claims; none judges; none produces conclusions—but then neither does the brain.

The greatest of discoveries, the most fantastic of suppositions, the most daring theological and metaphysical speculations can eventually be written in the form of a series of openings and shuttings of circuits, carried out by a computer. Not expressed or accounted for in such a series is the fact that it begins and ends when it does, that it is just this particular series that is accepted, and that the initial material is divided in that one, rather than in any number of other possible ways. When the functioning of a complex unit is expressed in terms of the functioning of its parts, one leaves unexplained why just those parts, in just that arrangement, with just that beginning and ending, are selected. Where the initial content had its bunchings, beginning, ending, divisions, and unions intrinsic to it, a series substituted for it has these only in the mind of a programmer and in his program.

The mind in its most general and constant form, is a structure expressible as the law of non-contradiction, 'x-is-not-non-x', exemplifiable everywhere and by everything. It can be specialized as 'a is not-non-a', 'a is-not non-a,' or as 'a R's non-a'. When account is taken of the fact that a specialization of x can itself be quite complex, and that any relation can specify the R, the structure is seen to be general enough to permit of its being specialized in countless ways. Used in judgment or inference, the components of that structure are distinguished and specialized to yield specific rules. The human mind, as the locus of these, is a relation able to connect other epitomizations, specializing them at the same time that it uses them.

One may place major emphasis on the relation, the terms, or the articulated whole of them together. If the first, one attends to the mind. If the second, one has material for claims about the terms severally or together. If the third, one perceives, expects, imagines, believes, or doubts, depending on the degree of intrusion on and the direction in which the mind is pointed.

The use of mind, apart from all content, yields an understanding, bare, readied, awaiting filling. Content for it may be worked over or passively received, and the result worked over or received, and so on endlessly. The active and receptive involvements follow one another, with the consequence that the mind is both brought to bear on what is distinct from it, and made to yield to what it confronts. A man is thereby enabled to make contact with what is external, to be enriched by means of this, and to be prepared to deal with it.

Although the mind operates in privacy, it uses content originating apart from it. Wherever the content is obtained, its limits will be there. If the content is obtained from or through the agency of the lived body, the mind will be involved in observation, perception, and cognate activities. If it focuses on the imposed relations, it will be involved with what holds multiplicities together.

A mind does not function well when other epitomizations overrun it. It may function poorly, too, when other epitomizations are not insistent enough or not ready to present to the mind what is available to them. The mind enables a man to become more complete by mastering what there is. The result is promoted when thinking is allowed to be guided by an inclusive end, or by having it engage in inquiry, seeking to realize such an end—and best of all, when both occur.

Descartes was so anxious to pass from "I think" to "I exist" that he left himself insufficient time to examine all that was entailed by his "I think". Thinking, he said, was possible only to a human whose I was identical with or exhaustively involved in the thinking. The reductions are not easy to accept since men are then denied to have selves or I's when they do not think, or are supposed (as Descartes himself did say) to think always. Later Descartes held that 'thinking' was intended to include believing, doubting and the like, but he did not say how or why these are types of thinking. Nor did he make provision for the existence of a person when none of these evidently occur. Men surely are persons even when asleep, in a stupor, and at other times when they are not thinking.

Once the mind is in existence, it may be possible to remember what had once been thought by following the direction of the thinking that had been engaged in. The act requires no knowledge of the nature of thinking, and no grasp of the nature of mind. The memory of a thought requires only the recovery of the thought. We are not thinking afresh when we remember; instead we are trying to recover what we had once thought, trying to reach what had been constituted by a previous act of thinking.

But if this is so, we are not only able to think, but can know what it is to think, for such thinking can be set in contrast with what we do when we try to remember what we had thought.

What we know is objective, not because the mind has been abandoned or something in it had been projected or hurled beyond it, or because the mind is not private, but because it lives the body, and in doing so passes beyond the confines of the body to make contact with what exists outside privacy. We know what is outside our mind by using our mind. The use is private but the outcome is in contact with what is independent of that privacy.

Naive realism holds that men know an objective world just as it is, adding and subtracting nothing. Since it acknowledges that men are knowers while discounting the role of their minds, in effect it supposes that men are at best private blotters or mirrors, apparently unable to make any errors. A related position is offered by Kant in his view that the I is a mere logical accompaniment of knowledge. The reciprocal of these views is a subjectivism with its insistence that everything known is a function of privacy. The realist and the subjectivist both suppose that privacy is and remains pure and apart, the one taking all content to be unaffected by it, the other taking the content to be entirely subject to it. The two are matched by another Kantian view that whatever is known is a function of a knower who produces of an objective world, and by the Hegelian view that whatever is known is a function of a more or less hidden Absolute. But individual knowers are both subject to what is available, and contribute to making it articulate in the form of knowledge.

A man may be overwhelmed by the obstinacy of things, unable to leave an ostensible characteristic mark of himself on them; may take the world to be outside his range; or may see no connection between the two except that provided by impersonal laws. The world will then be untameable or alien. His body, as in that world, will express nothing of the fact that he lives that body, or of what he does by means of it. Nor will his privacy be evidenced by anything he does. Intelligible privately, he will not be intelligible publicly. His public manifestations will then have to be dismissed as irritating intrusions of a subject. That will not make them cease to be present.

'Objective' content may be in the privacy, in the body, or in the world beyond. The acknowledgment of that fact allows one to accept something like both earlier and current usages of 'objective'. In the *Century Dictionary*, C. S. Peirce defined the 'objective' as "perceived or thought; intensional; ideal, representative; phenomenal; opposed to *subjective* or *formal*—that is, as in its own nature." He went on to remark: "This, the original meaning which the Latin word received from Duns Scotus, about 1300, almost the precise contrary of that now usual, continued to be the only one till the middle of the seventeenth century, and was the most familiar in English until the latter part of the eighteenth." The original meaning refers to what is private, and allows for an extension to what is not caught up in the mind; the current meaning credits content the same degree of detachment from a subjectifying privacy that the original did, but goes on to take it to be in the body or the world beyond. Both meanings can be accepted, the one remarking on the private and the other on the public or bodily locus of what is 'objective'. One will, of course, not then accept the part of the earlier meaning which has 'objective' comprise what is 'representative'; nor will he accept that part of the current meaning which has 'objective' be without any bearing on the mind. Instead, he will hold that 'objective' may be either private or public, and can be brought into relationship with what is in the mind.

Were all thought a function of what is experienced, there would be no prescriptions, no theories which were more than generalizations or blind guesses, and then, of course, no knowledge of what was governing private acts. Men can be trained to think along lines that others prescribe. Training in vocations and professions has as its task the production of mental habits which guide men to the same desirable results achieved in the past. Carpenters, plumbers, lawyers, and physicians are trained to think in the way others have successfully thought. Athletes and engineers undergo similar training. We would like all to adventure at times, but on the whole we want them to remain quite close to the patterns of thinking of their predecessors, and to provide maximum accommodation for what occurs when they do what their predecessors did. Logic is to be used by them as an agency for making such accommodations fit in with what is coherent and justifiable.

Offering formalized structures in which beginnings and endings are related by necessity, logic formulates those rules which are specifiable by any enterprise, and which are to be followed if one is to move surely and directly from accepted beginnings to acceptable endings. One must learn to learn how to 'read' those rules, just as one must learn how to read a design or a map. The reading involves a restricted type of thinking, since it requires one to stay within marked-out paths. The 'words' are different, but once mastered allow for quick learning.

It is not too difficult to train children to infer properly nor is it difficult to have tasks carried out by machines. More difficult—and more difficult even to understand—is the act of using guides in order to infer with surety. Inferences are acts. Occurring apart from, and in accord with warranting rules, they differ from the act of just following rules, although both start with and depart from a beginning to arrive at and close with an ending, which the rules present together. An inference gets to a justified conclusion; by following rules one arrives at what is only a prescribed outcome.

A guiding rule need not require a linear move, or a union of a number of linear connections. It could require a convergent or dialectical move; it could demand that one proceed in other ways. There are at least eleven ways of using rules—eleven types of inference (*First Considerations*, pp. 144–45)—and most likely, more. It is perhaps sufficient to note that historical discovery is guided by the principle that multiple fragments are to be dealt with as converging on a common origin, and that legal activity is guided by the presentation of alternative formulations among which one must decide at the outcome of an adversary proceeding. Inferences which conform to such different guidances differ from one another in the kind of justification that can be provided for them, in the ways they proceed, and in the kinds of conclusions they enable one to reach. All accord with, but are also to be distinguished from their respective guiding, prescriptive rules. If an inference is to begin with a statement actually true, it will have to turn this away from whatever enabled it to be true. Only then can the statement be converted into a true premiss from which one can move to a justified conclusion. An inference begins with what is just a supposedly true premiss when an original reference is either not known or is ignored. Were there never such a reference, inference would begin with what had no commerce with anything specific outside it and, so far, would not be pertinent either to science or to practice.

Where, in a rule, beginning and ending constitute a single unit, in an inference one starts at one end and replaces that with which he began by what is reached at the other end. The act of inference arrives at the end, specified by a guiding rule, by moving from the beginning that the rule connects to the end. As just enabled to function as the start of an inference, a statement is a detached item, not yet used, and therefore quite distinct from the beginning marked out in a rule, since it is there joined to a required conclusion.

Somewhat as a car is driven along a road, departing from one position and arriving at another, both already marked out on a map where they are connected, so an inference is carried out in a thinking, departing from one specified place and arriving at another in accord with a rule. Because one leaves what one accepts as being true in order to arrive at what is to be accepted as true and is to replace that with which one began, inference is at once desirable and hazardous, needing to be guided by rules which specify what conclusions are acceptable.

The detachment of a premiss, the use of it at the beginning of an inference, the replacement of it by a conclusion, and the reference of this to the world from which the premiss was derived, are all part of an act of thinking. We can conceive this to consist of more limited thinkings involving the detaching of content, the turning of the content into a premiss, and so on. Or we can view the entire occurrence as a single act. In either case, the thinking will take place under conditions set by a guiding rule.

Against the background of a rule, thinking is occupied with the production and use of a premiss, the passage toward a conclusion, and the achievement and referential use of this. The thinking is unsatisfactory to the degree that the conclusion deviates from what the rule requires, and is to be corrected by new efforts to arrive at the required result. The thinking may be quick or slow, roundabout or straightaway. Sometimes it may involve nothing more than a fresh and separate concentration on the conclusion in the light of what a rule requires—the kind of thinking involved in doing sums or following commands. Usually, thinking must be made to pass through various intermediate points distinguished in the rule.

A thinking which is occupied with presenting a rule-endorsed outcome, and thus one which may be reached in a leap, should check and be checked by a thinking which proceeds from an acceptable premiss to a conclusion along the prescribed path of a rule. When the conclusion is important, the move to a foregone conclusion is to be emphasized. If one is more concerned with warranted and tested activities, it is preferable to follow the rule closely. A reasonable man gets to desired conclusions, a rational man follows warranted rules, but an adventurous one relies on a creative effort to turn available content into part of his mind in ways neither he nor anyone else can anticipate. Fresh thinking is needed if one is interested in discovery.

The content that is brought within the compass of a mind may have been derived from other epitomizations, from the body, or from what is beyond these. It may still be directed there. A man 'puts his mind on' or 'gives his mind to' what he confronts when he reaches to what is to be explored. His mind then functions either as a single unit, requiring the new items to find a place within it, or allows itself to be modified by what else is encountered. New material is dealt with in a set way or on its own terms. What had been learned governs what is being learned, or what is being learned is allowed to function as a guiding rule. Each emphasis needs to be checked by the other.

To try to deal with new material, without taking advantage of what one had learned, is to try to recover an innocence that one's development and knowledge actually preclude. It is to give what is present equal weight with what had been encompassed before. Whenever we lean too much in one direction, an effort should be made to lean in the other. The effort is encouraged by remarking on the neglected, novel, or familiar. A better use of privacy will make use of old material while attending to the new.

Understanding is challenged by dissatisfaction, curiosity, or questioning, provoked by what has not yet been brought within the mind. What is beyond the mind prompts consideration of what has not been mentally prepared for. The saddened, the depressed, the discouraged, the dull, the uninquisitive, and the smug keep mainly within already attained mental patterns. To change them, one must lure them or provoke them to try thinking along different routes. It is difficult to do this for those who are long set in what had been for them successful ways of thinking.

As having a status and a power of its own, the mind is somewhat like the 'active reason' signalized by Aristotle. Some of his Arabian commentators have supposed that this was completely impersonal, and apart from all individuals. What belonged to a man, they thought, was a comparatively feeble, passive instrument, the creature of experiences. But passivity is just a stage at which a truth-claiming mind is when it is awaiting use. Mind is active as a claimant; it is activated when used, whether on content, on other epitomizations, or on the body and what is beyond it.

Other interpreters of Aristotle are inclined to treat Aristotle's rather unclear account of 'active reason' as a God-given possession of individuals. But they fail to make evident how, despite its identical nature and content in every case, it could have a different being or role in different men. What is common to a multiplicity of men is indeterminate; if it is employed differently in different cases, it is because it is inseparable from a determinate content, a determinate body, and various privately used powers.

A mind which fails to relate any epitomization and understood content properly may be biased toward one or the other. Yet if the mind were to have no other function than to keep them in balance, it would be unduly limited. To overcome the limitation, more provision would have to be made for either the content or the epitomization. This will not occur unless new opportunities are offered, there is some equilibriating government of both, and something required or valuable is to be gained by the act. Gains are possible because all epitomizations are indeterminate in themselves, needing to be readied and, so far, made able to accommodate what intrudes. Each, to be itself to the full, must turn intruders into possessions. Relating content to other centers allows the content to be objectively articulated; expressing the mind enables this to benefit from the presence of what had already been distinguished.

Daily language is used with considerable accuracy when one says, "I am keeping something in mind." It is not the linguistic use here or elsewhere that dictates to fact. Language is molded by the community to keep it in some accord with what is accepted as existing apart from the language. Were the act of keeping something in mind to crowd out all other ways in which the mind functions, there would be a store of wanted material, but one would never get to the point where this was in fact used. One would imitate in privacy the scholar who spends his energies collecting needed books, manuscripts, references, paper, and pen, and then finds himself unable to do anything. An occasional painter in that predicament dips his thumb into his paint and makes a mark on his canvas, thereby beginning an act of painting. His example tells the rest of men that one way to escape from just keeping things in mind is to have the mind inquire or infer. Whatever was then acquired could of course still be 'kept in mind' just as the thumb mark of a painter could set a problem as difficult to solve as the one that was faced when he just had his materials ready for use. Blocks in the way of intellectual creativity are not automatically removed by engaging in some new act. What is needed is an exploration of avenues other than those which end with keeping something in mind.

It is easier to keep things in mind than to make use of the mind. Fatigued, one is not prone to do more than keep something in mind or keep to routes followed in the past. There will be an effort to change if one is more tempted to engage in new adventures than to just prepare or repeat. A luring prospect is desirable. Some men make themselves inquire by keeping before them the prospect of fame. No one device is suitable to everyone. Each must find for himself the most effective way to get somewhere between sheer retention and sheer guidance, or forever be only ready to begin to use his mind.

The rationalists' denigration of imagination has been overwhelmed by the romantic insistence on imagination as the best of agencies for grasping what is so. But there surely is no need to suppose that when imagining one is engaged in irrational, unfathomable activities, is in the grip of impersonal forces, or is not thinking. A refusal to acknowledge or abide by rules may still allow one to arrive where he ought to be.

A direct and constant involvement of any epitomization with mind produces a grooved mind. Later attempts at such involvement, while not forced to follow the route that had once been followed, will sooner or later groove the mind still more. Even free, fresh, spontaneous thinking crosses an area that had been crossed before. Inevitably, it is confined and paced by habit. Shakespeare soon enough began to write Shakespearean plays and verse. The fact does not stand in the way of the acknowledgment of the different uses to which he put his genius or the degree to which he was able to vary the expressions of his habits. Nor does it deny his ability to move outside the orbit of what he had already achieved. Each work added something unpredictable to the Shakespeare canon, but in retrospect we can see that it was not foreign to the rest, and even that it was somewhat foreshadowed. Knowing this, a shrewd forger can produce a 'Shakespearean' play. Unlike a living Shakespeare he will, of course, necessarily keep himself confined within the style of the canon so far established. If he did not, no one would accept his work as 'Shakespearean'. That limitation was not antecedently accepted by Shakespeare; if it had been, he too would have produced Shakespearean forgeries.

By taking possession of the mind, it is possible to avoid unknowingly following its established patterns. The act requires a directed application of other epitomizations, and is itself subject to habit. This may be welcome. It surely is desirable, if we seek to benefit from whatever we are readied to do.

Conceivably, the mind can itself be known through an act of thinking. When this occurs a second mind is not created, somehow additional to the first. If there were, a third mind, directed toward the second, would be needed so that one could know this, and so on without end.

A mere thinking is not guided. Its outcome may be discrepant with what is in fact confronted. The thinking may apply to what is past or future, to what is presupposed, or to fictions. It may go astray. Proceeding without criticism or constraint, it yet may be attentive to what is occurring, and even to have this determine the kind of content that will be accepted.

We try to improve the thinking of children, and sometimes would like to improve our own. If we have recourse to rules, prescriptions, and controls to govern the thinking, we could lose some of thinking's characteristic spontaneity and the discoveries to which it sometimes leads. If thinking is not to be recapitulative but exploratory, it should start, move, and end without being bound by what had been achieved earlier. It is best trained when well aimed, and confined to what has multiple facets and yields multiple tests for the correctness of its results. When practical, it seeks a way out of a baffling situation. When appropriate to a work of art it may start at any point, and attempt to arrive at others, under the guidance of the work itself. When appropriate to previous great adventures in thought, it starts with problems previously faced, but it still should seek its own way to the same or to better solutions. Its adventures are to be corrected and redirected again and again by comparing what is confronted with what is thought.

To require one to arrive only where others had already arrived is to deny thinking its right to be creative. Still, we usually have immediate practical concerns, and wish to use the mind in quite limited ways. We then are glad to arrive at a slightly new thought that is at least as satisfactory as an old. If we need a base in terms of which subsequent acts are to be performed, we make use of memory. Rarely do we remember just in order to have once again what we had faced before. What is wanted is what had stood us in good stead; we want to keep it in mind, awaiting a desirable use.

Athletes, craftsmen, mathematicians, explorers, and inventors may have poor memories, but they all have much in mind, vivifying it, bringing what is needed to the fore readily and effectively under the stimulation of slight cues. They contrast rather sharply with those who, with ready memories, are able to attend at once to what is in mind in a determinate, dated form.

So far something indeterminate is in mind, one is expectative; if that which is in mind is determinate, one is retrospective. Where the conversion of the latter into the former requires abstraction from an actual determinateness and the facing of the result as that which is to be used, the conversion of the former into the latter requires the indeterminate to be given a determinate setting, enabling it to be remembered as what had been expected. Having remembered my appointment, I now wait to see my friend at the expected time and place. Having waited in vain for him to appear, I cushion his expected presence within the determinate place and time of which I now take note; later I will chide him for not having been just where and when I had expected him. At these and at other times I judge, and in that act measure the degree of achievement possible, the degree to which full power is exercised, or the degree to which a desirable achievement is approximated. I refer to the first when referring to a man's intelligence; to the second when speaking of him 'putting his mind' to a task; and to the third when thinking of what is intrinsically intelligible.

Men differ in their mental powers; what one is able to achieve through the use of mind another cannot. It is also true that what this man can achieve he does not, failing to use his mind to the degree that it could be used. Refusing to think, he allows himself to be swept along, to react, or to respond emotionally. He lacks motivation, is too relaxed, fails to use his mind. As a result, he may achieve less than another does who has an inferior mind, but who applies himself more diligently.

Sometimes we exaggerate and suppose that achievements in some particular direction evidence an ability to do as well in other directions. It is not necessary to make this supposition in order to say with warrant of some man that he does not put his mind to work to the degree he can. The criticism is to be distinguished from one directed at his failure to be sufficiently occupied with the available content.

If a man uses his mind splendidly without making any apparent effort to do so, we suppose that he could have achieved more had he tried harder. We may be mistaken. He may not be able to do better with deliberate or great effort than he does when he allows his mind to roam. But it is sensible to assume that he will do more justice to his task if he makes an effort to use his mind. We get a man to put his mind to work not by simply prompting him to make better use of it, but by attending to content as deserving or requiring the better use, thereby prompting him to be engaged in thinking rather than in some other act.

Using past achievements as a measure offers a good way to compare what is being done with what had been done. But it does not let us know what could be done. What has been achieved may be less than one might achieve. Often the only measure we have of what might be done is provided by what had been done. But occasionally we also note that severe tests have not yet been faced. And in the case of children, we know that most grow and become able to think better than they once could.

Intelligence measures a capacity to use one's mind. The evidence for this is something done. If one has grown he will of course not be adequately evaluated by tests which attend only to what he had once achieved. If we are to know where success always gives way to failure, we must know where capacity has been maximally expressed. But unless there is no possibility of further growth, the privacy behind that capacity will be able to increase it and thereby provide new ways to use the mind.

A level of intelligence sets limits beyond which one is not able to perform well through the exercise of thought. To raise the level is to grow psychically. Apart from the accompanying gains of physical maturation and the benefits generated by discipline, we have no knowledge of how such growth can be promoted, any more than we have a knowledge of how to make a great runner out of a good one. All we are able to do is to provide occasions for good performances, provocations for the exercise of unused power, and opportunities to use that power to a greater degree than before. Men privately make themselves better; all that others can do for them in the end is to provide occasions for their self-improvement.

The great thinkers of the world make evident what can be thought. After it has been thought, it is often not too difficult to follow their lead and to think along their lines. It took the genius of Newton and Leibniz to invent the calculus; it is now within the competence of school-boys. Such men mastered content that before was unknown, vague, chaotic, or dismissed as absurd. They produced what can be understood by others. Not to be able to understand what they made available is to make evident the degree one falls short of having a fully developed capacity to use his mind.

In the history of intellectual discovery, there is progress from what was once unintelligible to what is now intelligible. A rationalist moves beyond that point to contend that the intelligibility of anything is intrinsic to it, in no way dependent on the achievements of men, and that the role of great thinkers is but to make the intelligible assume a communicable form. Would not the thinkers then have to lay hold of what was not communicable to others, and make it so? Would we then not have to content ourselves with saying that there was something inexpressible which some men converted into the known? Would we not have to maintain that thinking was never discovery, that it was always fully creative? Dewey would hold not only that a rationalism must answer these questions affirmatively, but that the fact provides a warrant for pragmatism or instrumentalism. His own view, though, fails to distinguish between two meanings of 'intelligible', one of which refers to an intrinsic rationale while the other refers to what men understand. God is thought, by some theologians, to be 'intelligible' only in the first way. What is intelligible in this sense may never become so in the second, since we may be incapable of comprehending it.

The rationalists' contention can be nothing more than an expression of a belief unless he can show that there is a rationale in whatever there be. This can be done. It requires a reference, though, to a power able to impose a rationale everywhere. That power need not be conscious or divine. If this reference is not made, all that can be properly maintained is that what has not yet been made intelligible in the second sense might already be intelligible in the first.

The problem for lesser men in relation to what greater thinkers understand is similar to that which the greater have with respect to what they have come to understand for the first time. Both are faced with what is not yet understood, the first because a rationale has not yet been discovered; the second because what is already intelligible has not yet been converted into something understood. The second, on his own, must make what he confronts subject to his thinking. If he fails, we can do no more than prod and urge him to try harder, which is to say, try to get him to use the intelligence he already has; or try to prompt him to increase his capacity to understand.

i. Resolution

A prospect is a real possibility, a relatively indeterminate condition pertinent to what is present. Action is needed if the prospect is to be turned into
a relatively more determinate entity in a succeeding present. The action
adds determinations to the prospect, but need not be directed at it in order
to do so. Prospects are realized even by actions which are occupied solely
with altering what is present.

Privacy faces at least four different types of prospect: *goals* which one is
inclined to realize; *objectives* which have sought values; *ends* which are
worthy of dedication, and a *good* which should govern what men decide
and do. Goals are prospects for *preference*, objectives are prospects for
choice, ends are prospects for *will*, and the good is the prospect governing
responsibility. The first three are pertinent to resolution, an epitomization distinct from but able to be exercised at the same time that the mind
is. They involve different exercises of freedom; exhibit resolution but in
different ways; and express a person exercising a distinctive epitomization,
involved with a distinctive kind of prospect. Consequently, if the three are
bundled together, and indifferently dealt with under such headings as
'freedom', 'decision', 'choice', or 'will', important distinctions will be
overlooked.

Animals occasionally decide which route to take, what objects to
select, with which other animals they are to mate. They do not forge
decisions on the basis of what they learned about the functioning of their
own or other bodies. Men can. Men can also make decisions about what
is wholly private. Some of those decisions may never be carried out in
fact. Since they would not be known to have occurred unless something
were publicly manifested, to know of them one has to look to what is said
or done. The fact makes it seem reasonable to assume that decisions are
bodily occurrences unnecessarily supposed to have predecessors in the
form of privately forged acts. If that assumption is made, one would still,
of course, have to admit that what was publicly decided had at least been
privately initiated, particularly when the decisions are preceded by assessments of possible outcomes. The admission would not yet compel the
acknowledgment of a distinctly human, independently functioning privacy. But such a privacy one will be forced to acknowledge when acts are
found to depend on resolutions. These are private activities ending in
decisions which make determinate what is both sought and realizable. It
is necessary to acknowledge resolutions in the form of preferences,
choices, and will, if some things publicly done by men at different times
are to be made intelligible.

Both men and animals add determinations to some of the prospects that are pertinent to what is present. The realization of the prospects may not serve the body as it is by itself or with others. Men can use them without regard for what in fact will ensue, contenting themselves with making use of the prospects to determine for themselves what they will do. If the results are carried out in fact they will surely affect the body's course. But the resolutions will have been produced before, and perhaps in disregard of the body's nature, requirements, or roles.

When bodily acts are directed at the realization of prospects which had already been resolved upon, evidences of a distinctively human private activity are provided. To know just what occurs, we must of course know how men's bodies function when unaffected by any resolution. The additions that are found to be bodily present have then to be of such a nature that they can be traced back only to a preferential election of a means serving to bring about a goal, the chosen fulfilling of an obligation on behalf of some objective, or the willing pursuit of an end to which one is dedicated.

A resolution is a private activity ending in a decision. Although determinations are then produced in a relatively indeterminate prospect, the result will not be fully determinate. If it were, nothing would be added when a resolution was carried out in and through the body. Determinations are added to preferences, choices, and acts of will when these are bodily sustained.

To express a preference is to decide in favor of some means promoting an accepted prospect. Initially, the means was just a nuance in an undifferentiated content. When that content is related to a prospect, the preferred means is compelled to stand away from the content in which that means was an undifferentiated part. By so standing away, the means attains the status of an elected agency for realizing the prospect. The resulting preferred means could be wholly confined to the private decision; it could be expressed in a particular controlled bodily act; or it could be privately elected and aquire bodily form.

When men prefer, their preferences are qualified by the fact that they could have decided in other ways instead. And could they simply duplicate bodily what they privately preferred, there would be no need for them to make decisions, except to guide or to anticipate what was bodily done.

Like preference, choice is occupied with the election of means. The means is isolated by affecting a less remote by a more remote prospect. Unlike preference, choice elects the means when and as it fastens on a remote prospect as that which is to be insisted on for an indefinite time. If realized, that remote prospect will compensate for whatever values were in fact sacrificed in previous decisions and acts.

It is possible to produce a series of detached preferences, but choice inevitably keeps one related to the past and the future. Although something like preference is expressed by animals, none is able to choose, since none can subject itself to the demand that it attend to and realize objectives which compensate for values lost.

Will, like choice, takes account of values. Unlike choice, it faces a prospect which is to affect not only a less remote prospect out of which a means is to be isolated, but the body as well, making this too be directed toward the realization of that prospect. The presence and action of the will is at least tacitly acknowledged in accounts which emphasize practice over theory, though these too often go on to speak as though the will were a private faculty used solely to make a difference to some matter of fact instead of being, as it is, a private resolution directed at a prospect which affects privacy and body at the same time. That prospect is made as available to the body as it is to the privacy.

Preference is evidenced in the use of that one of a number of possible alternatives which is most emphasized by a desired goal. Choice is evidenced in the justification given by an accepted objective set of values to one of a number of possible alternative means. Will is evidenced in the production of what best promotes a prescriptive end. In all, a prospect is used to enable one to separate out and thereby make determinate what before was only a nuance in a single, less remote content.

Before a prospect is used to make an election of a means for it possible, one is faced with a less remote prospect, a content in which such a means is an unseparated, nuanced part. Were there only a number of distinctive alternatives amongst which one had to decide, one of the alternatives would just be selected. That alternative would be given a new role with the rest of the content either left as it had been before or endowed with the new determination, 'not selected'.

As just electable, a means is only a part of some content, itself made subject to a more remote and more indeterminate prospect. The bringing to bear of the latter on the former makes both of them more determinate—the latter by turning it into a controlling future, the former by becoming divided, with one portion in the role of a means to the more remote prospect. With these considerations in mind, the characteristics of the three modes of resolution can now be more clearly distinguished.

Even if a man were occupied solely with preferring one of two apples for eating, he would be faced with two prospects. In one of these, the paired apples would not be separated. In the other—the more remote—ways of eating would not be. Approached apart from the position of the prospective eating, the apples make up a content in which neither is favored. The prospective eating, on being imposed on that content separates out one of the apples as being more suitable for eating. Bringing the more remote prospect to bear on the prospectively eaten apples, as not yet separated from one another, yields a preferred apple.

The apple that was separated out was viewed as having a desirable color, smell, availability, or some other feature. There is no reflection needed here. The prospective eating and one of the to-be-selected apples makes a more congenial unity than that prospect does with the other apple. As a consequence, the prospective eating is turned into a guiding future making one apple preferred for eating.

The selection of one apple rather than another comes at the end of an act of resolution. An indeterminate 'paired-apples' is made determinate in the form of 'this-apple-selected-for-eating'. Nothing here is completely determinate. There is no fully determinate apple selected to be eaten, no fully determinate rejected apple. Nor is 'eating' in 'this-apple-selected-for-eating' fully determinate, though it is more determinate than it was when it was not connected with the apple.

Selection, like election, is a private act. It does not set one of the apples physically apart from the other. It does, though, make a difference to them, since it provides both with a more circumscribed future than they have when one of them is elected. To keep them within the introduced limiting future, the prospective eating which governs the selection must continue to be united with one of the apples. Otherwise, this would lose the status of a to-be-eaten-apple.

What the apples might do or become is more confined because of a selection. Whether or not a selected apple is eaten, as a result of its selection, it has a nature that is not identical with what it had apart from the selection, or as just available for a selection.

The restriction that a selection imposes is not absolute. The selected apple could be lost, tossed about, taken by another. The restriction on what will subsequently be true of it holds only as long as it is subject to a conditioning by the prospective eating. If a selected apple could be entirely torn away from all relation to its selection, the apple would once again face a distinctive future. That future would not be identical with the very future that had been faced before there had been a selection, both because some time had passed, giving the apple new opportunities, and because the fact that it had been selected makes it more apt to be selected again. Hidden away, it is still the apple whose sheen and color made it the object of a selection. It will rot after a while, but this will be the rotting of what had been selected.

A faded beauty may now look like one who never had been a beauty, but even apart from all memory on her part or anyone else's, hers has a past from which it can never be entirely sundered. If she had not been a beauty but was thought to be so, what she now is would be affected by the fact that she had been thought to be a beauty. That the nature and career of anything in the world is not necessarily physically altered by the fact that men had viewed it in a certain way does not mean that it does not have a different future as a result, since it will have been made to be together with certain other items, and given a career in contexts where it continues to exist together with those others. If a prospective eating is imposed on an apple, this will continue to be affected by that prospect. Because of that prospect, the apple cannot thereafter be entirely freed from the status it achieved as selected or not selected.

There may not be any object which is the counterpart of what is elected, but a selection always terminates in what is actual and separate. One selects through an act which affects an independent, actual object, the selection turning this into one which is in fact set apart from others. An election sets apart only something distinguished in some entertained content.

The outcome of a private election must be imposed on an actual object if this is to be actually selected. Were one of the apples picked up following its election, the picking up would be something new, not a continuation of the election. It would make the apple not just elected, but an apple selected because it had been elected. Since elections occur independently of references to what is in fact available or done, they always end with what is less determinate than the outcome of a selection.

As related to what is not present, privately or publicly, the future has various determinations. Could the future be disconnected from all that was present, it would lose all relevance and be no more than a phase in an all-inclusive possibility, with no other relation to what now is than that of allowing for its continuance. The denial that there are real possibilities affecting what is now happening therefore comes down to the denial that the future is relevant to what is present. A real possibility is needed to make what is present be a precursor of what is yet to be, while what is present makes a limited portion of the entire future be that which actions are to realize.

A relatively determinate 'a preferred-apple-for-eating' emerges out of the combination of a prospective eating with entertained content in which apples are not yet subject to an election. The imposition of the prospective eating on that content gives one of the apples a preferential standing. If that elected apple is selected, both apples as existing objects will acquire additional but diverse determinations and roles. Both the election and the selection occur privately. As just apples on a tree, the apples were neither elected nor selected. Picked up, a selected apple is given a new position in the public world.

As present actualities, the apples are, of course, distinct, with distinctive determinations. Is this not to grant that the apples were fully determinate to begin with, and that one of them is then given an impossible additional determination by being selected, while the other is given an equally impossible additional determination by being rejected? No. When awaiting election, they are conceived to be joined and in that guise related to a prospective eating. Apart from any election, each is merged in an entertained pair. The members of that pair are made more determinate when distinguished in an election, affected in a selection, and made subject to an action.

Strict determinism ignores these various factors, as well as those which present entities have because of their relation to their pertinent possibilities. In its universe whatever is—whether it be present, past, or future, whether or not it be elected, selected, or acted on—is fully determinate, bounded off from all else. Nothing there is ever produced, changes, or becomes. But in this universe, what is present is subject both to privately and objectively operating prospects, making what is present be more than what is just present. Only if it could be wholly detached from all possibilities could a present item be fully determinate.

Determinations are introduced by free acts. These start with what is present and convert what is possible for them into a controlling and finally a realized eventuality. By providing determinations, one limits the determinations that can still be acquired. Consequently, were there an omnipotent power its exercise would result in a perfect determinism, since it would then no longer be possible for future determinations to be added. But then, or course, no actuality would ever become or change. There would be no causation, action, or coming to be and passing away.

A more remote prospect adds determinations to a less remote prospect, only so far as the two have distinguishable natures—the less remote because it is directly relevant to what is happening, the more remote because it is relevant to the less. The future is not broken up into distinct moments by those prospects; a separation out of a prospect by what is present, sets that prospect in contrast with others with which it was connected, and in contrast with the future which continues beyond it. The more remote prospect is made distinct from other equally remote prospects by being related to a prospect which is being realized. Resolution brings the more remote to bear on the less, thereby turning the more remote into a goal, objective, or end, to be attained through the agency of the less.

A preference enables the prospect of eating to add determinations to paired apples to make the pair yield an apple elected for eating. Were the apple chosen instead of being preferred, there would be an obligation to do something in consonance with an obligation carried from the past. Were one to go further and will to eat the apple, a prospect such as remaining in good health would have been used to enable one not only to elect an apple but to make the body act so as to promote the realization of that prospect. Preference, choice, and will use wanted, obligating, and prescriptive prospects, respectively.

If a preference has been exercised, the election of one alternative will have been guided by some such objective as the satisfying of hunger. A preference could, of course, be exercised by one who refuses to eat, since the prospective satisfaction of hunger might make waiting, preparation, or rest preferable. One can take distasteful medicines to get better; tasty medicines may not be elected even though one wants to get better. The preference is produced by making prospective health yield a means to it. That preferred means is distinguished because the prospect it is to serve is marked out and effective. Once it is distinguished, the means remains so, but the more remote prospect is distinguished from the rest of the future only so far as it continues to be related to the preferred means.

When one chooses, both an alternative and a compensatory objective are elected. The election of the alternative is one with the subordination to a new objective or with one already in force. A subsequent failure to act in consonance with what the objective requires makes a man guilty for a failure to make good the losses in value which the election of that alternative involved. The choice can be made without regard for the preferential status of the alternative chosen; the chosen item can be identical with the alternative that is preferred; it could require the election of what is not preferred; or it could be in consonance with a preference and go counter to what a previous choice requires.

An obligating objective is defined by the losses that previous decisions required; it is to be subsequently used to enable one to compensate for those losses. Freely bringing the obligating objective together with an undifferentiated set of alternatives, one chooses the alternative required by that objective. That alternative may be onerous or disagreeable. It is chosen because the obligating objective requires it as that which is at once a means to that objective and helps make good a previous loss in value.

Although possible, it is rarely that one decides to prefer rather than to choose, or to choose rather than to prefer. If he made either decision he would have to subject an elected act of preference or choice to another preference or choice. Here, also, the deciding would have its causes and effects, and work itself out freely.

Quite soon, in the course of his life, a man is obligated to realize an objective because of a previous choice. A new choice will have to conform to what that objective demands, or he will have failed to choose in consonance with what he had chosen before. The obligating objective does not, as a goal of a preference does, add to what otherwise would be a relatively unappealing means, so as to make this means the most appealing of alternatives. The obligating objective instead binds, demanding its realization as a right, and exposes a failure in character if it is not realized. The obligation continues to be binding, since it is a function of what a man, by his own past decisions, had made into an inseparable part of himself. The first choice that one makes has an obligating objective which previous acts define; all subsequent choices should be for the sake of realizing objectives in which the losses involved in previous choices are made good by an obligated man.

To know that a choice has been made, one must know that an obligation had been created, and that one is therefore required to elect an alternative that most satisfies this. It is to recognize that what is to be done demands a compensation for the losses that some previous decision involved. The obligating objective evidently makes both the chooser and his chosen alternative into its sanctioned agencies.

If no account is taken of values lost, and if an election of an alternative is not seen to compensate for the loss, no knowledge that a choice has been made will be possible. We most readily know that a choice has been made when a man expresses the fact that he is living up to an obligation and therefore is directed toward an objective required by what he had previously done.

Since, as in the present, a man joins what he had done and what he is obligated to realize, the acknowledgment of something as evidence that he has made a choice is one with the recognition that he is a free being, though not necessarily one who decides correctly. The acknowledgment that he is a free being, obligated to realize an objective because of what he had previously done, is quickly made. Yet it requires nothing less than a recognition that he privately links what he ought to achieve to what helps him achieve it. Did he just link a past with a future, he would of course also exercise a private power, but he would so far not be different in principle from any other kind of being. But when he chooses, he gives what is in the past and future of the chosen the status of a past and future deliberately unified. What otherwise would have been just a past and future external to an indifferent present thereupon becomes his past and future, sustained by his present chosen alternative.

Politics and law focus on public acts, though rarely with an explicit acknowledgment of the character of men, privately maintained. Without paying attention to the demands of politics or law, a man makes choices and judges others in the light of the choices they make. Few stop with judgments which refer only to what others are observed to do; almost everyone uses the present acts of others to begin a move toward them as obligated. The obligating objective is usually assumed to be one which a society or perhaps a religion endorses, with the consequence that the act is taken to express an election which is or is not in conformity with the demands of the society or religion. Since social or religious demands do not often coincide on all points with what in fact obligates men because of what they had previously decided, men's resolutions are rarely in full accord with what their society or religion underwrites. To know what a man ought to choose, it will usually be necessary to replace the obligating prospect which a society or religion endorses by an objective that in fact justifies an election of a particular means, enabling a man to compensate for values previously sacrificed. If he brings about what is commonly endorsed, he is to be judged as being more or less moral, while living up to the standards set by a society or religion.

Were a man to live up to what an obligation requires, he would decide as he should. But we do not know that some one has done this unless he provides evidence of the fact, perhaps in a report affirming that an obligating objective determines what he is choosing. Unfortunately, we cannot be absolutely sure that the report is accurate, not even if it is provided by one who is apparently trying to be as honest and exact as he can possibly be about what he had decided. And, even if he reported correctly just what he had done, he may not have decided as he should. A man's decision can fail to match what his obligations demand whether he reports poorly or well.

We hold on to both past and future items through a resolution and thereby unite them in the form of a justified alternative and obligating objective. That we do this seems beyond question. Exactly how and why we so act is more difficult to see. Conceivably we might have just noted what another does, and copied him. Nothing less than a knowledge of the losses in value that an election involves, and the kind of outcome that must be achieved in order that those losses are made good, is needed if a man's character is to be adequately judged. This is done by measuring his use of societal, religious, or any other standards by what would be decided by an ideal man of native excellence, one whose choices make good whatever losses in value his previous choices involved.

A man may not choose properly at some particular time because of a failure either to recognize the objectives that are operative in his decisions or to decide as those objectives require. When he fails in the first way, he is defective; when in the second, deficient. As the one he does not decide as a mature man should; as the second, he is a mature man who decides wrongly. His character varies according to the degree with which resolutions conform to what is required.

There are no perfect men. All are deficient some of the time, allowing an objective that justifies the choice of an alternative to have its place usurped by a less justified objective. Did this not occur, men would never fall short of what they themselves ought to and are trying to do. But, while no man always lives up fully to all his obligations, since it is he who decides it is he who necessarily obligates himself. He alone is chargeable for not later sustaining what warranted the election of the alternative chosen. Not necessarily defective, he is deficient again and again, always able to be but not always succeeding in remaining faithful to what is involved in the choices he made.

A man provides evidence of his decision in an act expressing the fact that he elected an alternative with the help of an obligating objective. Usually, there is no waiting for that evidence. Instead, he is judged at once to be obligated by the nature of his past choices, leaving for later the decision as to whether or not he is defective or deficient, the one because he makes the wrong decision, the other because he does not sustain the objective that would justify his decision.

The evidence that a man is obligated because of what he wrongly chose is found in what he publicly does. This is available only to those who know right from wrong. Just as no one sees that a promise has been made or broken unless he understands how promises are expressed and what a violation of them is like, so no one can know that another has chosen wrongly unless he understands what a choice is.

If a man made a publicly noted promise but did not do what he had promised, we would not yet know that he was guilty for having failed to live up to an obligating objective. To know that, we must know that he did not simply break the promise but wrongly chose to do so; he must be known to be one who ought to have kept his promise, whether or not he or others care that he did or did not.

Evidence is imbedded in what is independent of the source of that evidence. An indentation in the sand provides evidence of a human foot if it not only has the shape of a human foot but depended on the pressing of a foot in the sand. If one knows nothing about the capacity of sand, he would not know whether or not the indentation was evidence of anything. If he did not know that the indentation was a footprint, he would not know that it provided evidence that a foot had been impressed there. To judge that the sand was indented by a foot, one must distinguish the sand in its usual state from what it now is, and trace the difference back to its cause. To be able to attend to the evidence, one has to know that there is something present—the indentation—which has a different nature and source from that in which it is. Evidence imbedded in physical objects could be identified only by one who had knowledge of such objects and the ways they act. Evidence imbedded in what is biological, similarly, could be identified only by one who had a knowledge of living beings and what they do. Evidence imbedded in moral, ethical, sacramental, or metaphysical objects, could be identified only by those who have knowledge of governing prospects and the decisions these make possible.

Does not such a view require one to say that a sane man cannot know what an insane man is like, and what it is that he does? If it did, it surely would be suspect. But a sane man need have no more difficulty in knowing the source of insane acts than he has in knowing the source of anything else. He is not required to duplicate the source, but only to move toward it sympathetically and to understand it. Since wickedness does not stand in the way of the production of good concepts, there is no necessity that bad men be unable to understand what is good. No less than better men, they can find, in what is publicly available, evidences of what was properly elected by others.

Where a causal act proceeds from an antecedent cause toward a subsequent, actual effect, realizing this through the introduction of determinations in that effect as merely possible and entailed, an election uses an indeterminate prospect to help make determinate what is to realize this. The production of the determinations, and therefore the election of some alternative, has its causes. It may be necessitated by what precedes it. But, from the position of that which is being made determinate, the production and election are necessarily free. Freely made decisions are necessitated by what occurred before; the free realization of a prospect ends with an actual, necessitated effect.

Three hard problems stand in the way of the ready acceptance of this view: (1) All action occurs in a present, where everything is in the process of becoming determinate. Could a present action affect what is only prospective? (2) If an alternative is elected, it must have lacked the determinations which the election introduces. Is what is elected as prospective as is the objective to be realized through its agency? (3) If a prospect serves to introduce determinations in what is to realize it, will not what is not yet, act on what is past for it?

1. Were a prospect at some temporal distance from the present, it would of course be outside the present. But prospects are not remote from what they condition. They are where the conditioned is. The possible future is not separated off from the present by a time which is stretched out over a spatial line. Related to the present as a condition to what it conditions, it is *for* the present. To take the possible future to be at a time subsequent to the present is to confound it with a realized future, a future that occurs at a moment that replaces the one now present. A correlative observation is to be made about the past. This, too, is not at a distance from the present along a spatial line. Nothing in the past takes up room or has duration. What makes up the past are not extended objects, but residual determinate, unextended facts, sustained by what is present.

2. Election gives the elected the status of an isolated alternative. Before then, it was without boundaries, not entirely separated from others, lacking sufficient determination to be able to stand apart. It was there as a component of an *a*-or-*b*, not as an *a* disjoined from a *b*.

The action of a man, at its inception and throughout, is directed at an indeterminate prospect. It does not follow unit move by unit move. Already connected with the prospect, its successive stages intensify, concretize, make the prospect more and more determinate. The connection never breaks up into momentary unitary steps. If it could, there would be a warrant for taking each unit step to have a beginning separable from its ending. Each of the unit steps could then be divided, and so on without end. What now is takes up an undivided stretch of time. This may, like the now of a dynasty or a war, extend over a plurality of other occurrences, without being divided. Within the range of such a now there are other, shorter nows in a sequence, each member of which is as indivisible as the now of the dynasty or war.

3. A future prospect is used to enable one to make determinate and thereby elect a member of a conjunctive disjunct of possible alternatives '*a*-or-*b*-or-*c*. . . .' By being imposed on the entire conjunctive disjunct, the prospect makes one of the conjunctively disjunct items stand away from the rest as elected. There is here no acting backward from an actual future time to the present, but only the free making a prospect act as a necessary factor in the constitution of what is to be present and elected.

The determination that the prospect introduces is produced through the free, constitutive combined activity of the prospect and a conjunctive disjunct. Together they produce a necessitated decision.

Odd or novel as the view may sound, it is inescapable, even when one turns from privately produced decisions to what occurs in fact—unless it makes sense to say with the Laplacians that what will be at the next moment is already existent there (and yet has somehow to make an appearance when that next moment somehow becomes present), or with Humeans that what will be just pops out at a later moment without reason or warrant and therefore may not pop out at all, leaving an empty future which inexplicably becomes present.

Like preferring and choosing, willing ends with the election of an alternative. But instead of electing an alternative with the help of an appealing objective which it serves, or because it is demanded by a justifying objective, will elects and makes an alternative effective because it is demanded by an end that governs the way in which the body acts. A preferred alternative can remain solely within privacy; a chosen alternative has a bodily expression; willed, a body is directly affected by the very end that is privately focused on.

Privately, all that occurs when one wills is the use of an end so as to make the body act in ways which promote that end's realization. There is here no controlling of the body by the privacy, no making it go one way rather than another, no first a deciding and then a carrying out, no impetus given by a freedom operating on a passive or resistant body. Instead, there is a necessitated but freely produced focusing on an end which in turn dictates how the body is to act.

It is possible to will what is bad for oneself, for the body, or for others. It is possible to will what one prefers or what one chooses, and to prefer or to choose what one wills. The will is then more or less strong, more or less able to make the body act as it requires. A perverse or bad will makes the body act in injurious ways. No less than a good will, it depends on a privacy freely occupying itself with a prospect which makes the body act. The goodness or badness of the will is unfortunately independent of its strength. The best of wills may be impotent, the worst of wills powerful. A will that is bad or perverse may be no less effective than one that is good, since the two differ only in the kind of end that is being favored.

Bodies have no aims, no power to direct themselves at prospects. The fact does not stand in the way of their being affected by them. Although the prospects have no power of their own, enabling them to make a difference to the way bodies act, although by themselves they can do no more than restrict the range of eventualities that are open to the body, they can guide the body when they are willed to do so.

A willed end directs the body toward a prospective end privately insisted on. The recognition of the role that is here played by the end makes it possible to bypass an age-old and insoluble problem, hinging on the question of how one can, through an act of will, infuse energy into the body, control it, and change its course. No such infusion occurs. Instead, the will identifies a particular prospect which may not have been relevant to the body, and makes this a condition for it. Sensitivity and other epitomizations also make the body into an agency for realizing privately adopted prospects. The main difference between will and them is that the will, in addition to living the body by making it into an agency, also governs the body by means of a possibly worthy or regrettable end that is to be reached through the body's aid.

Were it not possible to limit and empower the future through acts of will, there would be no bodily effort made to realize what is taken to be good. Must one then conclude that a bird flying thousands of miles south to a nesting place has a will? Where it seeks to be is a good for it and, apparently, keeps its body directed toward it. Although its destination seems to be fixed and to limit the direction in which the bird will fly, what it does can be fully accounted for without requiring a reference to a willing by it. Bodily composition and stimulation apparently suffice to keep the bird on a steady course until it reaches its destination. There is therefore no need to credit it with private resolutions. A man, in contrast, can empower any number of prospects, treat any one of them as an end. There is none that he necessarily insists on; there is no outcome that he inescapably acts to realize as the good.

Evidence of an exercised will is most readily found in those ordered acts of the body which need not have been emphasized or controlled on behalf of the body, the species, or society. It is available only to those who already know that the acts could have been differently ordered, might not be preferred or chosen, and are directed toward the realization of an end privately adopted. They must know that an actual sequence of bodily acts is not necessary but is nevertheless necessitated by a prospect privately fastened on. And the evidence must be shown to be persistently imposed on the body by the prospect.

The conditioning of a body by will is discovered when one finds an ordered set of bodily acts directed toward a single outcome whose realization does not benefit the body, the species, or fellowman. That the will is directed at that prospect is known by the prospect's insistent effectiveness against the moves needed to benefit the body, the species, or fellowman. So far as the willed demands coincide wtih what these require there is of course no knowing what had been willed.

No one can succeed in fully anticipating what particular efforts will produce. The full concreteness of anything is beyond the reach of all prediction and preparation, having details no conclusion could encompass. Even details filled in by the imagination will be general, lacking the obstinate, externally produced, intensive multiplicity of the details to be found in what exists. Those details are not irrationalities, beyond all knowing; there is nothing in any occurrence which sets a limit beyond which knowing cannot go. But what is concrete cannot, though, be exhausted by any set of concepts. Knowing must attend to what is endlessly knowable, always more than what can be caught in any formalization or conceptualization. When one wills, as surely as when one acts, the result is more than one could have anticipated, and will always be more than what is articulately known.

A good will is directed at a prospect that ought to be realized. So far as it is good, the will cannot avoid being so directed. Could a will be good in and of itself, what it fastened on would then have had to be fastened on by it. But no will is good apart from a willing of what is good. By fastening on an end that ought to be realized, whether this be a good for oneself, for others, for all, or for something indifferent to their interests, a will makes itself good. It could not do this, of course, if it did not express a privacy which acts so as to make a worthy end govern the way in which the body functions. Must one then not be good in order to be able to will the good? If so, a good man would be like a bird that had to fly south on the onset of cold weather, since his condition would dictate what prospect would be effective. But a good man freely wills a good end and rejects other prospects, even when these are more attractive, more promising, or more widely endorsed at the time.

A preference for the alternative of eating what is available is guided by some such goal as satisfying hunger. It could be made by one who dislikes the taste of food. If a choice is made, the election of that alternative will be inseparable from an obligating objective, and therefore from a context where charges of guilt are relevant. The choice can be made without regard for the food's suitability or unsuitability for eating. If a man wills to eat, his eating will be required by a persistently imposed end. To increase our surety that the election was made for one of these reasons rather than for another, we would have to increase our surety that it was preferred, chosen, or willed, and thus was elected because it promoted what was attractive, obligatory, or supposedly good.

Preparations, promises, and the answering to the demands of a willed end can be expressed in a common language and through other exhibitions of social cohesion. What cannot be known by attending to these is whether or not an election was governed by the use of an appealing, obligating, or willed prospect. It is not enough for others to hold that one acted in one of these ways. Nor is it enough for a man to believe or say that he had done so. If others say he is incompetent because he prefers inadequate means, that he is guilty for having chosen wrongly, or that he has a bad will because he did not govern his body by properly using a good end, there would still not be sufficient grounds—even if he confirms their judgment—to conclude that he had an independent privacy which was able to make decisive elections. To obtain that conclusion, the body's course must be shown to depend on the presence of a controlling prospect which plays a role because it appeals, obligates, or provides a common prospect for both privacy and body.

It is the individual who decides. How he decides is properly said to be his doing, even when the exact way in which the decision is made and the carrying it out are neither known nor supervised. Just as he need not know how his muscles and tendons work in order to be accountable for striking a blow, so he need not know how or even why he privately acts in certain ways in order to know that these make a difference to his character. Caused, carried out, and with consequences not understood or sought, his acts could have gone another way had he made a different use of the prospect in terms of which he was proceeding.

Just as one justifiably deserves rewards and punishments for what is publicly done, so he justifiably deserves praise and blame for what he privately initiates. The way in which he privately acts, how his privacy continues, stops, or modifies the body's course, may be beyond prevision. Nevertheless, he deserves praise or blame for what he decides to do.

Because of his resolutions, a man is able to publicly act so as to realize an appealing prospect, is prompted to publicly act to realize an objective which obligates him, and is conditioned to publicly act so as to realize an end which is privately fastened on. Because his preference, choice, and will carve out possible agencies, they are like actions which emphasize what is to be rather than what has been or is. The warrant for our assurance that any of them occurred warrants the assurance that a man acted privately and freely.

A man, for Aristotle, was primarily a member of a society, which was supposedly civilized despite its acceptance of slavery and its subordination of women. Since he thought of the body as having to be guided in its course by decisions which find a proper balance between understood opposite tendencies toward excess and defect, his view required that both understanding and resolution play a role. He did not, though, take sufficient account of the range of resolutions open to a man. Ignoring both choice and will, his work dealt only with preferences for means to happiness, treated as that which had an appeal rather than that which was intrinsically good. A stronger Aristotelian 'ethics' would have made room for the exercise of both choice and will. It and a Kantian 'ethics' would then be supplementary, the Kantian emphasizing what privacy accomplishes by itself, the Aristotelian what privacy expresses in and through the body. Since neither takes into account dimensions of privacy other than the person, strictly speaking they do not offer us an ethics. An ethics must take seriously the existence, nature and functioning of a responsible self. There are some indications in Aristotle's references to the theoretical reason, and in Kant's categorical imperative, that the idea is not alien to their intent. But it is still necessary to go beyond even what they could have said, for their approaches keep one confined to what men ought to decide to be and do. An ethics (still to be considered) also has to speak of what men could make themselves become by using what could make them as perfect as men could be—healthy, privately and publicly.

What is not attended to is sometimes said to be unconsciously grasped. What was once known is sometimes supposed to be stored in a hidden reservoir; what makes one understand and particularly what makes the understanding be affected by and have an effect on other epitomizations is sometimes taken to be the outcome of the working of a distinct agent, the Unconscious. Understanding and resolution, in particular, are often spoken of as though they were loci or expressions of what is below consciousness. There is, of course, more in a privacy than what is understood. And some operations of the understanding occur without supervision or control. But though what is privately done may not be consciously produced, this does not mean that it is the work of some subterranean power expressing itself in all one's acts. To suppose this is unnecessarily to place behind the specific things men do a kind of lake pierced by many sudden fountains—or, alternatively, it is to take a man's privacy to be a neoplatonic One in miniature, somehow able to pluralize itself.

Each privacy is a constant, but it is operative only in the form of specific epitomizations, whose occurrence depends on the activity of the body, on some previously achieved epitomizations, or on epitomizations able to occupy themselves with tasks having no public role. Repressions, displacements, distortions, and hidden memories are derivates, following on what was once consciously entertained. Pushed back into the privacy, they may be elicited again, sometimes in the form they once had. That fact has perhaps led to the view that they are in the privacy in the very form they have when they are expressed.

Members of a conjunctive disjunct are not identifiable with the members of an actual disjunct. The former lack, the latter have boundaries of their own, and are able to act apart from one another. A variegated aboriginal privacy, whose differentiation is one with the distinguishing and separation out of what was before inseparably merged, is therefore quite different from an imagined privacy where separated items are viewed as slipping back intact into it. Since a person and his epitomizations allow for the recovery of what had once been distinguished in them, were the likelihood of being recovered a mark of what was unconscious, it would be necessary to hold that there are many different manifestations of this, able to affect one another in multiple ways. One would also have to suppose that, in each of these manifestations, there were well-demarcated powers which had not yet been expressed. What a man was, apart from any expression, would then be exactly what was expressed, but just hidden for a while.

Analytic philosophers take 'analysis' to be a purely intellectual act, emphasizing what was already distinct. There can be little question but that analyses often serve intellectual purposes. That, though, is far from showing that the analyses are the results of intellectual acts, or that, if they are, that these occur outside the provenance of decisions and simply make evident that what had been in existence before was already fully determinate. It is one thing to distinguish. It is another to make what is distinguished distinct; that requires the maintenance of items apart from one another, outside the control of the act. A capacity to make decisions is then presupposed.

Analysis begins with conjoined items, and proceeds by exercising a decision to separate them from one another. When the items are effectively conjoined through need or other direct involvements, or when they are subject to conditions which affiliate them, subject them to laws, place them in fields, or grade them, analysis has to break through to them as they were when apart from one another. That means the items must have some integrity of their own; otherwise analysis would be identical with creation.

Analysis, at its best, replaces an irrelevant conjunction with a disjunction. The conjunction, even if only of aggregated items, was dependent on the operative presence of a humanly imposed or objective condition able to hold them together. In the absence of such a condition, one would have to deal with each item separately. The fact is readily overlooked in accounts of analysis because the analyst tacitly assumes the position of a condition which allows distinct items to be together, and then takes note of what he finds. His assumption of that position actually incorporates a twofold decision: to take a stand where the various items are just alongside one another, and to refer to distinct items. His resolutions usually express preferences, though it is possible for him to choose to or to will to analyze, and thereupon obligate himself or require some such bodily activity as the production of diagrams. Analysis, strictly speaking, though, is only a moment in a resolution, merely distinguishing items, where a resolution goes on to fasten on one or more of them while allowing the rest to remain together.

Although it makes sense to acknowledge a kind of decisiveness in animals, coming to expression in well-calibrated acts appropriate to what is in fact present, there is no evident need to suppose that they are able to engage in analyses. They sharply distinguish mates and enemies, and focus on needed food and drink. But none of these requires that they privately set distinct items alongside distinct items. They cannot in fact do so, for they have no privacies which they can utilize apart from their bodies. Buridan's ass, if a true ass, never did attend to paired bales of hay which he could conceivably analyze out into distinct bales. Instead, he moved toward one of them because he was inclined toward it at the moment.

It is now possible to resolve an old controversy as to whether or not thought precedes resolution. Thomists maintain that thought comes first for, they say, resolution would otherwise be blind and arbitrary. Scotists maintain instead that resolution precedes thought, since one can decide to think. Their controversy was centered about the role of mind and will in God, the Thomists holding that God does what he knows to be good, the Scotists holding that what God does is necessarily good. Both supposed that there is a God and that he has a mind and makes decisions. Putting aside the fact that both accepted a revelation of a special kind, and were dealing with a mind and resolution quite different from what a man might have, it becomes apparent that their dispute has to do, not with what is known and resolved, but just with what is initially confronted. When one considers an undifferentiated set of items and then makes one or more stand apart, thought precedes resolution. When one assumes the position of a condition, enabling one to attend to items as independent of one another, resolution precedes thought. A God, presumably, might sometimes do the one and sometimes the other—granted that a divine thought and resolution are different from one another.

j. The Person

Sensitivity, sensibility, desire, need, orientation, sociality, understanding, and resolution epitomize a person. They are not distinct faculties, marked out, tensed, ready to be expressed. They become distinct in act, and once in operation, continue to be active for indefinite periods. All the while, the person continues to have an integrity and a conditioning power of his own, able to govern them in relation to one another, and able to be affected by the promise that other epitomizations of the privacy will be elicited.

A person is always publicly manifested in the form of sensitivity, but there are times when his other epitomizations are not expressed or have no discernible bodily expression. While expressing himself in his body, a man may also act independently of his body, his kind, or his society. He can therefore achieve results which may not enable any of these to continue or to prosper.

Not until one attends to the evidence that a man has native rights does one reach the point where the complete nature of his person can be clearly known. Since some of those rights originate with his self and its epitomizations, an examination of his rights must be deferred until the self has been understood. Until then, all that can be said with confidence is that a person can publicly show that he is living his body by means of the epitomizations of his person.

When a man makes aesthetic discriminations, acts to promote the species, and takes on roles, he makes use of and is sustained by his body, without being oriented or controlled by it. Although subhumans also promote their species, and though some of them could even be said to make aesthetic discriminations and to have distinctive tasks to perform, they do not have private lives. They cannot, therefore, encompass their epitomizations in persons, cannot make different epitomizations affect one another, can make no choices, can exercise no will. If they understand and prefer, it must be in ways which differ from man's, if for no other reason than that their preferences and understanding are involved with promises different from those with which human preferences and understanding are involved.

Because only a man is a person, only he can be encountered by other men in acts which thrust indefinitely toward an independently functioning privacy, insistently expressed in and by means of his body. Only a man can be confronted as a 'you'. Since that you is maintained from within, where native rights are possessed and whose public forms others are to protect and support, one who knows him knows him to be a private as well as a public person. What he publicly is, is both faced as a publicly available you, and passed beyond toward a privacy insisting on itself.

We are able to encounter persons because they are public, and because we pass beyond their public guise toward what presents this. When we seek evidence that another is a private person, we trace part of what he is in public back to its private source. We may have doubts at times whether he is alive. But if we know that he is alive, we already know that he is a person, publicly and privately, because we directly move from his public person toward his private person, and sometimes also use the private to understand how the public is to be regarded.

Were men just bodies, they would not be persons. Were their persons wholly private, their rights could never be denied. Were their persons wholly public, they could be exhaustively known through observation, and would be unable to discriminate, want, seek, evaluate, infer, or decide. Were the private sides of their persons simply and directly expressed in public, there would be no rights which they did not publicly urge. Were their private persons entirely independent of their public persons, they would not be necessarily present as you's. Were they just persons, they would not have I's or responsibilities. Were their persons unrelated to their selves, they would not have rights expressed through their persons. Did their persons not precede their selves, they would have been responsible when infants.

Our grasp of another, even when his expressions show that he is privately undergoing pain or pleasure, does not stop abruptly at his sensitivity. We readily pass beyond his expressed sensitivity toward the sensitivity as private, and sometimes even beyond this toward other epitomizations. Although his person will not yet be known to be distinct from the various epitomizations of it, and will never be known as it insistently begins to express itself, we can get enough knowledge of his person to be able to say that he deserves respect, and that he has private rights that need public expression and support.

Each man is able to attend to the public person he is making manifest by approaching it as present in a public world. When he does this, he too inevitably passes beyond his public person into it as privately sustained. He too then uses what he observes as evidence of himself as private, at once expressing itself, sustaining what is publicized, and effectively countering his own advance into himself.

Since a man moves inward from what he himself sustains, what he confronts is himself in the guise of a me. And that is quite different from himself as a you, for a you is never, while a me is always known by the same private being that sustains it. Since both are confronted in public and have the same public guise, the knowledge a man has of his own person is consequently in one sense like and in another unlike the knowledge that others have of him. He may observe exactly what they do, and he may reach no further into his own privacy than they do. But he alone sustains what he publicly faces; what he reaches toward and sustains is both reached and sustained only by him. A you is confronted by one privacy and sustained by another; the very same privacy confronts and sustains a me.

A you is always part of another; a me is always part of oneself. A you is approached solely from without, the surface of what is more recessive; a me is also reached from without, but as both the limit of what is more recessive and the beginning of a move toward that very recessiveness. A you is an other for one who observes and passes beyond it toward its private source and sustainer; a me is observed only by the very being who presents and sustains it.

We know something of what the me of another is like, not because we are acquainted with it, or because we somehow not only observe it but provide it with a sustainer, but because what we learn about his you coincides in part with his me. What we cannot obtain is the qualitative difference that his sustaining makes to the public content which we both face. We can never make contact with his me, for we cannot start from and sustain anything from the side of his privacy. It is also true that we cannot know his you except by approaching him from a position external to him. He, of course, cannot know himself as a you at all. Any attempt to do so would require him to make use of his I, and as a consequence make him reach himself as a me. Just as he alone can know himself as a me, only others can know the you that he presents. Neither the me nor the you is available except to persons, the one by the very person who sustains it, the other by those who are external to the being who presents it.

When men have difficulty in determining whether or not someone else is a person, it is not easy to decide whether it is then also being inconsistently supposed that the man who is being confronted is faced as a you and can face himself as a me. What is clear is that no animal can do either; none knows either you's or me's. Myths, stories, and a belief in the transmigration of souls, though, seem to support the view that persons could occupy animal bodies. If the animals are credited with human speech, taken to be guilty of wrongdoing, or assumed to be able to acquire a human body once certain conditions are fulfilled, their bodies, by that very fact, will be denied to be just animal bodies, able to do nothing more than act or have the potentiality to act in subhuman ways. In effect, one will have already allowed that the supposed animals are humans, somehow hidden by bodies not really theirs. They might run on all fours and be mistaken by all to be just animals but, as they eventually disclose, the animal-like behavior that they exhibit has no bearing on what they are, intend, or do.

Each man is both a private and a public person. His private side is never reducible to what is just incipiently public. If it were, he would not be able to provide evidence of thoughts, resolutions, and rights which may never be publicly urged or acknowledged. If a man neither urges nor acknowledges these he will, of course, provide no evidence of their presence. But once he yields evidence of them in the course of the expression of his privacy, they can be known to exist. No evidence of them may thereafter be available. But at no time is he ever less than a person, both private and public, the one expressed as and evidenced by the other. His private person is his public person freed from the contributions of the body, intensified, less and less accessible, able to become public through diverse expressions which the body sustains and may qualify.

Subhumans express what they must. Men are able to refuse expression to what they could express. We know that they express their private persons, just so far as we are able to see that their well-functioning bodies sustain what does not benefit those bodies. We come to know about deep-lying private powers when we learn that the bodies also act in ways which do not promote the species, a continuance in an environment or milieu, or roles in a society. Encountered as public persons, what men manifest can be used as the beginning of a direct, convergent, intensive move toward epitomizations of their private persons, or as the beginnings of inferences to the nature of those persons. Even when one attends only to a human's cry of pain, one inevitably impinges on a private person coexistent with oneself.

The distinctions we make when understanding what we are doing and what we are, offer a good clue to what we are to look for in other men. Conversely, distinctions between what others do and what they are help us to understand ourselves. We learn something, too, when we attend to those who are ill, unhappy, or in distress, especially when we seek to discover how those states can be overcome and successes increased or preserved. This is best done by keeping clear the difference between what a man is as public and private, by attending to the intensive connection between them, and by recognizing that they can affect one another's functioning. We learn about others in part by reflecting on what we know about ourselves. We learn about ourselves in part by reflecting on what we know of others. But we also know about others because we attend to them, and know about ourselves because we attend to ourselves. If all we knew of others rested on what we knew of ourselves, there would be little point in asking questions, observing, or conversing. And if all we knew of ourselves was a reflection of what we learned of others, we would never have to attend to ourselves.

It is possible to know that something has fallen short or is amiss only if one knows what ought not to be and, therefore, that what occurs stands in contrast with what should have been instead. Calling attention to what may be amiss in a claim, a sceptic shows that he knows that men can be mistaken. Unavoidably, he then assumes that he knows what must be rejected. Claiming that something is misconstrued, he tacitly refers to what is true. If he does not make that reference, he is not a sceptic, but one who does not yet know what to affirm or deny. The better grounded his scepticism is, the more surely will it be grounded in what ought to be acknowledged by all.

Scepticism rests on suppositions which it cannot call into question without undermining itself. It is viable only as a surrogate for a state of wonder or hesitation. But, unlike them, it issues no challenges and grounds no inquiry. If it stops with its initial claim, it rests with a man who is able to question and who thinks he knows what a proper answer to this would be. Were his question directed toward one who could answer, it would be expressed by one who was at least a person awaiting answers from another who is acknowledged to be a person as well, and therefore with a right to be dealt with honestly. Sceptical or not, a man is and functions as a person and deals with others as persons. He can add that he does not yet know how he or anyone else knows if some claim is warranted. If he just stops there, he states a fact about himself which he neither questions nor denies. If, instead, he goes on to say that everyone else is in a similar state, he makes an as yet unjustified claim about all men and the nature of human knowledge.

To be a human is to be a person, at once private and public, affecting the body and insisting on himself through and by means of this. Related forms in animals are so persistently directed at what is bodily pertinent that they cannot even ground the promise of a self. Those animals, of course, have effective privacies of their own—otherwise they would not feel pain or pleasure. Unlike man's, their privacies are not able to initiate activities which are directed toward non-bodily prospects. Producing shelters with good balance and proportion, they have no interest in these for their own sakes, to be enjoyed and not simply used. Animals have no obligations. Able to exercise a kind of preference, none can choose or will, for these would require them to attend to prospects to be realized, sometimes in opposition to what must be done if the animals or their kind are to continue or to prosper.

Each epitomization of a person has a distinctive innermost limit, able to be expressed independently of the rest of it. *Consciousness* is the innermost limit of sensitivity. Were a person always incipiently or actually manifest, his consciousness would be wholly keyed to what his body was undergoing or to what was being confronted. *Susceptibility* is the innermost limit of sensibility, allowing a man to make discriminations in any content. *Want* is the innermost limit of need; were a person entirely involved with his body, he would want only what was within the reach of that body. *Appetence* is the innermost limit of desire, enabling a man to occupy himself, not with what promotes the species, but with what might allow him and others to continue. *Status* is the innermost limit of orientation, allowing a person to take a stand in himself apart from his place in an environment or milieu. *Dignity* is the innermost limit of sociality, where a man can maintain himself despite changes in his society and in the face of its demands. *Contemplation* is the innermost limit of understanding, enabling a man to attend to ideas without concerning himself with their truth or use. *Resoluteness*, finally, is the innermost limit of resolution, serving to keep private activities in accepted grooves. All are possible only to men. Resoluteness, in contrast with the others, also represents the entire person. It here plays a role somewhat like that of the I, which, as will be seen, is at once an epitomization and a representative of the self. Because resoluteness has this role, a man's bodily expressed sensitivity can not only be charged with consciousness and other limits of the other epitomizations of his person, but can present his entire person in a condensed form. A wine might not be just tasted, consciously tasted, or tasted as something appreciated; it might not just satisfy a want or be tasted because this is what a man's status requires him to do. The tasting could be sensitively carried out with consciousness, susceptibility, want, appetence, status, dignity, contemplation, and resoluteness, some more prominent than others at different times.

Once a man charges his sensitivity with the various limits of the epitomizations of his person, it is difficult for him to return to the stage where his sensitivity is exercised in complete independence of those limits. Consequently, he will continue to act as a social being, with the distinctive resoluteness of a person even when he is feeling simple pleasures or pains. If mature, he will supplement and sometimes enrich the result with epitomizations of his self. But well before then, he will carry the promise for this, and thus be one who could become more mature.

TWO

The Self and Its Epitomizations

a. Autonomy

Societies, states, and other organizations usually take a man to be accountable because he is identified as the primary source of desirable or undesirable public occurrences. Sometimes they hold him accountable because he is a convenient or traditionalized object of reward or punishment. All the while, he may or may not have caused the accredited occurrence or outcome. He may even have had nothing to do with it. It may have come about against his vehement verbal and physical opposition, despite his decisions, and regardless of his needs.

A man might claim that he deserved a reward that was not given to him or, more rarely, that he deserved a punishment that he did not receive. He then refers to a private autonomous act by which he took upon himself the status of being accountable. This he could do independently of any attribution of public accountability. But if others do not take him to be worthy of rewards and punishments for what he autonomously initiates, he will usually go on to judge them as incompetent, unperceptive, not able to distinguish what happens to occur from what in fact was begun by a free agent.

Legal references to 'intention' stop short with publicly ascertainable acts of preparation, as indeed they must if they are to be of service to a publicly conducted legal procedure. But one can privately intend without ever making any preparation to carry out what was intended. There is a signal difference between what one then does and a wish. A wish idly considers what one would like to have occur, and for whose realization accountability is not assumed. The wish may have multiple connections with other private occurrences; it may affect them and be affected by them; it may have surfaced because of deep-lying causes; and it may lead one to will and act. But as just occurring within the privacy, the wish does not add to what is autonomously begun. A private intention does.

To determine whether or not there has been a private assumption of accountability, one must know if there had been a bodily expressed preparation to act, and be able to trace this back to a private initiation whose outcome merits reward or punishment. Usually, a man is taken to have assumed accountability when he says he has done so. It is believed that he did so, too, when he is taken to have exercised preference, choice, or will. But we can be confident that he has assumed accountability only if we can learn, through his speech or action, that he rejected publicly provided rewards or punishments because they were undeserved. Such a rejection clearly expresses an autonomous acceptance of accountability.

A man may claim to have assumed accountability for something different from what he is publicly taken to have originated, or for which he is punished or rewarded. This does not mean that he in fact assumed accountability for it. But if one does not allow that he could do this, it would have to be said that his rejection of a publicly ascribed accountability has no private ground; that the private ground is not autonomously produced by the self; or that there is no way of knowing that it exists. The first of these reasons does not allow that rejections of legal, social, or conventional accusations and punishments, or of endorsements and rewards may be valid, reasonable, or honorable; willful, perverse, or in error. It requires us to deny that a man could try to deceive, or could try to avoid a judgment of his intentions. The second acknowledges that a man has a privacy, and perhaps even a self, but does not grant that he can make himself act in publicly desirable or undesirable ways. The third, although it does not deny that he can initiate something other than what is publicly credited to him, denies that an inference to autonomy is possible, and therefore that one could know that a man can reject a publicly ascribed accountability because it conflicts with what he privately initiates. Together, the three stand in the way of the fact that an assumed accountability is at once private, produced, and knowable.

Public accountability automatically characterizes anyone who is made the object of reward or punishment. The very act of rewarding or punishing him makes him publicly accountable, whether or not anything else is said or done. It makes no difference if the rewards are expressed as honors, privileges, benefits, or by signs of admiration or approval, or if the punishments take the form of restraints, fines, or disqualifications, rather than physical injuries. To be rewarded or punished is to be made into a publicly accountable being.

Responsibility (as we shall see), like the autonomous assumption of accountability, does not depend on others. That one does or does not receive praise or blame makes no difference to responsibility. One is responsible if he privately acts for or against what ought to be. He thereby makes himself worthy of honor or condemnation—and that is different from deserving praise or blame, and also, of course, different from receiving reward or punishment. Worthiness waits on no one else's judgment or act; a man makes himself worthy by what he privately does with what ought to be. He may be worthy of respect but be blamed or punished; he may be worthy of condemnation but be praised or rewarded. If he is held to be publicly accountable, and therefore rewarded or punished, it is not necessary for him to have initiated praiseworthy or blameworthy acts, or even to have initiated acts which deserve reward or punishment according to prevailing social standards. Rewarded or punished, he is held accountable, even when he does not deserve praise or blame, or should not be honored or condemned.

It is possible to deny that there is autonomy, and yet make good use of the idea of accountability. We do that when we punish animals. If a drunkard climbs the fence of a bear's enclosure in a zoo and is killed by the bear, the bear is held accountable. No matter what is done with the drunkard, the bear is shot. No one supposes that the bear autonomously began what it did. It is also true that a man might not be held accountable for some of the things which he originated autonomously. Modern societies and states refuse to hold a man accountable for minor deceptions practiced on his own children. So far as the societies and states are concerned, he may deliberately make and break promises to them with impunity, though smaller groups or particular individuals may still hold him accountable, and punish him in ways which might have widespread approval.

Modern theologians take God to act autonomously, but none holds him to be publicly accountable. If he were, it is hard to see in what sense he could be rewarded or punished. Though there are recorded instances of men who refuse to obey a God's commands, as well as reports of generous sacrifices made in thanksgiving to a benevolent God, these could not possibly affect him if he were a perfect being. What is perfect needs nothing, and is beyond the reach of any finite act. Praise can not reward God. Rejections of him, say through violations of his edicts, through blasphemies or by refusals to give him his supposed due, cannot injure him.

Public accountability occurs within the frame of a social morality. Its occasions, instruments, and termini are determined by traditions, conventions, and commands. When the rewards and punishments have no other ground except the caprice of those able to reward or punish, they are unjustified. If the rewards and punishments are other than those which the prevailing morality requires, they are unjustly bestowed. Injustice contravenes the demands of a prevailing social morality; justification finds its ground in such a morality. An autonomous man may devalue what is done to him both because it is taken to be unjust, not what is morally proper, or because it is supposed to be unjustified, not what the society authorizes.

As autonomous, a man begins actions which express what he is independently of others. He stands apart from his body and person, specializing his self in an act which makes him deserving of praise or blame, not because it does or does not satisfy his conscience, or because he is legislator and subject in one, but because it more or less expresses what any self should. That 'any self' is at once more and less than an individual self: more, because it is not limited by a particular body or person, though its presence presupposes theirs; less, because it is only a facet of an individual self. When one acts autonomously, it is the 'any self', what his self has in common with all others, which is specialized in the act.

A start has a purely formal relation to a mere terminus; a beginning is in a tensional relation to a prospective ending. At its start, the autonomous act of one man is like another's precisely because a start, unlike a beginning, is an abstraction. A beginning is a part of a single act and cannot therefore be separated from the unitary activity of an individual self with its unduplicable insistence.

In every enterprise men struggle to make a start give way to a beginning, converting what, in its concreteness, is not well bounded or clear into what is appropriate, usable, on its way to being completed. As long as a painting is just confronted, as long as it is not seen as a unit with its own integrity, it is dealt with as at the start for an appreciation. An actual appreciation requires one to begin to attend to its nuanced unity over a period of time. A passage from a start to a beginning is possible; as a consequence, the start becomes part of a move to that beginning. There is no regress latent here, for a passage from a start to a beginning occurs only if the prospect of the beginning operates on the start to make that start part of that beginning.

Just as we begin with a painting in which a start is not just an abstractable feature but is part of the act of appreciation, so we begin acts as 'any self' without first starting with what is common to all selves. Our action as 'any self' is an integral component in our beginning as a distinctive self, progressing toward a purposed end.

Children have selves. Their immediate awareness that they are being dealt with unjustly makes that evident. The fact that the scope of their judgments is quite limited, and that they too often pivot about needs, makes apparent that the self of a child is not yet the self it could be. The child is nevertheless autonomous, and so far on a footing with other humans. It too is a member of a kingdom of ends in which each human is a unit alongside every other. It is that position which the de-individualized aspect—the self in the guise of 'any self'—occupies, giving the individual self the status of a unit coordinate with others, while the individual self enables the 'any self' to be embodied in what is done.

Unless one knows how a society functions, it is not possible to determine, from a knowledge of the acts for which men make themselves to be privately accountable, whether or not they are publicly accountable for those acts, or even whether they are accountable at all. The fact that their condition has been improved or worsened provides no indication that they were rewarded or punished by their society. It surely does not provide an indication that they had been rewarded or punished by some God. But men's ready belief that their improvement or worsening is due to the acts of a society or God perhaps reveals an awareness of the fact that their own acts have private grounds, and that a proper response to them requires proportionate rewards and punishments. It is tempting then to suppose that what men do is always met by appropriate responses. But there need never be such responses. The final proper reward for being right is being right; the final proper punishment for being wrong is being wrong.

Because societies have no explicit laws, no well-codified sets of demands, one learns best what they permit and forbid by living in them. The admonitions and corrections of elders channel the activities of the young along the well-grooved paths trodden by those who lived before. When the society changes, its ways of determining who is accountable also change. With different kinds of activity, at different times, and over the course of their histories, different demands are emphasized. Men who fitted well within older patterns are discommoded. They are then somewhat like the young they had taught and corrected, men who are punishable for failing to do what is socially required.

Holding oneself to be accountable for what one is being held accountable is a quite different act from assuming accountability. By holding himself to be accountable, a man endorses what his society does; by assuming accountability, he initiates acts that he would like his society to endorse. The holding oneself accountable stops with the acknowledgment that one's society acted properly. But if accountability is assumed, one privately sets out to do what presumably should be done.

An autonomous man assesses what his society demands and does. By holding himself accountable, he yields to its ways. The assumption and the holding are both private acts, but where the one is the autonomous work of a private self, the other does no more than offer a private endorsement of what society independently does. Although it may be couched in terms of right and wrong, that endorsement is not the act of a self; it is instead the act of a person, primarily expressing a preference, usually qualified by understanding, and having some effect on how he chooses and wills.

Although Oedipus had no knowledge of the fact that the woman he married was his mother, even he took himself to be accountable for the act, and punished himself in accord with the outlook of his society. Had he seen himself to have autonomously initiated a horrible act—a possible view in the light of his recorded outburst of temper with a consequent murder of his father, and his impulsive threats—he would have distinguished his individual self from the common 'any self' it incorporated, and could therefore have ended by despising himself. Had he merely found himself to be accountable according to the standards of his society, he might have quietly accepted the punishment that was due him.

Some men do not fit well within their societies. Some oppose their societies deliberately. Others are just unable to function in them. The same treatments are usually accorded all, whether or not they are autonomous and have assumed accountability. In order to know whether they have done so, one must move beyond a society's concerns and attend to what does not and cannot interest it.

A reasonable man knows the main activities and outcomes for which his society holds him accountable. But it sometimes requires a council of supposedly wise men, or those who are knowledgeable in traditional practices, to decide hard or unusual cases. When men are held to be sources or occasions for the occurrence of what is societally endorsed or rejected, it is not often known whether or not they did in fact produce it. Only rough judgments can usually be made about causes of socially significant acts. Sometimes the question is ignored. When kings and generals are rewarded for victories achieved by others on a battlefield quite far away, or are pulled down by failures committed by underlings, no effort is made to justify the acts by claims that the kings or generals were in fact causes, or were even essential.

Well before a state arises, there are societies. And after a state has been established, the society which preceded it may continue to be. The state's organization, specified authorities, articulated demands, identified agencies of enforcement, and distribution of rewards and punishments will rarely coincide with those that the society provided.

Conventions, superstitions, habitual practices, rituals, and rites of passage, marriage, and death are carried out by men who are held accountable by their societies for acting or failing to act in rather precise ways and sometimes in considerable disaccord with what a state prescribes. If a state were to set itself in rigid opposition to a society's well-intrenched patterns, more likely than not it would find itself sullenly defied, and eventually overthrown. All the while, both the society and state may act in ways which do not accord with what an assumed accountability requires.

Law is an agency of a state. By its means the state articulates demands, one set of which deals with what men are required to do or refrain from doing. To be effective, the law must be backed by the threat of force, with a consequent punishment for violators, and occasional rewards for those who do what, or more than what, is demanded. Despite references to intent, law, since it seeks to confine itself to publicly available data, does not go beyond the attribution of public accountability. Yet most men, again and again, quickly pass from the legal accreditation of accountability to the supposition that accountability had been assumed, or that an act had been responsibly initiated. Over the course of criminal law's thousands of years of more and more refined formulations and decisions, men have come to suppose that law is properly carried out only if it terminates at those who are at once the causes of proscribed acts and have assumed accountability or are just responsible for them.

Since, by and large, men have no clear understanding of how to determine what a cause is and exactly how it operates, they have to rest with a rough-hewn, unquestioned supposition that every mature man can privately initiate or resist initiating what directly affects the welfare and lives of others. The more important the occurrence, the more likely it is that there will be a passage from the assessment of others as having assumed accountability—and thus as having acted in public on the basis of an envisagement of what a society or state endorses or rejects—to an assessment of the actions of men in the light of what ought to be done, regardless of what the society or state decrees, or how either of these acts.

Although in the minds of perhaps everyone, justice in criminal law is not wholly sundered from a grounding of a publicly acknowledged cause in a privately responsible being, legal justice concerns itself only with a publicly attributed accountability. Law's justification is that it enables a state to function consistently, fairly, and efficiently. It requires a state to encourage and restrain, reward and punish, but not necessarily those who are the primary causes of what is done. A state and its laws ignore the question whether or not the acts were preceded by private intentions or deliberation.

The determination of accountability tends to be made on the basis of what will maximally promote peaceful, public interplay, regardless of the virtues, vices, causal power, or actions of those involved. One law, consequently, may set a limit to the time when a man will be held accountable for his debts. Another law may require an employer to recompense employees for injuries the employees had themselves caused and for which they may or may not have privately assumed accountability but for which they are responsible. A third may demand taxes of all those who have incomes above a certain amount, regardless of how these were acquired, even taking men who are engaged in illegal enterprises to be accountable for payments to the same extent that others are. When lawyers speak of intent, understandings, misrepresentations, fraud, and the like, they stop with anticipatory, publicly discoverable forms of what is publicly done, even while the rest of men move on, in cases of vital importance, to make judgments about responsibility.

When modern states deal with mass murderers, those who eat their young, or who commit other horrendous crimes, it is customary to set up tests to determine whether or not the perpetrators can give some indication that they had assumed accountability. Putting aside the question as to whether or not the tests show what they are supposed to show, it is not to be overlooked that a man might have assumed accountability for certain acts and not for others. It is conceivable that a mass murderer may know right from wrong in the quiet of his cell and still not have assumed accountability for his crimes. He could be mature, thoughtful, careful, and still not have been able to avoid, in one particular case, what he would rather not have done. It is not possible to determine from a study of the acts for which men are held accountable whether or not they autonomously produced them, unless one can find that those men can distinguish right from wrong. That distinguishing differs from the demand of the M'Naghten rule for determining legally pertinent accountability, for it is ascertained—not as the rule is, through publicly administered tests—from actual evidence that social determinations of right and wrong were privately judged to be incorrect.

By the M'Naghten rule, men are punishable if they show that they know what is legally right to do but do not do it. That condition could well be met by one who acts autonomously. Yet such a man might not do what a state endorses; knowing what this is, he may not do it because he deems it to be improper. A strict application of the M'Naghten rule would compel one to take such an objector to the prevailing mores to be mad. In practice this difficulty is bypassed by limiting the use of the rule to homicide cases where what is done is wrong both from the position of society and from that of an autonomously acting self.

Men are held to be criminally insane when they are held to be publicly accountable for serious violations of socially established norms of behavior—and therefore to be justifiably confined—but not to have privately initiated and accepted what is traced back to them. The men might of course have made themselves privately accountable, but may not have accepted their publicly accountable acts as continuations of the assumed accountability. Theirs may prove to be a persistent and dangerous condition. Similar radical disconnections between the two accountabilities are not altogether unknown to the rest of us. Again and again, we not only fail to make proper provision for a private accountability or to give the result a satisfactory role relative to other private powers, but fail to continue an assumed accountability into a public act and thereby connect it with a public accountability.

In the attempt to blunt criticism, men occasionally speak of deliberately disconnecting an assumed private from a public accountability. They say that they do their public duty, or that they go about their public work well aware that they then fail to live up to a private accountability. This is the defense of the bureaucrat, the party man. Apparently, he is not aware that he voluntarily accepts a condition which a slave is forced to adopt. Excessive modesty leads others to claim that publicly accountable acts for which they are rewarded are independent of those for which they are privately accountable. Sometimes they speak of themselves as mere instruments used by some benign power. But if they were, they would be involuntary slaves of a noble lord. Where the bureaucrat takes privately and publicly accountable acts to occur in separated domains, the overly modest man does not allow that what is publicly credited to him is ever rightly credited to his privacy. The opposites of those who disconnect the two accountabilities in the attempt to avoid criticism are men who suppose themselves to be privately accountable servants of a beneficent master. The opposites of those who overmodestly deny that they are publicly accountable for public outcomes make a similar denial with respect to undesirable public acts, excusing themselves as having been caught up in unfortunate circumstances beyond control. The avowals and disavowals have strong ethical and moral coloring. All of us are alert to them, particularly when expressed by outstanding public figures. Even when it is affirmed that all human action is a function of genetic constitution, education, tradition, environment, or other forces originating outside men's privacies, public figures are judged by others not only in terms of what they do, but in the light of what they avow and disavow. Without hesitation, the statements of public figures are often taken to reveal something of what they are privately.

It is not often that we readily accept other similar reports as being correct. Why here? Is it not because the men add explanations supposedly justifying why they are to be differently assessed from what their acts would require? If we accept their reports, we take some part of their public acts to be excluded from our assessments. Their reports of what they do are then used to tell us how they are to be judged. If we did not accept their reports as true, we would have to take the men to be lying or to be confused.

One who falls short of what the rest are able to do can still be credited with an equal dignity. We do not know how to do much to help him act as well as the others do, but occasionally we can do a little. Were the problem in principle beyond solution, we would not only have to take both the criminally insane and those out of control to be different in kind from the rest, but would have to attribute their improvements to accident. Yet it is no accident that some men, finding that they have lost control on some crucial occasion, prepare themselves to avoid a repetition.

Churchill thought that the Nazi leaders should not have been brought to trial, but instead should have been summarily shot. Granted that we know that they caused or occasioned or in other ways were accountable for the horrors which still challenge our comprehension, Churchill was more correct than those who went through the pretense of determining whether or not those Nazis knew what they did. The performance of unspeakable crimes is warrant enough to subject the perpetrators to serious constraints and, in a period of war, to summary death sentences. Such treatment carries with it a judgment of public accountability.

Private accountability has its own nature at the same time that it is subject to modification and control by other private powers. Through the agency of the person, it may come to expression in public acts. It can be present apart from consciousness—a fact which it is customary to acknowledge under such headings as 'instinct', 'drive', and 'conatus'— working to overcome distortions, gaps, and incoherencies in what is privately done.

Although we rarely attend to our private accountability, we occasionally catch a glimpse of it when, in anger or when careless, we manifest what we would rather not exhibit. Our condemnation of ourselves for what we publicly did at those times points to us as accountable for what in fact we would rather not have allowed to escape into the open.

Man alone can make himself be privately accountable. His private accountability can be well prepared for in a concessionary act by which maximal room is provided for what his private accountability brings about. If only minimal room is provided, he will express himself authoritatively. When in between these two extremes he is dignified.

A concession need not be conscious, deliberate, or willed. We learn of our own and of others' concessions primarily by attending to what is publicly done, and noting the persistence of the type of private activity that this carries out, often in the face of serious obstacles. A man may find himself conceding to act accountably without knowing how or why. If he is tempted to speak in biographical terms, he will talk about genetic dispositions; if in ethical, of native excellence or corruption; if in religious, of divine determinations. But then it will be difficult, if not impossible, to understand how his concession could be changed, redirected, strengthened, or weakened. Fortunately, a lack of understanding of how one concedes or how a concession could be changed does not require the supposition that the concession is unavoidable or unalterable.

The concessions of little children are either faint or non-existent. Usually, we find it comparatively easy, with the help of threat or punishment, encouragement or rewards, to have them change the type of acts in which they engage. More likely than not, we then attend only to what they might accountably do in public. Sometimes, though, threats and punishments, encouragements and rewards prompt the children to prepare for an assumed accountability in better ways. Although mature men have a greater power than children, they also have more indurated and established habits, making them less ready than children to provide opportunities for their latent, greater powers to be expressed.

We are now faced with the paradox that a child can mend its ways, perhaps more easily than most adults, even though its privacy and its body are poorly articulated, and neither well-known nor well-trained. The paradox is weakened with the recognition that what a child expresses is readily altered, thereby making it relatively easy for other private powers to be elicited, and the child enabled to act persistently in other directions.

Genuine attempts at self-reform begin from privacy and particularly with an assumed accountability which had been well prepared for. Because children are comparatively unformed, they neither need nor are able to engage in such reform. Indeed, neither they nor adults can be rehabilitated, if by that one means an alteration in their concessions by the imposition of external constraints, or by the promise of desirable goods. These devices are effective only so far as they elicit private powers, individually possessed and capable of being individually used.

The removal of temptation, strong discouragement, and an encouragement of various acts, though they may result in a radical change, do not yield what they should, even when they make one reluctant to engage in what is undesirable. A substitution of desired behavior for a changed concession always leaves open the possibility that the undesired activity will reappear under new conditions. A burnt child does not make such a substitution; it stays away from fire under many different conditions, because the memory of the burn leads to new responses for an indefinite time.

When authority has been lost, it is difficult to recover it; and when it is strong but narrow in range, one tends to take an assumed accountability to be distracting and even wrong-headed. Fortunately, the situation is not hopeless. Sooner or later, one calls on hidden reserves. Changes externally produced make a difference to the expression of private powers, and even the most listless of men has imperious appetites and needs. Easy to state in principle, the corrections may be heartbreakingly difficult to elicit in fact. But were they not at all possible, the fanatic and the lethargic would belong to a different species from the rest of us. Once it is seen that everyone has moments when he is too zealous or too lax, it is not difficult to recognize that he differs from others only in degree. If more persistent, less flexible, more withdrawn, or self-centered than others, he still is not different in kind.

By avoiding the extremes of both concession and authority, one is able to reach a point of a proper self-respect, a just evaluation of his private value. Pride, arrogance, and smugness mark a mistaken self-respect. Self-contempt, self-abasement, and the minimization of one's own value err in the opposite direction. Yet there are cultures and times when one is endorsed and the other condemned.

Apart from the undesirable acts which the distortions might encourage, there is nothing much to regret in either a man's exaggeration or minimization of his private value. Nevertheless, we resent the exaggerator, taking him to offer a challenge to us, to tempt fate, or to defy whatever God there be. And we are sorry for the minimizer, taking him to denigrate man unnecessarily. Despite the fact that the first might be quite happy and even might act on behalf of others, while the second, though perhaps not joyous or sure of himself, might have found a position where he can function best and with maximum satisfaction, we want them to change their ways. Neither of them, though, usually pays much attention to critics, the arrogant taking them to be jealous or treating their judgments as having comparatively little worth, the self-abased taking them to be bad teachers who recommend foolhardiness, or who want one to overlook serious personal faults. The critics, to be sure, might be jealous, but still right in resenting the exaggeration. They might offer bad advice, but still be right to pity. Granted that this is so, and putting aside the dubious supposition that the exaggerator is asking for trouble and that the minimizer is cheapening man, a problem still remains. Why are we so strongly affected by these deviants? A plausible answer is that the one apparently gets what is desirable unwarrantedly, while the other makes an unnecessary sacrifice. Why should we care, as long as they do nothing to us? Is it not that we take both to incarnate a judgment of our inferiority or superiority relative to them? Whether or not they attend to us, when we attend to them, we see from their walk and talk, their emphases and attitudes, that they implicitly take us to be relatively less or more than they. This would not disturb us did we not take them to measure us.

We find it hard to discover by an examination of ourselves whether or not we are holding ourselves to be higher or lower than we should. We therefore look to others to provide us with a measure for ourselves, objecting to those who exaggerate or minimize themselves because they do not seem to take us to measure them. Disturbed when we take them to measure us, we resent them because they are apparently not disturbed in turn. We try to escape being measured by them through laughter and pity, thereby tacitly confessing that we are not trying to change them. But when irritated beyond control, we try to humiliate, embarrass, disgrace the exaggerator, hoping to make him become aware of the weak hold he has on his own destiny. Or, aroused to compassion, we try to support, encourage, or love the minimizer, hoping to make him awaken to his value. We then make evident that we believe both to have reserves whose expressions provide a needed balance.

b. Responsible Action

Things and animals, and sometimes men as well, it has already been remarked, are often held accountable for outcomes for which they were just occasions, causes, or convenient objects of reward or punishment. Unlike men, things and animals cannot assume accountability, since they have no separately operating privacies. As a consequence, they cannot be guilty—and therefore, of course, cannot be innocent. They deserve neither praise nor blame. We recognize a man to differ from them when we face him as a fellowman, and therefore as one whose privacy operates as an independent power, initiating acts guided by prescriptive prospects. While we take him to be accountable in the very act of acknowledging him to be the object of reward and punishment, we know that he also assumed accountability only if he makes evident that he takes himself not to deserve the rewards or punishments he receives. That fact he makes manifest in his protests, acts of disobedience, and in his publicly expressed assessments of others, their functionings, and their instruments, severally or together.

When a man takes himself to deserve rewards and punishments different from those which are bestowed, he implicltly reports an assumed accountability—and incidentally, that he has a self, since this is epitomized by that assumed accountability. He is not judged to be responsible, though, until he is taken to be one who is required to produce what finally ought to be. He is properly judged to be so, of course, only if he is in fact responsible. And this he is, once he reaches the stage where his individual self can make what is common to it and any other into a representative of that self. Did this not occur, not only would each self be radically individual—as it in fact is—but there would not be anything which it had in common with other selves except general features and a subordination to controlling conditions. Were different selves just instances of something common, they would exhibit this, but would not be the selves of individuals or be in possession of what was common to all.

A man need not know that he is responsible or that he acts responsibly. It suffices that he has epitomized his self in the form of a responsibility, and thus is at a stage of development beyond where he can be autonomous. The fact that he is responsible makes his every act objectively right or wrong. Even when he acts 'irresponsibly', he is still responsible for what he does.

A man's responsibility does not await anyone's acknowledgment or depend on his acting voluntarily. He will not, however, be known to have a responsible self except so far as one can find and make use of evidence showing that he has developed beyond the stage of being a person, and has then made himself be like every other self, within the confines of which he expresses what he uniquely is, and where he is to be assessed in absolute terms.

The most satisfactory evidence that others are responsible for what they do is provided by their public acknowledgment that someone else is responsible. By taking another to be responsible, they reveal themselves to be responsible as well, for only those who are responsible can take others to be so.

In the ordinary course of life, responsibility is not often focused on, though it is not altogether neglected. Usually, others are assessed as more or less measuring up to some conventional standard. The standard, even in primitive societies, demands much that responsibility itself requires. When fairly clear at its center, it can be well used in most cases; when blurred, its applicability will not be evident. The standard offers little help when one is faced with hard or borderline questions. It is, moreover, usually adopted without sufficient awareness that it may have been affected by established social classifications and traditions. To escape from these limitations one must use a final good to measure all else.

The traditional view that man has a created soul allows one to affirm that this is subject to absolute demands. Assuming that the demands are made by the creator of that soul, they are supposed to have an insistence and a justification which turn the denial or neglect of those demands into a blasphemous opposition to what the creator prescribes. The view not only makes men responsible for what is alien to them; it supposes that they, despite their finitude, are somehow able to withstand a divine and presumably imperious insistence. But surely, what men ought to do is not what some other being—no matter how noble or powerful—demands, but what they have made themselves responsible for in the very fact of having selves.

We know that others are responsible without first attending to ourselves, and then supposing that those others are like us. We attend to what they say and do, taking no time to think or to make comparisons between them and us. When we come to judge ourselves, we make use of publicly available evidences, jsut as we do when we judge them. Although we alone may have access to that evidence, and though each of us comes to it from a private position, it is in the public world, having been exhibited there through the help of our bodies. Considerable reflection and sophistication are often needed to enable us to determine exactly what we privately produced or what was added to this. Still, we have little difficulty in finding some evidence of privacy and, in a single move, passing beyond that evidence toward its more purified, intensive, unitary, private source.

It has already been remarked that no animal's feelings, need, or desire epitomize a person. All the more surely, an animal cannot have a self, and therefore cannot assume accountability or become responsible. None can attend to ideals, truth, beauty, science, politics, ethics, or art. Nor can its privacy be articulated in the form of a plurality of powers able to act on one another, apart from what its body is or does. Able to provide miscues, it does not know how to deceive. Never self-conscious, it knows no shame. None ever blames itself, or should. To say that we do not know

whether or not men are different from all other kinds of living beings is to
forget these truths and, among other things, to confess that we do not
know whether or not men alone are responsible beings. If one goes on to
hold that all that is or can be known is what is public, is caught in a
common language, or is a function of economics, history, biology,
chemistry, physics, instinct, tradition, or custom, one incidentally maintains that no one can be, or can be known to act responsibly. We honor
those who make these and similar claims when we say that they are
speaking irresponsibly, for we then take their acts to fall short of what is
endorsed by a distinctive, human responsibility that characterizes them as
well as others.

Unless what a man privately does is freely done, he does not act responsibly. Were his privacy a set of secret springs and sluices imitating in a
shadow world what mechanists think occurs in a public, observable one,
he might still be distinguished from all other kinds of beings, but he would
not be responsible. If the springs and sluices were peculiar to him and had
no counterparts or simpler versions in what was subhuman, he would be
quite distinct from them but, like them, would still not be responsible
Were his responsibility just an incipient form of what could be public, all
expressions of it would make it public. But men are responsible at times
for thinking, willing, or being autonomous, and for other private acts.
Their failure to make the acts conform to what a final good requires, and
which they ought to realize, means that they are less good than men
should be.

Responsible acts have causes. They also have effects. Those effects are
achieved linearly or constitutively. Linear causes exist before their effects
do. Those effects are brought about, not by the causes alone, but by these
and temporally extended processes of causation which begin at those
causes and convert the effects, as merely possible and future, into later,
actual effects. As a consequence of a process of linear causation, a possible
effect becomes present and determinate and is sometimes able to function
as a cause for a subsequent effect of its own. The process of linear causation, whether taking place in a public world or within a privacy, freely
adds determinations to the possible effect which the cause necessitates
along the lines of natural laws. In contrast with a linear cause, a constitutive cause need take no time to bring about an effect. Its effect can be
present when it is. But in order for an effect to be able to stand apart from
its constitutive cause, it must be sustained by something outside it and the
cause. In a modified form, a failure to see this is at the center of the views
of those theologians and philosophers who, with Augustine and Descartes, take the universe to depend for its existence, moment after mo-

ment, on a constitutive act of God. Not recognizing any power other than God's, they are unable to show how the effects of his acts could be separated from him, and therefore be other than dangling appendages. From a different perspective and along a different route they therefore end where Neoplatonists inevitably do, with something derivative, incapable of being detached from its constitutive source and therefore unable to be an actual effect of this.

When a man privately initiates a public act, he acts both linearly and constitutively, and as freely as he does when he acts just constitutively. His freedom is consistent with a strict linear determinism, where this is understood to involve the occurrence of effects that are logically entailed by their causes and are to exist after these. But if a man acted only in this way, exhibiting freedom only in the form of a linear production of determinations in necessitated effects, he would do nothing more than make a possible effect be actual and present at a subsequent moment. He would not have acted responsibly. He may have been autonomous, privately accountable for public outcomes, but he would not have engaged in a responsible act, since he would not have acted under the governance of what ought to be. If what he does occurs solely within his privacy, his responsiblity will be exercised in private. If the resultant effects are expressed in public actions, evidence of the responsibility will be available, even if all that is publicly done is to wrongly claim that one had not acted responsibly.

A prospect is a possibility and therefore necessarily indeterminate. Some determinations are introduced into the possibility when this is privately used. Further acts are required before the prospect can be made fully determinate, realized as a bounded unit, set in a larger world. As still future, it is an unseparated nuance in a single possibility relevant to whatever is now actual. On being realized, it is disconnected, specified, and related by negation to the rest of the undivided possibility.

Aristotle acutely remarked that tomorrow's sea fight is not a sea fight now won or now lost by us, but only a possibly won-or-lost sea fight, a sea fight which is not yet determinately won or determinately lost by us. 'Won-or-lost' is a conjunct disjunct. The actual battle is a means by which each side introduces further determinations into this, and thereby changes it into a sea fight that is won or lost. It is tempting to stop at this point and maintain that one is here faced not with a possible won-or-lost seafight, but with a won-seafight or a lost-seafight. But these, too, are partially indeterminate until the battle has been fought. The battle determines whether the sea fight is won or lost easily or with difficulty, whether it takes minutes or hours. If one supposed that these determinations, and an endless number of others were already ingredient in the possibility, one would not yet have overcome the radical difference that separates what is merely possible from what is produced by some present act. Wherever and whenever something is responsibly begun, it has a determinateness it would otherwise lack. It has, though, less determinateness than it would have were it carried out. But at both times, an obdurate intensity is present which no prediction or articulation encompasses; at both times, adventures are undergone that were not otherwise possible.

Although decisions are often responsibly made, a responsible act is not equatable with a decision. Apart from the fact that a decision is the work of a person while a responsible act is the work of a self, and thus of a man who has matured beyond the stage where decisions are made, a decision makes use of an attractive, obligating, or fixated prospect, while a responsible act is constitutively caused by what finally ought to be as then and there pertinent to what is being done. If a responsible man does not act responsibly, which is to say, if he does not act as his responsibility requires, his responsibility still continues to be attached to the final good. Although defied in his act, his responsibility toward that good will affect the act, to make this what he ought not to have produced.

A decision may be guided by thought, consciously made. It could begin a chain of events which will not in fact lead to the realization of what ought to be. If it is made by a responsible being, his self will qualify what is decided, marking it as radically right or wrong, because assessed by what is absolutely good. That good is not itself very good; it is only a possibility of a perfect harmony of all beings and acts. Within its compass every occurrence has a place, but only as allowing a place for all else. Because there are many different kinds of beings and acts, and because there are many ways of harmonizing them maximally, the good that is an inescapable prospect for a mature man is no more than a largely indeterminate ideal. The fact does not stand in the way of the ideal's capacity to measure the worth of whatever is privately begun or publicly performed.

A particular act more or less meshes with what else there then is. To the extent that an act cannot fit in with others, to that extent either the act or both it and the others are defective relative to one another. Yet either or both may be what ought or ought not to be, as measured by a final good. This does not just endorse whatever particular harmony of items may have been brought about at some time; it allows for such a harmony only provisionally. A final evaluation takes account of all occurrences. What is done by a man living up to his responsibility in a given epoch may not be what the good finally requires, so that one who at a given time does what he ought may fall quite short of being as excellent as a man can and ought to be. An Aristotelian high-minded man is the best of Greeks, carrying out his duties and living a full life, but only as part of a seriously defective world, with its slaves, biases, poverty, classes, and limited range. He does what he ought at his time, but this is less than what the final good requires.

Good men are good in their settings. Whether or not they are also good absolutely depends in part on how good their settings are. If they live in the light of eternity, ignoring the value of the settings in which they inevitably are and where they inevitably act, they fail in still another way. The best of men has to do justice to whatever goods there may then be and to those that will be. Unfortunately, no one knows what will eventually ensue.

Practically, it is desirable to know what benefits mankind, not as a mass, but as a plurality of individuals within a common civilization where the arts, sciences, philosophy, industry, and peace all flourish. That ideal makes it possible to oppose and alter prevailing states of affairs, even those in which all fit well but at a lower level then they could. The final good needs for its realization the radical reconstruction and relating of established and even desirable harmonious, satisfying wholes so that a greater and greater, more and more comprehensive good can be realized, and in which the losses involved in modifying or abandoning what is satisfactory for a time will be more than balanced by greater goods in which all can share and from which all can benefit. What he ought to do at a particular time is to act so as to help realize the next stage of civilization, where all are better enhanced and harmonized, but in such a way that a still higher stage is made possible. Unable to do more than act when and where he is, a man should attempt both to preserve what is excellent and to enrich what falls short of this, thereby laying the ground for a more successful venture in the future.

No matter how well-organized—indeed, the more surely it is well-organized—what stands in the way of the achievement of a civilized life by all must be rejected; what is less than men could attain must be altered; what deserves to continue, no matter what the state of the world, should be preserved. Men will differ on just what is required of them. Even if equally good and wise, they will disagree about what is to be done now and what is to be done later, or on how successful one kind of activity will be and the price it will require in contrast with others. Life presents a stupendous challenge to the man who takes his responsibilities seriously. The fact that he is concerned with doing what he ought does not mean that what he does will be what best accords with what the final good requires then or later.

Character is the outcome of the accumulation of the various degrees to which acts have been controlled by the final good and therefore are responsibly performed. If a man has a good character, this will not prevent him from acting badly at various times. Not will a bad character prevent a man from occasionally doing what he ought. But if a man continues to act as he ought not he will build habits which will tend to make him give little weight to what he should initiate, just as surely as he will tend to act as he ought if he has built a good character.

No one has a completely and persistently bad or good character. It is no more possible for him to do only what he ought not, than it is for him to do only what he ought, even when this is limited to what he ought to do so far as his present knowledge and circumstance permit. A conceivable steady career in which he did what ought not to be done would require him to persistently use his mind and resolution properly, while a conceivable steady career in which he did what ought to be done would be disturbed by insistent expressions of the epitomizations of his person, the acts of his body, and the demands of autonomy.

A man is to be perfected, made excellent as a private and a public being. As the latter, he is to be perfected both as he exists apart from all others and as together with them. As apart, his possible perfection requires that he attain a harmony in his privacy, in his body, and between his privacy and his body. If he does this he will be hale, sound, i.e., healthy.

It is possible for a man to make the achievement of his health be the primary result that he attempts to produce. But if he does only this, he will be one who is and becomes less than a man should be, since he will then necessarily neglect to some degree the demand that whatever else there be also be perfected.

A responsibly governed activity is freely produced. The course and outcome of that activity need not be unexpected. As Bradley remarked, we are not surprised to find that an honest man acts honestly. The character he formed makes actions along that line more, not less likely, without precluding occasional acts of an opposite tenor. We cannot deduce what is to occur, but we can know what will be done for the most part, once we know the nature of the character that has been formed.

Incorporating our concept of the good in our judgment of what is done by a man, we make use of our own responsibility, not in order to engage in an act similar to his, but to affect our estimate of him. As a consequence, we will responsibly add an evaluation to our articulation of what he does, thereby making our understanding of him be responsibly governed. We could, of course, first find out what he does and then assess it responsibly. If we did, a detached observation would be carried out on our responsibility. But though we could do this, perhaps when we were trying to review his career and make a summary judgment of his character, we usually assess him in the very act of attending to what he is doing, while remembering a short course of activities, or some signal set of acts for which he had been responsible. In the one way, we would make a responsible judgment of him; in the other, responsibly judge him. In the one we would impose our responsibility on our private understanding before we moved on to attend; in the other, we would responsibly face what he makes evident. The one is not necessarily a more or a less reliable method than the other, or more or less the act of a mature man.

A responsible man is one whose self has developed beyond the stage where he can act only autonomously. He does not become less than or equal to those who are not responsible when he fails to act as he ought, but continues to be a responsible being, subject to a prescriptive final excellence, while doing less than he can and should. Had he not yet attained the stage where he was responsible, or were he unable to impose his responsibility on what he was doing, he would still be able to express his person through the agency of its different epitomizations. When we are uncertain as to whether or not any epitomization of his privacy is operative, we are also uncertain whether or not we are dealing with a human being.

If a man is drugged or driven to extremes by hunger, thirst, or punishment, is deranged, or is otherwise out of control, he is still responsible for whatever he did to bring himself to such a pass. If he did not contribute to the situation, he is still responsible for the judgments he passes on what happens to him. Unable at that time or later to pass a sound judgment, he will not be able to bring his responsibility to bear. When he allows the place of sound judgment to be usurped by superstition, faith, hope, fear, he brackets his maturity. But if in fact mature he is responsible for what he does, and therefore for his poor judgment and improper acts.

Responsibility, like other epitomizations, is not a fixed quantity or faculty. It comes to be. It can be bracketed, and it can be ignored. Usually it is effectively present for a considerable period. But whether it is or is not effectively present, it is always part of a mature man's privacy, relating him to a final good which assesses his acts as absolutely right or wrong.

The world sometimes overwhelms. Circumstances may be beyond a man's power to control. No one can withstand the force of a tornado or an earthquake, or check his fall from a height by an act of will. No increase in technology or knowledge will enable him to control the rest of the world. Not only is much of it outside his reach, but his use of it depends on its having an existence and force of its own. Separately and together with others, each man is in a world that goes its own way, sooner or later making evident its final mastery of him. The fact shows how mistaken are those who take man to create, constitute, or control through mind, will, or intention whatever else there be.

Were the world really man's creature, he would be responsible for allowing it to deny him the opportunity to act responsibly. Prevented from acting responsibly by this or that natural circumstance, he is still not deprived of the power to make responsible decisions, or to act responsibly in other areas. Even when forced to run precipitously by ferocious animals, sudden floods, or falling rocks, he may be able to act responsibly toward those in his care. Nor is his status as a responsible being necessarily compromised when he is precluded by circumstance from acting responsibly in the public world. He will still be able to act responsibly on epitomizations of a privacy not publicly expressed. Of course there are times when he cannot act responsibly, publicly or privately. He might not only be subjected to threats and displays of might, but to powerful physically enforced coercions by other men, society, or state, or to pains so great that no man, and surely no ordinary man, or he in particular, could possibly withstand them. He could not then possibly act responsibly.

Bodily functions can be slowed or speeded by emphases on sensitivity, need, or desire. Some bodily functions seem beyond the reach of these, and are carried out in sleep, when in a stupor, or when one is upset or indifferent. Some are quite insistent, perhaps never to be entirely denied. Though there are men who seem able to starve themselves to death, it is hard to find someone who can remain thirsty for long in the presence of water. There are also uncontrollable movements of the blood, chemical processes going on in the stomach, lungs, and heart. Even if it is granted that by some act of thought or will some of these can be radically changed, it still remains true that there are occasional spasms, emotions, and appetites which arise no matter what one decides or plans. No will is so strong, no intellect is so powerful, no virtue is so insistent but that the body sometimes acts without regard for their presence or demands. Evidently a man's responsibility has limits, outside of which there are not only controlling circumstances and coercions, but inescapable, unconquerable forces. His status as a mature being must be said to be held in abeyance by them, denying it an opportunity to be expressed.

It has taken a long time to get over the idea that a man is just a body through which irresistible instincts or drives make their way into the public world. We have slowly come to see that early deprivations may preclude later uses of the eyes, that the absence of love and talk, the infliction of serious and inexplicable punishment, the denial of opportunities to express curiosity, to use the imagination, to feel accepted, wanted, or useful can have deep, searing effects, standing in the way of the responsible production of various acts. The illustrations are not important. What is important is the fact that responsibility's range can be unduly limited by early experiences. The fact can be exaggerated. This is done when men excuse their failures to act in proper ways as being wholly due to what they had once undergone. It is one thing, though, to resist the exaggeration, and another to deny that men can sometimes be deprived of the opportunity to be responsible and to act responsibly.

Sentimentalists, thinking that they are speaking on behalf of the underprivileged and downtrodden, deny that these can act responsibly, and in a stroke place those they defend on a lower level than the rest of men, since they then tacitly suppose that those unfortunates lack the private powers the others have, or are not able to express them. Some moralists go to the opposite extreme and suppose that all men have had the same opportunity to develop channels through which responsibility can be expressed. With the same blunt finality that characterizes their opponents, they thereby deny that men need ever to differ in a capacity to carry out the same responsibility.

Evidently, there are points beyond which no man can act responsibly, privately or publicly, points beyond which he is not able to bring his responsibility to bear. But if he is a mature man, he is still a responsible being. All that we can properly conclude, therefore, is that there are times when his responsibility is denied expression by forces outside his control. Always related to a final excellence, when denied the opportunity to give this a role in his private as well as in his public life, he is prevented from being in act what he is intrinsically. He will still, of course, continue to express his privacy in some ways, in and through his body, since otherwise he would cease to be alive. But so far as he was prevented from expressing his responsibility in any way, he would be denied the status of an actual, functioning mature man. The absolute good would then measure the disvalue of what prevents the realization of that good by him.

A man's body is at once a biological organism, a living unit, a humanized instrument, and a publicized person. As the first, his body is one among other organisms, to be understood in terms applicable to all. As the second, it has a nature and function to be understood in terms which apply only to the members of the human species. As the third, it is in a milieu. As the fourth, it is under the control of and gives expression to his private person. Privacy is exercised in all four. In the first, it is primarily accommodative; in the second, responsive; in the third, considerate, and in the fourth, assertive. If he is responsible, his privacy measures, by the standard of an absolute good, all that his privacy is impressed upon.

No human body is only a body. It could be that only when dead, and then not at once or for long. Not at once, because the body is still part of the community, related to it by ceremony, law, and work; and not for long, because the body soon loses all semblance of a human body, and is eventually forgotten. But a man may be so subject to natural forces that he can mainly act only as a physical body. His biological activities may then play only an inconsequential or uninfluential role. Nor is his body only alive. It could be that only if it were just a unit in a species. Nor is it just humanized, for it is unique and privately controlled and used. A man's body is able to be and is used as an agency by his privacy to make possible the public realization of prospects privately faced. Without deliberation or consciousness, the privacy lives his body and thereby makes it a lived body.

Even infants live their bodies. Turning them this way and that with pleasure and surprise, they do something beyond the capacity of kittens or chimpanzees. The living of a body by one of these subhumans is a direct, continuous act, moving smoothly from privacy to body, a living which is incipiently or actually in the body; infants, instead, bring independently functioning privacies to bear. Even before it has a self, and therefore when it is just a person necessarily making itself publicly present, an infant's privacy is more than incipiently public. Some of its power is able to be specialized in the form of sensibility, in desires for what it cannot have, and in an orientation toward what it cannot make its own. But some of its privacy will not be used by its person. If later expressed in epitomizations of a self, that privacy will be expressed as autonomy, in responsible action, or as an I, and will be in a position to use an idios to determine how all other private powers are to function in relation to one another.

Whether or not it be agreed that an infant is responsible for anything it does, it surely will be allowed that it is immature. Since it is a person, it must have inextinguishable human rights, as well as a human sensitivity. As it matures, more and more specialized powers will be used by it. More and more use will be made of more and more comprehensive prospects. All along it will be more subject to circumstance, coercion, and uncontrolled bodily functionings than an adult usually is. Its boundaries are set by its body, species, milieu, environment, society and the cosmos, all dictating what it can express and do. The point beyond which it cannot act occurs within the limits where mature men can exercise responsibility.

If a man privately acts in ways which never obtain public expressions, we will not have evidence of what he privately began. If we are to be sure that he is responsible, we must attend to him within the limits where circumstance, coercion, and bodily functioning could be opposed by him in the attempt to realize what ought to be. This we can do if we ourselves express ourselves responsibly, and therefore if we approach him as able to stretch between things to do and what ought to be done. We are most successful in finding the evidence when he and we make dissimilar assessments.

Were a responsible act wholly confined to a self, there would be no publicly available evidence that it was present; references to it would at best report what one was able to discover in one's privacy. And if a responsible act were not forged in the light of what one's body could do, that body would only accidentally carry out what was privately begun. But sometimes a man does succeed in expressing his responsibility, sometimes even effectively restraining or redirecting his body in accord with this.

No one begins with a direct grasp or a clear understanding of another's responsibility. But all can come to know of the responsibility, once it is acknowledged that he is a fellowman, a fact evidenced by the acts for which he is justifiably held to do what is right or wrong.

c. The I

Hume—and after him, Kant—remarked that he never was able to observe the I he was supposed to have. The contention, of course, was sustained by an I. That fact both of them tacitly acknowledged, the one in his references to his ability to bundle together whatever he encountered, the other in his references to a transcendental unity of apperception which, though said to be just a logical accompaniment of thought, had the power to possess and impose universally applicable conditions on what was experienced. These powers, of which Hume and Kant seemed to know so much, are limited versions of the I, or of what the I itself owns, claims, grounds, or uses.

It surely is right to say with Hume and Kant that the I is not an object of observation in the way in which a perceived color or a palpable body is. But this does not mean that there is no knowing that the I is, what it is, or what it does. It is one thing to reject what has no evidential grounds; it is another to reject what all men use and into which all can move beyond any pre-assignable point. The fact that the I is not an object of a Humean sensing and is not constituted by Kantian categories does not show that it does not exist or that it cannot be known. To doubt it is to make use of it, as Augustine and Descartes observed. To look for it is to use it in another way—as Hume made evident when he remarked, "when I enter most intimately into what I call myself. . . ."

Presupposed by everything a mature man does, able to insist on itself in and through every private act, the sustainer and observer of the self-same me, the persistent locus of human dignity, the possessor of all which is one's own, privately, bodily, or publicly, the I can be denied to be present, effective, and knowable only at the price of denying that a man has reached the stage where he has a developed self, remains identical over time, and looks at the world from a unique position.

There are many ways of approaching the question as to whether or not another can be known to have an I. The easiest and the most common is to recognize that what is a you for other men is a me for the man himself, and therefore sustained by an I. That I is partly expressed in his replies to a treatment of him as a you. Even when he fails to show that he attends to himself as a me and therefore has an I, in taking him to be a you, he is faced both as one who can be a me for himself and, as one who, grounding the you he is for others, has an I. As we shall see, there are still other, equally sound, though not as often used warrants for acknowledging that he has an I, unique, self-same, and possessive.

The I represents the self, measuring and adopting the distance between what is responsibly required and what is in fact initiated. The distance marks the degree to which what is privately begun is ethically correct. By adopting the distanced requirement, the I becomes qualified as ethically good or bad. No one becomes ethically good or bad because of what someone else did; no one inherits another's ethical status. Only when a man has an I is he an ethical being, and he continues to be so as long as, and only as long as, he continues to have that I.

When Kant spoke of men as being members of a kingdom of ends, able to legislate for themselves what they are to do, he seemed to suppose that they were thereupon revealed to be at their highest pitch, true ethical beings. But, as he quickly saw, he had to add supplements to transform a man's being into one that was truly ethical—for Kant, a being that supposedly was free, immortal, and under the care of God. Since Kant allowed for no knowledge of these, taking them to be only 'postulated' in order to complete a theory of ethics where virtue is rewarded by happiness, he in effect both admitted and did not admit that there was a stage of ethics outside man's reach. It should have been admitted. Kant never came to recognize that only a self could be ethical in the required way, because Kant antecedently cut himself off from the acknowledgment of an I which both epitomizes and represents that self.

One already known to be responsible is seen to have an I when he covers the distance which separates what ought to be from what is being done. And he is seen to do this even when he does no more than certify that something is so. By his "I believe," "I think," "I know," or even just "I feel," he makes evident that he has an I, since what is claimed is not only that a belief, thought, knowledge, or feeling occurs, but that it is backed by the I. Conceivably, a man might be mistaken, not of course in affirming that he believes, thinks, knows, or feels, but in taking it to be the backed by his I. But if he is mistaken, there would so far be no warrant for holding that it was the very same being who believed at one moment, and thought, knew, or felt at another; no warrant for holding that he was self-same over the course of his life despite many changes in body, belief, thought, knowledge, and feeling; and no warrant for holding that he was an ethical being, no matter what he said or did. Some thinkers have accepted these reductive consequences as in fact describing what is the actual state of affairs. But in that very act, they show that they have I's. To want others to accept one's claims is to tacitly acknowledge that one is backing the claims with an I, and that one takes others to be able to do so as well.

"It was I who did what was wrong a while ago" requires the I to exist for an indefinite period. The I behind what was done is the very I that is behind what is now being said. But "I see a cat", though privately produced and sustained, despite its verbal form, is not necessarily backed by the I. It is one thing to see a cat, another to have the I involved in seeing it, and a third actually to set the I behind the claim that one sees a cat. "I see a cat" usually means only that the I is involved in an act of seeing, and not that one is claiming to be seeing a cat. Consequently, one is not usually discommoded on discovering that what had been noticed in the dark corner had been misconstrued. But there is a claim made when one says "I saw a cat"; one then expects others to take what is said to be a truth, and to do so because it has been presented to them by an I acting responsibly. There are of course times when claims are made in speaking of what one is seeing, particularly if it has some importance for others.

Even animals feel pain, though they lack I's. A man can undergo pains without bringing his I into play. Were a man to truly say "I had a pain," the I that is behind that claim will not necessarily have been behind the feeling. To make the claim, an I is needed as a sustainer. Were the I placed behind a claim about an occurrence which did not have an I sustaining it, that which was claimed would be given a new status. Where before it could have been carried by the sensitivity or some other epitomization, it is now carried by the I. To have a pain is to undergo a sharp, sensitive experience of negative value; to say truthfully, and therefore to really claim "I have a pain" is to set the pain in a domain of claims and counterclaims, truths and falsehoods, sustained by an I.

A man may find himself acting in uncontrollable ways. Sometimes what he then does is eminently desirable, leading one to speak of inspiration and the strange ways of genius. What is done might be accepted or opposed by his I. It will be possible to know this if one knows that he had accepted responsibility for the things he does.

If this is correct, we are forced to say that a fetus, a child, and perhaps a youth does not have a true, distinct I. At most, it can be maintained only that a fetus has a promise of an I, a child has one episodically while a youth might have one not well defined. A true I, when once achieved, continues to be present; it is a locus of identity, and not just persistent as privacy is.

Even such an apparently innocent remark as "I remember being there," involves and may be backed by an I, certifying that something in fact is being remembered. Because the claim of having remembered something has as part of it the claim that the very same I had been present at the previous time—for no one can remember anything which he did not himself confront—the remark requires the admission that the I had been copresent with what is said to be remembered and has continued into the present.

Since neither an embryo nor a fetus has an I, no one could possibly remember being the one or the other. A man, though, can be said to remember being a child or youth—but only so far as his recollection can be credited to a privacy which had been present at certain past moments. He will not remember either of those times in the same way that he now remembers what he did when he finally acquired a true, distinct I.

The philosophic view that the I is an empty accompaniment of what is being said has the virtue of recognizing its persistent presence. The more common supposition that the I is uninvolved with what else there is has at least the virtue of allowing one to affirm that the I remains unchanged over the course of time. Yet both go too far, a fact that is hidden by the negative form of the contentions. An I is not contentless or decorated with idle predicates. It has a different ethical weight at different times, absorbing its claims within itself on its own terms. A specialization of the self, it guides, intrudes on, and uses other epitomizations, making evident that it is not supererogatory. Without it, a man would not be able to claim every act and encountered object as his own. With it, he can intrude on his self and person, as well as on their epitomizations, to make all his possessions be tinged with an acquired goodness or badness. Once the I is distinctly marked out, he is properly judged in ethical terms for whatever he does. Most of these contentions would be accepted by Kant.

Allowing that the I is presupposed by ethics, Kant denied that it could ever be the object of knowledge. By that denial he meant to reject the supposition that it could be known the way in which physical objects could be known. And here he surely is right. But there are other ways of knowing, and surely other ways besides those which involve the use of his categories, schema, forms of intuition, and the like. He himself affirmed that what was real had degrees; had he gone on to affirm that one could begin with the acknowledgment of the real as having a low degree and as continuous with greater degrees of more unified private content, with which everyone is acquainted in the course of conversation, sympathy, love, thoughtfulness, and the like, he would not have had to postulate an I. Instead, he could have acknowledged it as present whenever anything was claimed as one's own.

The consciousness that another is attending to oneself is at best a prelude to self-consciousness, since it is possible for a man to note that another attends to him without thereby also becoming self-conscious. Teachers, actors, and politicians are rarely self-conscious when they see that others are carefully watching them. And when they are self-conscious, they still do not necessarily have a consciousness of their selves or of their I's. Children are self-conscious before they have distinct selves, and therefore true I's. And though men have selves, they rarely attend to them. A self-consciousness need not be accompanied by feelings of shame, guilt, or embarrassment. A man will perhaps feel ashamed when he sees a stranger looking at his exposed sexual parts, or when he is aware that he is suddenly come upon in a compromising situation. He then reacts either to a supposed reduction of what is an avenue for his radically primitive expressions to the status of something supposedly encapsulating his destiny, or to a judgment that he had neglected to act with the caution or control that a mature man should exhibit.

We take others to be self-conscious when we see them inadvertently blushing, making embarrassed attempts to hide or cover, or offering apologies or excuses. We come to know that they are self-conscious so far as they thereby show us that there is something they do not want us to know about them. Their expressions are treated by us as exposures which make evident something not altogether desirable in them, while revealing who they really are. Issuing from a deeper ground than that which the familiar allows one to surmise, a betraying expression makes that ground suddenly available to others.

Starting from his I, a man may use private and public agencies deviously, thereby misleading those who take what is most obtrusive to be a good beginning for understanding what he is privately. But once we learn that some of his expressions are being used to hide from others just what is intended or done, we will know that he is using some of his expressions for a purpose, privately entertained.

No one is a you to himself. Each is a you only for others. Still it is *his* you. Unlike others, he does not simply pass beyond what he has made public toward a private source of this, but faces what is public as that which he sustains as well. He provides what others can face as a you, without his needing to know this. If he, too, attends to his body, he will face it as his, and move through it toward himself as its sustainer. When he attends to himself, he uses his I to publicly reach toward the I, through the me which that I is sustaining from within. He does not have to know that he has the role of a you for others. But since, when he attends to himself as a me, what he attends to will coincide in part with what others face as a you, he can know something of what others see as a you in the course of his own knowledge of himself as a me.

There are some who try to understand another man by attending to him as though he were like a mirror image of themselves but somewhat distorted, or as if he were like an animal but part of a group to which animals do not and perhaps cannot belong. But a mirror image does not sustain what is present by means of a more intensive, possessive, insistent private power, able to approach itself as a me. And even when one forms an alliance with an animal while excluding all human company, one is confronted with the fact that the animal cannot face itself as a me, and therefore cannot have an I.

In knowing another as a you, whether or not one addresses him, and thereby expresses a respect for him as having a responsibility and a status reflecting the fact that he continues to be qualified by the stretch between what he ought to do and what he in fact does, one moves toward him as deserving respect. Were we indifferent to him, we would not accord him the status of a man, except where indifference itself serves as a means for expressing an evaluation of him.

It is doubtful that we could ever attend to a man and still be totally indifferent to him. If we could, we would have to go through radical changes in attitude in order to attend to him when he suddenly begins to speak, bleed, or stare at us. Even when he is abused, even when he is bestial, he is faced as able to present himself in a way no other being can. He will, so far, be shown a respect appropriate to one who has made himself present as a you for others. An indifference which precludes according him the status of a man keeps one from confronting him as a you. Contempt is more metaphysical than indifference, and for that reason cuts deeper.

Occupation of positions in space, time, or causality, expressions of feelings of pleasure or pain, agreeableness or disagreeableness, need, desire, orientation, and sociality are modes of presentation. The occupation of an extensional region ends with a submission to it, other expressions adding qualifications to what is encountered. A you, in contrast, while publicly available to others and affected by what else occurs, is oneself in a public setting.

A man has the status of a you without wanting to have it. It is his even when he is not conscious, or when he is not doing anything, for a you is himself as confrontable by others. This, of course, it cannot be except through the agency of a lived body, a body privately governed and used.

Were there no I, there would still be a body; it could be enriched by the person; but it would not be given the publicized form of a possessive, self-identical power, able to carry the burden of responsible acts, well or poorly performed. So far as a you is possessed by an I, a man is faced as having the dignity of a human with his you at the limit of a self-presentation. Since, when we speak to infants, animals, and things, we do not suppose that they have I's which hold on to what is being publicly presented, the 'you' we might employ in speaking to them, while not entirely free from a reference to a manifesting privacy, will function primarily as a locative. We come close to making this use of you when we speak to men who have been identified as carrying out public roles. Busdrivers, waiters, toll collectors, and tenders of machines are dealt with primarily as publicly functioning and located. Usually, it is only when something goes wrong that they are dealt with as genuine you's. We are then aware of the fact that what we had confronted and which continues to be present and possessed privately should have been brought into better focus by us and them. To know others as men is to know them to be presenting themselves under the limitations of public conditions, but not to be entirely contained or even expressed there. What is publicly confronted is what each presents. If he is mature it is possessed by his I.

Each man knows himself, not as a you, but as a me. To do this, he starts from his I and moves outward into the public world so as to arrive at his own public presence. If he did no more than this, he would confront his me as a kind of it, a mere stop for a public reference. Instead, at the same time that he attends to himself as public, he moves toward what sustains this from within. The meeting place of the attending and the sustaining is his me, reached both from the outside and from the inside by his I. That I acts as a referring, perceiving power at the same time that it sustains what is referred to. It is not then split in two. The attending and sustaining are both carried out by the same, single, persistent I. When a man attends to his me, he not only comes to that which he also sustains, but penetrates beyond it toward what is sustaining it.

If a man did not attend to his me, he would not observe himself. If he did not sustain it, what he observed would not be himself continued into the public world. Just as he moves beyond the you of another, so he moves beyond the me which is his alone toward what sustains it. But if his me is accessible only to his I, how could another know it to be present unless he could adopt the position of that I?—and that surely is impossible. How do we know that there is another I which confronts, sustains, and possesses another's me? The answer has already been suggested. What is attended to as a me, is partly known as a you by others. Those others converge on that you, beginning from public acts, gestures, appearances, and speech, supplemented by a rejection of other possible objects of reference.

To know that one who is being faced in the guise of a you can be attended by himself in the guise of a me, is to know him to use his I so as to refer to and sustain what he is publicly. Knowing that the you is sustained by him, he is known as having an I, persistently possessing whatever it reaches.

A man can be approached from many different angles. What is confronted from one angle is no mere profile. Were it one, it would not be known that there were other profiles still available. And there would be no warrant for supposing that whatever other profiles were confronted were profiles of the same being. If we are to concentrate on one expression, others must be held away, set in contrast with it. Boundaries, placed about that to which we attend, exclude as well as include, keeping what we focus on in relation to others at the same time that all are grounded in a single obduracy.

What is perceived is unitary, insistent, and obstinate, with its own contours, nature, rhythms, and career. We never stop at its surface. Inevitably we move beyond it toward that which is presenting it. We do not see a sheer red, but a red *of*, a red belonging to something. That red *of* is not altogether separated from a shape *of*, a size *of*, and sometimes a smell *of*. When we perceive, we move beyond what is a mere red, shape, size, or smell, toward what insists on itself in and through them. When we know another's you or our own me, we can and do usually penetrate further than we can and do when we attend to colors, or sizes, or smells. A confronted you or me leads us toward the I which presents and sustains these.

d. The Self and Its Epitomizations

The self does not inevitably impinge on the person. Nor is it as readily discerned, unless one approaches what is publicly expressed as being laden with values, revealing something of the ethical character that was in part forged apart from the body, and sometimes without regard for it or for that with which the body might interplay.

Fetuses are persons and, of course, so are infants. But one must be at least a child to have a self. To have that self epitomized, one must mature. Well before that time, there are momentary assumptions of accountability, engagements in responsible acts, and perhaps insistent expressions of the I. Once the self's epitomizations have been expressed, the self can be ignored only at the risk of our no longer being able to distinguish a self, able to engage in private acts affecting character, from a person, more or less resolute with inalienable rights.

We have already seen that one can be held to be publicly accountable for desirable or undesirable occurrences, identified through the provision of rewards and punishments. The accountability presupposes neither intention nor consciousness, freedom nor control. The being to whom it is credited may deserve neither praise nor blame. It need not even be a man. Any being, even an inanimate one, can be held accountable solely because this is the conventional or easier thing to do. Although we do not usually speak of rewarding or punishing a physical thing for the occurrences we take it to cause, reserving 'reward' and 'punishment' for those in whom we think a desirable change in attitude can be induced, our rejection and alteration, cherishing and preservation of things are readily brought under these rubrics. If the practice be thought to be too loose, one should also abandon references to rewards and punishments when dealing with animals, and be content with references to 'conditionings for' and 'conditionings against'.

'Reward' and 'punishment' in their narrowest use carry a note of commendation or condemnation, usually by others in the same group. Their occurrence need not be known to those who are rewarded or punished. Consequently, there need be no hesitation in speaking of rewarding and punishing animals high up in the scale of development, leaving it a matter of taste whether or not to extend the term to lower animals and things. In any case, rewards and punishments of men, whether or not known by those who provide them or by those who receive them, or both, need not have anything to do with desert or cause.

There is no such ambiguity with autonomy. An assumption of accountability is possible only to men, and then only after they have de-

veloped sufficiently so as to affect a representative resolution that this is
carried out by one who sees himself to be deserving of reward and
punishment for what he sets himself to bring about publicly. And if a man
acts responsibly, he tries to realize what will make him deserving of praise
or blame. Since accountability, autonomy, and responsibility are independently exercised, it is possible for a man to take himself to be deserving
or to be in fact deserving of commendation and yet be deservedly
punished and blamed; and for him to deserve commendation and be
deservedly rewarded and praised.

Autonomy is a distinct epitomization of the self, able to be carried out
independently of other epitomizations, and independently of what other
men or society decided or do. Inevitably it impinges on resolution, guiding this in the light of what is envisaged and, therefore, involving the
mind. It can also be freed from that involvement, and then be brought
back again to bear on it in a more developed form. A responsibly produced
private act depends on the presence of what ought to be realized, whether
or not it is ever realized or even promoted. One is therefore responsible for
acting both in ways one ought not and in ways one ought. The action may
be wholly private. If it impinges on autonomy, it makes a man open to his
own assessment and to the assessments of others as deserving praise or
blame.

Responsibly produced acts may be carried out with reference to what an
assumed accountability does. They may yield nothing more than the
consequence of imposing what ought to be on what is privately confronted. They can then be brought to bear on an assumed accountability
to make this not only affected by a responsibly used end, but to be directed
toward the realization of this. Because responsibly produced acts can
enrich an assumed accountability in this way, responsibility reveals itself
to stand higher than autonomy. This does not mean that it arises later.
What governs and enriches need not originate later than that which is
governed and enriched.

The I apparently comes to be at the same time as the other epitomizations of the self do. Also, it represents the very self that it epitomizes. Like
the other epitomizations, it also comes to be under the prompting of a
developing body. Not a substance, a logical supposition, or an unknowable, the I can be felt, known, willed, obligated—indeed made subject to
every other epitomization. But it usually dominates them, insisting on
itself as their possessor. To take it to be an unknowable at the heart of every
private act is to deny oneself the opportunity to say that it is at all. There is
a difference, though, between the I that is known and the known I—not in
content, but in their roles in knowledge. The known I is the I as subject to

the conditions of knowledge; the I that is known is the object to which the known I is referred, thereby making the known I true of it.

One might allow nothing to be taken as an object of knowledge but that which conforms to the conditions which a rigorous science, a formal language, or cosmic categories provide. Although, as has already been observed, the restrictions are unwarranted, they still allow one to make some contact with the I as the unity at which the articulated knowledge of a mature man converges.

Whatever is experientially known is the adumbrated unity in which the components of knowledge are conjoined. By providing those components with a unity of his own, a man makes them into an articulated, unified item of knowledge. The unity that he provides should match the unity to which the components are attributed. He will claim as true what he articulates. If he is making a claim about his I, he will back the claim with his I and have it adumbratively terminate in his I. But surely a little child, caught in an obvious lie, will sometimes insistently urge that what it says is true. If, as has here been contended, the child has no true I, it must be doing something different from what a mature man does. It could be said to be making a claim, even a claim that something is true, but only as one challenged by others and defending itself against a social judgment. The child will then be seen to be trying to maintain a public position and not, as a man does when he makes a claim, to be in possession of what is held to be true for anyone.

It is one thing to say or even to insist that one has a toothache and quite another to claim that one has it. The latter alone is supported by an I as that which every other I could also claim to be a truth about the sufferer. One must be able to get far within oneself before one is able to claim what has a status apart from the claim, and therefore could be acknowledged by others as well.

What a man publicly expresses has many shapes and guises, differing considerably from one another. His expressions are to be referred to a self-same, insistent, possessive I if we are not to view him as though he were radically pluralized by those expressions or by the factors by means of which we articulate what we discern of him. He can move through his me toward his own I, and toward the I's of others through the mediation of their you's, but of course he can never get to his own I, or to the I's of others as they are insisting on themselves from an undivided base.

One moves toward an I against the ever-increasing resistance of a primary insistence behind his own me or behind another's you. But there is no point at which he must stop. And when brought to a stop, he thrusts toward and becomes aware that there is still more unified and resistant content beyond that point. Because he is acquainted with and knows the I in these ways, he is able to take men to be identical despite bodily changes or changes in the actions of different epitomizations; to be loci of obligations; and to be required to realize a final good.

The epitomizations of person and self are in an order of greater and greater privacy. Sensitivity is at one extreme, the I at the other. In between are the other epitomizations of the person and self. Each of these is able to act apart from the others. Each can be affected by those behind it, and can be used to promote outcomes outside their provenance. Each can act on any of the others. Even the I can be used by them. If one is speaking precisely when he says, "I am in pain," "I am hungry," or "I am frustrated," his I is being approached through his me.

The epitomizations of a person are able to affect the I directly. The I can be thought about, focused on, or deliberately related to some prospect. Consciousness and other pure forms of epitomizations can make the I an object of what has no necessary bearing on bodily occurrences. The I will still be able to possess and directly affect any of the other epitomizations. It will still be able to use them as pivots, and thereby treat them as private forms of me's through which it passes toward itself.

Although it is not clear that all the abstract possibilities for a self-return are ever actualized, many can be. A man can autonomously assume accountability for desiring to assume accountability, to take but one example. All the while, each epitomization retains its integrity, continuing to act in a distinctive way, with the higher members of the hierarchy able to maintain themselves in an unaffected guise to a degree not possible to the lower.

As the epitomizing representative of the self, the I enjoys an independence and a recessiveness not possible to other epitomizations. That it does, can be known by reflecting on the fact that it pivots not only at other epitomizations but at the person and self, at privacy itself, and at the idios, which a mature man achieves and exercises independently of these. Each in turn can function for the I as a kind of mediating me.

The daily acknowledgment that another has an I is as dogmatic as it is unreflecting. But it is less so than Hume's "every distinct impression is a distinct existent," since it does not claim to speak about all that is or ever will be. It is less metaphysical than Carnap's claim that all the points of space and time are unique, and therefore able to make the beings which coincide with them into unduplicables. It is more certain than the undemonstrable, familiar dogma that one's fingerprints are not duplicated anywhere and can never be; that contention, with a confidence rooted in ignorance, speaks of every fingerprint that will be at any place or time, and thus makes a hazardous empirical assertion assume the look of a universal, necessary truth.

No one starts with a profound metaphysical knowledge of himself as an I, or uses arguments to belatedly infer that another has an I as well. No one is even sure just what features or acts are peculiarly human. If he were sure, he would know with certainty what was common to all men. That would still fall short of telling him about his I, for this is his alone. It is also true that different I's are equally I's. Does this not mean that their I's must share common characters? Or could the I's be only numerically distinct, and yet paradoxically not be available for a counting? One or the other of these alternatives could not be avoided, were an I nothing other than the referent of an abstract concept. But an I is inescapably adumbrated in our judgments that others are men. It is also moved toward through a me, and through various private epitomizations, in acts which are themselves unique, outside the area of predicates or ideas. What is common to all I's is abstract, and referred to by means of abstractions, but each I is unduplicable and intensively rich, never just a locus of characters or a unit in an actual or possible enumeration.

An I can possess whatever is privately initiated. The movement toward it along a path of increasing density is not only unduplicable—as every other movement's course is—but is not possible to one who is not at once resisted, supported, and directed by the very I he is trying to reach. Although no one can ever penetrate fully into another I, whatever distance he does go is made possible by that I.

In childhood, dogs, birds, fish, and perhaps even flowers and dolls were spoken to, sometimes about matters one would not tell anyone else. They were then not necessarily taken to be human. Let it be supposed that they were. They would then have been misconstrued, but in such a way that the error clung to a truth, for to be able to anthropomorphize anything, one must already have some grasp of what humans are and can do. When a child lavishes affection on what is not human, and when it speaks to animals and things, it is hopeful, awaiting some human expression from them which would make it clear that they had understood what was being said. If this is what a child does, the child must have some inkling of what a human is and does, even while it fails to look for one properly, or in the right place.

To say that I know another to be human is to speak both boldly and cautiously. Boldly, for it closes out the possible alternative that what I reach might be less, or more, or other than human. Cautiously, for it does not claim more than what had made itself evident. The boldness is limited and the caution relaxed if nothing else is claimed than that I do sometimes discern something of what is beyond the expressions of those I address as 'you'.

Because I am aware of a distinctive, revelatory, publicly presented you, I am aware of a manifested I. Because I penetrate beyond the surface of the you, I am aware of a depth and power not yet publicly exhibited. Because I start with what another expresses, I am able to make a beginning of a move toward the source of what is expressed. The more deeply I move into him, the more closely do I approach him as the possessor of what was manifested. The more fully I, at the same time, hold myself away, the more am I able to recognize that he has an I correlative with mine.

An infant looks at its hand in the same way that it looks at the hand of another. Could it discover that when its hand is squeezed it meets this with a different expression of itself? Could it learn that it has an I by attending to the fact that the clapping of its hands depends on a single use of both hands? It could, if it had an I. But if it had, that I would be identical with the I it will have when an adult. But an infant's viewing of its hands, and its use of them gives way to other acts as though they had no common origin. Its seeing, using, and sustaining, unlike an adult's, do not require an origin in a single, persistent epitomization of a self. What it originates is well understood as originating at a number of different epitomizations, having a single privacy behind them which is less determinate than the self that an I represents.

Adults sometimes speak with intimacy and warmth to animals and things. They are deceived by ventriloquists. Such admissions leave untouched those times when no mistake is made. There are luminous manifestations, presented and possessed by insistent I's. I know those that belong to myself as surely as I know other men's. Occasionally, and particularly when I think I have done something worthy of high commendation, I may allow myself to reveal more of what I truly am. But even when I think of myself as remaining quite hidden, having other sides no one will be able to discover, I often reveal something of myself. Just as I learn about others by using what they do as evidence of what they initiated and from where, so they and I learn about what I am by attending to and using what I do as evidence of what I initiated. Even my good deeds are qualified in such a way that some of my unexpressed vices, tendencies, and views are not beyond all surmising.

What I discern in another I sometimes find inviting. But sooner or later my advance into him is stopped. This may prompt a return to myself. I also make such a return when, attending to him, I note that he is attending to me. Whichever occurs, I come to myself in a way he cannot. I am a you for him, relative to him, and maintained in opposition to him. When I try to learn what I am like from his position, I turn back to myself from where he is attending to my me. My return is then not entirely freed from his influence but, to the degree that I move toward my I, the return becomes more and more unaffected by him. Coming back through the medium of my me, I reach a depth beyond which no one else can go. I know it as that which is more powerful, richer, more unitary, and more basic than anything else at which I can arrive, once I understand it to be that at which all my intensive moves converge. But I do not then in fact reach my I as able to possess whatever there be.

One can point to a person, hurt a person, and provide public satisfaction for a person's rights. One cannot point to or hurt a self. Unlike a person, a self is wholly private. Well before there is a self, there can be sensitivity, sensibility, need, desire, orientation, and sociality, as well as a mind and resolution. But a self is needed if one is to assume accountability, to act responsibly, or to have an I.

A person is inevitably affected by or occupied with what is not private, modified by what is bodily undergone and by what had been done before. So far, we can find neither a warrant nor a ground for supposing that a man is self-same or even persistent over the course of a career. Still, what he is privately is no direct function of what he is publicly. When he publicly changes, his private person may be unaffected. This is not yet to say that his person remains self-same or even persists. Since the very same being who intended and committed a crime continues to be, no matter how many years pass, evidently that being is not just a public person, since this sometimes changes beyond recognition. Reference is being made not just to what may be obligated by what had been decided, but to one who is identical over time. Since we know that persons change publicly and that they can alter internally, and since we know that we are nevertheless self-same over our entire careers, no matter what our bodies or persons have undergone, and no matter how and in what way they have changed, we must have a knowledge of ourselves which reaches beyond both our bodies and our persons.

The I represents the self. It has the power to engage in a self-identification by means of which it is able to reduce all changes to the same constant result. "I am self-same" means not just that the I is unchanged, but that it recovers itself while making maximum provision for the effects of various epitomizations. When the I makes use of consciousness and responsibility, it turns their changing forms and content into intensifications of itself. By possessing what he responsibly does, a man is therefore able to make it part of a self-same I. The responsibility is his, made part of his constant I, no matter what else he might do.

Although we always succeed in making ourselves self-identical, we may not always give our identity the best possible expression. The I may be so overrun that it is unable to do more for a while than remain self-identical only at its center. Eventually, though, it will make whatever intrudes become an integral part of itself, changing it into just a nuance. To bring its self-identity to the fore, the I must insist on itself. This it may not do successfully except after considerable time and effort.

When we ask ourselves whether it was really ourselves who did such and such, we make evident, not that we think that we are altogether different from what we have been, but that we cannot detect the self-identity behind what we responsibly sense or do. We have such a failure in mind when we try to make someone recognize that he is guilty for having committed a crime. We do not want him merely to recognize that he is obligated to make good the losses in value which are due to him, that he was responsible for the act, or that he is now responsible for it. We want him also to admit that he is the very same being who initiated the act. Were we content with making him realize that he was obligated, we would take him to be self-same only in the sense that he was required to do something in the future because of what he had done in the past. If we supposed that he was responsible for what he did, we would not yet have a warrant for supposing that he continues to be responsible for it. Although he could conceivably become responsible for it again, he would not remain responsible for it over time unless he were the very same, identical being who had initiated the act. Were he just responsible later as he had been before, he could still be quite different from what he had been, particularly since he may have repented and reformed. We are asking him to recognize that the responsibility he had for a particular act and its consequences is his now because he is now the very being he was then. His admission that he is still guilty for what he had responsibly done tells us that he recognizes that his responsibility has been incorporated in an identical I which makes the responsibility for the act remain as it had been, even while he is engaged in new activities.

If a man is unable to accept as his present responsibility what he had responsibly done in the past, we must find agencies by which to awaken in him, not a better sense of responsibility nor even a feeling of guilt, but a better sense of his I and its inseparability from his responsibility. Aware that if his identity is not acknowledged, it will not play a proper role, we do not wait until he doubts or denies his responsibility for what he had done.

Instead, we help him bring his identity to the fore, and see that it effectively intrudes on what he does. There is perhaps no better way of doing this than by making him see that much which is laudable had him as its source and that he could be the initiator of other admirable acts. His identity is not a feature of a substantial soul or mind, which may have originated elsewhere and may have an existence after death. Just so far as such a supposed reality is a self-contained, irreducible unit power, it stands in contrast with the body, or has this as its creature. In the one way, the unity of man as he now exists is lost; in the other, the obstinate, not altogether mastered body is denied its independent functioning in a world outside one's control.

Identity presupposes a grounding I. Relative to responsibility, that I is possessive, dominating, and able to act in other ways as well. Relative to the I, the responsibility is a condition adopted, allowed to permeate, giving the I an additional coloring without limiting its activity or altering its nature. The possession of the responsible status changes the I from the innermost insistent epitomization of a self into an insistent force which does not merely act but reduces everything it touches to the status of an aspect of itself. The I, to be sure, acts in diverse ways. Everything it does can be said to originate from the same point and, so far, to be one of a number of expressions of the same unit. The actions of this are diverse because different situations enable them to be so.

The justified rejection of the idea that the I is a substance, or that it is indifferent to all else, does not warrant the supposition that it exists for just a moment, reverberating perhaps with the nature and acts of a different I that preceded it. It is self-same despite change, overcoming what is different. Nor is one warranted in supposing that the I, though distinct from the self, once existed outside that self, or that it continues to exist after this life is over. Because identity depends on the presence of the I, it begins after a life has begun and may stop before it ends. And because it has come to be without the aid of mind or memory, its presence cannot be credited to nor made coextensive with either.

We signalize the persistence of a man when we use his proper name. He may change that name, of course, but as long as he can be addressed by it, he is one who is acknowledged to persist. Although in early childhood, a proper name serves to do little more than to mark out a particular, localized body from which the child has come to expect various actions and products, this is enough to provide a starting point for the child's use of a proper name, since the expected outcomes are faced as having been privately begun and not just publicly encountered. A proper name takes one to a being who is acceptive of that name. Once that fact is well-established, the actual changing of a name will have little importance.

The persistence of a man requires nothing more than the presence of his privacy. This continues throughout his life unchanged, as the indeterminate source of the various epitomizations of it, and what these in turn are epitomized by. That persistence is quite different from the self-identity that is due to the I, for this is insistent on itself everywhere, reducing to itself whatever impinges on it.

Each epitomization of the self is able to be and to function in contradistinction to others. A fully developed self has them in full flower, coordinated by it. Consequently, the self has the twofold status of a common originating source and of a version of this in the form of a relation between different epitomizations of itself. If any of the epitomizations has not been fully developed or exercised, or if the self has not provided them with an effective coordination, the joint but independent functioning of the I and responsible acts will fall short of what it could and should be. As a result, the two will be too much involved with one another, or one or the other will fail to provide a satisfactory counterfoil. A man will then not have a multiply expressed I, or will not act responsibly before or after he has an I. Or, where the two are in existence and fully operative, he may not have them working together properly.

Both the I and responsibility begin acts which need supplementation from other epitomizations. But they also do and ought to interact with other epitomizations and with what is in the public world. They deserve to function concordantly. To the degree that they do not, to that degree the one or the other must be prompted to express itself more vigorously, or must depend on the rectifying act of the self.

There is a rational connection, provided by the self, between the I biased in one way, and responsibly begun acts biased in some other. The self becomes determinate so far as it relates these oppositional biases and thereby achieves an articulation. An incompletely articulated self lacks an epitomization, or fails to have this in a supplementary role. And when the provided relations between its epitomizations are operative, the self continues to exist as an effective power, able not only to offer some rectification for whatever distortions occur but to contrast with the person which, with it, epitomizes a more basic privacy.

Not all men reach the stage where they have I's that carry the outcome of a particular use of responsibility. But once they reach that stage, they never fall back to living on a level sustained earlier. It is not possible to return to a more elementary stage. The ability to act responsibly may be weak; the epitomizations involved in it may not be distinguished. Responsibility may be denied to exist. It may be blocked by other epitomizations. But as long as there is a self, it never is annihilated, any more than the I is. All one can do is to avoid having responsibility achieve adequate expression, or fail to have his I insistently operative to the degree that it can be. Made subject to a resolution, the responsibility and the I can be helped to act in ways they had not before, and then can take over so as to function as independent powers, even making that which had previously empowered them to submit to their dictates.

A man's private life could pass idly before him as a series of adventitious occurrences, no more relevant to him than what is taking place in the external world. At the limit, nothing would be accepted as being part of him. We may then want him to take over, to identify himself with something, to accept it as his own, to carry his I out into the public world. Our prods and punishments may force him to spurts of effort, but more likely than not they will have no persistent effect, for the fault usually lies in a private failure to be insistent. It is also true that a man can be most insistent privately and yet refrain from acting. He may live an intense private life with only a minimal involvement with what else there is. When this occurs, it will be helpful to alter public situations so as to enable his self-identity to operate in public somewhat as it privately does.

The I tries to turn whatever is encountered into intensifications of itself. The effort is subject to two serious limitations: Other items are irreducible, and what is taken from them is different in nature and career from that which would assimilate them. The double difficulty measures the value they have relative to the I. The greater the value, the less should something be changed in order for it to become incorporated in the I. From the standpoint of the I, the world is tragic, containing evil just to the extent that it continues to be in irreducible opposition to what an insistent self-identification requires.

The I is always able to be known as being more than what is publicly expressed, since a penetrative advance into it is blocked more and more effectively at a greater and greater convergent intensive depth, with a singular persistent unity at the limit. It makes no difference whether one seeks to reach one's own I or the I of some other; one always starts at some expression of it and moves toward it intensively and convergently beyond any pre-assignable point, but without ever arriving at the I as that which is insistently expressing itself, and possessing whatever it reaches. It can be said to be known in the way in which we know whatever is adumbratively reached by a thrust beyond whatever content we stop at. But only it is moved toward as singular and insistently possessive.

Animals can be feared, seen as somewhat absurd, and even pitied.

None though, can be made to feel contemptible or despised. Such states require one to be in a world of men. The most cold-blooded, callous murderer is together with the rest of us. He is a unit in a human domain, where he always remains. It should therefore be possible for each of us to find within himself a capacity for every vice that he made explicit and exploited. Otherwise, we and he would not be members of one mankind. But he is to be condemned and we not, because he, and not we, initiated deplorable acts.

There is a cohesiveness to men which sets them apart from all other beings. The contention is readily distorted. One might suppose that it holds only because we are biologically alike, capable of interbreeding or something similar. But we are allied as humans, subject to a common, specialized form of a governance that bears on all that is human, a governance which in turn specializes a more comprehensive way in which all actualities are together. Humanity is a universal, restricted to those who are capable of penetrating one another to a depth not possible to other beings. Within that frame we oppose one another to constitute a single set of selves, more or less compatible.

e. Recapitulation

Evidences of human privacy are available in the form of public occurrences, imbedded in what is alien to them. Were they not imbedded in what was alien, there would be no place to look for them. Nor would there be a need to, for we would be immediately in contact with the privacy once we attended to the evidence. Evidences are publicly available in what enables them to have careers and locations they otherwise would not have.

Evidences of privacies are specialized continuations of privacies, bodily sustained. Were there no bodies, there would be just undifferentiated privacies doing nothing. Whether the evidences be of a sensitivity or of an I, or of anything else in between, they can be isolated and used without reflection. When the evidences are separated out, they are found to be then and there connected to what is evidenced. This completes the evidences, thereby enabling one to move intensively into and to know their sources.

Sensitivity is a readiness to discriminate through the agencies of the different senses. Each of these is keyed to different kinds of data. None is able to deal with what is below or above a particular degree of intensity. Behind and effective on all is an Aristotelian 'common sense' which allows one to know that what was encountered by means of one sense is also encountered by means of another. Because of that common sense, it is possible to know that what is seen is the very same object that is touched. Evidence for sensitivity is to be found by isolating an insistence intruded into bodily withdrawals, advances, struggles, and relaxations.

Sensibility is a bodily sustained privately initiated power, discriminating what is agreeable from the disagreeable, independently of the sensitivity and without regard for what promotes or hinders the body's functioning. Evidence for it is imbedded in bodily acts which enable one to attend to qualitative differences apart from any role they might play in practice. Only one who knows that the discriminations are worth making will find in bodily acts evidence of a privacy attending to aesthetically significant differences.

Need is a bodily expressed private insistence toward what enables a body to prosper or persist. Evidence for it is imbedded in bodily efforts carried out even at the price of pain and the denial of pleasure, and whether or not something is agreeable or disagreeable.

Desire is a bodily sustained private striving, serving the species. Evidence for it is imbedded in bodily acts which may not help the body to prosper or persist, and may at times even jeopardize its continuance or prosperity. If one does not know that it is desirable for men to act on behalf of their kind, he will not be able to find in their bodily acts evidence that they have privacies acting on behalf of their species.

Through *orientation* a man is able to occupy a niche in an environment and a position in a milieu. His body is thereby kept in consonance with a plurality of others which need have nothing to do with his pleasure or pain, agreeableness or disagreeableness, need or desire. Evidence for it is imbedded in what enables the body to be together with what is relevant and congenial to it.

Among the more developed animals, something like *sociality* is operative. Their struggles for power and territory, for mates and food, are not altogether separable from an effort to assert themselves or to achieve a place in a group. But they neither focus nor insist on a sociality, or bring it to bear on other dimensions of their privacies. A man, in contrast, uses his sociality to interlock with others for mutual benefit. His sociality is a representative private effort at union with others. Evidence for it is imbedded in bodily acts which serve a social objective. The acts may not benefit his body or his species. Only one who knows that it is desirable for each man to act as a representative of all will find in the bodily acts of another evidence of his sociality.

Thinking is a controlled private process of drawing conclusions. Neither the process nor the outcome may be of benefit to the individual or to any other man, to them together, to the human species, or to any group. Only one who knows it is desirable that an individual conclude correctly even about useless matters will be able to find in bodily sustained utterances and acts evidence that a man has a mind.

Resolution is a private election of an alternative with the help of an appealing goal, an obligating objective, or a willed end. The evidence for it is imbedded in bodily acts directed toward the realization of what appeals, obligates, or is pertinent to the harmonious functioning of both privacy and body, regardless of its bodily, species, common, or intellectual value. Only one who knows that it is desirable for such realizations to occur will be able to find in bodily acts evidence of an individual privacy governing the body by means of prospects.

No man's privacy is exhausted by his person. Each begins his life as a human by epitomizing his privacy in only one of the ways needed to fully articulate it. Faced later with new channels provided by a maturing body, and provoked by obstacles then encountered, his privacy is epitomized as a *self*. That self may remain unexpressed, without epitomizations of its own, for quite a while. Yet it can be known to be present by attending to and following the lead provided by the new evaluative distance introduced between what is privately begun and what is bodily done. When that self arises what is present is faced as having value.

Autonomy is a private taking of oneself to be deserving of rewards or punishments for what is publicly done. Evidence for it is imbedded in bodily acts which express an opposition to an attributed accountability. If one does not know that accountability can be assumed, he will not be able to find evidence of an autonomous initiation of what is publicly said or done.

Responsibility makes one worthy of praise or condemnation for having done what is objectively right or wrong. Evidence for it is imbedded in bodily acts directed toward the realization of what finally ought to be. If there is no knowledge of what this is, it will not be possible to find evidence for responsibly produced acts.

An *I* is a persistent, possessing, private power, representing the self. Evidence for it is imbedded in bodily occurrences expressing acts privately initiated by an ethical being. Only one with an I can identify the evidence and therefore come to know that another I is functioning in these ways.

Evidences for man's different powers are found only by men. And they are found only in men. The double fact that one does know a good deal about the privacies of others and yet cannot know of those privacies without making use of his own, grounds the familiar paradox that the very men who deny that there are privacies or that these can be known, look to others for honest reports, just assessments, cooperation in inquiry, the pursuit of ideal ends, and other public exhibitions of privately initiated activities. They also offer their denials to those others as honestly presented and perhaps justified for reasons that the deniers privately endorse. At one and the same time these men theoretically abjure and practically make use of their own privacies and what these enable them to do with the evidences that enable them to know of the privacies of others.

It is not hard to make use of evidences of privacy. The use requires only an increasingly intensive progress toward their unitary origin. This is achieved every day by great numbers without effort. But it is quite hard to identify all the evidences with surety and to use them well in effective, deeply penetrative acts. The penetrations are slowed by the resistance of the privacies, and quickly come to a stop in content where one cannot distinguish what one is doing from what is being encountered. If an abstract knowledge of privacy is sought, one must conceptualize the evidence and then reason in accord with the intensive stretch that connects evidence and source.

Evidence is found imbedded in what is alien. It has the status of evidence only so far as it is turned away from this toward what it evidences. Once this turn has been made, the movement to privacy, either through penetration or by an intellectual process of inference, has already begun. The freeing of the evidence from its lodgement in alien content is already part of a movement into privacy, for it is that very privacy in its thinnest guise. We engage in it when we take what we hear to be asserted, affirmed, or maintained, as a truth, doubt, thought, or assessment. By freeing it from its involvements, we purge and thereby allow it to evidence its source. We do something similar when we take a raised closed hand to be a threatening fist, a nod to express approval, or a living body to be lived. All take us at once into an insistent individual privacy. The step has a conventional length; custom dictates just how far into another's privacy it is acceptable to go. The step, though, can be shortened or lengthened, or broken down into a number of smaller steps, at the end of each of which a study can be made of what has been reached. The lengthening, shortening, and subdividing enable one to move different distances into a privacy. One, though, is already in contact with the privacy, as soon as the evidence is freed from its alien bearer, and therefore functions as evidence.

These summaries all need and deserve much more elaboration and supporting arguments than they have received. The upshot is that little more has been done than to open up a field for further study. But that perhaps is enough to have made it possible to obtain a secure knowledge of the way a man's privacy acts on and through his body.

PART TWO

THREE

Reconstructions

a. A Necessary Task

In the first part of this work, evidences of different epitomizations of privacy were focused on in order to ground a knowledge of the nature of privacy. The results provide a guide for determining the contributions both privacy and body make to the existence of an actual functioning lived body.

Distinguished factors in a man's public existence yield evidences of the source of those factors. The isolation and use of the evidences make it possible to answer the question, "What are the major divisions of privacy?" once it is seen that privacy is the source of those very evidences. What is then not known is how and why evidences of privacy were made available. To learn this, it does not suffice to attend to actual occurrences, and there distinguish components that had been intruded on or through the body. In that way one learns only what occurred. To know how and why evidence of privacy was made available, one must use as evidence a distinctive type of activity—a living of a body—which benefits the individual maximally only if it is sustained and helped.

A lived body is the product of a sustaining and an intruded factor, the one provided by the body and the other by privacy. What is to be discovered is how and why these are joined together to constitute a lived body. Without that knowledge, one might know the outcome but not know the manner or the reason for its occurrence. Conceivably, the body and privacy might be treated as being so independent of one another that their possible union was beyond comprehension. This seems to be what Descartes did. Having defined them to be separate substances, he could not explain why they should or how they could ever make contact with one another. He could not even show that it was possible for them to be related. Yet, since he knew that the possibility was in fact realized in purposive action and perception, he had to allow that they were joined. That concession is less than what is needed if their union is to be more than a chance product, due perhaps to the accidental meeting of expressions stemming from both sides.

Distinct entities are able to interplay with one another only if they exercise independent powers. Had they no such powers, the entities would be at best distinguishable parts within a whole. But if they exercise independent powers, the entities could together produce what is quite different in nature and act from both of them. It is not always possible to know from a study of the workings of independent powers what will result from their juncture. One can, to be sure, know what ensues when separate moving bodies act on one another. It is possible to determine the outcome in advance of their meeting, once we know their different velocities and the angles from which they approach one another. This is a consequence of the fact that there is here an exercise of just one type of power, so quantified that combinations result in the production of another quantity. But the meeting of privacy and body is unlike the meeting of two bodies; privacy and body exercise two different kinds of power, one of which cannot be quantified.

For different powers to interplay, six conditions must be met: (1) They must be subject to a common governance; otherwise they would not be together and therefore be in a position to act or to resist. Instead, they would be distinct universes, separated from one another by an unbridged gap. (2) They must be independent if they are to engage in correlative acts. When diverse acts are performed by a single being they reveal it to have separately functioning but not oppositional powers, or to have single expressions diversified by being carried through independently used channels. (3) Each must be pertinent to the other; otherwise neither will dictate the extent and manner in which the other can be effectively insistent or resistant. (4) Their functioning must be mediated by a common agency; apart from this, what one of them does will have no way of making contact with the other. (5) They must make a difference to one another; otherwise nothing will have been insisted on or resisted. (6) The outcome will be new, since it will be produced by a distinct, fresh juncture of the different powers.

Because they meet the first requirement, both privacy and body are to be understood to occur under conditions neither provides. The second requires that common characterizations apply to them in different senses. It is never enough, though, to acknowledge what enables items to be together; nor is it ever enough to characterize them as independent of one another. One must also show why and how the items are pertinent to one another—the third requirement. This is our immediate topic, the fourth, fifth, and sixth being dealt with later.

Neither commands nor refusals to move are pertinent to the solution of Fermat's last theorem. The insistence of the one and the resistance of the other occur in a domain where it does not. Entities must be pertinent to one another if they are to be able to interplay. They can be effectively insistent only on what is ready to accommodate them; they can be effectively resistant only if they are ready to answer to what intrudes. Privacy and body are pertinent to one another; the insistence and resistance of the one are pertinent to the resistance and insistence of the other.

In a number of memorable efforts, Kant sought to show how purely logical concepts could become the categories used in knowing what was encountered in space and time—and how what was in space and time could be understood by means of the categories. A similar problem was arrestingly dealt with by Hegel in various ways, each purporting to show that every thesis was inescapably related to an antithesis, and all were inescapably related to an Absolute. Neither made evident how any item, when it stands away from another, could be pertinent to this. Kant never did explain how logical forms and content, or logical forms and space and time, were able to be joined. In his transcendental deduction he made an extraordinary, original attempt to show how they were in fact joined. What he had first to show, though, was that they were able to be joined. This he did not and apparently could not do, in part because he did not recognize that the question 'How is (scientific) knowledge possible?' has two meanings—'What are the essential factors and relations in (scientific) knowledge?', and 'How are the required factors able to fit together?'. If all we understand is that various items are interconnected, we will be able to understand what is analytically so; we will not yet understand how the situation to be analyzed could have arisen. We will know that the knowledge we in fact have is possible, but not know how that knowledge could be. We will know that certain factors are to be brought together, but will not know that they are of such a nature that they could fit together, either in their original or in a transformed state. But once we learn that they are pertinent to one another, we are in a position to show how they can be brought together. Hegel did not even try to explain why his categories were able to form a set of interlocked items, because he began with the idea that each was already pertinent to others.

An empiricism which takes mind or any other private power to be the product of what is bodily undergone offers a de-cosmologized Neoplatonism in reverse, putting experience where the other would refer to spirit or the One, and mind where the other would put matter. A rationalism which takes what is experienced to be a confused form of what is rational carries out a Neoplatonic motif in epistemology. On neither of these variants—as is true of the original Neoplatonism—is there anything to resist the supposed primary reality. Privacy by the one and the public by the other are turned into functions of what is other than themselves. To avoid this, what was taken to be derivative must be recognized to be in fact correlative and, therefore, distinct, pertinent, readied, and interactive, able to form a union with the other.

Both empiricists and rationalists begin with a union, and attempt to understand it by accepting one of its constituents as alone primary. Aristotelians, instead, insist on the presence and functioning of what is private or rational, as well as on what is experienced or bodily. But they too fail to take both sides with equal seriousness, and in the end just affirm that there is a joining of the two to constitute what is different from either. The question, how or why the joining could or should take place, how an insistent body could or should accommodate a private living of it, is rarely asked by any of them.

The empiricists' difficulties crop up again in materialism, which seeks to explain mind and other forms of privacy in terms of the interaction of material units, just as the rationalists' difficulties reappear in the existentialists' attempt to explain all that is experienced in terms of the exercise of private powers. To take account of both the private and the bodily, the formal and the material, the rational and the empirical, one must allow that they are not only independent and related, but are necessarily pertinent to one another and, therefore, are in a position to act and, through an interplay, to produce something else.

Pertinence is a consequence of the fact that items which are to be together must be receptive to one another. Only beings which could not be affected by others could be completely unreceptive, and therefore without pertinence to any. Relevance adds to pertinence a conditioning which enables the items to be together as harmonious or in conflict; items can continue to be pertinent to one another in a steady way even when relevance changes in degree or kind.

Omnipotence requires that there be something with an infinite capacity to receive it. It therefore necessarily differs both from a power to create everything, and from a power to overcome everything. An absolute creator has nothing pertinent and therefore relevant to it, while that which is able to overwhelm all others must face them as offering some resistance to it, and thus as not wholly passive, and therefore as having some pertinence and relevance. Omnipotence, in contrast with both, requires that there be others, and that these be absolutely passive with respect to it. But so far as their passivity was relevant to the omnipotence, those others would be pertinent to it, determining where it will act and to what effect. Omnipotence, evidently, is a self-contradictory idea.

The pertinence of an entity to another makes this be less than all there is. There is no reaching out to that other. An entity is pertinent to another because and so far as that other is receptive to it. What is true of the other is true of the initially acknowledged entity. The other is pertinent to it, and it is receptive to that other.

Every entity is both pertinent to and receptive to every other. If it were not pertinent, it would not make any difference to it; if it were not receptive, no difference could be made to it.

Kant not only failed to show how the factors required for knowledge were pertinent to one another, but was biased toward one of them—his categories—taking their other—the forms of intuition and their content—to be passive. He thereby prompted both the Fichtean move to deny independence to the forms and content of intuition, and the Hegelian move to attempt, with the help of the Absolute, to produce those forms and content from, and yet have them interact with, their counterparts. On the other side from Fichte and Hegel are Locke and his successors, for whom reason is passive and encountered content active. Such one-sided views end with the paradox that what is passive has the extraordinary ability to make the active conform to it, while leaving the active without the power to do anything to the passive except receive it. Active and passive, as a consequence, interchange places. The paradox can be avoided if, with pragmatists, one starts with the interplay of items and then treats them as having no other reality than that of focused elements in single, indissoluble ongoings. But one would then have no explanation of why the interplay occurs, unless it be to overcome a poorer form of the interplay, where the distinguishable items fail to mesh properly. In such a view, there is not only no accounting for the failure, but once there was a perfect fit all activity would stop. Instead, one should begin with the acknowledgment of distinctive factors independent of but pertinent to one another; one will then be in a position to see how their interplay can yield units in which the factors have subordinated roles. The factors will rarely have equal power and efficacy. One of them will usually have a more effective role than the others. In any case, no neat balancing of diverse factors or of their contributions holds of privacy and body. A privately initiated pertinent living makes a receptive body lived; a pertinent living body enables a receptive privacy to live it. Because privacy is more active than the body, the first of these expressions is to be preferred. But when we come to consider the obstacles that the body sets before privacy, and the avenues it provides for privacy's public expression, the second way of speaking will be found to be more appropriate.

b. Pertinence, Privacy, and Body

Every living body is a lived body, i.e., a product of the intrusion of a privacy on a body which has a nature and activities of its own. The most primitive of living bodies is the outcome of the intrusion of a living on what is thereby made into a single lived body. There, the intruded is enabled to function in a new way. Other types of living body are the products of the intrusion of a higher order of living on lived bodies of another sort.

The human privacy which lives a body, thereby making it lived, continues to exist apart from the body. So far as it acts on the body, it turns this into a distinctive, single, unitary, lived body. Sensitivity provides the most primitive way in which a body is lived; other expressions of privacy act on a body already lived by sensitivity.

Before privacy can act on the body, the body must be receptive to it, able to accommodate the privacy, able to give it a bodily role. If the body could not do this, it could not be lived.

A pain in a foot is not a single, inchoate throb; it is different from other kinds of pain, acquainting one with the foot, contributing to the nature of the foot's activity, and identifying the foot as one's own. The body accommodates the sensitivity with a stress at the foot, and is thereby lived by sensitivity. The sensitivity varies in tone because the body is receptive to the sensitivity in a number of distinct but limited ways, each effectively qualifying it.

In advance of privacy's acting on the body in a particular way, the body must be ready to accommodate it, though not solely on privacy's terms. Were the body completely resistant, the privacy would not be able to affect the body at all, and this would so far lose the benefit of being lived. But were the body completely passive, privacy would lose the benefit of the body's ability to allow privacy to use the body. Able to add to and be added to, the body is turned toward sensitivity and other epitomizations as acceptable by that body under limitations.

A body does not prescribe to a privacy the manner or degree to which this will manifest itself. But so far as it is receptive to the privacy, the body will allow the privacy to be bodily expressed. Although the privacy can make use of the body only because and so far as the body enables it to do so, the privacy of course impresses itself on the body in its own way. It can be present superficially or thoroughly, overlaying the body or filling it out, making it mainly a carrier, or providing only a minimal opportunity for the body to be expressed.

Pains and pleasures are felt to be pains and pleasures of the body when sensitivity is expressed, because that expression is intruded on a body which is receptive to the sensitivity. But sensitivity does not intrude on the body in a constant way. While remaining constant as private, its expression fluctates in intensity. A pain in the toe may be felt as slight or great, and may change rapidly from one to the other. Something similar holds true of other epitomizations. And whatever the epitomization, its content will be affected by the body which the epitomization lives.

Only an expressed epitomization unites with a body, the body setting a limit to the difference that can be made to it. Increased pressure on a toe will usually occasion greater pain, but the addition will not be necessarily concentrated at the toe or occur only when the toe is subject to the pressure. It may be felt elsewhere or throughout the body, and may be so felt even when the toe is no longer acted on.

Cutting off nerves will preclude the occasioning of pain at various parts of the body, but the cutting neither interferes with the pertinence of the body to sensitivity nor affects the degree to which that sensitivity will be expressed. Cutting nerves does not destroy a lived body; the body is still lived at the places from which the nerves were severed. Though the discriminative power of sensitivity is dimmed at the disconnected areas, it will still directly intrude on them.

As an alternative to this view, it might be maintained that blood, cells, or other bodily agencies provide a foothold for a living of the body, without thereby making this sensitized or requiring the use of nerves. But then one presupposes that some private expression, either more primitive or more advanced than sensitivity, lives the body. But what is more primitive is an undifferentiated privacy, the privacy as not expressed, while what is more advanced presupposes sensitivity. If one gives up the view that sensitivity provides an initial and persistent way of living a human body, to hold instead that before and apart from sensitivity's expression, an indeterminate, unspecialized privacy is an integral part of the body, permeating it without being expressed there through some epitomization, the body will have to be lived by a human who is not yet a person—and that is not possible. Were one to hold instead that it is a person not yet epitomized who lives the body, there could conceivably be a person who never was and might never be sensitive, be in need, have desires, or be epitomized in other ways.

If a person could be denied expression by cutting off nerves in the body, one would have to allow that his body could cease to be a human body, or that it would remain human but be lived by an undifferentiated person. Only the second of these alternatives is consistent with a supposition that a loss of sensitivity still allows a person to be bodily present. But if we to suppose that an undifferentiated person just fills out the emptiness which a blocked sensitivity leaves behind, and if we are not to allow that such a person could suddenly become present late in life without ever having been present before, we would also have to grant that an undifferentiated person was present in the body all the while. Since only pertinent epitomizations of a person are expressed in and through diverse bodily channels, only the supposition that an undifferentiated person always accompanies the sensitivity but may remain when the sensitivity is not expressed, is tenable. But then, though a man might initially begin as sensitive, by surgical operations one would be able to turn him into an undifferentiated being, a state he had never been in before, even when an embryo. The resulting lived man would no longer have any particular tasks, limited objectives, desires, needs, and so on, though his body would continue to be as differentiated and as complex as it had been before.

A body makes it possible for a privately initiated expression to affect it in ways which reflect the fact that the body continues to maintain itself while it is being intruded on and used. The epitomized privacy acts on the body so as to constitute with it a single, lived, controlled body inseparable from an unexpressed, more intensive form of the privacy.

The body gives sensitivity an opportunity to make the body sensitized. The public features of the result and the public features of the body before it had been so sensitized may be alike in every respect. One could not then tell by attending to its features whether or not it was the body of a person. To look like other humans is not yet to be a person. Effigies are not persons. To look quite unlike other humans is not to cease to be a person. Human monstrosities are persons. Still, a person differs from a non-person. A sensitized body acts differently from a body that is not sensitized; it withdraws and advances, in parts or as a whole, where it would not in the absence of sensitivity. Advances and withdrawals are, of course, not restricted to sensitized beings. Magnetized bars attract and repel one another. But advances or withdrawals do not alone characterize a sensitized body. This also suffers and is satisfied. These require that it be privately lived.

Men make evident that they have pains and pleasures by grimacing and by speaking, as well as by moving toward and away from what is affecting their bodies. But these evidences are not essential to the occurrence of the pains and pleasures. Pains and pleasures are not dependent on the evidence that allows others to become aware of their presence. There is such evidence, of course, because sensitivity made itself manifest with the help of the body. The fact causes difficulty only for those who allow for nothing unless it be a purely public occurrence, or who require one to attend to such an occurrence as something wholly detached from what might privately accompany or produce it.

We move directly toward and penetrate to some extent into the privacies of others when we confront them in extreme cases of danger or enjoyment. When the evidences are not so conspicuous, we are less inclined to do this, or do it with less insistence and effectiveness. The penetrative moves are limited by that into which they are made. There surely are times when no one makes such a move; times when others are entirely oblivious of what someone else is undergoing; times when a man may not attend to what he is experiencing. He and we will nevertheless conclude that he had been sensitive, that he had in fact undergone pains and pleasures, once he and we acknowledge that his body is sensitized and therefore is a body of a person. If we know that a man is still alive, we know that he is still sensitive, that his sensitivity has been brought to bear on a body that is pertinent to it, and that the result is a body which has a career not possible to that body as not lived by sensitivity. The situation is not altered in principle when epitomizations other than sensitivity live a human body.

Even if we could find no act or feature in a human body which was different from those possessed by what is not alive or is not human, we can know that the body has been sensitized, and therefore is the body of a human person able to have pains and pleasures, if only dimly and privately; for once we learn that he is sensitive, we know that he will continue to be so as long as he lives. We know, too, that he will persist throughout that time because throughout that time he is a single person. What we will not then know is whether or not he is self-same, with the very same distinctive I. To know that we would have to have evidence that took us beyond his person.

We can, as we have already seen, determine when a man first comes to be, if we can determine when it is no longer possible to have identical twins. At that point, there can be a single person, with a constantly maturing, more and more privately qualified, complex body. Only if we allow that one can pass back and forth from the state of being a person to the state of not being one, and that he therefore will sometimes have and sometimes not have native rights, could we be warranted in holding that he does not have the status of a person as long as he is alive.

A living body contributes to the constitution of a lived being. If that being is human, the other constituent of it may be an epitomization of the self. Whether it is or not, it will always include an epitomization of the person, whose most persistent and primary expression is sensitivity.

That on which privacy is imposed must have a nature of its own, if privacy is to be expressed there. Were the body which privacy lives completely passive, were it a kind of Aristotelian matter or a Kantian manifold, it could not sustain the expression of whatever might intrude on it. It would completely give way before the intruder. The body on which privacy intrudes has a nature which helps determine the kind of responsiveness that will be exhibited by the lived body.

The nature of the body which is to be lived has to be receptive to the privacy, neither too flexible nor too rigid. Were it absolutely flexible or absolutely rigid, it could be joined to nothing at all. The body gives privacy an opportunity to help constitute a single nature in which the privacy provides a meaning, and the body provides a localized subject for this. Apart from an intruded privacy, a living is articulatable and envisageable as subject to biological, chemical, and physical laws. As intruded upon by a freely expressed privacy, it is subject to those quite different laws that govern lived bodies.

We must learn in the course of experience what objects are dangerous to our bodies, what congenial, what injures them, and what nourishes them. But apart from all such learning, we immediately know that what we taste is pleasurable or not, and that what is bodily suffered is usually painful. Were that knowledge obtained from an observation of our bodies in the same way that we learn about pins, fires, weights, and the like, we would have to infer that we felt a pain in a toe. But inferences are precarious, and may take a long time to complete. A very young child can know that it feels a pain in its toe; it surely has that knowledge without engaging in a process of inference. What it feels may of course turn out to have a cause in some other part of its body. That result, instead of compromising the claim that it can have a direct knowledge of what is occurring in its body, supports the claim, for what will then be discovered is that the pain felt in the toe can sometimes be controlled by doing something to some other part of the body. A pain in a toe remains a pain in a toe, no matter what is learnt about the bodily causes of that kind of pain. A podiatrist may determine that the pain has its cause in some other part of the body, but he does not and cannot nullify the fact that his patient is feeling a pain in his toe—not of course that toe as observed by the podiatrist, but still that very toe as providing a privately reached localization for the pain that is being felt. What is felt is a pain-in-a-toe, and it remains so no matter what one discovers through observation.

Theories which radically separate sensitivity and the body, never allowing one to be pertinent to the other, are faced with what for them must be an inexplicable fact: a man can and does distinguish a pain in his toe from a pain in his finger. The theories inevitably arrive at such a pass because they assume that pains and pleasures are private occurrences completely alien to what publicly occurs. As a consequence, some thinkers will be tempted to ignore the pains and pleasures, and attend only to what can be expressed in a public language, or to what can be known by taking account of a body's parts and functions. One outcome of such efforts will be the neglect of the fact that one can continue to distinguish a pain in a finger from a pain in a toe even when it has been clearly shown that there is nothing amiss with either the finger or the toe.

Every body is resistant. That resistance is an insistence as countering an intrusion. As resistant, the body is and must be pertinent to whatever might affect it. Otherwise, it will make no difference to intruders, and therefore not even be able to support them, locate them, or enable them to have a bodily role.

The resistance that a body exhibits toward other bodies is different in kind from the resistance that it exhibits toward privacy. But the body will have to be pertinent to those other bodies just as surely as it is pertinent to the privacy; otherwise those bodies would not be able to act on it. It will, of course, resist those other bodies in a different way from that in which it resists the privacy, since this acts in a non-physical manner.

The kind of resistance a body exercises depends on the kind of intruder it encounters. Once it is supposed that a lived body is like every other, only more complicated and flexible, and that it is related only to other bodies, it becomes impossible to understand how it could go in directions which are neither determined by other bodies nor of benefit to it.

A body is given a direction by the privacy that impinges on it. Its resistance is then not so much overcome as enriched. The recognition of that fact need not invoke the spectre of vitalism, or require the conception of a new type of action.

The resistance of a living body is directed toward an intruding privacy which can live it in still other ways. Could the body put up an absolute resistance to the privacy, preclude the intrusion of the privacy altogether, it would not, with it, be able to constitute a lived body. Could the body not resist the privacy at all, it would give that privacy no role in a conjoint product. There is no knowledge, decision, or intent in that body. Its pertinence to privacy is a consequence of the fact that it can make a difference to the privacy's expressions. Were one to deny that the body could be pertinent to the privacy, one would also have to deny that it could even be related to the privacy, for such relation requires an imposition on and a support by what sustains the related term.

A man's privacy is expressed in and through his body, but not entirely. As not yet involved with the body, his privacy has neither direction nor public roles; its pains, pleasures, desires, and needs are just privately undergone. The privacy can have direction and public role only if it is possible for it to have them, and that requires the body to accommodate the privacy, make privacy's thrust pass through limited bodily channels. Privacy is thereby enabled to be expressed in a public space and time, facing specific obstacles and opportunities. The outcome is quite different from the directionality which the body acquires from the privacy. The body enables privacy to become an exhibited power; privacy enables the body to be used to realize prospects privately entertained.

Nothing in privacy requires that it direct the body it lives. Nothing in the body requires that privacy act so that pains are reduced and pleasures increased. But a body not pertinent to privacy could neither be living nor lived, while a privacy not pertinent to a body could not make use of that body. Because they are pertinent to one another, they are able to benefit one another.

The direction that a lived body initially or subsequently follows will result in benefits only some of the time; it can end with the annihilation of the lived body. That some directions are better than others is slowly learned; habits, thoughts, and decisions help determine which of the many often unfocused efforts made by a lived body will prove of benefit to it. The pertinence of the privacy to the body guarantees no more than that the privacy can be expressed there, to make the body directed toward what it might require but not encounter.

A living body is an organic, complex unit, within which one can distinguish a single unity and a multiplicity of governed parts. This is still far too little to acknowledge, if one is to do justice to the presence of even pains and pleasures. These mark the fact that the body is also sensitively possessed and owned. It is possible to possess and not own, or to own and not possess. A thief possesses what he does not own; money in a bank is owned but not possessed. Were a body just possessed, it would be something used and adjusted to, but there would be no claim to it. Were it just owned, it could conceivably be taken over by someone else.

The body is lived because and so far as there is a privacy able to possess it. One reason it is not to be injured or to suffer is that it is privately owned. Because it is both possessed and owned, it is immediately felt as more or less conforming to privately grounded claims.

If ownership of a human body is not allowed, there will also be no acknowledgment of the body as carrying the rights of a person. There will be no torts, no murder even, but only injuries, destructions, abuses to a body. This may be a body more complex and wondrous than the bodies of others, but it will belong to no one. Yet even an animal privately owns and possesses its body. Unlike a man, though, the animal's privacy is not able to be turned away from that body, not able to engage in acts which have no bodily import. Its privacy has no rights to its body other than those it expresses or will express there; it is too much the possessor of its body to be able to benefit from the fact that it also has the status of an owner.

As able to be possessed, an unsensitized living body is open to a privacy which can lay hold of it. As able to be owned, it is open to the privacy as making a claim on it. As both together, the body is lived and thereby owned. This would not be possible were the body not initially pertinent to the privacy. Were it pertinent to the privacy only as what could be possessed, it could be used as though it were something alien. Were it pertinent to the privacy only as that which could be owned, it could be claimed, but the claim might not be satisfied. The body is pertinent to privacy as that which maintains itself apart from the privacy, thereby giving the privacy something to claim and use.

As owned, a body is not changed in nature or functioning, though there will be a difference to the kinds of relations it will have to some other beings. Possession of the body, though, affects its nature and career, making it subject to the dictates of an accommodated privacy.

Were there just an essence, mind, form, or reason on the one side, and an existence, matter, or sense datum on the other, we would have a problem of understanding how the two could ever be together, but there would be no need to ask whether or how one owned or possessed the other. One side, it might still be urged, due to its superior nature or irreducibility, had a right to possess and own the other, but this would not suffice to show that it could exercise the right, that it did in fact possess or own the other. Privacy exhibits itself as that which owns the body on possessing it.

Privacy intrudes on a body which is able to accommodate it. Even if the body could not initiate any acts, even if it merely reacted to the intrusions of privacy, it would function as a single unit in accommodating the intruder. The fact that privacy takes the initiative, that it intrudes on the body, does not mean that the body makes no difference to it.

A lived body is the joint product of an expressed epitomization of privacy and a living body, each making a difference to the other. To credit the body with the ability to make a difference to the privacy is, of course, to go counter to a long and honorable tradition which maintains that bodies are essentially passive and in any case that they cannot make a difference to what is private, not even to give this a public role. But absolute passivity is a nullity. A body must always be above the supposed limit of such an absolute passivity. There is no genuine action by privacy except with reference to what can make a difference to it.

Both body and privacy are active, undivided units. Both are receptive. Both are divisible into a plurality of subordinating and subordinated factors. Neither just awaits the other; each also acts. But the body does not act on privacy until privacy impinges on it. It then not only resists privacy but makes this function in new ways. The pertinence of the privacy to the body makes it possible for the resultant lived body to have an intensity, identity, responsiveness and direction, and to be possessed and owned, while the reciprocal pertinence of the body to privacy makes the privacy be subject to contingencies and to have a career in a world of bodies.

What is absolutely passive, as has been noted, would be unable to make a difference to anything that might impinge on it. It would seem, though, that it might be possible for something to be through and through active, sheer energy, with only a limited duration and location, brought to a stop by a counterforce. But so far as it was able to be counteracted, it would be passive, pertinent to and awaiting the counteraction. The point is obscured when quanta are quantified and thereby treated as aggregates of smaller units, since quantities lose their distinctive boundaries when they come together. By subtracting one quantity from another, it is possible to obtain another quantity in which neither of the others is to be found. But interacting quanta can retain their identities. The quantified energy of an actual, complex, lived body is the outcome of a union of a pertinent quantum of privacy and a pertinent quantum of bodily energy.

A privacy that was not accommodative would not have expressions whose nature and occasions could be affected by the body. The distinctive functions of the body would make no difference to it. Although the privacy could make use of the body, it would not be a privacy of that body. But so far as privacy is accommodative, it is receptive to the body. Privacy does live the body, insisting on itself and making the body its agent, but that living of the body is inseparable from its acceptance of that body.

The body remains a body when lived because the epitomization which intrudes on the body also accommodates it, thereby enabling the body to remain a body and not be a privacy in a bodily form, or just a completely pliable instrument. A body is always more than a hindrance or an agent for privacy since it gives privacy the status of an effective determinant of what is bodily done.

Privacy allows the body to continue to be, but as sustained by what is not bodily at all. The resultant lived body is no more dependent on the privacy that lives it than the privacy is on the body that is being lived. An expressed privacy and a living body are correlative, analytic components of a single, complex, lived body.

Because it is accommodative of a body, the task and course of privacy will be partly determined by that body. Since privacy governs the body, it nevertheless lives this as its own. It is also accommodated by the body. The more surely that the priority of privacy over the body is affirmed, the more surely must one look to the body to accommodate it; and the more surely one affirms that the body is pertinent to the privacy, the more surely must one affirm that privacy accommodates the body. Consequently, to understand the human lived body, reference must be made to what is lived and to what could live it. A privacy would not be able to intrude on a body unless that body made provision for it. Privacy needs the receptivity of the body in order to be able to be a privacy for it. But if privacy could not accommodate the body, privacy could not be affected by the body and, by that very fact, would be without a bodily role. Yet there are some who speak as though there were minds or souls or some other form of privacy altogether alien, unaccommodative of a body.

Every expression of privacy acts as a quantum, an undivided unit. Imposed on the body; it is therefore able to unify what is then lived. Because it is pertinent to the body, it provides the body with a new ground which will be filled out by the body in its own way. The union of privacy and body that results acts and interacts, and can be associated and contrasted with others. Because the privacy has limits set for it by the body, it is not able to be in full control of the body. Since the body is in a world of bodies and is there subject to determinations outside the governance of the privacy, the body will affect the way the privacy publicly functions.

The pains and pleasures undergone by sensitivity provide occasions for giving different weights to different bodily occurrences. Categorizing what bodily occurs, the pains and pleasures are something like taxonomic devices, ways in which what bodily occurs is divided into a limited number of sustained classes. Recording what is bodily occurring, they accentuate the dependence of private determinations on what is outside privacy's control.

It is possible to live a body as an occasion for classifying bodily occurrences as painful or pleasurable, without living it as that which compels one to take account of bodily occasioned pains and pleasures. And one can be forced to feel pains and pleasures without living the body as painful or pleasurable. It is also possible for the two types of experience to occur together, each containing the other as a subordinated factor; at such a time, the body, while lived painfully or pleasurably, will be accepted as a source of pains and pleasures. These ways of having pain and pleasure can subordinate and be subordinated by other bodily pertinent aspects of privacy.

Although everyone distinguishes different kinds of pains, remarking with ease on the difference between those felt in the stomach from those felt in the mouth or ear, it is remarkable that so many philosophers have been content not only to lump all pains together on the one side and all pleasures on the other, but to ignore their bodily pertinence. Although justice is then partly done to the fact that pains and pleasures are private occurrences, and that they have categorizing roles, allowing one to group together a large number of diverse occurrences, what is not made evident is why privately felt pains and pleasures should be in some accord with the adventures of a body, itself unable to feel.

Were sensitivity not pertinent to the body, there would be no feeling of pleasures and pains which were a consequence of the ways in which the body happens to act. Yet, a knowledge of the body itself often makes it possible to predict when pains and pleasures will be felt, and even to know to what part of the body they will be attributed. But what is not then known is that they are felt, that there is a sensitivity which is being made to undergo them.

Sensitivity cannot anticipate the adventures of the body. It cannot be prepared for the particular stresses which the body introduces. The failure is exhibited in two ways. It must await the action of the body, and it is not in perfect accord with the actual contingent ways in which the body functions. As a consequence, there are bodily occurrences that are not recorded in pains and pleasures, and for which there may not be provision made in the sensitivity. The pertinence of the sensitivity is with reference to a body whose different parts have different degrees and kinds of resistance, not all of which are brought into play when the body is affected by the sensitivity.

Conceivably, every change undergone by the body could be recorded by a properly prepared sensitivity. That sensitivity, while unable to anticipate every bodily occurrence as having a positive or negative value for it, would record every bodily occurrence as pleasurable or painful. This, though, could occur only if the human body were equally resistant everywhere, able to make itself in all its complexity distinctively felt by an insistent sensitivity.

What here holds of sensitivity has its counterparts in accounts of every other epitomization, both of the person and of the self. Privacy and body are neither altogether alien nor altogether in harmony. They are turned toward one another, but there is no pre-established consonance guaranteeing that every change in the one will be matched by a change in the other. An epitomization is pertinent to the body without thereby becoming perfectly attuned to the differences in the ways in which the body acts. Because, on its side, the body also has a reality, and because this is pertinent to the sensitivity only as a single, private expression, the being which results from their union is a privately sensitized, lived body.

Privacy can be both misconstrued and well understood. In either case one can predict consequences from what one is able to understand of it. It is, in short, intelligible. That intelligibility is an aspect of it, dominating and being dominated by other aspects. All specialize the intelligibility at the same time that they make this operate within their limits. As a consequence, an understanding of the intelligibility of any epitomization will usually require the envisagement of the other aspects.

The pertinence of privacy's intelligibility to the body makes it possible for the body to benefit from the intelligibility when that body obdurately blocks the advance of the epitomization. Because the intelligibility of privacy is already prepared to become the intelligibility of a lived body, it will be able to relate different parts and acts of the body in new ways, thereby giving them a new import. What may be bodily connected as cause and effect, oppositional, supportive, and the like, the pertinent intelligibility might relate as similar or different. Although the initial bodily connections will still remain, functioning more or less as they had before, they will be given a new meaning by being intelligibly related in new ways. The lived body, consequently, will have a rationale that is different from the intelligible connections that its constituents provide.

Different bodily occurrences are intelligibly interrelated by an epitomization that is pertinent to them. Pleasures and pains, although they are bodily distanced and occasioned, are intelligibly interconnected by sensitivity. That sensitivity is always operative, but only in special cases is it concentrated in the form of an intelligible base for diverse sense modalities. At other times, sensibility can do no more than subjectively join them in a constant way, while living them as intelligibly together in the body.

Because privacy is substantial, it is already able to face the alien demands of a body. Because privacy is real, it is already prepared to take some account of what is not predicted. Because privacy is intelligible, it is prepared to use different bodily occurrences as so many units to be related as parts of one experience. Because privacy is also unified, it is able to order different bodily occurrences as better or worse. All involve a reference to a body which is able to make a difference to the privacy.

A privacy is pertinent to bodies other than the body with which it in fact unites. But it cannot be prepared for those bodies except through the mediation of the body that it lives. Apart from that mediation, it could, though, be said to be indifferently pertinent of any body whatsoever, for every body is a possible occasion for the privacy to encounter content. That content is present in ways and at times not within the privacy's power to determine or control. Were one to hold that a bodily occurrence is what is privately felt, there would then be nothing in principle to stand in the way of the claim that it is possible to feel what is occurring in a body which is not one's own. But a man has an irreplaceable relation to his own body, not because that body is most insistent—often it is not—but because of the way it accommodates his privacy. One cannot therefore properly speak of his privacy as pertinent to every body in the same way that it is pertinent to his own, even if one supposed that the involvement with them was overlaid with a specific reference to his body. His body is not just a member of a world of bodies; it has a specific pertinence to his privacy, and his privacy is accommodative of it. In turn, his privacy has a special pertinence to that body, a body which is accommodative of it.

We sympathize and share in the rhythms and sufferings of others. We make direct contact with other men as persons on a footing with ourselves, and do so without hesitation. That sympathy and sharing is mediated by our bodies. When we sympathetically live in accord with another, or when we directly deal with him as a person, we do not have to sacrifice the intimacy which we already enjoy with reference to our bodies. Instead, we use them as mediators enabling us to extend our private expressions to what is at a distance.

The bodies of others and the privacies that live these are reached by our privacies. We can do this only if mediated by our bodies, and thus with the others' not having an import for us that our own have. If others cannot reach us except via our own bodies, our privacies can be only indirectly accommodative of those others. In any case, we would never be able to grasp anything other than our own bodies, and therefore would never be able to apprehend what was apart from us, could we never use our bodies as mediators.

A body is voluminous, occupying a position in a public space and time, understandable in terms of the reception, retention, and transmission of energy inseparable from all other bodies and their energy. How could such a body make a difference to a privacy, in no way extended in public space, not within a public time, unable to use the energy of bodies? It could not, unless the privacy were pertinent to it. Together with that body, the privacy constitutes a single, complex, existent, lived body, because the body accommodates the privacy. Because the privacy is distended, indivisibly voluminous, and therefore able to be accepted by the body's extension, it is possible to know what is occurring in the body and in what is related to this.

Were there no way for a man to approach his body from the outside, he could still be able to discriminate his pains and pleasures as being occasioned by his body, and would be able to engage in other private acts passing beyond the confines of that body. But he can also pivot at objects external to his body, and thereby arrive at his body as that which he privately quickens and possesses. Well before that time, and independently of it, his privacy will be subject to perturbations due to the limits set and the adventures undergone by his body.

No one knows what another is privately undergoing except so far as the other provides him with guides, criteria, reports, and signs, or bodily evidence. Whatever is reported will be couched in a common language of words, gestures, and acts, making it possible to learn what the other is expressing and perhaps what he is attending to. But though he can alert us to what he is undergoing, he cannot present us with it.

While viewing his own body from without as other observers do, a man, in addition, comes to his body as a limit privately reached. He will not get any closer to that privacy or to its limit at the body by tracing an occurrence at his skin through the nerves and eventually to the brain. These are as remote from the privacy as the skin is. Privacy is not separated from body by a spatial distance. There could be no distance between the limit at which the body stops and the limit at which the privacy ends; there is only one limit, faced in one way from the side of the privacy and in another way from the side of the body.

The voluminosity of an insistent epitomization, like the distendedness of the Augustinian soul in time, is wholly private. The limit it shares with the body belongs to it on its own side. One would not be able to make contact with his body if the limit of his privacy were not the very limit that the body faces from its side. That two-faced limit would not be possible if the epitomization and the body were not pertinent to one another.

A lived body is a unitary outcome, subject to a privacy which accepts the body as that which is to be governed and used. The privacy, as pertinent to the body, has a restricted range and role, and provides the body with a distinctive way of being unified. The unity of a lived body, consequently, has its functions and range confined by the body that it organizes. The organization that it provides cannot be observed. It is neither an organ nor a bodily part. It is also more than a condition instantiated by the body.

To account for the fact that the body is lived as a single complex, it is not necessary, in addition to the body's own organic unity, to invoke another organization which coincides with this. The lived body has only one unity and that is provided by the privacy. As able to provide the organizing unity for the body, the privacy is pertinent to the body and therefore ready to unify it. Although the body as living has an organization of its own, it is under the governance of a different privately imposed unity which lives the body as a unity at the same time that the body is lived by means of other epitomizations.

An aggregate of items, when in an organism, does not cease to be an aggregate; nor does it undergo a change in membership. One could add or subtract any one of the items from the aggregate without affecting the others, merely increasing or decreasing the number being considered. But when one imposes a unity on them, the items are joined together in such a way that an increase or decrease in their numbers affects the nature of the outcome.

The unity which privacy provides on making the body a lived body has effects that can be known by others. A foot is withdrawn, a hand reaches down, emphasis is placed here rather than there. While each occurrence is initiated from the position of the privacy, each is publicly expressed with the help of the body. What cannot be observed is a privately produced interrelating of the items.

The structure and functioning of a body are not identifiable with its unifying organization. A structure orders bodily parts in relation to one another; functioning involves a sequential activity by different parts. A unifying organization, in contrast with both, is a unity privately imposed, making the body a lived unitary body.

The alteration that is required in order for an epitomization to unify the body so that it lives the body, is quite general, making no reference to particular parts or regions of the body. It continues to be pertinent as the body changes in detail, content, and course. When it is accommodated by the body, the organization is specified through the agency of particular bodily occurrences. These specifications cannot be known in advance of their occurrence; what can be so known is only a type of occurrence. How could that which was private ever make contact with what was exterior to it? How could a body, acting in accord with the laws of bodies in a cosmos, even have contact with a singular privacy? An answer to this question, Kant seemed the first to see, requires that the disparate entities in their different ways be integral to a single mediator. Kant held that this was time. Some of his successors, the absolute idealists, thought it was the Absolute. Each view enjoys an advantage over the other. Although Kant did not recognize any other mediator besides time, he did recognize that the mediated items continue to be distinct from one another, with natures and careers of their own. Although some of the idealists did not allow for any mediator other than their Absolute, they did maintain that this took on many different guises, each able to mediate different items. But the one could not explain why there was a time, and the other could not explain how there could be anything to be related. The problem requires for its solution not only the acknowledgment of a number of relations, but the recognition that the terms in the relations are aspects of what exists and acts apart from those relations.

The difference between a controlling condition and a relation is between what makes an effective difference to independent items and what simply terminates at them. Where the conditions govern entities independent of them, the relations which specialize the conditions are continuous with what terminates the relations, the terms. As the idealists say, the terms are internally related. But they are present only so far as they are sustained by entities outside the relationship. Relations are internal to aspects of what continues to exist apart from the relation.

In their roles as terms, neither privacy nor body is identifiable with itself as active or even as able to act. The relations connecting them do not encompass them as interplaying; they can interplay only so far as they are not terms in relations. Both privacy and body provide terms for two asymmetrical relations, in one of which a term functions as a beginning and in the other of which it functions as an ending for any act that might use the relation. The actions of privacy and body traverse these different relations from a beginning to an ending term. Each moves through its own term as a beginning to arrive at the term of the other as an ending; each is able to act on the other because it acts through itself and the others as terms internally connected. The actions of privacy and body pass through the relation to the sustaining body and privacy respectively; as a unit source of acts, each expresses itself through the medium of itself, functioning as a term.

Why do privacy and body not just absorb the portion of the relation that terminates in them, thereby precluding the terms from being part of those relations and thereupon preventing themselves from being acted on by the other? This would be a possible state of affairs were privacy and body in control of the terms that they provide. But the terms are in part a function of common governing conditions, and arise when the conditions are specialized as relations having a limited range.

We have here the principles which permit of a solution to such traditional problems as the ways in which form and matter, soul and body, mind and body, thoughts and the external world, theory and practice, state and the individual, can be effectively together. Each of the paired items has its own integrity and ways of acting. Each is pertinent to the other. Each is related to the other in the guise of a beginning or ending term, internal to a connecting relation. Each acts through its term along the route of the relation, to terminate in the other as sustaining a correlative term.

A mind is not a substance residing behind mental acts; a body is not a substance undergirding bodily acts. Each is both a unitary sustainer of a term and a power operating through the term, and terminates in the sustainer of a correlative term. Both mind and body have integrities of their own; each acts on the other via specialized forms of the very conditions which enable it to be at once distinct from and together with the other.

There are as many types of action as there are types of relation which privacy and body are able to traverse. A number of the actions can occur at the same time, some proceeding from the privacy and others from the body, the joint product being expressed as the action of the lived body.

A private action not only makes a difference to the body, but the body makes a difference to it. As a result, privacy and body are joined in an unpredictable twofold way, analyzable into a plurality of concurrent but independent actions going from privacy to body, and from body to privacy. Without a knowledge of that twofold action, we would have no satisfactory explanation of how privacy and body could make a unity. But the nature of the unity which they together constitute is not exhaustively analyzable into its constituents, since those constituents affect one another on being unified.

If one frees the word from necessary references to irrationality, to excitement, to what is wholly private, or to what is wholly public, one can characterize the union of privacy and body as 'emotional'. We get an emphasis on private excitement when we stress the action of the privacy, and an emphasis on bodily turbulence when we stress the action of the body. But their union always has the two of them together in a new dynamic way.

Once it is noted that there never was a time when privacy was unexpressed, or when the body was unresistant, it becomes evident that from the first a human being emotionally unites sensitivity and body at the same time that his privacy continues to have a portion not yet bodily expressed, and that the body has capacities to interact with other resistant bodies. Each type of expression of the privacy changes the nature of the lived body. At its most mature, the body is lived responsibly by an I which possesses and owns it. Within the compass of that lived body, it is possible to discern other subordinated ways of living the body. A reductionism, which takes the lived body to incorporate or sustain only sensitivity, need, or desire, treats that body as though it were impenetrable by other private expressions. But there is no more difficulty for responsibility or the I to live the body than there is for any other expressions of privacy to do so. The living of a body by these is produced through acts which involve relations similar to those that are involved when a body is lived by sensitivity or the other epitomizations of the person.

What enables one to distinguish expressions of privacy are the prospects they serve. Sensitivity enables the individual to attend to what may occasion pain and pleasure and thereby promote the welfare of the body. Other epitomizations enable the body to bring about results which may not benefit and may even be detrimental to the continuation or prosperity of the body. Were it not for that fact, it would be desirable to speak of all expressions of privacy as differing only in the body. If we begin with the acknowledgment of a lived body, we begin with a privacy and body emotionally joined, and then have to face, not the question of how what is not human is made human through the intrusion of privacy, but how a lived human body is lived more intensively, or in additional ways.

The problem of explicating the way in which a privately initiated need acts on a body does not differ in principle from the problem of explicating the way in which a privately initiated resolution does. They differ, though, in the kind of lived body they intrude upon—need intruding on a body that is sensitively lived, and resolution intruding on what is lived in other ways as well.

Expressions of privacy make use of the body on behalf of an effort to effectively control what they can. Different ways of living the body are required when the body becomes too complex to be governed in the way it had been, and therefore would, apart from new expressions of the privacy, no longer be as completely lived as it had been before. The new expressions are resisted by the body as already being lived in the older way. Sensitivity could then be said to be maximally insistent, and responsibility or the I to be so minimally, or conversely. But all can be equally insistent. It is because they differ in the prospects they face that the expressions of privacy differ in the degree to which they affect the body.

An alternative view of considerable plausibility holds that every epitomization of human privacy is expressed always, at least to a minimal degree. That alternative allows one to hold that men are always social beings, and that the difference between the least and the most mature is a matter only of degree. It makes it possible to recognize the identity of an individual at his most immature with himself when most fully developed bodily and privately. It also makes it possible to assimilate the Aristotelean and medieval claim that each individual has a single distinctive soul, able to make use of available bodily avenues. Nevertheless, the alternative should be rejected. There is no evidence to ground its supposition that an embryo or even an infant is responsible, can make decisions, or seek to realize ideal ends. The achievement of the status of one who is involved with what is far outside the confines of his body awaits the development of that body and the use of it as an agent for sustaining and supplementing his effort to realize what is beyond bodily reach. If we reject the alternative, we are still able to understand a mature man as able to express private powers which depend for their presence on the prior existence of a promise grounded in epitomizations possible to the immature. Our account will then be more empirically tempered, more in consonance with what is known of growth and learning, better aligned with what is known of man's discovery of himself in nature, and in better accord with the hard-won knowledge that some humans fail to get much further in their development than to express their persons. When we come to man as fully matured, the difference between the two approaches is almost lost, since both allow one to say that man at his most mature may express all his powers through the agency of his body.

There is only one body that a man lives at any time, all previous forms of his lived body providing only analytic components. As lived sensitively and in other ways by the person, the body, therefore, can be only conceptually distinguished within the body that is lived by the self. Something similar occurs when a man carries out a public office. Although he continues to live his body, that body is an analytic component within his living of that body as privately occupied with carrying out a public role. His pleasures and pains may be as intensive as before, but they will be qualified in new ways. Surely a pain in a slave's toe is the very same kind of pain that is felt by a king? Or more sharply, must a pain in the toe undergo a change in quality, rhythm, degree, or character when a man takes an oath of office? One answer is within everyone's experience—a change in outlook makes a difference to the quality of what is sensitively undergone. To know that one is at the doctor's office, to decide to go to the doctor, to know that there are possible remedies available which one can apply without a doctor, all make a difference to the quality of a pain, often reducing its tensions and intensity, and sometimes increasing them. The two cases are of course not completely parallel. There need be no private change produced by taking an oath of office, while there is one when expressions of privacy live the body in new ways. A man can continue to live his body as he had before no matter what role he has, but if he expresses a new epitomization of his privacy, the body on which this is imposed is changed. To live a body responsibly is to live one which occasions pains and pleasures qualified by responsibility. The living of a sensitized body by responsibility or some other power, consequently, precludes one from feeling the pains and pleasures he had before. By living a body that had been lived in another way, he makes the body that had been lived in that other way into a component of the body that is then being lived. The fact is not readily recognized, in good part because higher forms of living a body are not expressed in constant ways, thereby allowing for the living of the body on a lower level in between the times when it is lived on a higher. Might one then not go on to say that greater degrees of sensitivity or other epitomizations of privacy are interspersed by expressions of lower or even of minimal degree? One could, could one overcome a difficulty:

Both a man in a stupor and an embryo, and apparently even a newborn infant, have bodies which are only minimally sensitized. Unable to focus on particular regions in their bodies, unable to express their sensitivities differentially through different bodily channels, they are provided only with occasions for diffused pains or pleasures. More differentiated forms of pain and pleasure arise with the achievement of better differentiated bodily areas, either because attention is directed there, or because the body has grown in complexity.

Might the difference not be equally well explained were one to suppose that the same degree of sensitivity is always expressed, accompanied by different degrees of an ability to focus on this or that bodily part, thereby giving pains and pleasures sharper boundaries and setting them in contrast with the other portions of the sensitivity? There surely is nothing foolish in such an idea. But it does require one to allow for different degrees in the expression of the power to focus on particular bodily regions. Consequently, it just replaces the idea of different degrees of an expressed sensitivity having a minimal in a diffused form, by the idea of different degrees of focusing, with a minimum in an inability to focus well or at all. Nothing in principle is gained by making the replacement; something is lost, in fact, for one then gratuitously denies that sensitivity has degrees.

What arouses acute pain in an infant may not do so in an adult; a man's habits, ideas, associations, and the like may dim what would be intensely felt by one less mature. One must therefore hold either that an infant has a greater degree of sensitivity than an adult—and one will then have to acknowledge degrees of expression once again, but suppose that the highest forms occur earlier than the lowest—or that the sensitivity suffusely expressed by an infant is localized by the adult and there cushioned and modified by the rest of the sensitivity and perhaps by other private epitomizations. The second of these alternatives alone allows one to recognize that a pain may be made to wax and wane by attending elsewhere and even to another pain. Were the change credited entirely to an attention added or subtracted, or to the degree of resistance to which the body is subjecting a constantly expressed sensitivity, it would still be true that the outcome would be sensitively felt to a degree it had not been before.

If the explanation of the occurrence of different degrees of pain and pleasure is credited to different degrees of expression on the part of some power other than sensitivity, one is forced to go beyond the obtrusive fact—an experienced difference in degree—to other supposed factors. The refusal to allow for the substitution of these for what is initially acknowledged, allows one to go on to affirm that there is a minimal degree to which sensitivity is always expressed, and that additional expressions of greater intensity help produce a fluctuating, diversely focused expression of sensitivity and, therefore, a way of living the body which can vary throughout the day as well as over the course of a life. What is true of an expressed sensitivity seems to be true of most of the other private powers.

Privacy is single and undivided. The self and person are specialized powers of it, distinguished in act. In turn, the various epitomizations of the self and person actively specialize these. None is a faculty, an isolated power. If it were, the individual would be pluralized even before he did anything. Different epitomizations are differentiated, but only when expressed.

Why not, it might well be asked, carry further the idea of difference in degree, and apply it to different expressions of a particular epitomization of a person or self, and to the person and self as well? Why suppose that sensibility differs from sensitivity, and need from sensibility, and so on, in any other way than in the degree to which they express a common privacy living the self-same body? Differences in kind, such as are here being insisted on, seem to divide a man radically, setting up different compartments in him. Yet men evidently live their lives without sudden breaks, while expressing different kinds of epitomizations. Why then not join most other thinkers in their supposition that every expression of privacy expresses one kind of private act to some degree, e.g., feeling, rationality, or desire? Putting aside, for the moment, the question as to which one of these different forms of a supposed single type of expression is to be chosen, one is confronted with the fact that the epitomizations are being viewed solely from the position of an indeterminate constant privacy. From that position, different epitomizations are so many specializations of it. One then ignores the different prospects which are inseparable from the different epitomizations. Different prospects are distinguished by epitomizations functioning as so many different active powers.

Expressions of a particular epitomization differ in degree because they have the same prospective terminus. Epitomizations differ in kind because they face different prospects, and therefore make different uses of the body. Each turns the body into an agent which, sometimes in opposition to the body's own requirements and satisfactions, enables one to promote the realization of the prospect. The different degrees of effectiveness that are given to a prospect make expressions in or through a body vary in degree.

Why not press on, and hold that privacy itself has some such objective as self-completion, self-articulation, or the realization of a final ideal, and that the different prospects which are pertinent to the different expressions of privacy differ from this solely in degree? Because it would still be necessary to acknowledge a difference in kind between privacy itself, with an all-inclusive prospect, and the specializations of that privacy, each with its own limited prospect. The specializations differ from the privacy in determinateness, direction, activity, and career, and may not only come in conflict with one another, but often have to be privately reconciled or rectified. If one attempted to reduce the difference in kind to a difference in degree, one would still be faced with the fact that the control exerted by a supposed prospect for privacy differed in kind from that exerted by the prospects for various epitomizations.

It is not possible to reduce all differences in kind to differences in degree because prospects, despite their unrealized status, have distinctive natures and make distinctive demands. The conclusion would lead to the acknowledgment of a plurality of possibilities, distinguished from one another as though they were so many actualities merely transported into the future, were those prospects separable from the expressions to which they are relevant. When and as different expressions of privacy are distinguished, so are their prospects, each controlling and guiding the expressions.

There is a difference between a body lived by sensitivity and one lived as well by, say, a resolution. Although the latter is not within the provenance of all humans at all times, their unity and persistence are not jeopardized by that fact. It is the same man who is and was sensitive, who prefers, wills, understands, or expresses other epitomizations. He will not yet be self-identical, if he still lacks an I, and therefore is not able to reduce whatever he encounters to a single, constant result. But he will persist, express the same single privacy throughout, whether or not he has an I.

Men, and only men, are persons. Without losing their status as belonging together in the same species, they can still differ from one another quite radically. The fact is so far in accord with the conclusions of those religious thinkers who divide mankind into the saved and the damned, and with the conclusions of those ethicists who sharply separate off men who are virtuous from men who are not. But the differences among humans are not solely differences in privacies, as some of these religious and ethical thinkers suppose. Men insist on different kinds of expressions when living their bodies in different ways. As a consequence, they differ from one another not simply as privacies, and surely not as just biological beings, but as men who live their bodies through the imposition of privately initiated expressions. Since a man who once lived his body responsibly in addition to living it sensitively may not do so at another time, he evidently can change in very distinctive ways while continuing to be the same person. But if men are distinguished from one another in this fashion, are we not forced to hold, with the religious and ethical thinkers just referred to, that men can belong to completely different classes? No. Two obstacles stand in the way. Sometimes men change, and quite radically: a noble man is able to intend and carry out great evils; a vicious man can decide to do good, and can do it; sinners become saints and saints sinners. Also, all men have the same kind of privacy, and are therefore able to express themselves in the way others do who are at the same stage of development.

All men are equally persons with privacies unlike those possessed by other kinds of being. Each, too, is unique with his own privacy, his own epitomizations of this, his own expressions, and his own lived body.

FOUR

The Primary Private Power

a. The Daily World

A resolute phenomenologist stops with what is privately faced. A resolute behaviorist, instead, stops with what is bodily observable. When the former accepts the very data that interest the latter, he still differs from him, since instead of seeking to control or to produce it, he is content to describe what he finds. Both he and the behaviorist would like to avoid references to anything beyond what is observed; but once it is allowed that what is now observed may be subsequently observed, and once it is seen that observations are made by persistent, presumably honest and conscious observers, account will have to be taken of something more than the observed. This will lead to a reference to persons and selves, and eventually to the indeterminate privacies which these diversely specialize. An advance is made on both behaviorism and phenomenology when it is recognized that public data are privately observed and analyzed, and that explanations for what is publicly acknowledged are privately produced and claimed.

Epitomizations by person and self do not exhaust privacy. This has a status apart from them as their common ground. As a man matures, another specialization of his privacy achieves a distinctive role. It is both widely known and not really known at all. References are made to it by almost everyone, although in quite different and sometimes opposing ways. Philosophers, theologians, and mystics have spoken of it again and again as providing man with some access to eternal truths, realities, or mysteries; their 'acting reason', 'anima', 'soul', or 'spirit' was understood by them to make contact with, to lose itself in, or to adopt what is forever. The accounts diverge, in part because they suppose that there is only one eternal entity, and then attend to different aspects of that one specialization of privacy which can be occupied with what is forever. In effect, they treat as one what is in fact many, and focus on different facets of what is actually undivided.

Most men hold that there is only one reality which governs all there is. Many identify that reality with a deity of some kind. Others take it to be a final substance, a pure being, a sheer, intelligible perfection, nature itself, emptiness, or an absolute. Two questions arise. Are they referring to different realities? Does not a man take account of every one and use them to enhance the other specializations of his privacy? I think the answers to both questions will be seen to be in the affirmative, once we acknowledge the *idios*, that specialization of privacy which is occupied with whatever final realities condition everything else—although we will not fully understand what the idios does unless we know what finalities there are, and the roles they could play in a privacy.

By accepting whatever conditions everything else, the idios becomes enriched, and attains a position where it can enrich and reconcile other epitomizations of the privacy with one another. To do this, it makes use of all the finalities, under the limitations which those epitomizations impose. The finalities are present and operative apart from the idios; they act on and are countered by whatever actualities there be. The use of the finalities by the idios is an additional fact, dependent on the existence of a mature man.

No actuality can make itself be relevant to, independent of, rationally connected with, distanced from, or in an evaluational order with others. Its togetherness with them in these ways depends on common conditionings by different finalities. Those finalities are not all-powerful; if they were, the very actualities they were to keep together would be so overwhelmed that there would be nothing left over to be related. Because actualities can oppose them, the finalities are able to act on them and make them be together.

Actualities are together with one another in a number of ways, each due to the conditioning presence of a distinct finality. There is nothing amiss in the supposition that the actualities might have been together in fewer, other, or additional ways than those that in fact prevail. But just what these might be we do not know. There is no deducing of the universe, unless it be from something else no else real, itself unaccounted for; or unless the universe is itself abstract, formal, a logical conclusion, with no place left for the individual engaged in the deduction. The finalities to acknowledge are only those and all those that are evidenced by conditions which in fact govern actualities.

The governing finalities are where the actualities are. Together, expressions of the finalities and the actualities constitute the 'mixed', a world of appearances partly grasped when we attend to what daily confronts us. The finalities and actualities are not separated from their contributions; they are those very contributions in a more intensive form. Consequently, when we seek to reach actualities or what governs all of them, we move, not to distant realms, but intensively into what was already present in a more attenuated guise. The acknowledgment of actualities and finalities is one with the acknowledgment that the mixed is a product of what they jointly constitute.

Finalities need actualities. Were there no actualities, the finalities would not express what they are in depth in a plurality of distinct ways. The need of finalities for actualities, however, is neither greater nor less than the need of actualities for the finalities. The idealistic attempt to deal with actualities as though they were limited forms of finalities is no more warranted than the empiricistic attempt to deal with finalities as though they were actualities, generalized and verbalized.

The movement from the effective presence of actualities to their privacies is convergent, from what is less to what is more self-contained and powerful. It is the reciprocal of the move which takes one to the finalities from the evidence of them that is provided by what they contribute to the mixed. When the former move is into man, one starts with his lived body. A complete account of him will go on to consider not only the different ways in which his body is lived but also how his idios is able to enhance and harmonize his various modes of living the body. The latter part of the task is still before us. It can be best carried out if it is preceded by an examination of a number of views—some already confronted—that might get in the way.

All of us, again and again, encounter a multiplicity of items. We progress toward an explanation of them by converging toward their more intensive, deeper, more effective sources. This we all do when we listen to one another; use a proper name; recognize that there are other humans; or acknowledge that others are persons and have selves, and that they express sensitivity and other epitomizations in and through their bodies. To recognize these facts is to oppose a dominant philosophical and scientifically endorsed view of the world which, since the time of Galileo, has held that the ultimate and only real units are indivisible cosmic entities.

Logic, science, and technology tend to favor explanations which start with unit entities, and try to understand all else as the product of their external juncture. As a consequence, the ways in which those units are bunched together, the fact that they are sometimes controlled by the more complex entities in which they function as parts, and the origin of the privacies of men and other living beings are not only unexplained, but are turned into inexplicables. When it is supposed that the only reality is a colorless, soundless host of unobservable entities, all compelled to act in accord with implacable, mathematically formulatable laws, with everything else treated as an aggregation of such units, as an aggregation of aggregations of them, or as some distortion of these, the perceived and even the perceivable will be taken to be illusory, subjective, mind-created, or mind-dependent. In different ways, a number of thinkers have found fault with this view, and for good reasons. It makes no provision for the reality of the observer, his instruments, and the machines he makes and uses, or for observable beasts, birds, trees, flowers, streams, oceans, and mountains of which one is forced again and again to take practical, and should take theoretical account. Why dismiss them? What is gained by making them give way to what no one could in fact observe? The behavior of complex beings and their gross parts cannot be explained by attending solely to what is within their confines, or by envisaging aggregations of irreducible unit entities. Although a flexing of an arm requires the use of tendons and muscles functioning in accord with the laws of mechanics and is, therefore, presumably explicable as a result of the way in which smaller units act together, it is still true that they are tendons and muscles, and not just collections of units; that the arm is flexed when neither the tendons nor the muscles or their gross or final parts is attended to; that there are laws which help us to understand and to predict what the tendons and muscles do; and that the explanations are sought and brought into play by individual men independently of whether or not they flex their arms. An adequate understanding of the action of muscles and tendons precludes a reduction of these to smaller units. Similar reasons stand in the way of an attempt to achieve a satisfactory understanding of organic beings by attending to the nature and functioning of their muscles or tendons or any other parts.

For some purposes one could take this or that context to be superior to others, allowing for a better understanding or grasp of what is real or supposed. But there is no compelling reason for holding that the preferential context must contain material entities or combinations of them, unless one is occupied solely with what is material. The reverse claim, giving preferential status to spiritual or mind-like items, is no less and no more justified. Better than either, if we are concerned not with the objects of a special discipline but with what is real no matter what the grade or kind, is a view which recognizes that both kinds of items are together in unified complexes whose nature and functionings express something of both. It is these unified complexes we daily confront and with which we begin our inquiries; it is to these we return to check the soundness and viability of our views; it is these we should seek to understand. The admission does not require a rejection of science or a denial that physical entities are real.

S. A. Alexander and Whitehead were acutely aware of the issue. Alexander tried to make provision for both ultimate units and complexes by supposing that the universe was built in layers, in which those that contained the comparatively simpler and physical preceded those that contained the more complex and non-physical. But it is difficult on his view to see how there could be such a reality as a man who was at once unitary and singular, encompassing a plurality of both private and public parts whose activities he affects as surely as they affect him. Whitehead followed Alexander's lead. Supposing that the most basic realities were at once simple and complex—simple in having only a momentary existence, complex in taking within themselves the past and prospective future in acts of coming to be—he, like Alexander, failed in the end to take account of persistent, individual actualities, with privacies of their own, able to express themselves in and through complex bodies. He did advance considerably beyond Alexander in many other ways, not the least of which was in his recognition that there was a 'non-physical pole' in every actuality. But neither he nor Alexander clearly distinguished a realm occupied by actualities from one where they appear. Nor did they clearly distinguish a cosmos of units from nature, lush and variegated, containing those units, combinations of these, as well as living persistent individuals with bodies within which smaller, cosmically governed ones could be found.

Other views—existentialism, in particular—have tried to turn the entire matter around. Instead of holding that there are real, ultimate units, or anything else for that matter other than men and what interests them, they take men to be radically private beings, and nature to be either non-existent or a human creation. Where their opponents cannot make provision for themselves as unitary, persistent men, and for what they use and observe, the existentialists cannot show how it is that a man could be hurt or killed by an unthinking thing.

Today there are some who, eschewing all speculative thought, start and end with a community. Others take men to be irreducible units whose life seems to be exhausted in a use of a shared language or other communal activities. All that can be observed and allowed, it is claimed, is community-toned. Anything supposed to be true is then just what is agreed upon by most, or by the most powerful or important members. Despite the fact that these thinkers inescapably make use of their own privacies to claim, communicate, and to forge their views, they hold that all we can use are what is available to others or is generally acceptable. No provision is made for men who use a common language. On their own accounting, no men could possibly privately assess the views or make private use of anything.

Were one forced to make a choice, it would be better to acknowledge the reality of complex entities, and not the reality of indivisible units; and better to acknowledge the reality of either than to allow for nothing more than communal realities. We, and what we daily confront, must be real, if there is to be anything used by any of us, or if there is a difference between observation and fantasy, knowledge and opinion. But we cannot avoid the acknowledgment of indivisibles as well, without precluding a physical explanation of the functioning of chemical units. It is, of course, true that one can hold on to any hypothesis, no matter how far-fetched, by making corresponding changes in different parts—a point made some time ago in *Reality*—or, by extension, by changing other claims which are organically connected with it. One can, therefore, as readily deny that there are ultimate units as that there are men. Nevertheless, if we are to understand what is daily encountered in terms of the realities to which present evidences lead and daily encounters presuppose, we must take a stand with the fact that there are men, subhuman beings, non-living beings, items within all of these, and finally ultimate, irreducible units. We must also affirm that all are finite, interacting, making a difference to one another, each with its own privacy. A freedom to entertain any hypothesis must not be bought by denying or ignoring what we daily know or at which we can arrive by using evidence available to all.

It is not necessary either to affirm or deny that whatever men or other complexes do might be intelligibly expressed by restating what occurs in terms of their parts and, ultimately, in terms of irreducibles. The restatements will presuppose the accuracy of the original account. In the end the restatements will have to be compared with the originals to see how well the restatements do justice to them. Restatements do not make data vanish, or expose them as having no natures or reality of their own. They reinstate them in another context.

We should begin with the familiar objects of every day as together with one another in various ways, and then try to grasp what we daily know in better ways, on more reliable terms, and on a larger canvas. Inevitably, we will move quite far away from our starting point. If we portray what is ultimate, really there, we will not necessarily then be in contact with this. A philosophic inquiry has a referent only if its outcome is brought into contact with the familiar world, and then made to move, under its guidance, to the reality about which the inquiry speaks. The realities we theoretically know are in fact reached only so far as our theoretical knowledge is begun with, sustained by, and mediated by what we daily know.

We move away from the daily world in the attempt to have more sharply demarcated, systematically organized, defensible knowledge. What we arrive at is different from that with which we began. But we arrive at it so as to understand the world where we had begun. We can do this if we both move beyond it as far as the evidence there requires us to move, and if we recognize that what we finally acknowledge is to be brought into relation to the real of which it speaks through the mediative help of the somewhat inchoate but inescapable world in which we daily live.

The objects of every day are together in space and time; they are interactive, law-abiding, and related to one another in other ways. To sharpen the issue, let us attend to just one of these. Space, as distinct from the items which are together in space, is a common condition for those items. It enables them to be together in symmetrical relations at various distances. As able to be together in space, the items are distinct from what they are as in the space, since as just able to be together, they do not yet occupy a spatial region and are, therefore, neither large nor small, near nor far, high nor low, neither to the right nor to the left.

Every actuality bodily occupies a region of space. Were it extended to begin with, there would be two extensions in the same place, one provided by the actuality and the other by the space. Were the actuality unextended, it would never take up room, and an infinitude of them could exist anywhere. So far, they would be indistinguishable from the angels of the medievals. Like those angels, they would have to take on alien guises if they are to be confronted, and so far would not be known as they really are. Since they could not themselves have the status of located items in a public space, they will remain unreachable things in themselves. To be able to be located in space, an actuality must be able to occupy a portion of it. This it can do, because it is distended, i.e., indivisibly voluminous, and able to interplay with a divisibly extended space.

An occupied space is a place constituted by a subdivision of extended space and a distendedness. As private, the actuality is distended; as public, it is in a limited region, privately bounded off from a portion of the publicly available space. What is publicly locatable is what has privately occupied a located region of space; the distendedness which enables it to do this is but an aspect of its privacy.

One moves from the objects of every day to a condition such as space on one side and to a private distendedness on the other, and from these to their empowering sources, the one omnipresent, the other finite, in the course of a metaphysical inquiry. Alone, this provides no explanation of why the components of public objects are what they are; what status they have apart from the objects they constitute; or why they come together. It must be supplemented by ontological, transcendental, and dialectical accounts. The first treats finite entities from the position of finalities; the second reverses that procedure and deals with final realities from the position of actualities. The third sets the ontological and transcendental in opposition. The first two, without the dialectical, are unable to account for the interplay of oppositional powers, while the dialectical alone would not allow one to know why oppositional activities come to rest where they do.

Finalities could conceivably yield actualities through some kind of self-division, but the distinguished items would then have to be held away from the finalities—and that requires the help of the actualities. Actualities could conceivably yield finalities through some kind of solidification, but the outcome of the solidification would be able to function on its own only if it were empowered—and that requires a reference to finalities. The irreducibility of each stops the incursions of the other. That dialectical result coincides in part with what commonsense men daily know. It is, in fact, the daily world, as freed from distortions and humanizations.

Although it is convenient to speak of privacies as being 'behind' bodies or acts (and of conditioning finalities as being imposed on actualities), it cannot be overemphasized that privacies, like finalities, are where they in fact operate. They are effective counterforces which qualify, and may be able to own, possess, control, and guide the bodies on which they impinge. None is a faculty or object; all are prescriptive, explanatory, and insistent. Privacies are 'behind' bodies or acts only so far as they are the sources of what is manifested in and through these. Their expressions are those very privacies diversified.

What is important in daily life and other limited settings does not cease to exist because it does not play a distinctive role in a larger world. The larger world does not preclude the existence of areas where special conditions prevail, any more than these preclude a nature where living beings have their niches and where they struggle to survive. Nor does nature preclude the existence of a cosmos where all unit bodies are dynamically together in common extensions in which and through which privacies are expressed, and the potentialities of bodies realized. All three are equally objective. None should be put aside as illusory.

The cosmos is the daily world, freed from specialized conditions, purged of all subjectivity, spread out far beyond the reach of man, and encompassing all unit actualities. Those actualities are subject to common, encompassing, effective conditions, of which governing laws are one instance. There is nothing amiss, though, in speaking of organic beings as existing in the cosmos as well as in nature, provided that it is also granted that in nature those actualities are subject to more limited forms of those conditions, that they have their own distinctive kinds of privacy, and that they are involved with limited numbers of others in an environment and in other areas. They will then be seen to be subject, at one and the same time, to wide-ranging laws, and to more specific forms of these.

We know that there are complex bodies. We can divide them, and sometimes we can separate out smaller bodies within them. We are forced to acknowledge that there are also ultimate, inanimate units in order to understand the functioning of the least complex of entities; to master the workings of known complex physical and chemical entities; to allow for occurrences which are not confined within complexes; and to deal with what is from a cosmological standpoint. Those ultimate units are atomic monads. The body of each is indivisible with a distinctive privacy behind it, empowering the body and expressing itself in and through this. Failure to acknowledge atomic monads compels one to leave the action of the bodies, their encompassment within larger controlling unities, and their occupation of space at least partly unexplained. Almost inevitably we are tempted to read into the atomic monads those features which are manifested in the complex objects. The temptation must be resisted if we are to avoid saddling ourselves with unjustified beliefs. There is no warrant for saying that atomic monads have minds or even that they have feelings like ours, though less intense. They are not tiny, dim-witted men.

We do not know whether or not the smallest of units that are acknowledged by scientists today are atomic monads. That they have magnitudes, stretching out in space and time, and therefore can be conceived to be divisible, does not preclude them from being the smallest possible. But the fact that we do not know how to divide them, and that we have not found smaller ones, does not mean that they are in fact the smallest. A unit is ultimate if there are not within it other entities distinct from one another and able to exist and act outside those confines. Even if such units existed only within the compass of some larger, and vanished once they were separated from this, they would still be ultimate, just so far as they themselves did not contain within themselves smaller units which could interact with one another, and perhaps with it.

Atomic monads take up room and endure for a time. If they did not, they would be extensionless points, incapable of being together with others in a common world. No matter what the size or shape of complex beings, whether they are alive or dead, good or bad, their rate of fall is determined by the atomic monads in them, each acting independently of the others. The fact does not preclude the effective expression of feelings, desire, and other epitomizations of a person or self in and through a confining complex body.

Atomic monads do not affect private experience, nor an occupation with prospects on the part of a privacy. But they do affect and are affected by the complexes which encompass them. If they did not, the fall of a man would leave his body behind, while a sudden leap by him would leave the atomic monads behind.

One generation finds that its predecessors stopped with what later was discovered to be quite complex. Since there is no predesignatable mass, magnitude, or state which necessarily belongs to an atomic monad, and since every observable can be divided at least mathematically, there never can be any surety that bedrock has been reached. At every stage of scientific investigation, we must be content to take as ultimate what experiments, observations, and theories together presuppose and demand, leaving open the possibility that some subsequent discovery may require that what had once been taken to be ultimate is complex, comprising still more ultimate units. Still, it is possible now to say something true about the ultimate units, by showing how more complex actualities could not be what they are if those units were not of such and such a nature—at the very least, that they are indivisible individuals, privately distended and publicly extended.

Atomic monads acting in concert make it possible for more complex beings to come to be. Their acknowledgment enables us to understand how it is possible for human gametes to give rise to zygotes, followed by embryos, fetuses, and viable human beings. Whatever the complex individual, references must in the end be made to a primal dunamis. Through the joint action of atomic monads, a portion of the dunamis, which they individually fractionate, is separated out as a privacy and a unitary body. The dunamis, under different designations and in different ways, was acknowledged by Schopenhauer, Bergson, Jung, and Whitehead. They were one in their rejection of Aristotle's view that what underlies all actualities is a passive matter. One consequence of Aristotle's supposition—which they did not explore—was his inability to explain how one type of actuality could arise out of another; another was his inability to account for individuals, or to make individuality intelligible. His view, that there were 'fixed species', each without origin, was required by his supposition that at the root of all actualities was a primal impotence.

Consequently, what was supposedly common to all beings was not seen to be the source of complex actualities. It also was not seen that the different privacies provided the dunamis with a multiplicity of ways in which it could be manifested—although the correlative view, that bodies together enable what is final to have a cosmic role, and that what is final enables bodies to be related, was occasionally glimpsed.

b. Possible Worlds

Separate actualities and finalities, and unions of actualities and finalities necessarily affect one another. The outcomes of these interplays could have been different from what they in fact are. No particular result is necessary. Whatever occurs might have been otherwise. Considerations such as these led Leibniz to ask why there was Something rather than Nothing. The question has been repeated by Heidegger. But it still is not clear. If the Nothing is set over against the actual world, it is the Nothing of that world. If it is not set over against it, and thus is not faced with what is real, it is just a logical possibility, reducing the world, if taken to be alternative to that possibility, to another logical possibility.

Given a pair or a larger set of logical possibilities, there is no reason why any one of them should have any standing that the others do not. A world which was a member of such a pair or set would be no more concrete or real than the Nothing with which it was contrasted. If, instead, one acknowledges the world to be real, one already acknowledges what is more than a possibility. One then faces real possibilities, possibilities which are relevant to and can be realized only through some act carried out in the world.

The alternatives 'Something or Nothing' are not on a footing if 'Something' is more than a logical possibility, more than what is not self-contradictory. If there were many logically possible worlds, any conceivable item would have a place in at least one of those worlds. But for any item in our world, a possible world would be one in which at best something relevant to that item could have a place. It is a tautology to say that the item is rigidly designated. Everything in this world is self-same relative to whatever is a possibility for it.

Leibniz thought that one logical possibility was that of the best of all worlds. God, being good and powerful, made this real. Leibniz failed to make clear that for God to do this, he not only had to credit that logical possibility with a dignity denied to all other logically possible worlds but, in addition, had to add something to it to make it be more than a possibility. A logically possible perfect world is no more real than a logically possible imperfect one. If our world is real it is more than either, for it is then more than logically possible. It could not be set alongside logical possibilities, whether of a perfect world, an imperfect world, or a Nothing, without denying it its reality.

A perfect world could be a real possibility for the actual world. No God, though, could face that possibility in the way the actual world could, since only the latter would have it as its real possibility. Faced with the possibility of a perfect world which he wished to make real, a God would have to treat it as an impotent possibility. He would then have to realize it or enable it to be realized through the action of an already existing actual world or an actual Nothing. But neither of these can realize that possibility, granted that either can be at all.

If Nothing and the world were just logical possibilities, a creating God would have had to ask himself why the possibility of the world should be realized rather than the possibility of the Nothing. But were there no realities besides God, the possibilities would forever remain possibilities unless God could somehow make something be outside himself. To do that, he would not have to attend to any further possibility, but he would have to make himself be less than perfect, faced by what is not himself.

Logical possibilities have the status of real possibilities only so far as they have been transformed so as to be realizable by what is already actual. For Nothing to be, it has to be brought about by someone or be put in place of something. A Nothing in fact is something more than a logical possibility. If God gave this reality, he gave it something of himself. If God alone exists, there could not be just Nothing. At most, Nothing would be just an idea in him, without a counterpart. If he faced the possibility of having a Nothing or the possibility of having a world in addition to himself he would face them not as logical possibilities, but as possibilities for him to realize. Were they pertinent to his goodness, creativity, understanding, will, and the like, they would be real possibilities for him, one of which his creative act would transform into an actual Nothing or an actual world. Only the latter has its own possibilities to realize. Before he acted, there would not be an actual Nothing which he might or might not fill, any more than there would be an actual world which he might or might not allow to realize possibilities. Instead, he alone would be.

Were God a creator of all else, he would produce something, but not in place of a Nothing which was already present. Such a God faces only the possibility of something to be made by him.

The only Nothing that is relevant to this world is the nothingness of this world. This is not an alternative to the world, but a possible consequence of its activity. It would have to be produced out of and replace the real world if it is to be the nothingness of that world, and would necessarily differ from a merely logically possible Nothing, because it had somehow acquired reality—enough in fact to exclude all else. A Nothing which was able to be instead of this world would have to replace it, and therefore would have had to become real. But it could not become real unless somehow it was given reality, either by the world or by some being outside the world. If it were given reality by the world, the world would, as Aristotle observed, still remain, unless conceivably it could in that very act destroy itself, and thereby be both cause and effect together.

A variant of this issue is contained in the attempt to speak of possible worlds, worlds alternative to this—another idea of Leibniz'. But when one speaks of possible worlds, one refers to those that are only logically possible. Those possibles are not alternative to our world but to other possibles. A really possible world is relevant to our own; it can come about only through acts performed by what is in this world. Such a really possible world is future to what now is, to be realized through the workings of this world.

Since logically possible alternative worlds are all on a footing, if our world is viewed as one among the logically possible, it has to be denied the reality that it has. If, instead, our world is acknowledged, logically possible worlds would be alternative to one another, but not to this world.

No items in this world are necessary. Every one of them can be replaced. If one is made to vanish, it will be through the act of some other, and then in such a way that something else is left in its place. The elimination of a contingent being yields not Nothing but something else. There always is some actuality or other, just as surely as there always are finalities which enable them to be together.

The actualities that are in this world together constitute a necessary whole. Let it be supposed there are just two, *a* and *b*. From the position of *a*, any *b* would be identical with *non-a* and, from the position of *b* any *a* would be identical with *non-b*. From the position of either one, there is an exhaustive disjunction of items. Only the ignoring of their being together as real entities will make it possible to view them as entirely indifferent to one another.

Actualities have their own integrities. They are individuals with unduplicable privacies, but they are so only so far as they are also together in a single world where each has the status of an *a* over against the rest in the guise of what is not *a*. The fact that *a* can be replaced by *c* does not show that the world as it now is is not an exhaustive set of entities, and surely does not show that both *a* and *b* are just logical possibilities. Contingents in their severalty, they still cannot be replaced by a logical Nothing.

There are no possible worlds alternative to this, but only different occurrences that might have been brought about, and different occurrences which might eventually be realized, the realization in both cases presupposing possibilities inseparable from what is actual. To explain why something is thus and thus and not different, one must refer to actual causes in this world.

c. The Idios in Act

We learn that there are final, conditioning realities as well as complex actualities by identifying and using their attenuations, after separating these out of the appearances they help constitute.

We learn that there are at least five final conditioning realities—or if we distinguish space, time, and causality as irreducible and unitary, seven —by tracing to their sources five (or seven) types of relationship.

We learn that there are monadic, atomic actualities when we see that these alone can always be indifferently together, all others vanishing if we overlook their unitary complexity, encompassing what otherwise would be indifferently together.

We learn that the atomic monads are different from one another, once we attend to the fact that each is an object with which all the other atomic monads are related.

We learn that the atomic monads are distinct units, once we see that each is a locus of all the final conditioning realities.

We learn that there is a continuity between the privacy and body of every actuality, once we see that every act has an origin in what is not fully manifest in public.

We learn that there is freedom in every actuality, once we see that every act is partly constituted in the course of its occurrence.

We learn that actualities are able to persist once we see that their privacies are not exhausted in the production of any act.

It is necessary to acknowledge the presence of insistent privacies in all actual beings, if we are to understand their functioning. Were the privacies of these not insistent, there would be no countering of final conditions with a consequent limitation of the range and specialization of these conditions. Were the privacies not unduplicable, making limited, insistent demands which are only partly expressed and necessarily diversified when expressed and, in the higher forms, able to be specialized as a plurality of distinct private epitomizations, there would be no individuals, nothing in reserve, nothing able to decide and think, but only inert entities which enabled universal conditions to be localized and have the role of relations.

All bodies, even those which cannot be physically divided and thus are ultimate, are mathematically divisible. A privacy is not divided or divisible in these ways. It remains single and singular even when it has specialized epitomizations and expresses these. Both ultimate units and complex beings are at once indivisible as privacies and mathematically divisible as bodies.

The privacy of a man is initially specialized as an epitomized person which is expressed always as a sensitivity, and may be expressed in other ways as well. The various epitomizations of his person, and later, the epitomizations of his self, may come in conflict with one another. The conflicts are overcome in part by the person or the self, and are finally subject to the idios. This, through its acceptance and use of final conditions, is able to control the other epitomizations of the privacy in ways that the person and the self cannot. But it is not always successful.

The idios is both receptive to and makes use of all the conditions originating with the finalities. The receptivity and use differ from one another both in function and result, the one providing an opportunity for the conditions to contribute content, the other enabling the idios to take the conditions into itself on its own terms. Were the receptivity to occur without the use, the idios would be passively subject to intruded conditions. Were the use to occur without the receptivity, the conditions would remain external to the idios, not enrich it. Both take place at the same time. But since they are independent of one another, the idios is constantly faced with the task of combining them. The result is a more or less successful governance of all of a man's epitomizations. The more the epitomizations hobble one another, the more is the idios called upon to act on them, and the more is it therefore occupied with making receptive use of final conditions so as to be able to harmonize the different epitomizations.

To the degree that the idios successfully receives and uses the conditions, to that degree a man will become *self-sufficient, self-mastered, self-guiding, creative,* and *self-established.* Each state depends on the effective reception and use of a distinctive final condition.

Self-sufficiency is a state where one is able to be and act without the help of others. It does not have a necessary reference to the satisfaction of appetites or to the possession of any particular items, for there is no ascertainable end to these. Instead, it requires the receptive use of a condition that allies and contrasts all items, keeping them together as more or less relevant. When accepted and used by the idios that condition enables the different epitomizations to become more or less relevant to one another.

The healthier a man, the readier he is to become and act as self-sufficient. The contention seems to oppose obtrusive facts. Men who come closer to enlightenment than the rest often appear to be far from healthy. Some claim that they have conquered or denied their bodily desires and have kept other activities under full control, so as to be able to concentrate on becoming more intimately involved with what is ultimate. Since they distinguish themselves from their disciples who are actively engaged in struggling with their private and bodily propensities, evidently what is being claimed by the teachers is that they have passed beyond that stage. The work that the idios would otherwise have been called upon to do presumably has been made unnecessary by the teachers' reception and use of a final reality. Instead of denying that the healthier one is, the more he is able to become and act as self-sufficient, the fact is just bypassed. The determination of what is to be done by the teacher is left to his idios, as able to make him be self-sufficient. Evidently, the teacher has concentrated on the expression of that finality ('Substance' I have elsewhere called it) which enables each actuality to be self-centered and to have different degrees of relevance to others.

Self-mastery, like self-sufficiency, results in a man maintaining himself apart from all else. But where self-sufficiency involves a self-centering, self-mastery involves a self-bounding, the becoming a distinct being, affected by and incorporating the expression of a final Being. In self-mastery, use of a condition dominates the acceptance of it; in self-sufficiency, acceptance dominates use.

Were a man not at all self-mastered, he would not be coordinated with, not be on a footing with anything; his idios would not even be together with the idios of another as its equal. Were he not at all self-sufficient, he would be completely dependent on others for his being. Since an engagement with one condition is independent of an engagement with others, it is nevertheless possible for the idios to do more justice to one than to another. As a consequence, a man may be self-sufficient but exhibit little self-mastery, or be self-mastered while far from self-sufficient.

Although the idios is equally receptive of both conditions—indeed of all the primary conditions—and makes some use of all of them, it does not succeed in carrying out every task to the same degree at every moment. As a consequence, it does not deal with all the epitomizations with the same success.

So far as a man has achieved self-mastery, he is able to make both his privacy and body be independent of the privacy and body of others. That self-mastery is to be distinguished from the outcome of the exercise of a will, since it does not require consciousness. Like other forms of self-enrichment, though, it is promoted when other demands are reduced, and the will is used supportively.

Accepting the reality of a creating, good God, and the ability of men to freely elect good or evil, theologians have asked themselves, and have been asked by others, whether such a God might not have done better had he created men bound to do only what is good. They answered the question by saying that a man who can decide freely and therefore who can freely elect what is evil is superior to one who lacked a freedom to elect, even if that lack meant that he did nothing but good. At the same time, it was held by these theologians that God was free but could not do evil. It is not clear whether or not it was also supposed that God could not do evil because he found it to be repulsive, because his freedom was exercised outside the sphere where good and evil are distinguished, or because his goodness excluded the presence of evil. Perhaps it is just as well that these were not distinguished, for on the first of these alternatives, God would not tolerate evil, on the second he would not do anything about it, and on the third he would not allow a place for it in what he was supposed to have created.

If evil is really outside the reach of God's knowing or acting, it is evidently nothing that concerns him. It is not reasonable to suppose that any man would be subject to a divine punishment for somehow producing what is outside God's scope. Be that as it may, a man acts freely when he accepts and uses any condition.

If a man is receptive to and adopts a condition grounded in a final rationale, he freely becomes *self-guided*. He is then like a God whose freedom is exercised outside the area where there is good or evil, differing mainly in the degree of power at his command, his imperfections, and in his ability to act freely on other epitomizations. A good God always does what is good, no matter how evil it seems to be to men. Apparently, this is what Job learned from his conversation with him—and perhaps also that what God does becomes good because God does it.

A reference to God in philosophy should be just an occasion for examining a limiting case. It is here made to help clarify an intelligible governance of what privacy does. Nothing in the understanding of man need be jeopardized if God's reality is denied, ignored, or understood in non-traditional ways. On his own, whether or not there is a God, a man accepts and uses a universal rationale, and thereupon guides himself to act properly on the various epitomizations of his privacy.

Unlike both self-sufficiency and self-mastery, self-guidance demands that the idios keep a good balance between the acceptance and use of a final condition. We would like to become more completely self-sufficient and self-mastered, but do not have much success. We can, though, make ourselves well-guided almost at once by putting our minds to work on behalf of the idios when this makes acceptive use of a final rationale.

Spontaneity exhibits an uncontrolled spurt of energy; innovation provides a pivotal point enabling activity to change direction; invention reorganizes what is available so as to produce a new object able to bring about new results; originality is freedom expressed beyond the control of established rules and ways. *Creativity*, in contrast, is controlled, operates on behalf of what is to be completed, promotes the achievement of excellence, and brings about what no submission to rules could have yielded. Though it has within it something of all the others, it is no amalgam of them. Creativity in root is the product of an acceptive use of a distinctive final condition, enabling one to incorporate values one would otherwise lack, and to spell out the result in one's own way.

Most men's creative power is not properly channelled through needed epitomizations. Nor are most men sufficiently trained or sufficiently free from routine conventions, public opinion, ambition, self-consciousness, and a knowledge of what has already been achieved by others, to be able to express their creativity with results that match those produced by prodigies. Not mature enough to be able to enrich themselves with what is governing and qualifying them, prodigies nevertheless are able to combine a number of powers to produce great results. A mature man though, can make himself creative beyond the capacity of even great prodigies, since these can get no further than to exhibit a combination of spontaneity, innovation, invention, and originality. He may not be able to put the creativity he acquired to good use, but the prodigies, in contrast, have not acquired enough creative power, and surely do not know how to use it to most effect. A child actor does not understand just how he is or should be envisaged from most other positions, since he does not understand what it means to be in them. A child musician, poet, painter, chess player—there apparently are no child architects or child directors of films or plays—has not yet come to the point where his spontaneity, innovation, invention, or originality is enriched by a grasp of what is at once vitally benign and malign.

Creativity is the result of a receptive use of conditioning by Existence, specialized as space, time, and causality. Did a man not make these his own, there would be a discrepancy between what he makes public and what he privately is. He would be just a distended occupier of a region who was being subjected to alien conditions. A similar discrepancy occurs when he fails to make a good bring about a sharp contrast between what he privately and publicly is. Such a sharp contrast sometimes occurs when he fails to be creative.

A great creative man is caught up in projects whose full magnitude and complexity he does not fully grasp until he has worked at them and given them an articulate, finite form. His achievement makes possible the supervening of beauty, goodness, and truth in a finite region. Usually he pays little attention to these, even while he keeps at his work, until they become clearly manifest.

Although a creative man is not necessarily more self-sufficient than others, he is as free from distractions as one who is self-sufficient. Nor is he necessarily the master of himself though, like a self-mastered man, he uses limited powers to make something important. Not altogether understandable even to himself, what he does has an intelligibility that routine occurrences lack. And though not enhanced in the way a self-sufficient, self-mastered, or self-guided man may be, he could be enhanced as much or more, and thereby enabled to produce what none of these can. He need not be in a frenzy, subject to the muses, a creature of passing fancies and vagrant images. But he must channel his creativity through limited and well grooved avenues, if he is to use materials with skill and confidence. If a man does not persistently try to achieve an excellent result by supplementing superb craftsmanship with great creativity, his results will be seriously limited, and perhaps radically flawed.

A mature man can act creatively. If he fails to give his creativity adequate expression, and therefore does not enable it to take advantage of avenues which have led others to great outcomes, he will of course not produce anything particularly new or important. The adventure has its own dangers. The effort to produce a great work easily leads to the expression of creativity along routes used before and, therefore, makes it come into the open as just a moment in an habituated activity.

A man can become more and more creative the more mature he becomes, but he does not produce anything great unless he is in control of subordinate powers, and persists in a making and remaking until a controlling excellence supervenes. A study of past creations will not teach him how to be more creative. At best, it will acquaint him with the residues of past creative acts. Nor can he be taught by other creative men in such a way that he will necessarily be more creative. At best they can help him avoid the errors that are due to ignorance, incompetence, conceit, lack of imagination, or a failure of dedication. To engage in creative activity, a man must make his various epitomizations subject to the enrichment he achieves by his acceptance and use of Existence as a final condition.

Self-sufficiency, self-mastery, and self-guidance benefit a man as he exists by himself. Creativity, apparently, does not. When not employed in bringing about something outside himself, we sometimes speak of a man as being lax. But creativity is also involved in genuine appreciation, and in support of others who are engaged in creatively producing works of art, expressing virtue, or using their minds. All epitomizations benefit from creativity, through their unavoidable linking with it and through the effect it has on them.

When creativity does not come to realization in something excellent, it continues to play an important role in determining how various epitomizations of privacy are to be interrelated. A mature man, consequently, can fail to produce good public work because he spends his creativity in producing a new unity of self and person. Or he may be too habituated, too much involved with limited practices and goals to be able to use his creativity well. It is also true that unless he is a good craftsman, he will rarely exercise his creativity in other than incidental and quite limited ways. Creativity has little fruit if not carried out in acts quickening specific channels already distinguished and controlled. The fact that men, as they grow older, often become more routinized, unimaginative, less creative than they had been does not require a denial that they still have as much creativity as before. It shows only that they do not, and perhaps cannot, make the best use of available channels.

In addition to making himself self-sufficient, self-mastered, self-guided, and creative, a man can also move toward a position from which he can steadily assess what he does as better or worse, depending on the degree it diverges from what he established himself to be. His *self-estab-lishment*, like the others, is achieved in acts which are not altogether controlled or consciously exercised. Like the others, it is the outcome of the acceptance and use of a distinct final condition. This, an assessing unity, enables him to provide a measure of the value of what he does and to pass judgment on the more limited assessments made by his I. Were he not self-established, he would tend to assess his epitomizations, actions, other beings, their acts, and the world about in conventional, habitual, practical, obligating, or deliberately adopted terms. He may, of course, assess anything or assess nothing. His achievement of a stage where he can make final assessments still leaves him free not to make them or to assess them wrongly or even perversely.

Even if a man fails to change the judgments he is accustomed to make, or does not lead a better life than others who are less mature, he will still be better than he had been if he attains the stage where his idios enables him to measure all else from a primary, constant position. Before he reaches that stage he may have assessed and acted well because his assessments and actions were guided or determined by others. It may be better for the rest that he so function. It may even be better for him that he do so, not only because he will then be able to live more compatibly with others, benefitting from their work and sharing in common enterprises, but because he will be able to be in better accord with what his body can do and be. But he will himself not be as self-established as he would have been had he acted in terms of a measure which enriched him.

As a man matures, he establishes himself more and more. By accepting and using a final, unifying condition, he makes himself into a final assessive ground. His consciousness of what others prefer, his pursuit of limited goods, even the exercise of a perverse will, cannot stand in the way of his establishing himself as a measure in terms of which these are assessed. If his assessments are not expressed in appropriate acts, if his explicit judgments and decisions conflict with others', he will be self-discrepant, judging and deciding in some independence of his matured, enriched idios. He will not have attained the stage where he had established himself as able to measure himself and others in final terms. To reach that stage, he must express himself as an ultimate, assessing ground, able to make himself effective in and through his other epitomizations.

Artists, the religious, scientists, philosophers, and similarly occupied men, whose achievements sooner or later increase the store of civilization's goods, usually neglect areas where others also produce what is valuable, spiritually, socially, and economically. They differ from these primarily in having at least tacitly pledged themselves to produce what is excellent. The pledge justifies their neglect of tasks satisfying other needs, just as long as they remain occupied with producing what has at least as much value. They are most successful when their idios governs their resolutions.

It is possible for a good man, accustomed to doing good, sometimes to do what is bad, knowing it to be what ought not to be done. His act is assessed by himself in absolute terms. More or less persistently, with more or less success, he then exercises control over the avenues through which he expresses his assessments. When he fails to impose himself as an absolute measure, he will realize more limited and perhaps regrettable prospects. Evidently, there is gain in a man attaining a position from where he can evaluate all things. But if he makes his final assessment effective, he will sooner or later come into conflict with other men.

The difficulty can be met on a number of levels. His idios could provide a base for a coherent ordering of all his epitomizations, and the living of his body. Or its assessments could be used by decisions which are in consonance with the decisions of others. Or what he publicly does could be made to conform to what is commonly approved. Were he to follow an act by others of the same kind, there will come a time when he will acquire a character reflecting that practice. There is no exact point at which this occurs. So far as he tries to govern his epitomizations, he will not be devoted as much as he otherwise could and should be in order to become enriched through the reception and use of final conditions.

Were there no idios, there would be no effective position from which a man could take final conditions into himself and thereby govern all the epitomizations of his privacy. Because the idios has as its task the receptive internalization and the self-dictated use of the conditions, it is necessarily engaged in a number of activities. But, apart from the aid it can call on from thinking and other epitomizations, it is unable to combine its different endeavors and achievements to any considerable extent. Yet that result must be achieved, if a man is to be at his best.

Although a man might have no clear knowledge of his idios or how it functions, he can be conscious of his own transience. This is enough to make him be receptive to and to try to use what is forever and can enoble whatever it governs. The more mature he becomes, the more is he able to benefit from the reception and use of those final conditions. At each moment, in order to be able to receive and use them on his own terms in an effort to benefit from them maximally, he must face them as equally present and important. His failure to be maximally enriched by all of them at one moment, fortunately, will not preclude success at another. But to assure success, his idios must be ready to receive and use them all.

Accounts of man as an ethical being, as a member of a society or a state, as a worker, artist, or religious being, take him to be already matured. He is then supposed to be somehow already in possession of the powers and agencies by which he is able to know, assume a role, or be occupied with what he takes to be ultimate. Psychological theories of learning and education try to discover how he attains to these levels. But if they restrict themselves to observations and reports, they will not be able to tell what it is that expresses itself in the observable ways, who is reporting and how, or what promotes smooth functioning. Reference should be made not only to various private powers but also to the idios' ability to harmonize deviant and conflicting acts.

The idios is the last position reached in a progressively inward move from a publicly evident, to a self-sufficient, self-mastered, self-guided, creative, and self-established man. As enriched, the idios provides evidences of the existence and nature of final conditions. Starting instead from a metaphysical knowledge of the finalities, the idios is identifiable as enabling various conditions to have effective roles in the governance of the other epitomizations of the self and person. In the first way, one comes to the finalities in a process of evidencing; in the second, they are found in condensed forms as common controls of what is privately begun.

Once the idios is acknowledged, the furniture that has been traditionally crowded into a mind, or just piled up in no apparent order, can be put back into its proper places. To do this, it is necessary to acknowledge the power of the idios to govern all the epitomizations of the self and person, and thereby make itself evident as the harmonizer of all.

The idios, while able to function apart from the body, needs the body's prospering in a public world in order both to come to be and to be free to focus on the task of enriching itself and other private epitomizations. As a consequence, murder, starvation, slavery, debilitative work, and the denial of the opportunity to function well, all become identifiable as radical violations of human nature, private and public.

It is quite possible for a man who committed a crime to be so appalled by what he did that he will be almost incapable of another, while some innocent man might be so attracted by what was done that he will be prompted to commit such a crime himself. A positivistic approach to men, which concerns itself only with deterrence, would require that the latter and not the former be punished. Who is not outraged by the prospect? Is this not because all are aware that the act had a private origin, and that the first and not the second man is guilty for that crime? The private origin of an act, of course, is not alone to be considered. It is, though, a crucial factor in a sound judgment of merit. The limits of a purely positivistic approach to law, politics, and man must therefore be set at the point beyond which merit and consequently a governing privacy are to be acknowledged. Man's knowledge of the role of that privacy in living a body in a world with others keeps a public justice from having more than a limited, utilitarian role.

We reach toward the idios of others in sympathy. We thrust beyond their surfaces toward them as denser, more private, unified, in more or less control of what is done. We do not then lose all opportunity to conceptualize, to grasp them in still another way. Acquaintance and understanding are compatible.

Let 'idea' refer to any thought, 'concept' to a thought rooted in and directed at what is singular, and 'notion' to a thought referring to what is final. We can then say: When we confront another man we often have two ideas, one of which answers more or less to what we confront, and the other of which is used to express what he is in himself. If we observe well, and have able minds, the first of these ideas will be in good accord with what in fact is confronted, and the implications that are drawn from the idea will be in consonance with what both occurs later and is able to be confronted as the initial items were. If we deal with another as having a dignity; if we speak and listen to him, work or play with him, look to him for friendship, love, or respect; or if we admire or are in awe of him, we also usually displace the second idea with a concept of him as privately living his body by exercising powers having a source beyond our reach. In addition, we thrust, from what we confront in him, toward his idios. We can also do more. Knowing that an idios is behind our own self-guiding, self-sufficiency, self-mastery, creativity, and self-establishing, we can correct our concept so that it is in more accord with the fact that he also has an idios. We would just add something common, what is true of every individual, were it not that we see that our corrections are limited by what is encountered in our moves toward his idios, and that we have good notions of what is accepted and used by this.

Each man can get to know some others better and better, and finally arrive at a point where he has a rather firm understanding of them in depth. Each can take advantage of an idea of what he is able to observe and of some schematic idea or concept of what a man is. If he also has some notion of the conditions used by the idios, he can make the outcome of the juncture of the two ideas, or of an idea and concept, benefit from the notion. By taking advantage of the way in which the referent of a notion is connected with his idios, he will not only be able to give the referent a private base, but make this base be the object of a concept.

If a man has a concept of another's privacy, he has a singularized knowledge of him. Most of the time though, concepts are poorly forged, and ideas are grounded in poor observations and a faulty understanding of what it is to be a man. Despite this, most seem to have some idea of human privacy, forge concepts, thrust from what is conceived toward what is singular, have at least a vague notion of what will enable a man to be self-enriched, and bring the notion to bear on the objects of concepts.

When a man greets me warmly with a smile, I usually respond in a similar way, without reflection. It is hard to know whether or not I have an idea of what I then confront. The fact that I can recall and reflect on his greeting and his smile can be readily accounted for by taking the introduction of an idea to occur at the time of the recall. There is little doubt, though, that I have a concept of a smiling, warmly greeting man when I attend to him. Both the greeting and the smile are unreflectingly treated as continuing the approach I make to him. They converge toward his I. Once again, I could conceivably have just reacted to him. I may also be mistaken about him; he may be trying to lull or to deceive me. Whether he succeeds or not, I replace the idea of him as a warmly smiling man by the concept of him as friendly, aware that he is more than the object of an idea of a smiling man. My thrust toward him as friendly continues indefinitely on beyond the point where my idea applies.

For the most part, I am content to imbed my idea of another, greeting me warmly with a smile, in my concept of him as friendly, vaguely continuing beyond this into him as not yet fully probed. The union of the two has a richness and a use neither alone has. If, instead of being content with my concept of him as one who is in fact friendly and is expressing himself in one of the many ways in which such friendliness is exhibited, I would like to know him as a self-enriching being, I must sharpen the notion of the conditions with which his idios is occupied. If I then use the notion to enrich my concept of him, I will be able to arrive at him as an idios-determined, friendly object of my concept, expressing himself in a warm, smiling greeting. Should I find from his next acts that he is not in fact friendly, I will have to change my understanding of him, from one who is both publicly and actually smiling, to one who is engaged in a unique act of deceiving. To do this, I must use a concept of a deceiver in place of a misleading 'friendliness'.

As long as we continue to keep our ideas, concepts, and notions grounded in penetrative thrusts that reverse the order in which a man makes himself present, we will know him in general terms at the same time that we will understand him to be like ourselves and, therefore, to be at once human and unduplicable. The possibility that he may have a poor character or be ill we expect will become manifest in crises and inadvertencies. If they do not, his possible private deviance will be dismissed as of little importance.

Is it necessary to attend to the idios? If all we know or want to know is an origin on which we can count to express itself steadily and persistently, why should we try to understand a man as affected by his idios? The obvious answer is that if we had no notion of his idios, we would not know him to be a single harmonizing source of acts. We would then not know that his various epitomizations both diversify a single privacy and are connected in ways which we could not adequately express in ideas. We therefore would not be able to know what it means for him to be honest or deceitful, mentally healthy or ill, reasonable or perverse, since these are individualized ways in which he impresses himself on various epitomizations, all at the same time.

A man's acts could preserve or enhance what is good, measured in terms of a final standard of excellence, but the fact may not be noticed. Also, what in one society is taken to be deception might be treated in another as a testing or just playfulness; what in one society is taken to manifest a serious private malfunctioning may be treated in another as a sign of divine favor. Only because we have a sound concept and notion of what a man privately is, and an idea of what ought to be publicly done, can we confidently say that we may be mistaken in our understanding of what men are privately and may be able to do.

We can know when men go astray. But if they act as they should, we do not know whether or not they had privately governed themselves properly. Consequently, we come to know the secrets of men, more by attending to what they do wrongly than by attending to what they do correctly. Evil not good, vice not virtue, deviance not conformity, error not truth, yield the best evidence of what another privately is. So far as we can tell, good men are alike. But no one is at his best always. Each falls short in various ways. At all times, each is an individual, insistent on impressing his radically distinctive idios on the epitomized sources of his public acts, to make these function together in better ways. We would not know it was necessary to do this, did men always act as they ought. Evidence for the existence and functioning of the idios is most readily provided by those aberrational acts which can be traced back to improperly functioning, private sources whose activities can be redressed only by what can make receptive use of final conditions.

There is no higher demand to be made on a man than that he be a man. To satisfy that demand, it is necessary to know what it is possible for a man to be. And that requires an understanding of his idios, the power by which he can govern himself and thereby make his body act in ways which may at times not benefit that body, his species, or his society.

FIVE

Human Excellence

a. Remedies

A man is tired and relaxes. Asleep now, he is awake later. Having walked for a while, he rests. If such changes meant that he did not persist, he would never last for more than a very short time. There would then be no one who, after being quiet for a while, became restless, or who first thought and much later spoke.

If a man lacked an I, he would not be self-identical, one who reduces different occurrences the self-same result, but that would not mean that he could not express the same privacy again and again. Let it, though, be supposed, with a rigorous follower of Augustine, Descartes, Hume, Whitehead, and some Buddhists, that every momentary state is a distinct entity, radically cut off from all others. Who or what joins these in a man? How could they be credited, as they are, to the same being? If reference is made to a mind, this will itself pass with each act, or will remain self-same. If the first, the objects known could not be first present and then associated. But if the mind continues, its momentary states will not be radically separate; they will be together in it, all in the same private epitomization.

A man is able to act in different ways on different content at different times without jeopardizing his persistence. As a father, I am involved with my children; as a teacher I am involved with students. Sometimes the one interferes with the other. In my role as father I sometimes act quite differently from the way I do when I act as a teacher. My children make a difference to me not made by my students. It would not surprise me too much to hear someone say that I am a quite different person in my home from what I am in the classroom. What I encounter in these and other ways has different effects on me. That is one of the reasons why I behave differently in the two cases.

There are times when particular epitomizations, the expressions of these, or their outcomes are beyond my power to guide or control. They are insistently present, often to the detriment of other occurrences, to myself, to others, to society, and sometimes to mankind. They evidence the fact that they have a power exercised without regard for other epitomizations, expressions, outcomes, myself, others, or the situation in which I am. My refusal to be satisfied with them not only points up the fact that there are normative ways in which they should function, but that I am more than an aggregate of efforts, acts, or parts which only by good fortune happen to work in some accord at times.

When activities are viewed as aberrational, it is tacitly supposed they are to be overcome, qualified, or controlled, and that others are to be encouraged. When we speak of a man as being sick, mad, as having lost his wits, in a fit, and the like, we look for some way to prevent the occurrence from having full force, and try to prevent it from recurring. Sometimes the result is good for others or for society. If the result is a superlative work of art, an important mathematical proof, a great discovery in theoretical science, or if it involves the use of arms, legs, or other parts of a body to achieve results far beyond the point where others with similar training and opportunities have been able to go, we will tend to make reference to some special trait, to inspiration, to gifts, or to genius. The aberrational will be endorsed because of its benefits or desirability. It is hard, though, to see how a follower of Freud could avoid placing such a man in the same category with other aberrants, even those who seriously injure themselves or others.

Required to take account of different things, I deal with them in different ways, compensating for their differences by engaging in different ways of possessing them. My self-identity is maintained by reducing different items to the same outcome. I here add to the persistent constancy of my privacy, the reductive power of my self-identical I. The neglect of either the privacy or the I makes a mystery out of the familiar pair 'stimulus-response'. Were there no persistent privacy or self-identical I, there would be nothing which responded in different ways to the similar stimuli, in the same ways to the similar stimuli, and in different ways to the different stimuli. There would be just stimuli now and other occurrences later. Conceivably, the privacy or the I might be just a pivotal point. If it were, a response would be the reverse of a stimulus. But there would then be no one to learn, to insist on himself, to assume responsibility, or to maintain rights even when these were publicly denied.

When privacy is ignored, we have no alternative but to take a man to be just a recipient of whatever happens to occur. Were, instead, the identity of the I, with the reductive power of its act of possession, ignored, we would be forced to hold that a man was altered by the items he possessed. And if the acts of the I were ignored, one would lose the opportunity to account for the identity of a man who expresses himself in different ways in different situations.

Both animals and men are constant over time, but in different ways. The lowest grade of living being provides a convergent point for a multiplicity of influences on the way to the provision of a divergent set of replies. Higher animals express themselves from unitary positions. A mature man differs from both in being able to hold his singular, persistent privacy away from his body; in being able to have a person and self which originate diverse expressions; in having an I which remains unaltered no matter what it possesses; and in having an idios which enables him to govern himself. Whatever he encounters he subjects to himself as a constant presence, source, possessor, and control.

The idios never loses all control of the I or the other epitomizations of self and person, or of what those epitomizations empower, even when one of them is most insistent on itself to the disadvantage of others. When one of them gets in the way of others, the idios is challenged to achieve a better balance among them. Person and self provide less effective ways than the idios does for overcoming the incompatibilities exhibited by their epitomizations.

The more surely a man is able to eliminate or to reduce undesirable occurrences in himself, some of which are the effects of conflicts among his different expressions, the more surely does he provide a *remedy*. The more surely that his idios is in control and therefore the more he is able not only to prevent conflicts from arising but to overcome their bad effects, the more surely does he provide a *cure*, precluding what stands in the way of his being as healthy as a man can be.

Nine types of remedy are to be marked off from one another: (1) *denial of opportunity*; (2) *denial of satisfaction*; (3) *constraints*; (4) *threats*; (5) *habituations*; (6) *interspersals*, (7) *counteractions*; (8) *transformations*, and (9) *destructions*. Each at times successfully reduces a particular conflict or an unwanted outcome. But if it does not elicit actions by the idios, I, self, person, or privacy, what is done tends to be cosmetic only, hiding rather than correcting or replacing what is not wanted.

True remedies awaken internal productions of more encompassing and persistent corrections than could be provided from without. At their best, they promote rectificatory acts. But these are always *post hoc*, acting on what is already present and undesirable. Cures, too, are produced in the face of what is not wanted, but unlike remedies, they also overcome causes.

1. *Denial of opportunity*. Sometimes all that is needed in order to avoid headaches, anxieties, pains, allergies, passions, errors, or fears, is a change in place. One takes a vacation, varies the scene, has his direction changed, or is distracted. The undesirable occurrences are thereupon denied their usual or necessary occasions for reappearing. It is then tacitly acknowledged that a man is in part an environmentally determined being whose adventures are a function of the opportunities which the world and society provide. Opportunities, of course, are not only environmental or social. Thought provides opportunities for the exercise of sound choices and acts of will. But such interior opportunities are usually prompted by changes in exterior ones. One encourages thought through example or through the provision of rewards, and may sometimes succeed in promoting another's effort to think, choose, and will.

From Plato on, there have been men who have remarked on the fact that those who, like carpenters, attend to their daily tasks, not only have no time to consult doctors but find less need to do so than the rest of men. The view is close to that held by many doctors as well. The body, and less rarely the mind, if left to itself, it is thought, will tend to recover its health unaided. Men are being supposed to be natively excellent, but somehow corrupted by others or by the world in which they live. Each is thought to be pulled out of his Garden of Eden by forces outside him, and supposedly can return to it if what pulled him is removed, overcome, or counterbalanced. Whatever truth there is in that idea should not be allowed to obscure the fact that there are uncontrolled spasms, blinks, impulses, fantasies, hopes, and fears which we may sometimes keep from being fully expressed, but which we cannot always keep from arising.

What prompts or supports undesirable activities must be precluded if a man is to move toward a better state. The move itself, though, could lead him to try to achieve what is no longer a good state for him. No one should want to recover the innocence of childhood or the single-mindedness of the youthful athlete. An innocence not backed by sophistication, or a single-mindedness not backed by experience, makes one a prey to terror and error, and their accompanying pains. That is why we have guardians for those characterized by the one, and laws for those characterized by the other. A denial of opportunity should make it possible to achieve a better state, but this can be assured only if the denial is accompanied by the provision of other opportunities to overcome what is amiss.

2. *Denial of satisfaction.* It is a rare man who persists long in any direction if he is constantly frustrated; if he constantly fails to reach his goals, objectives, or ends; or if he does not find some satisfaction in making an effort. When private and public activities have already been begun, they can sometimes be limited or deflected by denying satisfaction in the course of the act, or in their evident outcomes.

If satisfaction accrues to an undesirable act, this should be countered by an effort to restrain or redirect the activity. When such remedial activity is not forthcoming it is necessary to remove what is disturbing. If the unwanted activity itself appears to be self-sustaining, being self-satisfied as it were, it is necessary to intrude on it with what can effectively change its nature or effectiveness.

A dominant tendency among some physiologists, biologists, and psychologists is to hold that a lack is expressed as an impetus or demand until it is satisfied. They are teleologically tempered, dealing with lacks in terms of prospects which control and complete. It would be more cautious to hold that there is something satisfying in the expression of a lack, particularly where the expression balances what is unsatisfactory in the lack itself. An unpleasant thirst is usually accompanied by a satisfying effort to drink. An activity which, unlike an effort to drink, is satisfying but not desirable, ending in what is regrettable, is to be countered by remedies which block the action and therefore the satisfaction.

Smoking and taking drugs satisfy. Some try to stand in the way of these by thinking, or by turning themselves in other directions, but to little avail. The activities can be stopped. Kept at, the activities take on something like the shape of aberrations, differing from these primarily in that they have been prepared for in outlook and habit, and are sometimes sought. They can be overcome by remedies which deny satisfaction to the activities and outcome, or by providing alternative, more satisfying activities and outcomes, and best of all, by both.

3. *Constraints.* Societies and states try to make various activities less satisfying, if not in act then in outcome, by imposing constraints in the form of threats, obstacles, and punishments. From their perspective, it makes no difference whether or not a man replaced a less satisfying activity by a more, as long as the replacement conformed to what the societies or states endorse. These do not ask if the conformity is or is not due to fear, is or is not deliberate or habitual. Indeed, in most situations it is better if men were to act out of habit, without reflection, rather than voluntarily, for habit can be relied on to a degree that volition and thought cannot, particularly in situations where conformity must be prompt. We want

men to stop at a red light instantly, without reflection. That we can assure by seeing that they obey unhesitatingly, through habit and the constraint produced by an indurated fear of punishment.

For the most part, men fail to act as they ought to act if they are to do justice to the nature and promise of their selves or persons, to the epitomizing expressions of these, or to their lived bodies. They do not properly insist on what had been neglected or minimized, or do not restrain what had been overemphasized. Here illness is a state of malfunctioning, where some part overrides or is overridden by others, thereby precluding a satisfactory expression of all together. Recovery requires rectificatory acts which overcome improper minimizations and exaggerations. The ability to elicit needed corrective or compensatory activities determines the degree of health that can be attained. In contrast with remedies which elicit better expressions, the rectifications prompt controlling acts. Cures produce a proper functioning, making remedies and rectifications unnecessary.

Cures are possible because a latent health can be prompted to express itself. Were this not so, being well and being ill would be just oppositional states, neither able to intrude on the other. Or only remedies would be possible, enabling men to function satisfactorily without the causes of the disturbances being overcome. Or men would automatically function properly under certain conditions. The first alternative takes contingent facts to be final, allowing for no cures. The second, because it denies that there is internal power or control, permits one to hope for nothing more than stopping for a while something unwanted. The third allows that, with a change in conditions, men might revert to their previous states. Cures, instead, presuppose an ability to determine what will be exhibited.

Public constraints are remedies, too often applied belatedly, when activities have already run their course and ended with regrettable outcomes. Occasionally, though, constraints are imposed in such a way that serious losses are prevented. Laws against conspiracy or defamation of character, limits placed on movement, speech, and action, when backed by force, sometimes stand in the way of the perpetration of crimes. Customary ways bring pressure on those who tend to deviate. And where all else fails, segregation, disqualification, reassignment, and the denial of a role in a community of interplaying individuals keeps aberrational activities within narrow confines, and sometimes prevents them from being carried out at all. Such remedies are directed at what is publicly expressed. 'Guilt', 'intent', 'knowledge' in their social, political, and legal uses, though they have some bearing on what is privately decided and done, refer to what is publicly evidenced and open to public control.

We use 'remedy' quite accurately when we say "The remedy for street violence is more severe sentences", though we are not as certain as we should be that the remedy we are recommending is correct. If it is, it will make the violence less congenial to its perpetrators. The constraints that are imposed, ranging from curfews to random arrests, from humiliation to imprisonment, are designed to keep the undesirable actions confined. The constraints, of course, cannot prevent the actions. Publicly applied remedies stop short at what is public. It is commonly assumed, though, that the disagreeableness of those remedies will so affect the men that they will change the ways in which they then act. The fact that this sometimes happens points up the truth that a man can be privately keyed to what occurs in his body, and thereupon change what he expresses in and through it. Constraints then serve not only as remedies, making certain acts more difficult, disagreeable, or even impossible, but also as stimuli, provoking private activities that guide and control what the body does.

4. *Threats*. A society or state that relies primarily on constraints tends to act too late or too severely. If it awaits what deserves constraint, it acts only after regrettable consequences have ensued. But if it does not await regrettable occurrences, it will keep men constrained to a degree they do not deserve. The theory that men are rightly denied the right to assemble, to speak, to live in particular places during times of crisis, drives one toward one extreme. The theory that a man is innocent until proven guilty drives one toward the other.

Laws in a state have a role similar to those which traditions have in a society. The more surely they set limits to what can properly be done, the more do they become like the remedies provided by social prohibitions. Sometimes such laws are very effective.

What is often called 'mental health' may have little or nothing to do with the mind, whether this be taken to be conscious or unconscious, since it may concern the roles which other epitomizations of privacy and their specializations—will or desire, perhaps—have in relation to one another. When the exercise of one epitomization precludes the proper exercise of others, there is a failure in private health. Without prompting, one may privately act to overcome the failure. Since there is not sufficient power to do so always, help must be given by remedies able to overcome some of the excesses. But if the idios does not intervene, any harmony that might be achieved through the application of remedies would be adventitious, and those achieved through the action of the person, self, or I would be only partial.

'Mental' health is best promoted when the idios controls the way in which independently functioning epitomizations act in relation to one another, and thereupon act as concurrent sources of what is done. We come to know of its control when we attend to the way in which expressions are privately forced to allow for others.

The persistent privacy, which is specialized as person and self, is not determinate enough to do more than provide a common center for its specializations. These may, at times, be expressed in oppositional ways. Only the idios is able to enrich the person and self, as well as their specializations. Only it can help them all be satisfied in a way that they could not on their own. For a man to be at his best, his privacy, person, and self, their epitomizations, the different parts of his body, and the body as a unit must act maximally and yet in consonance. This is possible if he is able to govern both his private acts and his body. And that requires the joint use of his idios and all his other private powers.

The idios is not able to force all epitomizations to be in harmony. Its control is not absolute. But it does have some effect on all, particularly when it is supported by the I. The I, then, instead of just being an epitomization of the self and representing it, assumes part of the burden of harmonizing other epitomizations.

The more successful one is in producing a harmony of all epitomizations, whether this be by the act of the idios alone or with the help of the I, the more surely will one be in good health, physically and spiritually, bodily and privately. This state the classical Epicureans and their rivals, the Stoics, both attempted to achieve. The latter though, minimized the needs of the body, while the former failed to take sufficient account of the final conditions which must be utilized if privacy and body are to be together and at their best.

A man whose privacy and body function in harmony with one another might still be in considerable dissonance with other men and with the world beyond. He might also not be occupied with what was of primary importance. The Epicureans tried to take these matters into consideration by aiming at the achievement of a healthy bodily and spiritual state in a company of friends. But men should also be together in a harmonious way with those who are not friends. And they should adjust themselves to the ways of a non-humanized world.

As long as we know that a man's bodily tendencies are being restrained, it will be possible to isolate evidences of some of the rectificatory efforts that are being privately made by him. But we will not know that he is trying to be excellent privately, bodily, and in the world, unless we also know that he is making use of his idios. This we can know once we see how his different private powers are being subject to a common control working on behalf of what is beyond the reach of any epitomization, the body, or any occupation with what else there may be in the world.

Evidence of the idios is provided when different tendencies are so restrained that they are together in a manner most suited to the realization of a prospect more comprehensive than any toward which they could be severally directed. Well before we know of the idios or what it does, we are able to recognize more limited adjudications due to the person, self, and I. Any one of these makes it possible to keep other private powers working well together. Each operates on them with a different degree of efficacy, and with reference to a differently functioning prospect.

The expectation that what one is doing or is about to do will be disapproved by others feared or admired, and who are able to follow their disapprovals with punitive measures, affects the nature and course of one's activities. When a remedy is brought to bear, it works in ways the disapproval cannot. Not just a stimulus prompting decisions or other private operations, or just serving to guide and control what is done, it still does not make contact with the activities at their origins. If it is to operate on what is private it has to elicit fear or other anticipations of what might be expected from others. The anticipations, despite their private sources, function as components of the remedies. They would have quite a different role were they not components in acts serving to limit or preclude what is not wanted, and, instead, just helped elicit agents governing and reordering different actions in relation to one another. Threats would then be partial stimuli, not partial remedies.

Remedies can be provided by oneself. Though men do not often threaten themselves, they can. Also, medicines can be taken to help one fall asleep or to avoid expected pain. In anticipation of, and in order to prevent the occurrence or full presence of something disagreeable, still other remedies can be sought or used. But even where what is not wanted is initiated elsewhere, a remedy can be self-applied. A supposed threat can be the outcome of an interpretation or guess about what others might do; a mistaken fear about what will ensue on the performance of particular acts may itself serve as a remedy, precluding or limiting what is done. Although operating within the individual, the fear here would be a self-produced remedy, sometimes limiting tendencies which might have been expressed in desirable acts.

'Remedy' has as its primary meaning the desirable reduction of an undesirable occurrence. To take anything which serves to brake or stop some activity to be a remedy is to deviate from that use. Since what does not contribute to the presence of what is desirable is not a true remedy, a fear or some other agent which just stands in the way of an undesirable activity, is not a remedy. Placebos are ineffective items believed to be effective. When their use helps to overcome what is amiss, they are true remedies or parts of them. Misconceptions of the threats of other men, society, or state having a placebic role are evidently also parts of or full remedies.

5. *Habituations*. By training, by a repetition of desirable acts in the little, and by discipline and self-denial, habits are formed. These may be overwhelmed by acts of will, or rendered impotent by some sudden occurrences awakening hidden impulses. They allow for exceptions, and for accidental or adventitious sequences of occurrences, while stabilizing emphases on particular tendencies. Honest men can lie; brave men can run away; drunkards may refuse a drink; the habit of eating when hungry can be modified by etiquette. Just as one can impose a momentary barrier in anticipation of some particular occurrence, so one can forge a relatively constant barrier, thereby producing a steady remedy reducing the likelihood of unwanted acts.

Bodily habits are not preparations but rather limiting ways in which preparations will be expressed. Not produced by privacy, they are the residuum of past adventures, providing channels through which the free activity of an epitomization will be manifested. No habits are so tight that they annihilate a free private act; but every habit sets limits to action unless it is expressly countered by a specific act overcoming it at that time. The act need not be deliberately performed.

A good habit mimics the way in which individuals privately rectify what is unwanted, since it makes aberrational activities yield to persistent tendencies. The habit therefore seems to exert a force on behalf of itself or of its possessor, and to thereby make the aberrational activity yield place to others. Since a habit is a more or less fixated connection between components of an act, but without power of its own, it is not altogether correct to say with Aristotle that habit is a second nature, for the nature of a man is fixed and effective. Impotent, a habit awaits use. Even if one were to modify the way a habit functions, he would not give it power. At most, he would turn it into a remedy functioning on behalf of rectificatory demands. Just as a doctor may deliberately and for the sake of a cure provide remedies which make the operation of the cure more expeditious or even possible, so a man may deliberately and for the sake of a cure build up habits which make it possible or easier for him both to avoid aberrational activities and to pursue another course. In addition to such corrections, introduced into aberrational tendencies and acts, and in addition to the supports they provide for private acts and the body as an organic unit, habits can serve as agents for a curative power which otherwise is not able to make itself felt.

References to the intent of a doctor or of the man who uses a remedy get no further than to an explanation of why the remedy is used. Its role as agent awaits a principal, a man able to take advantage of the remedy in order to be able to function well on his own.

6. *Interspersals*. Some remedies have no apparent role in correcting what is amiss. Instead, they seem to allow it to occur. Employed by good coaches and teachers, they function as interspersals, items introduced within aberrational tendencies or activities to delay their completion, or to deflect their course. Sometimes the interspersals are themselves attractive, prompting an interest in them with a consequent change in effort and direction. Confronted with an athlete who seeks adulation or fame, or with a student preparing himself to receive good grades or honors or to begin some career, instead of trying to get in the way, a good coach or teacher adds intermediates with an attraction of their own, and which could prompt a change in goal. If the habits and tendencies that had before been operative are thought to be not well-directed, the new items will be used to help the athlete or student to turn in other directions. The satisfaction of a task well done, with grace and success, or the pursuit of a new set of ideas or values is then made possible by interspersals seeming to promote a different outcome. What is interspersed could promote the original prospect. For too many of their charges that is the only purpose it serves. It is the hope of the coaches and teachers, of course, that the interspersed items will in fact appeal on their own terms. If there is any deception involved, it is in the failure to remark on the coach's or teacher's belief that what is introduced along the way is not a necessary part of the means to a particular outcome. One who wished to avoid all semblance of deception could well report on what he was doing and what he hoped to have it accomplish. Were this done, it is doubtful that its use would be objected to. Were one so scrupulous that he wished to avoid even the suspicion of the occurrence of a deception, he would have to distinguish in every reward, and even in the payment for labor, what was a full and just payment, and what promoted some other end. And then he would find that he had misconstrued human nature, for an incentive is often a stimulating remedy, answering to a desirable readiness in man to be receptive to what leads him to attain what is more satisfying.

An interspersal depends for its success on an individual's ability to be deflected, which is but to say on his readiness to accept the remedy as being of some value for him and so far, therefore, on his readiness to accept it as not just a remedy, a mere means to something else. Rewards sometimes function in this way. Given in response to some approved act, they are also intended to encourage similar acts by others as well. The more surely they are offered simply in appreciation of what is well-done, the more likely will they function as incentive interspersals.

Interspersals remedy by providing a pause or shift in what otherwise might have been a smooth transition. Though they fit in with what is being done, the satisfactions they provide may lead one to follow a new course. Their success evidences the attraction that beginnings have even when they open the way to goods other than those sought or which might otherwise be obtained. Not dependent on thought or on an insistence on some superior prospect, they make a difference to what is not wanted. Like all good remedies, those used on what does not terminate in items that will eventually satisfy fully, elicit support on the part of the individual. Somewhat like the sweet medicines given to children, they awaken cooperation by those who are to be benefited.

7. *Counteractions.* Some remedies serve only to awaken or to strengthen actions which limit or modify those that are being challenged. Interspersals, and other remedies, can be understood to have such a role. A counteraction differs from these in directly bearing on a particular unwanted activity.

Although epitomizations may just make use of what is bodily, and thus not act as remedies or provide for these, they can at times function as remedies for bodily occurrences, or begin acts which are bodily remedial. Bodily acts can also be modified and sometimes prevented by privately expressed inhibitions, rejections, and self-restraints, directly counteracting what is bodily occurring. This, of course, would not be possible were privacy radically separated from the body, or did it never express itself in the body.

Private activities can be countered by other private activities. So far as they are carried out independently and in the absence of control by something more basic, any one of them can provide a remedy for those that are acting aberrationally. Such remedies usually allow for a reassertion of the original activity, freed from its aberrational tendencies.

A remedy may stand in the way of a full, free completion of some other activity. It may itself have to be elicited, and what elicits it might be called 'the remedy'. But this should not be allowed to force a denial that the counteraction is remedial. It is desirable, therefore, to speak of what elicits it as being part of a single remedy, the other part being what is elicited and directly affects what is not wanted.

Like interspersals, counteractions mimic the action of one who subordinates various efforts on behalf of his own demands or for some prospect more inclusive or more remote than that which could be the terminus of any of the subordinates. Like interspersals, counteractions are specialized, limited occurrences. When the private production of a remedy is accompanied by consciousness or by an intent, it limits others, thereby allowing itself or other activities to proceed more effectively. The remedy here benefits itself, somewhat in the way the scolding by a parent produces a silence conducive to his continued reading.

There are times when private actions are countered by bodily actions. A soldier decides to stand his ground but finds that his legs have begun to run. If he has more sense in his legs that he has in his head, his legs will remedy his inclinations. Were it better for him, his fellows, or others that he not move, his running of course would not remedy anything. Instead, it would itself be in need of a remedy in the form of private resolves, public threats, constraints, and the like.

In some of the foregoing, no distinction had to be made between those remedies which change some undesirable occurrence and those that block or prevent it. An interspersal could as readily be brought under the one heading as the other. But since changing is quite different from blocking or preventing, one must sooner or later distinguish prohibitionary from transformative remedies. The prohibitionary gets in the way of what is not wanted; the transformative modifies it, turning it into something else. Sometimes the latter are spoken of as 'cures' since they seem not merely to get in the way of particular acts but to make them vanish. But they, too, are only remedies. Anger may bring another's undesirable acts to a quick close. It may also help transform them. A raised fist may be stopped in midair or opened in the course of a sheepish gesture to yield. Anger in both cases has the role of a remedy, underscoring the fact that not every remedy is desirable and may itself require remedies.

8. *Transformations* of what is private as well as of what is public can be produced privately or publicly. Two of the transformations—the private by the private, and the public by the public—seem obvious enough. A private transformation of what is public and a public transformation of what is private, though, seem to raise special difficulties. The distinction between these pairs is largely a product of a tradition which makes the members of each pair seem altogether alien to one another. The matter was already touched upon when dealing with counteractions. Transformations require us to face it again, but now, instead of attending to one type of power just standing in the way of the full exercise of another, we attend to the way this is turned into a different operation. The fact may not be noticed because attention is concentrated on just the last stage of the operation, perhaps because it is that in which we are most interested or

which alone we are able to alter. Not knowing the cause of the pain of cancer or how to prevent it, we try to make the pain vanish. If we succeed, our remedy, more evidently than in most other cases, will have little or no bearing on a cure. The cause of the pain may continue to be present, but no pain may be felt. The elimination of the pain is more than a cosmetic change. Admittedly, everything but the pain remains as it had been, but unless we are willing to say that the pain is still present, though not felt, the elimination of it must be recognized to involve a transformation of its occasion.

Interspersals can be treated as special cases of transformations, since they turn one activity into another. A transformational remedy, though, need not give an activity a more desirable form and, of course, need not be interposed just at the point where an activity begins to be undesirable. A transformation, of course, is not a remedy if it does not get rid of unwanted occurrences.

9. *Destructions.* It is not easy to determine whether surgeons remedy situations or just make remedies unnecessary. Their forcible removal of what appears to be the cause or occasion of what is unwanted seems to comport more with the latter than with the former idea, since it does not allow the unwanted to occur at all.

Remedies do not make a difference to the existence of a bodily part, but only to its functioning. Removing such a part of course will make its functioning in the body impossible, but that would at best allow us to say that a remedy could be the consequence of something else. Also, as has already been observed, there are remedies which are preventative and can be applied at the beginning of an act. Since there is nothing wrong in principle in understanding a remedy to have the role of never allowing some particular activity to get started, a surgeon's work could be said to provide drastic attacks, not on activities or tendencies, but on what sustains, grounds, channels, or allows them to be carried out. It would not even be amiss to view the destructions he produces to be parts of acts involving interspersals, transformations, and other remedies, differing from these mainly in incisiveness. Unless a remedy could not involve the removal of part of one's body, a surgeon's knife can have a remedial role.

When opportunities are denied for the carrying out of some unwanted activity, we have little hesitation in supposing that the situation has been remedied. If the opportunities denied are embodied in some object, the remedy is not compromised. If it were, most medical remedies would be misnamed. Remedies which involve the destruction of external objects, situations, energies, or bodily parts may result in undesirable changes in the way one will be able to function in ordinary circumstances; such remedies should, therefore, be used with caution and shown to provide the only known or likely effective agencies for avoiding the unwanted. And since it is also true that other types of remedy may themselves involve some destruction in the individual whose aberrational activity is to be blocked or overcome, one must go on to add a note of caution in the use of these others as well. Remedies are most desirable when they serve mainly as agencies for making cures more likely.

b. Cures

Even when a remedy involves the removal of an essential site or channel, or the bodily source of some aberrational activity, it stops short of where a cure begins. A cure does not simply exclude the unwanted. Blinding is not a cure for squinting. A cure produces the wanted.

A man's body has a nature and career which differ considerably from the nature and career of his privacy. His bodily organs and parts in turn function differently from the ways in which his body acts as a single unit, at the same time that its nature and career are affected by them. To be sure, his eye can be made to blink or to contract, no matter what he would like to do. But if it is his eye, if it is a living part of him, its blink is at least partly expressive of what is private. No bodily activity is completely separable from sensitivity or from some other epitomization of an effective privacy.

A cure precludes unwanted occurrences by subjecting their sources to private restraining powers. The exercise of those powers have no prescribed duration. Those that last for short times are just as surely cures as those that last longer. Sometimes a remedy may have a longer lasting effect than a cure does. One remedy for stuttering is the avoidance of an occasion or need to speak, but a cure for stuttering brings it under control. Although the remedy could keep one from stuttering for a much longer time than the cure, the cure will allow for progress to the point where stuttering no longer occurs, at least in normal circumstances.

Whether or not their actions are promoted by the use of remedies, cures require one to privately overcome conflicting or unwanted subordinate activities. Did one not have the ability to govern more limited powers and to dictate how they are to function in relation to one another, there would be no cures, since there would then be nothing which could limit the action of what is not wanted.

A full cure enables one to be in control of and, therefore, to adjust different acts so that together they maximally exhibit the nature of a unitary source. Its outcome is complete health, the establishment of a state where distinct operations together articulate the unity behind them all.

One can be healthy in body, in privacy, or in both. The first requires different parts of the body to function well, at the same time that the entire set of such functionings articulates the unity of the organism. The second has different epitomizations of the self or person governed by these, while these in turn are governed by the idios. Not until one is completely healthy privately, bodily, and the two are maximally adjusted to one another, is a man in the state he should be in.

Bodily cures await the elicitation of private powers directly bearing on the body. Cures for private disorders await the elicitation of more deeply grounded private powers. Either type requires that what is elicited help some limited portion of the privacy to function better in relation to some other. At both times, a controlling idios assures a proper functioning by what is not now dominant.

To help another, one must make available what he can assimilate in his particular, present state. His health depends on his ability to change that state. If he is so immature, hopelessly crippled, or distorted that it is not possible to do more for him than enable him to make his life pleasanter, and him more effective, there could still be a cure produced, just so far as he has been prompted to express his privacy in better ways than it had been expressed before.

When we cater to children, students, or patients, when we make those in institutions as comfortable as we can, and when we deal with prisoners as members of a confining institution, we provide remedies, not cures. By means of the remedies they, in their present positions, are enabled to function better in limited environments. The satisfactions they than obtain could be good counterparts of what the rest of men obtain in better and more open environments.

One is not helped much and may even be hurt if symptoms are removed but no provision is made for the exercise of a power able to control and to provide new, needed expressions. Even if the power is not known, or one does not know how to have it make a difference to what is being manifested, it may still be possible to present a man with what will provoke his governance by means of a persistent power which should be in control. We do something like this when we translate from one language into another, when we teach, and when we correct the misunderstandings of others in daily discourse. Here, too, modifications of what is presented are offered in the expectation that distortions will not only be corrected, but that private controls will be elicited and effectively expressed.

A wanted response is often prompted by sympathetically guiding tentative, partial expressions of it, and then providing assurances that no serious risk of failure will ensue. One thereby tempts a man to take over his own corrections by bringing to bear power that he had not yet used or had not used effectively. We succeed quite well in doing this when we help children develop. We have not yet learned how to do this with much success when dealing with adults.

If a cure is not provided by some other epitomization of privacy, it must come from the idios, and then be utilized by the self or person, or by their epitomizations. All cures are self-cures, the making oneself be in control of what is thereafter done.

A primary task is to find a way of directly enabling a basic power to act with more efficacy. If we know nothing of the way in which this can be done, we must be content with providing an altered way of acting for a while, changing what is disordered so as to enable an otherwise ineffective expression to be more successful. If the idios does not produce a cure, we must be content to restrain that on which it operates and thereby enable the idios to govern it more effectively.

Cure and will can have the same outcome; both can end in the achievement of health. But a cure cannot be counted on. Rarely are elicited insistencies sufficiently clear or strong enough to overcome all aberrations. An act of will, but one that is dependent on the I as occupied with the nature and value of an ideal, completing good, is needed. Although its best exercise depends on more knowledge and concern than men usually have, it can succeed where a cure does not or cannot, since it consciously and deliberately brings to bear a control which can be regulated so as to conform to what the situation needs. The two, of course, are not antithetical. Cure and will can even make use of one another. One can will be to cured and one can cure a will.

A complete cure awaits an insistence by the idios, making different epitomizations function maximally and in harmony. Left to itself, the idios does what it can but often enough without great effect. It is given additional power and thereupon is able to bring multiple activities into closer accord when made subject to a willed end. There need be no decision to be cured, but there must be an effort made to be in control. The fact accords with the wisdom of sages in many lands. But it also falls short of what that wisdom commonly encourages—the belief that a concentration on the desirability of a cure produces or promotes it.

Responsibility brings a good that ought to be realized by men to bear on what one privately initiates. A will promotes a desired end. If that will is good, it is expressed responsibly, and thereby governs privacy and body by what ought to be realized. An I is natively directed toward an even greater good, an ideal, completing whole in which every item is maximally enhanced in harmony with all else. The I is expressed responsibly when it guides responsible action by that ideal, completing whole.

One takes other men to be at their best when they express a good will, and thereby bring a final good to bear on what is present. Most men exercise wills that are not very good or are not very good for long. They are quite different from those who will to do evil. These, because they preclude the realization of what ought to be realized by insisting on what this opposes, exercise perverse wills. Such men deliberately set about to do wrong; they do not just stumble into wrongdoing or do wrong absentmindedly. That they may be uninteresting men, mere bureaucrats, unimaginative or banal, does not stand in the way of their setting about to do harm. They do evil and know it to be so. Himmler told his soldiers that the world did not appreciate how terribly difficult their work was, how hard it was for them to shoot down the defenseless men who stood there naked before them [convicted of no other crime but that of belonging to a despised race]. If the soldiers had before them the limited good of a thousand-year Reich of Aryans, and supposed that the willing of this involved the destruction of whatever stood in the way, their crime would be the willing of a limited good which required the destruction of what it could not tolerate. They would then allow the glories of the prospect to overwhelm their grasp of the values of what was present. One could not then properly accuse them of a much greater crime than that of being confused. But it is more correct to say that they destroyed what they knew it was wrong to destroy. They willed a limited good. That it was limited, they themselves made evident by identifying some actual things as standing in its way. If it were a final good, it would have made all that is serve it or fit within it. Their perversity lay in part in their refusal to will a final good, and in part in their violent rejection of what a limited prospect could not accommodate.

A perverse will fastens on a limited good as though it were absolute, and makes this determinative of all that should be done. Were the will subjected to knowledge and forced to attend to a prospective absolute good, an ideal excellence, it would be cured of its perversity. There is little hope, though, that such a cure will occur, in light of the attraction that a limited prospect has for a perverse will. An effective cure, though, would be provided could one focus on a prospect which precludes the acts needed to realize the prospect on which a perverse will fastens. For this, too, there is little promise, and for the same reason.

Some look to religion to provide a cure for a perverse will. But even deeply religious men find that they are not always able to counter the attraction of a decidedly limited prospect. An increased power, it will perhaps be urged, is exactly what accrues when one prays. Let the claim be granted. We would still be faced with the fact that a perverse will does not allow a man to take that first step. Such a will does not find prayer to be a more attractive prospect than what is perversely willed.

Cures can be aided by those remedies which weaken the force of what is not wanted. Punishment, example, and self-examination sometimes prove to be effective means for achieving this. The use of a good will, dedicated to the realization of a final good, promises more than a curative act can. But the use of will to realize a final good is precisely what a perverse will does not permit.

He who wills perversely could be helped to focus on the values that his will would otherwise destroy. He might change did he then discover that his perverse will prevented him from being the man he was trying to be, or to obtain the good he thought he was realizing. This, of course, would not yet mean that he was directed at what ought to be.

Although most men seem to believe that a perverse will can be cured, and that there are available remedies which make it easier for a cure to occur, there is no one sure way by which this can be be done. Our sorry experience with rehabilitation programs for criminals, some of whom give no evidence of anything more than an inability to adjust to dominant approved ways, indicates that there is little hope for great and widespread success in this direction.

War and politics occasionally use punishment and restraint to prevent what is supposed to be a perverse will from being carried out in public. Taking men to be fixated in various ways, they try to put a stop to undesirable public acts. Since no attention is paid to the question of whether or not what is stopped is being insisted on by a perverse will, those who are stopped are in effect taken to be just public sources of what is horrendous. It would be embarrassing for those who follow this lead to discover that the same view is held of them that they hold of those whom they punish and restrain, did they not treat the judgment of those others to be the inevitable outcome of corruption. Each side holds that it alone is doing what is right, and that the other cannot be changed. Each then goes on to suppose either that it itself is fixated in a different and in a better direction, or that somehow its members alone are able to will as they ought. In either way, each divides mankind into different species.

To act on an entity with success, one must have some appreciation of its nature, promise, and limits. To be most effective with respect to men, one must know what they cherish and how to trade on their concern for this, whether one seeks to enhance or to reduce them. The Nazis burnt synagogues and tore up prayer books because they knew these were precious to the Jews. The Nazis also knew that the Jews were men. That is why the Nazis engaged in humanly-debasing acts when dealing with them.

Were a man with a perverse will open to the persuasion of reason, he would be able to see that he stands in his own way, for his perverse will destroys the goods that a supposed excellent state of affairs, which he thinks he is going to realize, must preserve and enhance. But, caught up in passionately sustained endeavors which are believed to promote some important goal, not to be examined or understood but just to be pursued, and impressed with military success and the exercise of power, he brushes aside the fact that he devotes himself to the realization of a prospect which not only is not all-encompassing, but which requires him to destroy what is precious and can never be replaced.

For a man to exercise his will properly and successfully, he must not only attend to what others are and want, but must see himself and them as representative men. Otherwise, he would not even be able to converse with them. Each is allied with all others. He and they have representative roles. When any one of them says, "It is true that . . ." or "It is a fact that . . ." he lets others know that they can count on what is being said. The Nazis were able to tell effective lies because they spoke to their victims as men, able to understand and accept what was said as something seriously intended, claiming to be true. Even when no lies were told and the victims just lined up to be shot, they were dealt with as men who understood orders, and whose deaths were to be hidden or denied.

It is self-contradictory to view onself as a man and at the same time to take other men not to be represented by oneself and not to be representative of oneself. Men who have already defined the race of true men so narrowly as to exclude some others, cannot, though, be expected to change their ways by pointing up contradictions. Nor can they be expected to cure themselves, or to be persuaded by arguments. It is utopian to look to them to reform themselves. But if it is supposed that the situation in which they are could not have been prevented and that they therefore are necessarily perverse, perverse natively, one will distinguish oneself from them as radically different in kind. This is but to hold that those with perverse wills are not human in the same sense that the rest of men are. In the end, that is but to take oneself not to be a full man, since it denies that one is representative of them—and conversely.

The Nazis were men, though with perverse wills. Well before they were in control, their just complaints should have been satisfied, thereby enabling them to become men who were occupied with goods which had a limited but legitimate place in a world where good will prevailed. Others failed in not having so willed that the Nazis' initial justified claims were met. Of course, once the Nazis gained ascendancy, it was no longer reasonable to believe that they could be persuaded to will as men ought. To have some prospect of correcting a perverse will, one must deal with it well before it has been able to back its decisions with effective might and blind passion.

A perverse will runs its course almost beyond the power of anyone to stop it. But had a good will been brought into play before a perverse will was firmly entrenched and empowered, the perverse will could conceivably have been changed.

A good will must be exercised by others if social or political perversity is to be avoided or overcome; the prospects of concern to each individual must be at least those which a good will can use as a means. Such a use of a good will is not possible before one is in a position to use his idios to make himself all he can privately be. Only then will he be able to benefit his body, and live in an eminently desirable way, separately and together with others.

Physical good health is never the best state for one whose primary interest is justice, philosophy, art, or religion. A man can be so occupied with one of these as of such great value, that he sacrifices himself, starves himself, or neglects to satisfy other pressing and warranted needs. If he is said to be 'healthy', one will be using 'healthy' in a way which allows him to be recognized as being without health in another and more familiar sense. Health, as usually understood, is a desirable or necessary physical and possibly mental precondition for the occurrence or enjoyment of great goods. One who is healthy is able to devote himself to the pursuit of other goods with a vigor and persistence not possible otherwise. He will be most successful if his health is an ingredient in a more complex, high-grade activity. He can then be said to be truly healthy, one in whom beneficent governing powers have been merged with what they control. He will have true full health, though, only if what is controlled is what is distinct from him. While a cure depends on the ability of the idios to function as an equilibriating control over subordinated private agents, true full health characterizes a man who is not only able to function as a private being but is able to function well in the world and make it better.

A cure of the body depends to some extent on how this is lived. The fact has been discovered by those who have applied similar remedies to what seem to be quite similarly afflicted bodies, and then found that a persistent change in the manner in which the body was lived had been produced. Sometimes it is possible to prompt a change in the living of the body by relaxing it through drugs and in other ways, but one then usually provides only remedies which, for a while, overcome bodily induced tensions.

One need not accept Plato's way of dividing the 'soul' nor his supposition that the different parts of it are in an hierarchical order, to take advantage of his insight that a man is at his best when all his parts exercise their proper functions. Plato thought that this result was achieved when the highest-ranking subdivision exercised a rightful rule over the lower. He did not entertain the possibility that a number of them could be on a level, or that what should be in control was not to be identified with an epitomization of the self. The achievement of a balanced functioning of all epitomizations is the task of the idios. Without thought or deliberation, it acts steadily on all, gently trying to rectify the excesses of one by placing greater emphasis on others, and then in such a way as to avoid recurrences. It may be so effective that some unwanted factor or event never recurs, and nothing as bad or worse replaces it. One would not yet have warrant for saying that there had been a cure. A remedy could interplay with the cause of a symptom so as to suppress, modify, or eliminate its usual effect, without affecting what had the cause of the symptom as its effect. Unlike a remedy, a cure may allow symptoms to remain, having rendered them harmless or irrelevant, reporting nothing germane to a recognized illness. Flushing, a headache, even a searing pain might remain after a cure has been produced. If one then sought to get rid of these as well, one would have to provide a cure for a different cause than one had provided before.

We decide that a man is not functioning properly when his usual functions for continued life, growth, or other desirable outcomes cannot be readily performed or performed at all, or when his body deviates in appearance or activity from what is characteristic of others of the same age, background, and type of work. Over the course of history, we have learned how to stop or eliminate some of the unwanted effects, to leave individuals functioning somewhat close to a norm. That norm, though vague in details, unclear in its borders, unreflected on by most, is nevertheless fairly well enough understood by mature members of a society. In the face of a widespread disability, even one which has characterized most men throughout history, reference has to be made to an idealized form of a norm as that which men might eventually establish. Some such reference is made by those who seek to extend man's life span beyond the point where any has ever lived, or who try to eliminate diseases to which all men have been prone.

One type of cure is produced by the body as a unity, rectifying the ways in which different bodily parts and acts operate in relation to one another; another privately changes the ways in which the body is being lived; a third rectifies the ways in which subordinated expressions are related to one another. Best of all is an ideal cure, one in which the living of the body is so rectified that it enables a man to realize a good in which all other goods, private and public, are maximally together.

SIX

Rights

a. Native Rights

At all stages, from the moment that he comes into existence until he dies, a human has a privacy not fully determinate, not completely articulated, not exhaustively epitomized. Yet all the while, he is insistent, making his privacy effective in and through his body. Access to his privacy is made both by himself and others from the outside through his available, public, locatable, perceivable, embodied person.

Each epitomization has rights against the others. Those rights are limited forms of more basic rights, the rights to be, to function, and to prosper. All the rights are lodged in the person, and exist there even when there are no public expressions. As lodged in the person, the rights have the form of native rights with justified public expressions. A just society and state protect, support, and help men satisfy those rights.

A person is a locus of rights. Some of these originate in the person and its epitomizations. Others are carried by it on behalf of the self and its epitomizations. The rights in a person, consequently, are demanded by the person on behalf of itself and its epitomizations or on behalf of other specializations of privacy.

Each right is a claim to be, to function, and to prosper, and therefore to have and express a person, a self, or an epitomization of either one. Because some of the rights present in a person are claims made on behalf of a self, or by what specializes this, no knowledge of what a person is will reveal all the rights that a man has, even when these are present and are publicly presented by him through the agency of his body, or in petitions, demands, or requests. His body, as lived by his person, sustains the rights his person insists on, both those that his person carries on its own behalf and those which are his by virtue of his self. In addition, he has rights acquired by virtue of his place in the world, environment, milieu, and society.

If abstraction be made from a man's possession of his body, what remains is no longer a human body. It will not even be a single, complex unit, for such a unit has a distinctive privacy. It will then be even less than the body of an animal, just a whole or a colony whose career is a summation of the activities of its parts or members, or just an aggregate of units acting together. Such a whole or colony has at most a minimal right to be; it surely has no human rights. This does not preclude an attribution of publicly supported rights to them.

A human corpse is initially a whole and later an aggregate but, through society's conditioning, is made the object of respect and even reverence by others. Individual men, through memory and affection, also ascribe rights to it. Often they demand respect for those rights and protect them. These, of course, are not rights which the corpse itself possesses. But the rights possessed by a man are native, persistent claims made by him privately, whether he knows of them or not, and whether or not they are respected. Laying down the conditions for a just public world, the rights are not compromised if this not produced.

To know another as a you is to know him as a person. To know oneself as a me is to know oneself as a person. In both cases, the person is known as present, available to an external approach. I come to you from a distance; I reach my me from the outside. At both times, I privately engage in acts of attending. In the case of the me, I also sustain that at which I arrive. What I acknowledge at both times is a publicized person continuous with itself as still private. At both times, a locus of native rights is confronted, the publicized person having them in the form of claims against others, and the private person having them in the form of claims not yet publicly expressed. Because the two are inseparable, what I confront is my own or another's person, whose claims against others are in the foreground, sustained by the person as natively insistent.

Viable rights are private rights, able to have a publicly expressible form. Behind them are native rights. These, the viable partly express, usually in a modified form, answering to the transformations which the body provides. The viable rights may not be supported by others, or by a society or state, either because they are not known, because they are not urged, because they are disregarded, or because they conflict with others which have been sanctioned, spelled out better, or better understood. But they still remain, measuring the justice of others and the justice of the society or state.

The United States Constitution speaks of rights that are reserved by the people. It does not tell us what these are, it being apparently assumed that they are well-known. Whether or not they were well-known in 1789, they are not so today. Some of the rights we now have could be said to have been those that had then been reserved. If it be supposed that whatever new rights are recognized at some later time were the very rights that had been reserved at an earlier, a newly reocgnized right would be a native right belatedly identified. But what was recognized to be a right at some later time might just be what only then could be a genuine right. If so, some or all the rights supposed to be reserved by the people would not be genuine rights; men at a previous time would have only the capacity to reserve the supposed rights. If rights are really reserved, one does not just have a capacity to have them; one has the rights in fact. A state that does not satisfy their public expression will so far not be just.

Some of the rights that men now claim do not have public support. This they may acquire only when a sovereign power assures their protection and satisfaction. That power could credit men with only public rights, rights which those men do not privately ground. A child in ancient Greece did not have a right to publicly supported education; a child in the United States does. Neither has a native right to such education, but the child in the United States, unlike the other, has the right in a politically sustained form. It is bestowed by the state. Had the rights that men have all been bestowed on them, not only would the bestower be able to take away what it had given without necessarily doing anything wrong, but it could warrantedly refuse to acknowledge any of the rights that some or even all of its people insisted that they had. Because bestowed rights are not the only kind that men have, it is correct to say that some political systems are unjust because and so far as they refuse to give public support to certain human rights.

If a state does not allow for the expression and protection of some claimed rights, those rights might still exist. If so, they would be private rights which had no public standing. How could one know that there were such rights? How could one know that some rights are neglected or denied by a political body, if this does not explicitly say that it planned to back them? And, if there were rights which men never express, could one ever know that men had them?

We know that there are rights neglected, denied, or unexpressed, the results so far achieved permit us to say, because rights are intrinsic to different, known epitomizations, are located in the person, and are publicly expressed in demands which are urged in opposition to fellowmen, and sometimes against society and state. If this is so, why is it that the lists of rights drawn up by men over the course of western thought vary so much? How can it be determined just what rights there are, if they are not expressed, or publicly sustained? The answer to these questions is now fairly evident. The discovery of the primary ways in which privacy is epitomized is one with the discovery of the native rights that men have. We come to know what these are in a number of ways: using as evidences the acknowledged rights that are now taken to be worthy of public support; attending to the inverse of the public duties that men are required to carry out; envisaging a backing in men's privacies for the rights which were achieved over time, or which had been bestowed; or recognizing rights which are implied in the acknowledgment of other rights.

Hobbes thought that the rights men had were those which were guaranteed by a sovereign. He made one exception. Men, he thought, never surrendered a right to their lives. It is not altogether clear whether Hobbes thought that men never did, that they never could, or that they never should give up that right. Nor is it clear whether or not he thought that the right belonged to the men just so far as they existed apart from one another. What is fairly clear is that he did not see that if strangers can enter into a contract, they cannot be absolutely opposed to one another. Hobbes should have acknowledged that individual men, in and outside a supposed state of nature, have inalienable rights, whether or not these are ever identified or supported. The right to life is only one of these.

Why not deny that any man, as apart from all the rest, has any rights? Hobbes would perhaps answer that there would then be no rights to give to a sovereign. That answer leaves open the question whether or not there should be a sovereign, whether or not rights should or could be assigned to him, and whether or not he should be obeyed.

If a sovereign's right to men's obedience is a consequence of their having bestowed rights on him, they must have had some native rights in the first place. But if they can give up any of them, why may they not give up all, including the right to life? If it be maintained that they need that right in order to be able to benefit from the rule of the sovereign, one makes room for the claim that other rights, such as a right to health, or to express one's opinion, would also have to be granted. If the right of life is untransferable, surely such other rights are untransferable as well.

Why not be bolder than Hobbes, and deny that a man has any native rights, even the right to life? Might not a man, as Socrates held, be like an ox who belongs to a master having both the power and the right to kill it? The suggestion rests on the supposition that there is an absolute sovereign whose decrees are not to be gainsaid. Whether that sovereign be a God, an individual, a society, or a state, it will never act unjustly or err by going counter to the rights of men since, on the hypothesis, the men will not have any rights. Presumably that sovereign could be opposed. The opposition, though, would not be immoral, or wrong, or a violation of a contract; it would just be the expression of recalcitrant beings. Defying the only rights that there were, those beings would be brutes. But this they could not be at any time that they were in a position to make a contract and to transfer their rights.

If men do not have a right to oppose their sovereign, what that sovereign does will always be what should be done, unless it could somehow violate a higher law, or get in its own way. Relative to its subjects, it would not only have an unquestionable right to take the lives of some men, but would have the right to use any of them as it would. The men would then be taken not to have natures of their own or, if they had, to have natures which did not entail justified demands. Such a view should find nothing amiss in the ways men act on one another—as long as they serve the sovereign maximally. But a maximal service requires men to curtail their acts and to take account of what their fellowmen need, do, and claim. Otherwise, not all that should be done on behalf of the sovereign would be done.

If men are required to serve a sovereign, they must help one another, if only as a preliminary to all doing what the sovereign demands. Each would have to have a native right to be helped so that he could be of maximum service to the sovereign. If it be granted that the sovereign has an absolute right to the support of men, it must consequently be granted that each man must have the native right to become one who can support the sovereign. Granted, with Hobbes, that men have some native right which must be respected by the sovereign as well as by other men, one must hold, in contrast with Hobbes, that this is the right to function on behalf of a sovereign. From this point of view, a right to life would belong to a man only so far as he was under a sovereign, and then only in order to make it possible for him to do what the sovereign required. Since the rights to know, to make decisions, to be responsible, to be affiliated, and so on also enable a man to serve his sovereign, these too would have to be acknowledged, and for similar reasons.

This contention is at once bolder and more moderate than Hobbes'— bolder because it acknowledges that the right to live is not the only inalienable right; more moderate, because it allows all rights to be viewed as instances of a primary right to serve a sovereign. The right to life, of course, is more basic than others, since its satisfaction is a precondition for them. But that does not change the fact that it and other rights, on a strict Hobbsean view, are to be credited to men only so far as they enable them to be good subjects.

A Hobbsean account of rights and the role of the sovereign need not allow for rights possessed by men as existing apart from any sovereign. And it does not grant that men, as under a sovereign, have to be credited with those rights that enable them to be his obedient, effective subjects. Nevertheless, it affirms that men have rights when there is no sovereign, and—what it does not see—that when under the sovereign, they must have a number of other rights enabling them to serve him.

One might try to avoid this conclusion by imagining, along the lines proposed by Rawls, a just state which pays attention only to the different benefits men derive from their natural endowments, and which enforces rules both to promote their equal liberties, and to provide a more equitable distribution of benefits. No appeal would here be made to any native rights, not even to a right to life. One would appeal only to rationality or to a wish to achieve a fairer, more just state of affairs than would otherwise obtain. A failure on the part of men to promote the welfare of the disadvantaged would not point up native rights denied to them, but only reason or laws violated. No reference would be made to the question whether or not men had a native freedom to live or to think, or even to carry out a preference among publicly indifferent things. In short, one would begin by imagining men to be what they are not and could never be. If this be allowed, a host of other equally unrealistic suppositions would be no less viable. A sound political theory requires more than an exercise in imagination. At the very least, it should take account of men as they in fact now are, separately and together, and of the possible ways in which they could be improved severally and together.

A state is just if its guaranteed liberties support the public expression of native rights. Its decrees should be guided by the requirement that the state promote the maximum public satisfaction of those rights. A just state enables the underprivileged to have better opportunities to attain a better status; it also promotes opportunities for all to have richer private lives. If a state does not take men to be equal as persons, it will have no reason to enforce laws designed to bring about a more equitable distribution of goods and to help them all to be better as individuals, except so far as such activities promote the state's continuance or prosperity.

Behind the recommendation that equality be promoted by a state is the tacit acknowledgment that men are already equal as private persons, and that it is the task of a state to see to it that they become equal publicly. When that supposition is overlooked, one has as much warrant for holding, with Nozick, that men are entitled to whatever they have or can obtain, as one has for holding, with Rawls, that men are to enjoy the benefits that their superior endowments and opportunities happen to provide, as long as they agree to have the endowments and opportunities used to maximize the status of the rest of men. The present is closer to an older view, which holds that political men are to express themselves in mutually supportive and enhancing actions. But it also differs from that view in explicitly holding that men publicly and rightly insist on and deserve public support for what they privately and rightfully claim.

Two new questions must now be faced. If rights are inalienable, how could they belong to epitomizations which come and go, sinking back into a person or self apparently without a trace? And if everyone has at least the right to live, must we not also sanction the preservation of every embryo, fetus, or infant, no matter how imbecile or monstrous, and every terminal patient, no matter how terrible his pain?

The answer to the first question has already been anticipated. Every epitomization has rights; all the rights are carried by the person; if there is no distinguishable self, the only rights will be those which are native to a person and its epitomizations. An infant has no right to autonomy, for such a right awaits the attainment of a self. But an infant has a human sensitivity, and that means that it has a native right to live, to be free from pain, and to sustain a realizable promise to epitomize its person in other ways. Because its sensitivity is inseparable from such a promise, its sensitivity is different from a subhuman's, even one which, unlike the infant's, has a well-developed desire and a fixed niche in an environment.

The second question opens up the issue of conflicting rights. Disease-carrying rats and roaches, the imbecilic, the senile, the terminally ill, madmen, and wild beasts, all have a distinctive right to live. A human right to live is greater than a roach's, because it is the right not simply of a living, sensitive being, but of a person, and therefore of one who may be able to have a self as well. Those unfortunates who are unable to have selves still have, as part of their right to be persons, the right to acquire selves. They will, though, not have the rights of normal men, for these have actual, functioning selves and therefore have some rights that the less developed humans do not have.

When one right stands in the way of the exercise of another, the lesser evidently should give way to the greater. A subhuman's right to live should yield before the conflicting right of a human to live, for he alone is a person. If the human is defective, his rights must give way to the rights of normal men, when the two conflict and no other resolution is possible. The decision will be tragic, for one will have sacrificed a human who differs from the others only in not being a fully articulated person or in not being more than a person. The fact that one can justify the sacrifice of those with lesser rights for the sake of those with greater does not, of course, free one from the guilt which is entailed by the destruction or reduction.

The Constitutions of the United States and the Soviet Union explicitly state that men have rights. They both pledge themselves to respect those rights, and are able to back the pledge with effective force. They are not alone. Every state, whether it has a constitution or not, makes some provision in its legal system for the protection of the rights of some of the people under its governance. Indeed, it is a tautology to say so. What took no account of anyone's rights would not be a state but a coercive force. Anarchy precludes the existence of a state; tyranny is anarchy in ascendancy, under the control of one or a few men.

Normal men have the right to some material goods that they can call their own for a while. The so-called right to property extends that initial right to include the right to sell, bestow, and sometimes to consume, reduce, or destroy what is possessed. Men who do not belong to any group have no right to property because they have no group-sanctioned claims. They could possess and use, but they could not own. Ownership is a sanctioned relation which holds even when one is not in possession and even against those who are in possession. As has been remarked, we own the money we have in a bank, as well as the property a thief took from us and which he now has in his possession.

Inside a state, men have a right to property so far as a publicly expressed claim to own is there sanctioned and protected. It does not presuppose a private right. The right might be allowed solely for the sake of making service on behalf of a sovereign more palatable, effective, or expeditious. But if it were service on behalf of a sovereign that required men to be granted the right to property, the right would be theirs—even when the sovereign mistakenly failed to support it or so acted that it was limited, perverted, or denied. A sovereign who did not support the right would, on the hypothesis, deny his own right to have his subjects function effectively on his behalf.

Private rights to live, to know, and other rights grounded in the person, are doubly assured in modern states. These rights presuppose and are supported by men who have epitomized their privacies as selves and persons, each making essential claims to be and to prosper, and thus to obtain public support and satisfaction. If a state supports and satisfies the claims, it tacitly acknowledges that men have private rights whose public exercise is to be promoted and exercised.

Anarchism recognizes no other rights than those possessed by individual men. In some forms, it holds that whatever is in the world belongs to no one or, alternatively, to everyone indiscriminately. In some accord with Locke, it goes on to hold that a private right to property is both manifested and justified when one lays hold of or works on material taken from a common store. But since it makes no provision for a transfer of the supposed property, it reduces property to possession. But a right which reaches only to possession allows a man to put down what he had made his own, and for another to acquire a right to it just by laying hold of it. There will so far be nothing which legitimatizes turning over anything to others, particularly to those who have done nothing to make them deserve to receive it. A legitimatized transfer requires sustained rules or laws that make it possible not only to possess but to own, and therefore to be able to give something away or to exchange it for what has less value. Theories of entitlement, which take one to own whatever he might happen to have, necessarily fall short of making provision for property, except so far as this can be reduced to possession, and therefore to a minute fraction of what is in fact owned.

If allowance is not made for a sanctioned transfer, no allowance will be made for ownership and therefore for a right to property. At most, only possession for a while will be sanctioned. There could still be provisions made to protect one from theft—a denial of possession—but none governing gifts or exchanges. To allow for these, men must have the right to be persons together under enforceable common conditions. Unlike release by one and possession by another, a transfer needs the backing of conventions or laws which dictate how one is to deal with others.

Outside the provenance of any society or state are the stars, outer space, the oceans. These are owned by no one. This, though, does not mean that anyone can use them as he would, or can make his own what he might find there. What a man does even when alone is in part a function of what he had been enabled to do by his society or state, and to which he is so far bound. He discovers, uses, and possesses under conditions which the society or state provided, or which enabled him to profit from. His training, and therefore his ability to function apart from all, is a function of what had been obtained through the help of others.

The familiar maxim that there are no rights without duties, or duties without rights, prompts the ascription of rights or duties when none can be detected or otherwise justified. One has a duty toward later generations, though these do not yet have rights. The duties toward them involve actions designed to make the world a better or at the very least not a worse place than it now is. But as long as the others are still future, they cannot sustain any rights, private or public. A man can also have rights which are unknown; so far, they cannot be the object of any one's duties.

We credit contemporaries with rights just so far as we have duties toward them. Since we have duties toward the young, the infirm, the disadvantaged, the derelict, and the mad, for a similar reason they too will have to be credited with rights. At the very least, each will have to be granted the right to live as rich a life as he can, and the rest of men will have a duty to make this possible. Since we have a duty toward those who are to follow us, although they now sustain no rights, why not say that, although we have duties toward the unfortunate, they also have no rights? Or that if they have private rights which they do not express in any way, others cannot have duties pertinent to those rights? The suppositions shock, violating our sense of what is owed to them as humans. The shock points up the need to save the doctrine of the correlativity of rights and duties. Unlocatable rights which are correlative to prescribed duties should be said to be held in reserve by society or the state until they can be individually possessed, and unrecognized duties which are correlative to known rights should be said to await a time when a social or legal insistence on them will enable the rights to be exercised. Once we know either the duties or rights of men, we can then know what other rights or duties there are, even if only as held in trust for a while by society or state.

In ascribing duties to men, a society or state imposes a burden. The men are to take upon themselves the task of satisfying the rights of others. They are thereby acknowledged to have a private right to express what they can autonomously be and do. Duty, from this point of view, is the outcome of a right to be of help to others.

If men are credited with rights, they are given the status of beings toward whom others have duties. From this point of view, the rights are theirs because others have those duties toward them. Once again, the men will have been credited with the right to express what they can autonomously be and do.

So far as men decide how or when they are to carry out their duties, they have the right to carry out self-imposed, public, accountable acts. So far as it is they who determine what public form their native rights are to assume, they determine what the duties toward them will be.

Aside from ethical, and any possible religious duties, men have duties whose public satisfaction may or may not benefit either society or state. The autonomy that can ground those duties may not be socially or politically desirable, while conformity to what a society or state decrees may not be good for the men or for the society or state. A man has a private right to be part of a peaceful and prospering world of men, and has a right to accept duties directed toward the production and maintenance of that world. Since subjects are sometimes more perceptive than their rulers, if

they accept duties to promote peace or prosperity, they may have to insist
on rights which the rulers do not acknowledge or which they are inclined
to deny.

Over the course of time, rights which had never before been protected,
and sometimes even claimed, have been identified and backed by states.
The right of children not to work, and the right of women to vote and to
own property are rights which were not stated and certainly not protected
until recent times. If one held that the rights were native, always present,
but that a state had not advanced far enough to make it possible to
acknowledge or support those rights, it is incumbent on him to show how
it is possible to know of the existence of those rights. It is reasonable to say
that before the modern era, with its backing of public education, the new
structure of its families, its large-scale economics and the form that property has in it, the comparative underdevelopment of law, and the existence of absolute monarchies precluded the public acknowledgment of
those rights. If one is to be properly cautious, no more should be said than
that only when the time is ripe for their public expression are those rights
present and able to be publicly supported. While some rights are present
from the beginning of the life of a human person, and others come to
be when other epitomizations arise, these would be rights which existed
only when public opportunities to express them were brought into
being.

Females were once prevented from having the status of full-fledged
public humans. Now, because they have opportunities to develop as they
could not before, they can claim to have not only all the native but all the
public rights with which males had already been credited. What might
have been granted as a privilege for the females—a publicly recognized
advantage in the form of a favor or immunity to act publicly in certain
ways—would, by a change in circumstance, now have the status of both a
private and a sustained public right.

All private rights, it might be held, exist only when and so far as they
have become publicly viable in the course of history. Universalized, the
view would lead one to hold that there are no native rights, and therefore
nothing which can be justifiably insisted on in the face of a state's neglect
or opposition. But the existence of private rights is not jeopardized just
because they are not acknowledged, have no public support, or are not
recognized by those in power.

Lawyers and political theorists usually take a right to be a publicly
expressible, enforceable claim against others, and perhaps against the
sovereign. Strictly speaking, such a 'right' is no more than a privilege. It

need not have a private counterpart. What is publicly sanctioned is a genuine right only if it is grounded in a private right, whether this be native or comes to be at the same time that the right is publicly supported. The right to liberty—a protection from public restraints on movement, assembly, speech, and worship—even when hemmed in by restrictions serving to protect the state in times of war or stress, is an acquired public right. The existence of that right presupposes at least a concurrent private right grounded in the self. A right to liberty is a right to express that private right in public, and to have its satisfaction backed by demands on others that they perform corresponding duties.

Having come to know the native rights men have, one is in a position to see what other rights, if any, are entailed by these. The entailed rights might not themselves have a public role. It suffices for their acknowledgment that they are presupposed by rights already established. One of these is the right of the self to limit the actions of the I in relation to other epitomizations of the self. Others are the right of the person to control its different epitomizations, and the right of the idios to govern all epitomizations.

One of the tasks of a state is to give a public meaning and protection to native rights. The public rights it is to bestow are to be determined by knowing what the native rights are. As a consequence, it is possible to judge how advanced a state is by seeing how appropriate its sanctioned public rights are to the native rights that men have and express. And we can judge how just it is by seeing whether or not it gives everyone over whom it exercises jurisdiction the same public support for the same native rights.

Just as it can make public acknowledgment of the arrival of new powers in maturing humans, so a state can make public acknowledgment of native rights. It will, of course, not bestow those rights or produce their public expressions. It can do no more than provide the rights with opportunities to be publicly expressed and to see that they are then protected and satisfied. Those rights, though, may not be effectively supported by a state until men insistently call them to the attention of those who legislate, judge, and govern.

I imply that others have native rights when I refer to them as 'you's', for 'you' is a term of address applied to one deserving respect, and therefore to one who has the right to be taken to be a person. If used when talking to pets or things, even though this comes early in the speech of a child, 'you' is parasitical on a reference to humans, from whom the child learned the term. When used as a repetitive, marking out unit after unit, it is a substitute for a repeated use of 'one'. "You, you, and you", said of stones or fingers, one after the other, is not altogether separable from a feeble attempt to be humorous.

I become acquainted with your native rights to the degree that I become acquainted with your privacy. I move beyond the surface of your presented you, which is relative to me, to what presents that you. I find myself bucking a counterinsistence the more deeply I penetrate. Eventually I am brought to a stop. At that point I thrust forward indefinitely, more and more faintly, never arriving at a specifiable termination. When, as is here done, I reflect on the evidence that could have produced the you, and try to understand what the production is like, I forge an idea or concept of what had presented the evidence.

We are aware of one another as having native rights, all serving to articulate the single native right of a human privacy. If this is so, why have some of the greatest thinkers neglected to remark on that right, and on the other, more limited rights men also have? Why, if this is so, should there be any question as to whether or not a human fetus, or a man whose heart or brain exhibits no movement, has human rights? It is not enough to remark that we are able to penetrate beyond the you that another presents, or that we can produce an idea or concept of its source. None of us is able to make such contact with a fetus. As a consequence, there is a strong tendency to defend or oppose abortion by arguments about the supposed continuity or discontinuity of embryo, fetus, and infant, by referring to a woman's supposed right to do as she would with what grows in her body, or by calling attention to God's supposed commands. None of the views is so clear or well-grounded that its rejection or acceptance reveals someone to be inhuman, overly sentimental, or unable to carry out a process of careful thinking on a many-sided issue. No one knows just when a human person comes to be or passes away, but only that the one must occur after identical twins are no longer possible, and that the other must occur when the body ceases to function as a unit. This, though, all can know: if we are speaking of a human, we are speaking of one who has native rights which should be given social, legal, and political translation and support. Against this, it might be maintained that not even a full-grown man has native rights. If he had, the wisest of Greek, Hebrew, and Christian thinkers would have known them and consequently would not have condoned slavery, and would not have had difficulty in determining whether or not barbarians and other supposed primitives were fully human. Actually, the practices of these men partly opposed what their theories sanctioned. Their intermarriages, condemnations of murder, infanticide, and wanton cruelty, their encouragements to worship and the like, betrayed the living contradictions under which they lived and thought.

Aristotle insisted on a man's need to be with other men. He held that one who was altogether solitary, since he was no God, was an idiot living like a beast. Aristotle also emphasized the value of friendship. So far, Aristotle is quite modern. But were one to subscribe to the Aristotelian view today, he would surely list various virtues and vices that Aristotle did not envisage. Unlike Aristotle, he would recognize every human to have an I that was equal in dignity and right with others, without regard for gender or social position. It is not plausible to suppose that the difference between Aristotle's and our understanding of other men is due to the superiority of our insight. We do not, of course, know whether or not he made contact with persons in his own society in the very way we do, but was unable or just failed to do so when the men belonged to quite different cultures or when they had a presumably lower status. It is not implausible, though, to suppose that he was primarily interested in the kind of community that could conceivably be brought about when men function together excellently, and that this was enough to make him put aside a consideration of those whom he would not or could not take to be equals there. Still, Aristotle must have had many contacts with members of his own family. Even if he took them to be inferior to himself, he must have known them to be persons with equal sensitivity and other powers. At the very least, he knew his friends to be persons. It therefore seems reasonable to say that he differs from us today, not in his being unable to know persons, but in his not having been as ready as we are to allow that men with whom deep penetrating contact is not made are persons on a footing with those few who are directly and intimately known. We live in a larger world of recognized persons than Aristotle and most of our predecessors did.

A native right cannot be observed. It has no clear outlines, no obtrusive features. The native rights that we take a man to have, it might therefore be supposed, are just public rights which we have imaginatively duplicated in a privacy, without good warrant or gain. But were there no native rights, or were these not the source of what should be publicly supported, we would have no reason for criticizing a state as oppressive or cruel.

I am the equal of other men. No one is more or less of a person than I. I have the same rights they have. I can of course ignore their rights and they can ignore mine. I may give myself special privileges and dispensations, but the rights I have are still coordinate with theirs, whose private grounds I faintly glimpse when I insistently move against and through their counterinsistencies.

Despite the fact that I am often acutely aware that another is stronger, more courageous, perceptive, and patient, and that he is now involved in activities quite different from mine, I know us to be equal. Were this a consequence of the fact that there is a single universal 'man', which we share, we would at best provide localizations for a single common right, and we might then conceivably be unequal because of the way in which we sustained that common right. We have equal rights because we are equally human, but the equality could be due to neither of us, any more than it could be due to a universal which is instantiated by each or present in every one. Each, by himself, is incomparable. To account for the comparable equality of all of us, reference must be made to what can relate us, while we continue to remain apart, no matter what else is done. Were there no common controlling, equalizing power, we would be incomparably different, neither equal nor unequal.

b. Quasi-Persons

Equality is not the only relation which connects each man with every other. Men are also affiliated, are governed by common laws, are at various distances from one another, and are related as better or worse. These relations have one form when they connect men as private, and another when they connect them as public. Private men are equal to one another because their privacies are related by a common equalizing final condition; they are publicly equal because they are related as units in a common world. What they privately do and what is publicly done or allowed to them turns them into beings having different ethical and public standings. They are then related in more specialized and limited ways. They then also exhibit the fact that they are more than terms in relations, since they show that they are able to engage in acts which traverse the common relations in unique ways.

It was not foolish of the Supreme Court to say that a corporation is a kind of person, though it would be foolish to suppose that a corporation presents itself from a private position, that it is a person intrinsically, or that it is equatable with a human person. A corporation is only a quasi-person. Unlike those public rights, which are acquired in the course of a human life or over the course of the history of mankind or a particular nation and are accompanied by the presence of corresponding private rights, the rights of a corporation are those required if it is to function well in a modern capitalist state.

The rights of a corporation can be insisted on against particular decrees of the state, for a corporation has the rights just so far as it is a functioning unit in that state, apart from the decrees. Denials of those rights conflict both with the nature of the state and the nature of the corporation. Though the decrees are a just matter of special legislation and activities, the rights express what is essential to the being of a vital functioning economic unit in the contemporary world. When the rights of a corporation or a human person do not receive support from the state, the rights nevertheless continue to be and to deserve support, the one because the rights of the corporation are the rights of a unit in the state, the other because the rights of a person express what has a private sanction. A corporation can have a case against the particular practices of a state of which it is a functioning part. Men, in addition, can have a case against the state from a position no state determines, since they have rights which remain no matter what the nature of the state and, of course, no matter what its legislation.

The rights of a man are neither abrogated nor limited when he does not express himself properly, or when he competes with others. If he does not express his rights properly, he may be prompted to make amends. If his claims compete with the claims of others, there is a need to appeal to what is neutral to all of them. Since no state encompasses their privacies, recourse must be had to conditions and powers which can assess and adjust the men's publicly expressed claims.

The satisfaction of his rights is demanded by a man. Because his I is present in whatever it governs, his I demands that particular private rights be realized, of which the most basic is his right to be. This is constituted without deliberation, and is satisfied in being so constituted, so far as it is confined within his privacy. But when the right is bodily expressed, it is at once challenged and limited, since it is then made to assume the form of a demand requiring public satisfaction.

A man's native rights are publicly limited and qualified. Again and again, he is frustrated and defied, thereby tempting him to make a division between what he privately is and what he is publicly. Flagrant injustices, revolutions, the exhortations of rebels and religious men, the abasement and aridity characteristic of so much of public existence, might awaken him to the fact that he has rights which a change in circumstance or force do not affect. He may then make himself more insistently public than he had been before, demanding not merely the satisfaction of what is then publicly viable, but a satisfaction which he can privately savor and eventually make part of his I.

Present societies and states do not take every distinguished item to have rights. Many of the rights that they acknowledge today were only reluctantly granted. Those who speak on behalf of the rights of a forest or stream are evidently pointing to rights for which a state ought to provide support. An attempt to take the rights to exist only when they are acknowledged would require one to overlook the great age and constancy of the natural objects, their existence outside the human milieu, and the efforts that are being made to preserve them in something like the form they had before man began to make a difference to their continuation and welfare. They are not to be dealt with, as corporations are, under conditions provided by a state. If corporations are legal quasi-persons, forests and streams are natural quasi-persons, and are such whether there are states or not.

Corporations have rights only because they occur within a particular kind of state. The rights, too, are properly exercised only within the limits such a state sets. Since the rights of forests and other natural complexes are not dependent on the presence of a state or even of men, their rights, unlike the rights of a corporation, are intrinsic, though not able to be privately grounded or insisted on.

A forest owned by a corporation has legally endowed rights, because the two are related within a legal system. Since there is no way to turn a merely legal entity into a natural one, the owned forest, unlike the corporation, will have the rights both of a legal and of a natural quasi-person.

The United States Constitution's Eighth Amendment forbids the infliction of cruel and unusual punishment. It therefore offers some protection to the right of sensitivity. When the Constitution asserts that the people have a right to assemble peaceably, it offers some protection to men's right to make themselves accountable. Its provenance, of course, stops at the men as publicly present.

Legal machinery and the nature of legal evidence force a stop with persons as publicly present. All the while, the legal system and the evidence imply that there is more beyond what it is possible to publicly consider or control. The fact becomes conspicuous when laws make reference to 'intention', 'knowledge', 'deliberation', and the like. Although there is no usable, legal meaning for these which goes beyond publicly observable forms, those forms are not always sunderable from what is privately initiated. 'Intention' and the others legally express rights that depend on the presence or action of public agencies; behind them are rights which do not so depend and to which reference is constantly made by those who refuse to remain wholly inside legally defined situations.

c. Expressed Native Rights

Private rights are native rights; they cannot be limited or denied. All that can be done is to make or fail to make adequate provision for the support they need in order to have effective public roles. If not supported, the rights will still be present, still be capable of exercise within the limits of the privacy, regardless of what might happen in the public world. Not to be honored there is not to be allowed to translate them into public, viable forms. Illustrations of this denial are commonplace in repressive regimes, particularly those which set themselves in opposition to their outstanding men in the arts, science, religion, and speculative thought. The outstanding men certainly have no more native private rights than others. But because they have made themselves into richer private beings, what they effectively insist on is superior to what others can. Denying the distinguished men effective public rights denies to the rest an opportunity to have that richness made available to them.

Private rights are grounded in private, individual claims. Expressing the essential dimensions of the privacy, they are present in all. Although no man has more private rights than any other, and although some one may exhibit his in poorer ways and not in the contexts others do, he may still insist on them more forcefully, with the consequence that he will express the same native rights as they do, but in a way that they do not.

Rights are sustained and claimed by a person. Unless they are also insisted on by the I, they will be present in the person and expressed by him, but will not be persistently urged. The rights, as in the person, are distinct only so far as they are not entirely separated from their sources. Detached from those sources, taken solely as they are in the person, they are presented together. An account of the I's relation to native rights, consequently, will deal either with the rights which exist apart from the person, or will deal with them as they are insisted on by the person together with other rights.

Rights simply bestowed by a state help define the status of public persons within it. Possessed by individuals, the rights are theirs only derivatively and then only as long as the state continues to bestow them. The bestowed rights of a freedom of the press, a security against unreasonable searches, or a right to have a speedy and public trial did not exist before they were bestowed. A subsequent act of neglect, therefore, may result in their vanishing. As expressing nothing more than a decision by a sovereign power, there is nothing right or wrong in the bestowal of them or any other right, or in their subsequent withdrawal or neglect, unless such acts hinder the excellent functioning of or control by that sovereign power. The rights recognized in the so-called Bill of Rights are not all of the same type.

When it is said that a state denies rights to some men, distinguished from the rest by some feature not relevant to their functioning in the state, appeal is usually made to rights that should have been bestowed on those men. The appeal is warranted if the rights are required by the very principles which governed other bestowals. Those rights are to be distinguished not only from native but from acquired rights. As has already been observed, children as they grow older, like aliens who have met residency and literacy requirements, acquire public rights they did not have before. Females, once they have moved out of a state of subordination, are able to express rights that they could not express before, and should have those rights publicly supported in the same way the males' are.

Native rights should be translated into rights deserving support by the state. But the state should see to it that the satisfaction of the rights in their private forms are promoted as well. This will require the state to help men be individuals existing apart from it and one another, even while they are functioning members in it.

d. Ideal Man

An asocial man could be himself maximally only if he could abstract himself from his society and state. No matter what his attitude, they affect him. A 'public man', in contrast, makes maximum provision for the effects that his public life will have on him, maintaining himself privately as one who is primarily occupied with what he is and does together with other men. If one avoids both extremes, he will give maximum weight to every epitomization so far as this is consistent with a readiness to be most receptive to what is publicly achieved. He will then come close to being something like Aristotle's and Hegel's ideal man. For both of them, men are to be full members of a well-ordered society, and should prepare themselves privately to maintain themselves with quiet dignity while they benefit from their common existence within their society.

Neither Aristotle nor Hegel would grant that an asocial man could be an excellent man, since they take him to have a privacy which is the inverse of what he is publicly. Their theories stand in the way of their own recognition that a man should be occupied with knowing, making, appreciating, and with what is ultimate; if he is, he will surely act in ways which have little or no social significance and may even lead him to neglect social demands. The full recognition of that fact takes one from a consideration of the public person to a consideration of the private person, the self, and the idios. It is there that men sometimes occupy themselves with matters having no public role, and where they can know about and prepare to take advantage of whatever is publicly available.

Apart from society and state, men should make themselves be what they maximally can be. Indeed, they are urged to do so, on every side. Everyone is asked to be himself. From one perspective, of course, "Be yourself!" is a ridiculous command or recommendation, and that for a double reason. It is addressed to one who already is, and it awaits an action by him. From another perspective, it is sound, and may even prove to be most helpful, calling attention as it does to the fact that a man has the power to bring his idios and I to bear on every epitomization. If "Be yourself!" can help a man be himself with a force and persistence he otherwise would not achieve, a private act of rectification can evidently be elicited by so advising him. Either the advice will affect him in such a way that the needed rectification will thereupon be automatically produced, or his ability to understand and utilize what is said will prompt him to produce it. The first of these suppositions is not plausible, since it supposes that one can become the being he should be just by being advised to be so. The second, though, requires that a man be able to privately convert what is said to him into an occasion to be himself. To do that he must engage in an activity which depends on a still more basic power, working on behalf of a stage that is still to be attained. Negatively, he is being told not to identify himself with his achievements or failures; not to accept the judgments and the assessments of others without examination or qualification; and to stop self-denigrations. It is also apparently being supposed that if the advice is followed, he will become as he should be, either because his faults had obscured what was already present, or because his true state will have been given a needed opportunity to express itself adequately. The advice should be followed—if qualified.

A man is more than any work he does or any role he fills. No matter how satisfying or rewarding, the work and role are caught up in an external world, and have their natures and careers partly determined there. An identification of him with his work or role fails to take sufficient account of the intregity and insistence of his privacy.

Role and work help mold a man, at the very least channelling his activities, determining his opportunities, and setting conditions for what he might do there and elsewhere. A refusal to identify him with his work or role is not a refusal to grant that he exhibits and molds himself in the public world. Instead, it recognizes that what he privately is continues into what he is publicly, and conversely, the first providing a source for the second, the second producing limitations on the first.

A man's identification of himself with his achievements and failures is more frequent but less persistent than his identification of himself with his role or work, except in those cases where achievements and failures are important, crucial, or overwhelming. He becomes habituated to his work, fits into the contours of his role, and eventually ceases to know his own limits, but he can identify himself with his achievements and failures without letting these dictate what, how, or where he is to function. He may also mistakenly deny that the achievements and failures have anything to do with him, or may wrongly suppose that they are fully revelatory of his being or are even identical with it.

Some men dismiss their failures as being due to powers beyond their control. Others dismiss their achievements as of no moment. In contrast with both are those who are weighed down by some supposed signal success or failure. All ignore the fact that they are private beings who are not altogether sunderable from what is done in and with the body, and with what then ensues.

No one does or can identify himself solely with his successes. No one does or can identify himself solely with his failures. There seems always to be some inkling that one has a privacy not fully accounted for. If an identification with successes or failures were ever made, a man's being would be taken by him to last as long as the successes or failures were present or perhaps conspicuous.

Men betray themselves through inadvertent movements. Others often know them better than they know themselves. This would not be possible, did the others just stop at what was being publicly manifested. Success depends on their being able to use what they note as the beginning of intensive, penetrative acts. The penetrations are rarely deep and are always precarious, ending with content that cannot be entirely disengaged or adequately reported. Too quickly, moral terms and judgments are allowed to obscure what is discerned. Too readily, the approvals of others are accepted and their condemnations rejected. Fortunately, one occasionally comes to see that judgments which at first seemed incredible, downright wrong, or perverse, were right in the main.

If we have an uncertain grip on ourselves, we will be inclined to agree with others, and therefore to take ourselves to be more despicable or noble than we otherwise would. If, disturbed perhaps by this outcome, we turn to a trusted friend or a certified therapist, we will substitute another set of judgments for the first. The new, of course, might be more objective and perhaps be even better grounded and more judicious than the old. Sometimes it may provide us with agencies by which we can attain the stage where we will bring about results that will be subject to less adverse judgments. Unfortunately, this does not always occur.

To be himself, a man must not allow himself to be identified with the object of the judgments of others, both because those judgments, even when correct, never reach to his roots, and because they presuppose that he already is real apart from those judgments. The judgments of others are even less pertinent to him, his work, achievements, and failures than are those which are rooted in and express final realities that are and act independently of him. The most successful therapy frees a man from his therapist and at last allows him to function on his own.

The same man may both judge us and advise us to be ourselves, the advice following close on the heels of the judgment. The advice is good and often needed. When it is not followed, it is usually because it requires us to call upon hidden reserves in not altogether known ways, with unforeseen consequences and perhaps even undesirable ones, or because the accompanying constraints are felt to be overpowering, or our present state is thought to be desirable.

Sometimes men press hard on one whom they take to have broken a basic law of the state, a long-standing custom of society, or some fundamental ethical command. They would like him to admit that he not only did what he should not have done, but that he was untrue to himself. He is being asked both to confess and to reform. Occasionally, he may be spoken of as being corrupt, lacking moral sense and decency. If he is taken to have expressed his privacy he will be treated as one who is unable to initiate a type of act different from any of those he already exhibited. In effect, his humanity will be denied, and with this a responsibility for what he did. Instead of being condemned, he will in fact be excused, taken to do only what he must.

The advice that we ought not accept the judgment of others without qualification should guide the understanding of those others, alerting us to the fact that we are not yet entirely sure who they really are. But they may well be right. A serious wrong may have been committed. Our inadequate grasp of others should not be permitted to obscure that fact.

Helped perhaps by flattery or denunciations, men tend to accept the good or bad opinions they have of themselves as being right in the main. Whether or not they allow themselves to be misled by others, they are inclined to mislead themselves, permitting their own judgments to hide from them what they are. Their self-denigrations in particular are overly severe and often searing. A sound judgment of oneself should not result in a self-crippling. But the avoidance of this outcome is not to be identified with a refusal to lower one's estimate of oneself, particularly when this could well be a preliminary to the achievement, not simply of a sound judgment, but of a better state. Self-denigrations are appropriate if, by freeing one from conceit and misconception, they make possible a better functioning.

Recommendations should elicit what will enable a man to be himself fully. When they are forged independently of what he is or does, or independently of the judgment of others, they are not likely to help him. Usually, they are little more than awkward ways of referring to the fact that he has failed to be as excellent as he could be.

These reflections can be partly encapsulated in the well-known admonitions not only to be oneself, but to know and to give oneself. Self-knowledge is promoted by a study of the anatomy of individual privacy; the giving of oneself is promoted by an awareness that other men too have selves, persons, I's, and idios. To these admonitions one should add two others equally basic but not as widely remarked: respect yourself, take yourself to have the full value of a man, with distinctive powers and tasks to be cherished and exhibited; and remain yourself, distinguish the essential from the unessential, the native from the intruded, and try to have whatever is done express your constant, irreducible reality.

These admonitions emphasize the individual. They need supplementation by others emphasizing the fact that a man is also a public being who should help the rest become perfected in a well-controlled world.

Index